T0212932

Lecture Notes in Computer Science　　9434

Commenced Publication in 1973
Founding and Former Series Editors:
Gerhard Goos, Juris Hartmanis, and Jan van Leeuwen

More information about this series at http://www.springer.com/series/7408

Nir Piterman (Ed.)

Hardware and Software: Verification and Testing

11th International
Haifa Verification Conference, HVC 2015
Haifa, Israel, November 17–19, 2015
Proceedings

 Springer

Editor
Nir Piterman
University of Leicester
Leicester
UK

ISSN 0302-9743   ISSN 1611-3349 (electronic)
Lecture Notes in Computer Science
ISBN 978-3-319-26286-4   ISBN 978-3-319-26287-1   (eBook)
DOI 10.1007/978-3-319-26287-1

Library of Congress Control Number: 2015953248

LNCS Sublibrary: SL2 – Programming and Software Engineering

Springer Cham Heidelberg New York Dordrecht London

Springer International Publishing AG Switzerland is part of Springer Science+Business Media
(www.springer.com)

Preface

This volume contains the proceedings of the 11th Haifa Verification Conference (HVC 2015). The conference was hosted by IBM Research Haifa Laboratory and took place during November 17–19, 2015. It was the 11th event in this series of annual conferences dedicated to advancing the state of the art and state of the practice in verification and testing. The conference provided a forum for researchers and practitioners from academia and industry to share their work, exchange ideas, and discuss the future directions of testing and verification for hardware, software, and complex hybrid systems. Overall, HVC 2015 attracted 32 submissions in response to the call for papers. Each submission was assigned to at least three members of the Program Committee and in some cases additional reviews were solicited from external experts. The Program Committee selected 17 papers for presentation. In addition to the 17 contributed papers, the program included five invited talks by Patrice Godefroid (Microsoft Research), Stephen Bailey (Mentor Graphics), Mooly Sagiv (Tel Aviv University), Bodo Hoppe (IBM), and Yoav Hollander (Foretellix LTD). On the last day of the conference, the HVC award was presented to Armin Biere (Yohannes Kepler University Linz) for his contributions to SAT solving and its usage in verification. On November 16, one day before the conference, we held a tutorial day.

I would like to extend our appreciation and sincere thanks to local organization team from IBM Research Haifa Laboratory. In particular, Michael Vinov, the general chair, Tali Rabetti, the publicity chair, Tamer Salman, the tutorials chair, Revivit Yankovich the local coordinator, Yair Harry, the webmaster, and the Organizing Committee, which included Moshe Levinger, Ronny Morad, Avi Ziv, Karen Yorav, Sharon Keidar Barner, and Laurent Fournier. HVC 2015 received sponsorships from IBM, Qualcomm, Cadence Design Systems, Sandisk, Mentor Graphics, and Mellanox Technologies. Submission and evaluation of papers, as well as the preparation of this proceedings volume, were handled by the EasyChair conference management system.

September 2015   Nir Piterman

Organization

Program Committee

Roderick Bloem	Graz University of Technology, Austria
Debapriya Chatterjee	IBM Corporation, USA
Hana Chockler	King's College, UK
Flavio M. de Paula	IBM Corporation, USA
Rayna Dimitrova	MPI-SWS, Germany
M.J. Escalona	University of Seville, Spain
Adrian Evans	iRoC Technologies, France
Harry Foster	Mentor Graphics, USA
Franco Fummi	University of Verona, Italy
Alex Goryachev	IBM Research - Haifa, Israel
Alberto Griggio	Bruno Kessler Foundation, Italy
Aarti Gupta	Princeton University, USA
Laura Kovacs	Chalmers University of Technology, Sweden
Akash Lal	Microsoft Research, India
Martin Leucker	University of Lübeck, Germany
João Lourenço	NOVA LINCS - Universidade Nova de Lisboa, Portugal
Annalisa Massini	Sapienza University of Rome, Italy
Mayur Naik	Georgia Institute of Technology, USA
Jorge A. Navas	NASA Ames Research Center, USA
Hiren Patel	University of Waterloo, Canada
Pavithra Prabhakar	IMDEA Software Institute, Spain
Itai Segall	Bell Labs, Israel
Martina Seidl	Johannes Kepler University Linz, Austria
Ohad Shacham	Yahoo! Labs, Israel
Sharon Shoham	The Academic College of Tel Aviv Yaffo, Israel
Eli Singerman	Intel Corporation, Israel
Eran Yahav	Technion, Israel
Karen Yorav	IBM Research - Haifa, Israel

Local Organization (IBM Research – Haifa)

Michael Vinov	General Chair
Tali Rabetti	Publicity Chair
Tamer Salman	Tutorial Chair
Revivit Yankovich	Local Coordinator
Yair Harry	Web Master

Moshe Levinger	Organizing Committee
Ronny Morad	Organizing Committee
Avi Ziv	Organizing Committee
Karen Yorav	Organizing Committee
Sharon Keidar Barner	Organizing Committee
Laurent Fournier	Organizing Committee

Additional Reviewers

Bingham, Brad D.	Khsidashvili, Zurab	Salvo, Ivano
Chimento, Jesus Mauricio	Lavin, Mark	Scheffel, Torben
Goldstein, Maayan	Mari, Federico	Tronci, Enrico
Harder, Jannis	Meshman, Yuri	Zwirchmayr, Jakob
Ivrii, Alexander	Mover, Sergio	
Karbyshev, Aleksandr	Roveri, Marco	

Invited Talks

Between Testing and Verification:
Software Model Checking via Systematic Testing

Patrice Godefroid

Microsoft Research
pg@microsoft.com

Abstract. Dynamic software model checking consists of adapting model checking into a form of systematic testing that is applicable to industrial-size software. Over the last two decades, dozens of tools following this paradigm have been developed for checking concurrent and data-driven software. Compared to traditional software testing, dynamic software model checking provides better coverage, but is more computationally expensive. Compared to more general forms of program verification like interactive theorem proving, this approach provides more limited verification guarantees, but is cheaper due to its higher level of automation. Dynamic software model checking thus offers an attractive practical trade-off between testing and formal verification.

This talk will review 20 years of research on dynamic software model checking. It will highlight some key milestones, applications, and successes. It will also discuss limitations, disappointments, and future work.

Fight for the Future of Verification;
Live in it Today

Stephen Bailey

Mentor Graphics
stephen_bailey@mentor.com

Abstract. Functional verification is arguably the #1 challenge in the semiconductor and, therefore, EDA industries today. The pressure to verify ever larger, more complex systems within the context of schedules squeezed by market demands is tremendous. While it is impossible to predict specific inventions or innovations to come, it is possible to identify the challenges they must solve by understanding what is or will be consuming the most verification time. Specific areas of exploration include moving beyond chip to system level verification, SoC architectural implications on verification cycels and methodology and tying big data into verification automation.

Between Art and Craft: The Self-conception of a Verification Engineer

Bodo Hoppe

IBM Deutschland Research & Development
bohopp@de.ibm.com

Abstract. In the early days of verification, people wrote tests manually. This was done mostly by the designers themselves. The 90s marked the creation of software of automatic test generation. However, it was realized that stimuli generation, reference modeling and result prediction required dedicated skills.

With the progress of the field the required skills for contributing to the verification team became broader and included skills such as constraint solving, acceleration, and formal verification. Even more importantly, the verification engineer became independent. The opposite pole to logic design. And the job of a verification engineer became a career path.

Nowadays the boundaries fade again. A logic designer is expected to do formal analysis of his design, creating assertions and interesting coverage events and, last but not least, perform designer simulation to increase the initial quality of the logic delivery.

What are the most valuable talents for an engineer to have to be hired for hardware verification? The art of debugging? Thinking Logically? System Analysis? Programming? Creativity?

Going into the future, there is a strong need to rethink the self-conception of verification engineers and how they team up with the logic designers working in an agile environment.

Reasoning About Program Data Structure Shape: From the Heap to Distributed Systems

Mooly Sagiv

Tel Aviv University
msagiv@post.tau.ac.il

Abstract. Shape analysis is a static program-analysis technique that discovers and verifies properties of a program's dynamically allocated data structures. For example, shape analysis can infer that a linked list is acyclic, and prove that a program cannot free an element more than once. More generally, shape analysis provides a method to establish properties of systems whose states can be modeled as relations that evolve over time. A shape analyzer discovers quantified invariants of the elements of such systems.

In this talk, I will describe the road from analyzing dynamically allocated data structures to analyzing network protocols and other distributed systems. The survey includes both sound techniques and complete techniques. Some of these fundamental techniques inspired tools that are deployed in industry.

Contents

Hybrid Systems

XSpeed: Accelerating Reachability Analysis on Multi-core Processors

Rajarshi Ray[1]([✉]), Amit Gurung[1], Binayak Das[1], Ezio Bartocci[2],
Sergiy Bogomolov[3], and Radu Grosu[2]

[1] National Institute of Technology Meghalaya, Shillong, India
raj.ray84@gmail.com
[2] Vienna University of Technology, Vienna, Austria
[3] Institute of Science and Technology Austria, Klosterneuburg, Austria

Abstract. We present XSpeed a parallel state-space exploration algorithm for continuous systems with linear dynamics and nondeterministic inputs. The motivation of having parallel algorithms is to exploit the computational power of multi-core processors to speed-up performance. The parallelization is achieved on two fronts. First, we propose a parallel implementation of the support function algorithm by sampling functions in parallel. Second, we propose a parallel state-space exploration by slicing the time horizon and computing the reachable states in the time slices in parallel. The second method can be however applied only to a class of linear systems with invertible dynamics and fixed input. A GP-GPU implementation is also presented following a lazy evaluation strategy on support functions. The parallel algorithms are implemented in the tool XSpeed. We evaluated the performance on two benchmarks including an 28 dimension Helicopter model. Comparison with the sequential counterpart shows a maximum speed-up of almost $7\times$ on a 6 core, 12 thread Intel Xeon CPU E5-2420 processor. Our GP-GPU implementation shows a maximum speed-up of $12\times$ over the sequential implementation and $53\times$ over SpaceEx (LGG scenario), the state of the art tool for reachability analysis of linear hybrid systems. Experiments illustrate that our parallel algorithm with time slicing not only speeds-up performance but also improves precision.

1 Introduction

Reachability analysis is a standard technique for safety verification, analysis and synthesis of continuous and hybrid systems. Since exact computation of reachable states is in general intractable, set-based conservative computation methods has been proposed in the past with different choice of sets [1,2,7–9,12,22]. The reachable states are represented as a collection of continuous sets ($\subset \mathbb{R}^n$) with a symbolic representation of each individual set. Precision and scalability has been the two challenges with such set-based methods. The symbolic set representation plays a key role in deciding the efficiency of the reachability algorithm. Recently, algorithms using convex sets represented by support functions [12] and zonotopes [9] have shown promising scalability. Systems having dimension as large as 100

© Springer International Publishing Switzerland 2015
N. Piterman (Ed.): HVC 2015, LNCS 9434, pp. 3–18, 2015.
DOI: 10.1007/978-3-319-26287-1_1

have been shown to be computed efficiently with support-function-based algorithms.

The advent of multi-core architectures and many-core parallel co-processors like graphics processing units (GPUs) have provided tremendous computing power at our disposal. In this work, our goal is to leverage these powerful parallel architectures to speed-up the performance of reachability analysis and also possibly the precision of analysis. There has been prior work on devising parallel algorithms for discrete state concurrent systems in order to speed-up their performance on multi-core machines. Parallel state-space-search algorithms in the model-checker SPIN has been proposed in [6,13]. A GP-GPU implementation of the algorithms in SPIN has been proposed in [3]. However, no prior work is known to us on parallel state-space exploration of continuous and hybrid systems except for [17] which presents some preliminary results.

In particular, we consider the support-function-based reachability algorithm and propose two parallel versions of it. The first, samples the support functions along the template directions in parallel. This algorithm could be applied to any system with linear dynamics and nondeterministic inputs ($\dot{x} = Ax(t) + u(t)$, $u(t) \in \mathcal{U}$, $x(0) \in \mathcal{X}_0$). The second computes the reachable sets in slices of the time horizon. This algorithm can be applied to the class of linear systems whose dynamics A is invertible and the input set $\mathcal{U}$ is a point set. We also propose a GP-GPU implementation of the algorithm by following a lazy evaluation strategy. Our current GP-GPU implementation restricts $\mathcal{X}_0$ and $\mathcal{U}$ to be specified as hyperbox.

The organization of the paper is as follows. In Sect. 2, we present preliminaries on support functions and a reachability analysis algorithm using support functions. In Sect. 3, a parallel implementation scheme of the algorithm and our parallel state-space exploration algorithm is presented. We present our GPU implementation scheme in Sect. 4 to sample support functions in parallel in GPU cores. The experimental results are presented in Sect. 5 illustrating the achieved speed-up and precision. We conclude in Sect. 6.

2   Preliminaries

Since our work is focused on the support-function representation of compact convex sets, we recap the definition of support functions and template polytopes in Sect. 2.1. The reachability algorithm using support functions is discussed in Sect. 2.2.

2.1   Support Functions

Definition 1. *[18] Given a nonempty compact convex set $\mathcal{X} \subset \mathbb{R}^n$ the support function of $\mathcal{X}$ is a function $sup_{\mathcal{X}} : \mathbb{R}^n \to \mathbb{R}$ defined as:*

$$sup_{\mathcal{X}}(\ell) = max\{\ell \cdot x \mid x \in \mathcal{X}\} \tag{1}$$

where $\ell \cdot x$ is the scalar product of direction ℓ and vector x, that is, the projection of x on direction ℓ. A compact convex set $\mathcal{X}$ is uniquely determined by the intersection of the halfspaces generated by support functions in all possible directions $\ell \in \mathbb{R}^n$.

$$\mathcal{X} = \bigcap_{\ell \in \mathbb{R}^n} \ell \cdot x \leq sup_\mathcal{X}(\ell) \tag{2}$$

Definition 2. *Given the support function $sup_\mathcal{X}$ of a compact convex set $\mathcal{X}$ and a finite set of template directions $\mathcal{D}$, the template polytope of the convex set $\mathcal{X}$ is defined as:*

$$Poly_\mathcal{D}(\mathcal{X}) = \bigcap_{\ell \in \mathcal{D}} \ell \cdot x \leq sup_\mathcal{X}(\ell) \tag{3}$$

Proposition 1. *Given a polytope $\mathcal{X} = \{x \in \mathbb{R}^n \mid P \cdot x \leq Q\}$, the support function of $\mathcal{X}$ in the direction ℓ is the solution to the Linear Program (LP):*

$$sup_\mathcal{X}(\ell) = \begin{cases} maximize\ \ell \cdot x \\ subject\ to: \\ P \cdot x \leq Q \end{cases}$$

Proposition 2. *Given a hyperbox $\mathcal{H} = \{x \in \mathbb{R}^n \mid x \in [a_1, b_1] \times \ldots \times [a_n, b_n]\}$, the support function of $\mathcal{H}$ in the direction $\ell = (\ell_1, \ell_2, \ldots, \ell_n)$ is given by:*

$$sup_\mathcal{H}(\ell) = \sum_{i=1}^{n} \ell_i \cdot h_i, \text{ where } h_i = \begin{cases} a_i \text{ if } \ell_i < 0 \\ b_i \text{ otherwise} \end{cases}$$

where a_i and b_i are the lower and upper bound respectively of $\mathcal{H}$ in the dimension i.

2.2 Reachability Analysis Using Support Functions

In this work, we consider continuous linear systems with constrained inputs and initial states. The dynamics of such systems is of the form:

$$\dot{x} = Ax(t) + u(t),\ u(t) \in \mathcal{U},\ x(0) \in \mathcal{X}_0 \tag{4}$$

where $\mathcal{X}_0$, $\mathcal{U}$ is the set of initial states and the set of inputs given as compact convex sets, respectively.

We now discuss the algorithm proposed in [12] for computing reachable states using support functions. The algorithm discretizes time by a time step δ and computes an over approximation of the reachable set in time horizon T by a set of convex sets represented by their support functions, as shown in Eq. 5.

$$Reach_{[0,T]}(\mathcal{X}_0) \subseteq \bigcup_{i=0}^{N-1} (\Omega_i) \tag{5}$$

The convex sets Ω_i are given by the following equations:

$$\Omega_{i+1} = \Phi_\delta \Omega_i \oplus \mathcal{W} \tag{6}$$
$$\Omega_0 = CH(X_0, \Phi_\delta X_0 \oplus \mathcal{V})$$

where $\oplus$, CH stands for minkowski sum and convex hull operation over sets respectively, $\Phi_\delta = e^{\delta A}$ and $\mathcal{W}$, $\mathcal{V}$ are convex sets given as follows:

$$\mathcal{V} = \delta\mathcal{U} \oplus \alpha\mathcal{B} \tag{7}$$
$$\mathcal{W} = \delta\mathcal{U} \oplus \beta\mathcal{B}$$

α, β are constants depending on $X_0, \mathcal{U}, \delta$ and the dynamics matrix A. $\mathcal{B}$ is a unit ball in the considered norm.

The support function representation of Ω_i can be seen as an abstraction of its template polyhedra representations. A concretization can be obtained by computing template polyhedra approximations of Ω_i along a set of directions $\mathcal{D}$. Such concretization provides an efficient computation of intersection, plotting and other efficient operations over polytopes but at the expense of an approximation error depending on the number of template directions and the choice of directions.

The algorithm considers a set of bounding directions, say $\mathcal{D}$, to sample the support functions of Ω_i and obtains a set of template polyhedra $Poly_\mathcal{D}(\Omega_i)$ whose union over-approximates the reachable set. The support function of Ω_i is computed with the following equation obtained using the properties of support functions:

$$sup_{\Omega_{i+1}}(\ell) = sup_{\Omega_i}(\Phi_\delta^T \ell) + sup_\mathcal{W}(\ell) \tag{8}$$
$$sup_{\Omega_0}(\ell) = max\big(sup_{X_0}(\ell), sup_{X_0}(\Phi_\delta^T \ell) + sup_\mathcal{V}(\ell)\big)$$

Simplification of Eq. 6 yields the following relation:

$$sup_{\Omega_i}(\ell) = sup_{\Omega_0}\big((\Phi_\delta^T)^i \ell\big) + \sum_{j=0}^{i-1} sup_\mathcal{W}\big((\Phi_\delta^T)^j \ell\big) \tag{9}$$

3   Parallel State-Space Exploration

In this section, we present two approaches to parallelize the support-functions-based reachability algorithms in Sects. 3.1 and 3.2.

3.1   Parallel Samplings over Template Directions

The LGG (Le Guernic Girard) scenario of the state of the art tool, SpaceEx [8] computes reachable states using a support-functions algorithm with the provision of templates in *box*, *octagonal* and *p uniform* directions. A box polyhedron has $2n$ directions ($x_i = \pm 1$, $x_k = 0$, $k \neq i$) whereas an octagonal polyhedron has $2n^2$ directions ($x_i = \pm 1$, $x_j = \pm 1$, $x_k = 0$, $k \neq i$, $k \neq j$), giving a more precise approximation. The support function algorithm scales well when the number of template directions is linear in the dimension n of the system. When computing finer approximations with directions quadratic in n, we trade-off precision for scalability.

The support-functions-based algorithm is easy to parallelize by sampling the template directions in parallel [12]. However, there are implementation challenges. In this work, we propose a multi-threaded implementation with a master thread spawning worker threads for every direction in the template set $\mathcal{D}$. The pseudocode of master thread is shown in Algorithm 1. A global support function matrix M having R rows and N columns is allocated to store the computed support functions by different worker threads, where R is the number of directions in $\mathcal{D}$ and $N = T/\delta$ is the number of iterations. Each worker thread t_i computes the support function samples along a direction $d(i)$ in parallel. The results by thread t_i are written to the row $M[i]$ resulting in no write contention among the threads. An entry $M(i,j)$ stores the support function of Ω_j in the ith direction in $\mathcal{D}$ as shown in lines 2–3 in Algorithm 2.

The master thread waits for all the worker threads to complete. After all the worker threads have finished, we have a template polytope $Poly_\mathcal{D}(\Omega_i)$ for every convex set Ω_i which is obtained from the support function as shown in lines 7–9 in Algorithm 1.

Algorithm 1. Pseudocode of Master Thread

1: **procedure** REACH-PARALLEL-MASTER($\mathcal{D}$,N)
2:     **for all** $\ell_i \in \mathcal{D}$ **do**   ▷ Master Thread
3:         Spawn a thread t_i to sample sup of $\Omega_0 \ldots \Omega_{N-1}$ along ℓ_i
4:     **end for**
5:     Wait for all threads to finish.
6:     $R_{approx} \leftarrow \emptyset$
7:     **for** $i \leftarrow 0, N-1$ **do**
8:         $P_\mathcal{D}(\Omega_i) \leftarrow \bigwedge_{j=1}^{|\mathcal{D}|} d(j).x \leq M(j,i)$
9:         $R_{approx} \leftarrow R_{approx} \bigcup P_\mathcal{D}(\Omega_i)$
10:    **end for**   ▷ $Reach[0,T] \subseteq R_{approx}$
11: **end procedure**

Algorithm 2. Pseudocode of Worker Thread

1: **procedure** REACH-PARALLEL-WORKER(M,N,ℓ,i)   ▷ Worker Thread   ▷ Each
     thread gets an id $i \in [1, R]$
2:     **for** $j \leftarrow 0, N-1$ **do**
3:         $M[i][j] \leftarrow sup_{\Omega_j}(\ell)$
4:     **end for**
5: **end procedure**

Sampling with Thread Safe GLPK. It can be seen that when the initial set $\mathcal{X}_0$ in a location dynamics in Eq. 4 is given as a polytope, the convex sets Ω_i in Eq. 6 are also polytopes. Sampling the support function of a polytope is a linear programming problem. SpaceEx LGG scenario expects initial set $\mathcal{X}_0$ and $\mathcal{U}$ to be polytopes and samples their support function using the GLPK (GNU Linear Programming Kit) library [15], an open source and highly optimized linear programming solver library. In our parallel implementation we also assume initial and input sets to be polytopes and use GLPK package to solve their support functions. However, note that the GLPK library is not thread safe This is due to the fact that GLPK implementation uses thread shared data that suffers from race condition in multithreaded executions. To overcome this, we identified the thread shared data and made them thread local to ensure thread safety. The thread safe GLPK objects are used per thread to compute the support functions at different directions in parallel.

3.2   Parallel Exploration of Reachable States

In addition to the parallelization introduced in the previous section, we also propose another parallelization where threads compute reachable states in disjoint intervals of the time horizon in parallel. To bring in parallelism, our key idea is to compute the reachable states at distinct times in the time horizon and treat them as initials states for independent reachability computations. The reachable states from each of the initials states is then computed by an independent thread in parallel. For load balancing, the time horizon T is sliced into equal intervals of size $T_p = T/N$, N being the degree of parallelism. The limitation of this approach is that the input set $\mathcal{U}$ is assumed to be a point set and the dynamics matrix A is assumed to be invertible.

Proposition 3. *Given a linear dynamics of the form $\dot{x} = Ax(t)+u(t), u(t) \in \mathcal{U}$, if the input set $\mathcal{U} = v$ is a point set and the matrix A is invertible, the set of states reachable at time $t_i = iT_p$ is defined as:*

$$\mathcal{S}(t_i) = e^{AiT_p}.\mathcal{X}_0 \oplus A^{-1}(e^{AiT_p} - I)(v) \tag{10}$$

where I is the identity matrix.

Proof. Solving the differential equation $\dot{x} = Ax(t) + u(t),\ u(t) \in \mathcal{U}$ gives:

$$x(t) = e^{tA}x_0 + \int_0^t e^{(t-y)A}u(y)dy$$

$$= e^{tA}x_0 + \int_0^t e^{(t-y)A}vdy$$

$$= e^{tA}x_0 + A^{-1}(e^{At} - I)(v)$$

When $x(0) \in \mathcal{X}_0$, we apply minkowski sum to get:

$$\mathcal{X}(t) = e^{tA}\mathcal{X}_0 \oplus A^{-1}(e^{At} - I)(v)$$

Substituting $t = iT_p$:

$$\mathcal{X}(i(T_p)) = \mathcal{S}(t_i) = e^{A(iT_p)}.\mathcal{X}_0 \oplus A^{-1}(e^{A(iT_p)} - I)(v) \qquad \square$$

Let $\Phi_1 = e^{A(iT_p)}$ and $\Phi_2 = A^{-1}(e^{A(iT_p)} - I)$, the support function of the $\mathcal{S}(t_i)$ is given by:

$$sup_{\mathcal{S}(t_i)}(\ell) = sup_{\mathcal{X}_0}(\Phi_1^T \ell) + sup_v(\Phi_2^T \ell) \qquad (11)$$

The reachable states in each time interval $I_i = [iT_p, (i+1)T_p]$ starting from states $x \in S(t_i)$ is defined as $R(S_i)$ and can be computed sequentially using Eq. 6. Computation of $R(S_i)$ can also be in parallel over the template directions as proposed in Sect. 3.1.

Proposition 4. *An approximation of the reachable states in time horizon T can be computed by the following relation:*

$$Reach_{[0,T]}(\mathcal{X}_0) \subseteq \bigcup_{i=0}^{N-1} R(\mathcal{S}_i) \qquad (12)$$

Proof. $R(\mathcal{S}_i)$ is computed using Eq. 6 with a discretization time step δ with $\mathcal{S}_i$ as the initial set. Since S_i gives the exact set of states reachable at time instant $t = iT_p$, the correctness argument shown in [12] guarantees that $Reach_{[I_i]}(\mathcal{X}_0) \subseteq R(\mathcal{S}_i)$. Therefore, we have:

$$Reach_{[0,T]}(\mathcal{X}_0) = \bigcup_{i=0}^{N-1} Reach_{[I_i]}(\mathcal{X}_0) \subseteq \bigcup_{i=0}^{N-1} R(\mathcal{S}_i) \qquad \square$$

In Sect. 5 we show that computing the reachable states using Proposition 4 gives in some cases more precise results compared to the sequential algorithm in [11,12]. This is because the approximation error in the computation of Ω_0 in Eq. 6 propagates in the sequential algorithm. In our algorithm, since we compute exact reachable states at partition time points in the time horizon and recompute $\Omega_0^{t_i}$ using them, the propagation of the error may diminish.

4   Sampling Support Functions in GPU

It can be observed from Eqs. 8 and 9 that the support function of Ω_i can be computed from the support function of $\mathcal{X}_0$, $\mathcal{V}$ and $\mathcal{W}$. The support function of $\mathcal{V}, \mathcal{W}$ can be, in turn, computed from the support function of $\mathcal{U}$ and $\mathcal{B}$. Therefore, to compute the support functions of $\Omega_0, \ldots, \Omega_{N-1}$ along a direction ℓ, it suffices to compute the support function of $\mathcal{X}_0$, $\mathcal{U}$ and $\mathcal{B}$ along the directions $\ell, \Phi_\delta^T \ell, (\Phi_\delta^T)^2 \ell, \ldots, (\Phi_\delta^T)^N \ell$. Unlike the support function algorithm in [12] which computes the support functions iteratively using Eq. 8, we propose to compute the support functions in a lazy fashion which involves delaying evaluation until

---

Algorithm 3. Lazy evaluation of support functions

1: **procedure** EVAL-SUPPORT($\Omega[0\ldots N-1]$, $\mathcal{X}_0$, $\mathcal{U}$, ℓ)

2:      $D[0] \leftarrow \ell$;   ▷ Computing directional arguments

3:      **for** $i \leftarrow 1, N$ **do**

4:          $D[i] \leftarrow \Phi_\delta^T \cdot \mathcal{D}[i-1]$

5:      **end for**

                                                          ▷ Computing support functions in parallel

6:      Spawn thread T_i to evaluate i^{th} loop iteration;

7:      **for** $i \leftarrow 0, N$ **do**

8:          $Sup\mathcal{X}_0[i] \leftarrow T_i.evalSup(\mathcal{X}_0, D[i])$

9:          $Sup\mathcal{U}[i] \leftarrow T_i.evalSup(\mathcal{U}, D[i])$

10:         $Sup\mathcal{B}[i] \leftarrow T_i.evalSup(\mathcal{B}, D[i])$

11:     **end for**

12:     Wait for all threads to finish.

                                                          ▷ Computing support Functions of Ω_i

13:     $sum \leftarrow 0$

14:     $sup_{\Omega_0}(\ell) \leftarrow max\big(Sup\mathcal{X}_0[0], Sup\mathcal{X}_0[1] + \delta \cdot Sup\mathcal{U}[0] + \alpha \cdot Sup\mathcal{B}[0]\big)$

15:     **for** $i \leftarrow 1, N-1$ **do**

16:         $p \leftarrow max\big(Sup\mathcal{X}_0[i], Sup\mathcal{X}_0[i+1] + \delta \cdot Sup\mathcal{U}[i] + \alpha \cdot Sup\mathcal{B}[i]\big)$

17:         $sum \leftarrow sum + \delta \cdot Sup\mathcal{U}[i-1] + \beta \cdot Sup\mathcal{B}[i-1]$

18:         $sup_{\Omega_i}(\ell) \leftarrow p + sum$

19:     **end for**

20: **end procedure**

---

all the directional arguments are computed. The support functions are then evaluated in parallel in lines 7–11, as shown in Algorithm 3.

Observe that we need to run the same support function evaluation routine for a convex set but on different directions in parallel. We build upon this observation and propose to compute the support functions in SIMT (Single Instruction Multiple Threads) parallel architecture wherein multiple instances of a procedure execute in parallel but on different data. The modern day GPU (Graphics Processing Unit) architectures are SIMT in nature and we therefore propose to offload the support function computations to the GPU. A brief introduction to GPU architecture and CUDA programming model is given in Sect. 4.1.

4.1 CUDA Programming Model

We now briefly present the GPU hardware architecture and the programming model used to implement our parallel algorithms. As illustrated in Fig. 1, the GPU architecture consists of a scalable array of N multithreaded Streaming Multiprocessors (SMs), made up of M Stream Processor (SP) cores. Each core is equipped with a fully pipelined integer arithmetic logic unit (ALU) and a floating point unit (FPU) that executes one integer or floating point instruction per clock cycle. In our experiments we have used the NVIDIA GeForce GTX 670 having 7 SMs and 192 SPs for each SM, for a total of 1344 SPs.

The NVIDIA vendor provides also a special Application Programming Interface (API) called Compute Unified Device Architecture (CUDA) that facilitates the developing of efficient applications tuned for NVIDIA GPUs. CUDA extends the C and the FORTRAN languages with special keywords and language primitives that are suitable to achieve a high-performance hardware-based multithreading. We have implemented our parallel algorithms using the C extension.

The CUDA programming model consists in using thousands of light-weight threads arranged into one- to three-dimensional thread blocks. A thread executes a function called the *kernel* that contains the computations to be run in parallel using a GPU device. A CUDA program starts running in the Central Processing Unit (CPU) referred as the *host*. Whenever a kernel is launched from the host code, the execution continues then in the GPU. The max number of threads running a kernel is fixed at the launching time (this limitation has some exceptions in the modern GPU cards supporting dynamic parallelism).

Each thread is assigned to a SP and each thread block is processed by a SM. The thread execution model in CUDA is the Single Instruction Multiple Threads (SIMT). SIMT differs from the classical Single Instruction Multiple Data (SIMD) by the fact that the threads sharing the same instruction address and running synchronously are organised within a thread block into groups of 32 threads called *warps*. In a warp, the divergence of the threads execution in different branches due to *if-then-else* constructs, reduces considerably the level of parallelism and indeed degrades the performance of the kernel execution.

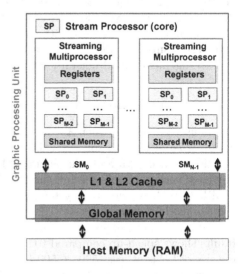

Fig. 1. GPU architecture

Threads can access different types of memory and their judicious use is key to performance. The most general is the off-chip global memory, to which all threads can read and write. Also the host can read and write the global memory and so this memory is usually used as a way of communication between the host and the GPU device. The global memory has slow performances and it is very important to access it in a coalesced way using a single memory transaction of 32, 64, or 128 bytes. The two caches *L1* and *L2* shown in Fig. 1 mitigates this bottleneck by storing copies of the data most frequently accessed in the global memory. Significantly faster levels of memory are available within an SM, including 32–64 KB of on-chip *registers* partitioned among all threads. As such, using a large number of registers within a CUDA kernel will limit the number of threads that can run concurrently. Finally, *local memory* is invoked when a thread runs out of available registers. In addition, each SM has a *shared memory* region (16–48 KB). This level of memory, which can be accessed nearly as quickly as the registers, facilitates communication between threads and can be used as a programmer-controllable memory cache.

Threads located in the same thread block can cooperate in several ways. They can insert a synchronization point into the kernel, which requires all threads in the block to reach that point before execution can continue. They can also share data during execution. In contrast, threads located in different thread blocks cannot synchronize each other and they essentially operate independently. Although a small number of threads or blocks can be used to execute a kernel, this arrangement would not fully exploit the computing potential of the GPU.

4.2   Computing Support Functions of Polytopes in GPU

As discussed in Sect. 2, when $\mathcal{X}_0$ and $\mathcal{U}$ are polytopes, their support function evaluation is equivalent to solving a linear program (LP). The Simplex algorithm [4,5] is a well known and efficient procedure to solve LPs in practice. There is previous work on implementing the simplex algorithm on CUDA executing in a CPU-GPU heterogeneous system. An efficient implementation of the revised simplex method over a CPU-GPU system is shown in [21]. A multi-GPU implementation of the simplex procedure is reported in [14]. However, the reported results shows speed-up compared to sequential CPU implementation only when the size of LP is at least 500 × 500 (500 variables, 500 constraints). The reason why performance is poor for small size LPs is the CPU-GPU memory transfer latency to copy the simplex tableau and therefore the time gain due to parallelization is predominant over the CPU-GPU memory transfer latency only for large instances of LP. Since the benchmarks we know are of dimension much smaller than 500, we did not go for a simplex-algorithm implementation in GPU.

4.3   Computing Support Functions of Hyperbox in GPU

When the initial set $\mathcal{X}_0$ and input set $\mathcal{U}$ are given as hyperboxes, which are special cases of polytopes, their support function can be computed using Proposition 2 instead of solving an LP with simplex algorithm. This also avoids expensive memory transfer of simplex tableau, a data structure used in the simplex algorithm, from CPU to GPU. Building on this observation, we implemented a CUDA procedure to compute the support function of a hyperbox. There are challenges to have speed-up derived from GPU due to issues like warp divergence, memory transfer latency and GPU occupancy. We map a CUDA block to compute support function along a sampling direction. Since CUDA blocks are scheduled to SMs, this ensures that all the GPU SMs are utilized when the number of sampling directions are more than the SMs in the GPU. Our block is one dimensional containing only 32 threads (warp size) since instructions in GPU are scheduled per warp which is a collection of 32 threads. The number of threads per block is kept to 1 warp-size since the task of computing the support function of a Hyperbox is lightweight. The maximum number of support function evaluation tasks that can be performed in parallel is limited by the number of directions that can be transferred to the GPU global memory. We attempt maximum parallelism by offloading tasks in batches of maximum possible size. The pseudocode of the GPU offloading routine is shown in Algorithm 4.

Algorithm 4. Offloading of Tasks in Batches to GPU

1: **procedure** GPU-OFFLOAD($\mathcal{H}$, $\mathcal{D}$, $numDirections$, Res)
2:     $gpuMemsize \leftarrow getGlobalMemsize()$;
3:     $sizePerDirection \leftarrow \mathcal{D}[0].memsize()$;
4:     $memsize \leftarrow numDirections * sizePerDirection$
5:     **if** memsize > gpuMemsize **then**
6:         $totalBatches \leftarrow ceil(memsize/gpuMemsize)$;
7:         $batchSize \leftarrow floor(gpuMemsize/sizePerDirection)$;
8:         $\mathcal{D}' \leftarrow malloc(sizePerDirection * batchSize * sizeof(double))$;
9:         $cur \leftarrow 0$;
10:        **while** cur $\leq$ totalBatches **do**
11:            $\mathcal{D}' \leftarrow$ copy $\mathcal{D}$ from $batchSize * cur$ to $batchSize * (cur + 1) - 1$;
12:            $gpuKernel <<< batchSize, 32 >>> (\mathcal{H}, \mathcal{D}', Res)$;
13:            $cur \leftarrow cur + 1$;
14:        **end while**
15:    **else**
16:        $batchSize \leftarrow numDirections$;
17:        $gpuKernel <<< batchSize, 32 >>> (\mathcal{H}, \mathcal{D}, Res)$;
18:    **end if**
19: **end procedure**

---

5   Experiments

The parallel algorithms are implemented as part of the tool XSpeed including the CUDA implementation. To measure the performance of our parallel algorithms, we experiment on two benchmarks and compare our performance with the SpaceEx's (LGG) scenario [8] and with an optimized implementation of the support function algorithm in [12].

5.1   Five Dimensional System

We consider a five dimensional linear continuous system as a benchmark from [10]. Since we require the inputs set $\mathcal{U}$ to be a point set for our parallel state-space exploration algorithm, we consider $\mathcal{U} = (0.01,0.01,0.01,0.01,0.01)$. We consider the initial set X_0 as a hyperbox with sides 0.02 centered at $(1,0,0,0,0)$. For the matrix A, the reader may refer to [10].

Figure 2 illustrates the parallel exploration with slicing the time horizon. The figure shows that a time horizon of 5 units is sliced into five intervals each of size 1 unit. Five threads compute the reachable sets in parallel starting from initial sets $\mathcal{S}(t = 0)$, $\mathcal{S}(t = 1)$, $\mathcal{S}(t = 2)$, $\mathcal{S}(t = 3)$ and $\mathcal{S}(t = 4)$.

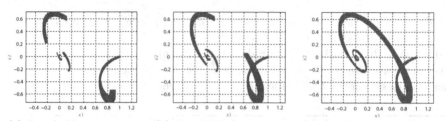

(a) Reachable states com- (b) Reachable states com- (c) Reachable states computed by individual threads puted by individual threads puted by individual threads
in 0.5 time unit   in 0.75 time unit   in 1 time unit

Fig. 2. Illustrating parallel state-space exploration in sliced time horizon

5.2   Helicopter Controller

To measure the performance on a high dimensional system, we consider the
benchmark of helicopter controller from [8,20]. This benchmark models the controller of a Westland Lynx military helicopter with 8 continuous variables. The
controller is a 20 variables LTI system and the control system has 28 variables
in total. We consider the initial set $\mathcal{X}_0$ to be a hyperbox and the input set $\mathcal{U}$ to
be the origin $\{0\}$.

Table 1 shows the performance speed-up in computing reachable states with
our parallel direction samplings compared to the sequential support-function
algorithm in a 4 core and 6 core machine with hyper-threading, namely Intel Core
i7-4770, 3.40 GHz, 8 GB RAM and Intel Xeon CPU E5-2420, 1.2 Ghz, 46.847 GB
RAM respectively. The results are an average of 10 runs for a time horizon of
5 units and a time step of $1.7e - 3$ units. A speed-up of almost 7× is observed
for the Helicopter model. The gain in CPU utilization shows how our parallel
implementation exploits the power of multicore processors effectively.

Figure 3 shows the speed-up obtained with the parallel state-space exploration with octagonal directions and time step of 0.0048 on Intel Core i7-4770, 4
core, 8 threads, 3.40 GHz, 8 GB RAM processor. The results from the SpaceEx
tool are obtained by running the executable available at http://spaceex.imag.
fr/ on the same machine, with same parameters. We show that selecting the
right partition size is important to obtain optimal speed-up. Partitioning beyond
a limit though give us high precision but degrades the performance as the
threading overhead outruns the performance gain due to parallelism. The threshold depends on the number of cores in the underlying multi-core architecture.
Figure 4 shows the gain in precision with box directions and time step of 0.01
and 0.0048 respectively for the five dimensional and the Helicopter benchmark.
The gain in precision is because the time sliced algorithm computes exact reachable states at time points in the time horizon and diminishes the propagation
of approximation error resulting from the computation of Ω_0 in the support-
function algorithm.

Table 2 shows the performance speed-up of reachability analysis when support functions are sampled in parallel in GPU (Algorithms 3 and 4) compared to

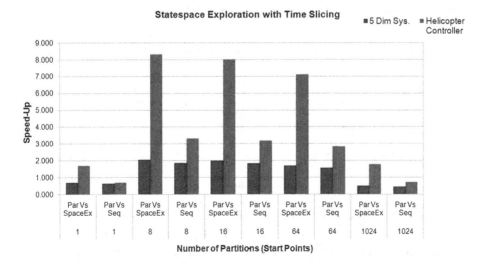

Fig. 3. Illustrating speed-up using parallel state-space exploration in time slices over sequential algorithm and the SpaceEx LGG scenario.

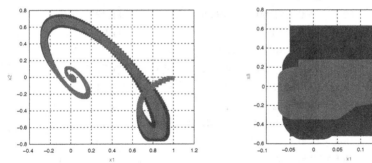

(a) Reachable states of the five dimensional model (Red-parallel exploration, Brown-support function algorithm)

(b) Reachable states of the Helicopter model (Red-parallel exploration, Brown-support function algorithm)

Fig. 4. Illustrating gain in precision with parallel state-space exploration over sequential algorithm.

sequential support function algorithm using GLPK and SpaceEx LGG scenario. The iters in the table refers to the discretization factor of the time horizon. The experiments are performed in Intel Q9950, 2.84 Ghz, 4 Core, no hyper-threading, 8 GB RAM with GeForce GTX 670 GPU card. We observe a speed-up of 9× to 12× over sequential implementation. A maximum speed-up of 53× is observed for the five dimensional and 38× for the Helicopter model respectively compared to SpaceEx on different parameters to the support-function algorithm.

Table 1. Speed-up and utilization gain with parallel support function samplings

Model	Dirs	4 core (8 threads)				6 core (12 threads)			
		Time (in secs)		CPU util gain (%)	Speed-up	Time (in secs)		CPU util gain (%)	Speed-up
		Seq	Par			Seq	Par		
5 Dim-model	Box	0.203	0.087	47.22	2.33	0.336	0.101	71.88	3.32
	Oct	0.937	0.337	68.75	2.78	1.532	0.401	74.46	3.82
	500	9.045	3.095	76.65	2.92	14.037	3.243	81.15	4.33
Helicopter controller (28 dim)	Box	2.418	0.571	71.05	4.23	3.36	0.608	79.96	5.52
	Oct	67.125	14.779	77.5	4.54	93.837	13.669	86.77	6.87
	3000	130.01	28.148	77.9	4.62	178.913	26.015	87.77	6.88

Table 2. Performance speed-up with samplings in GPU

Model	Dirs	Iters	Time (in secs)			Speed-up	
			Seq	SpaceEx	Par (GPU)	vs. Seq	vs. SpaceEx
Five dim. model	Box	1000	0.133	0.345	0.018	7.27	18.82
	Box	2000	0.287	0.686	0.028	10.01	23.93
	Oct	1000	0.717	1.399	0.06	11.87	23.15
	Oct	2000	1.462	2.8	0.119	12.30	23.55
	500	1000	6.695	24.171	0.576	11.62	41.96
	500	2000	13.329	39.58	1.114	11.96	35.52
	1000	1000	13.128	59.996	1.121	11.71	53.52
	1000	2000	26.022	94.204	2.219	11.72	42.44
Helicopter controller (28 dim.)	Box	1000	1.4	4.399	0.172	8.14	25.56
	Box	1500	2.077	7.263	0.249	8.33	29.11
	Box	2000	2.769	8.685	0.327	8.45	26.50
	Box	2500	3.444	11.014	0.405	8.50	27.18
	Oct	1000	39.089	123.794	4.246	9.21	29.15
	Oct	1500	57.632	248.769	6.321	9.12	39.35
	2000	1000	50.367	187.825	5.396	9.33	34.80
	3000	1000	75.086	311.652	8.054	9.32	38.69
	3000	2000	149.313	608.214	16.092	9.28	37.80

Observe that the performance of our algorithms improves with the increase in the number of cores in the machine and signifies that performance of XSpeed can scale automatically with future multicore machines and GPUs with higher degree of parallelism.

6 Conclusion

We presented a parallel implementation of the support-function algorithm and a time-sliced parallel state-space exploration algorithm. A lazy strategy of evaluating support functions to bring in parallelism is illustrated and implemented in CUDA to offload the computation task in GPU. We show that the performance of reachability algorithms for linear dynamical systems can be considerably improved using the modern multi-core processors. The use of GP-GPU has shown a promising performance gain in many scientific applications and we show that they can also substantially improve the performance of reachability analysis. The parallel algorithms and the GP-GPU task offloading are implemented in the tool XSpeed.

Acknowledgements. This work was supported in part by the European Research Council (ERC) under grant 267989 (QUAREM) and by the Austrian Science Fund (FWF) under grants S11402-N23, S11405-N23 and S11412-N23 (RiSE/SHiNE) and Z211-N23 (Wittgenstein Award).

References

1. Althoff, M., Krogh, B.H.: Zonotope bundles for the efficient computation of reachable sets. In: Proceedings of the 50th IEEE Conference on Decision and Control and European Control Conference, CDC-ECC 2011, Orlando, FL, USA, 12–15 December 2011, pp. 6814–6821. IEEE (2011). http://dx.doi.org/10.1109/CDC.2011.6160872
2. Asarin, E., Dang, T., Girard, A.: Reachability analysis of nonlinear systems using conservative approximation. In: Maler, O., Pnueli, A. (eds.) HSCC 2003. LNCS, vol. 2623, pp. 20–35. Springer, Heidelberg (2003)
3. Bartocci, E., DeFrancisco, R., Smolka, S.A.: Towards a gpgpu-parallel SPIN model checker. In: Rungta and Tkachuk [19], pp. 87–96. http://doi.acm.org/10.1145/2632362.2632379
4. Dantzig, G.B., Thapa, M.N.: Linear Programming 1: Introduction. Springer, New York (1997)
5. Dantzig, G.B., Thapa, M.N.: Linear Programming 2: Theory and Extensions. Springer, New York (2003)
6. Filippidis, I., Holzmann, G.J.: An improvement of the piggyback algorithm for parallel model checking. In: Rungta and Tkachuk [19], pp. 48–57. http://doi.acm.org/10.1145/2632362.2632375
7. Frehse, G.: PHAVer: algorithmic verification of hybrid systems past HyTech. Int. J. Softw. Tools Technol. Transf. (STTT) **10**(3), 263–279 (2008)
8. Frehse, G., Le Guernic, C., Donzé, A., Cotton, S., Ray, R., Lebeltel, O., Ripado, R., Girard, A., Dang, T., Maler, O.: SpaceEx: scalable verification of hybrid systems. In: Gopalakrishnan, G., Qadeer, S. (eds.) CAV 2011. LNCS, vol. 6806, pp. 379–395. Springer, Heidelberg (2011)
9. Girard, A.: Reachability of uncertain linear systems using zonotopes. In: Morari and Thiele [16], pp. 291–305. http://dx.doi.org/10.1007/978-3-540-31954-2_19
10. Girard, A.: Reachability of uncertain linear systems using zonotopes. In: Morari and Thiele [16], pp. 291–305
11. Girard, A., Le Guernic, C.: Efficient reachability analysis for linear systems using support functions. In: Proceedings of IFAC World Congress (2008)
12. Le Guernic, C., Girard, A.: Reachability analysis of hybrid systems using support functions. In: Bouajjani, A., Maler, O. (eds.) CAV 2009. LNCS, vol. 5643, pp. 540–554. Springer, Heidelberg (2009)

13. Holzmann, G.J.: Parallelizing the spin model checker. In: Donaldson, A., Parker, D. (eds.) SPIN 2012. LNCS, vol. 7385, pp. 155–171. Springer, Heidelberg (2012)
14. Lalami, M.E., Baz, D.E., Boyer, V.: Multi GPU implementation of the simplex algorithm. In: Thulasiraman, P., Yang, L.T., Pan, Q., Liu, X., Chen, Y., Huang, Y., Chang, L., Hung, C., Lee, C., Shi, J.Y., Zhang, Y. (eds.) 13th IEEE International Conference on High Performance Computing and Communication, HPCC 2011, Banff, Alberta, Canada, 2–4 September 2011, pp. 179–186. IEEE (2011). http://dx.doi.org/10.1109/HPCC.2011.32
15. Makhorin, A.: GNU Linear Programming Kit, v.4.37 (2009). http://www.gnu.org/software/glpk
16. Bujorianu, M.L., Lygeros, J., Bujorianu, M.C.: Bisimulation for general stochastic hybrid systems. In: Morari, M., Thiele, L. (eds.) HSCC 2005. LNCS, vol. 3414, pp. 198–214. Springer, Heidelberg (2005)
17. Ray, R., Gurung, A.: Poster: parallel state space exploration of linear systems with inputs using xspeed. In: Girard, A., Sankaranarayanan, S. (eds.) Proceedings of the 18th International Conference on Hybrid Systems: Computation and Control, HSCC 2015, Seattle, WA, USA, 14–16 April 2015, pp. 285–286. ACM (2015). http://doi.acm.org/10.1145/2728606.2728644
18. Rockafellar, R.T., Wets, R.J.B.: Variational Analysis, vol. 317. Springer, New York (1998)
19. Rungta, N., Tkachuk, O. (eds.): 2014 International Symposium on Model Checking of Software, SPIN 2014, Proceedings, San Jose, CA, USA, 21–23 July 2014. ACM (2014). http://dl.acm.org/citation.cfm?id=2632362
20. Skogestad, S., Postlethwaite, I.: Multivariable Feedback Control: Analysis and Design. Wiley, New York (2005)
21. Spampinato, D.G., Elster, A.C.: Linear optimization on modern GPUS. In: 23rd IEEE International Symposium on Parallel and Distributed Processing, IPDPS 2009, Rome, Italy, 23–29 May 2009, pp. 1–8. IEEE (2009). http://dx.doi.org/10.1109/IPDPS.2009.5161106
22. Stursberg, O., Krogh, B.H.: Efficient representation and computation of reachable sets for hybrid systems. In: Maler, O., Pnueli, A. (eds.) HSCC 2003. LNCS, vol. 2623, pp. 482–497. Springer, Heidelberg (2003)

Abstraction-Based Parameter Synthesis for Multiaffine Systems

Sergiy Bogomolov[1]([✉]), Christian Schilling[2], Ezio Bartocci[3],
Gregory Batt[4], Hui Kong[1], and Radu Grosu[3]

[1] IST Austria, Klosterneuburg, Austria
sergiy.bogomolov@ist.ac.at
[2] University of Freiburg, Freiburg im Breisgau, Germany
[3] Vienna University of Technology, Vienna, Austria
[4] INRIA Paris-Rocquencourt, Paris, France

Abstract. Multiaffine hybrid automata (MHA) represent a powerful
formalism to model complex dynamical systems. This formalism is particularly suited for the representation of biological systems which often
exhibit highly non-linear behavior. In this paper, we consider the problem of parameter identification for MHA. We present an abstraction of
MHA based on linear hybrid automata, which can be analyzed by the
SpaceEx model checker. This abstraction enables a precise handling of
time-dependent properties. We demonstrate the potential of our approach on a model of a genetic regulatory network and a myocyte model.

1 Introduction

Hybrid automata can model systems from a wide range of real-world domains.
Due to its behavioral complexity, the biological domain can particularly benefit from the expressiveness of hybrid automata [4]. However, biological models
mostly have highly non-linear dynamics.

Parameter identification is the problem where we want to find a parameter set for which a given property is satisfied by the system. In the biological
domain, this problem is of large importance considering the current limitations
on experimental measurement techniques [17].

In this paper, we present a novel approach to solve the parameter identification problem for the class of multiaffine hybrid automata (MHA). We reduce
the parameter identification problem to solving multiple *verification* problems.
In short, the algorithm consists of the following steps: We partition the parameter space into a number of equivalence classes. Given an equivalence class, we
show how the system behavior can be approximated with a linear hybrid automaton (LHA), which can be analyzed by the hybrid model checker SpaceEx [11].
In addition, we utilize a hierarchical search to start the analysis with coarser
regions and iteratively refine the partition based on the model structure. We
are also able to prune the search when we detect that our analysis will not find
any parameters in a subregion. We have implemented our approach and show
its potential on a genetic regulatory network and a myocyte model.

© Springer International Publishing Switzerland 2015
N. Piterman (Ed.): HVC 2015, LNCS 9434, pp. 19–35, 2015.
DOI: 10.1007/978-3-319-26287-1_2

Outline. The rest of the paper is organized as follows. In Sect. 2, we introduce some preliminary notions. Then we present our new approach, first the construction of the relevant parts in Sect. 3, followed by the hierarchical search procedure in Sect. 4. In Sect. 5, we evaluate the approach on two biological models. We discuss related work in Sect. 6 and conclude in Sect. 7.

2   Preliminaries

In this section, we introduce the notions used in the rest of the paper.

Multiaffine function. A multiaffine function $f : \mathbb{R}^n \to \mathbb{R}^q (n, q \in \mathbb{N})$ is a polynomial in the variables $x_1, \ldots, x_n$ with the property that the degree of f in any of the variables is less than or equal to 1 [15]. Formally, f has the following form:

$$f(x_1, \ldots, x_n) = \sum_{i_1, \ldots, i_n \in \{0,1\}} c_{i_1, \ldots, i_n} x_1^{i_1} \cdots x_n^{i_n},$$

with $c_{i_1, \ldots, i_n} \in \mathbb{R}^q$ for all $i_1, \ldots, i_n \in \{0, 1\}$ and the convention that $x_k^0 = 1$.

Hybrid automaton. A hybrid automaton (HA) [1] is a mathematical model with both continuous and discrete behavior. It is represented by the tuple $\mathcal{H} = (Loc, Var, Inv, Flow, Trans, Init)$. *Loc* is a set of discrete *locations*. *Var* is a set of real-valued variables $x_1, \ldots, x_n$. Each $\ell \in Loc$ is associated with a set of differential equations (or inclusions) $Flow(\ell)$ that defines the time-driven evolution of the continuous variables. A *state* $s \in Loc \times \mathbb{R}^n$ consists of a location and values of the continuous variables $x_1, \ldots, x_n$. The set of *discrete transitions Trans* defines how the state can jump between locations when inside the transition's *guard* set. The system can remain in a location ℓ while the state is inside the *invariant* set $Inv(\ell)$. All behavior originates from the set of *initial states Init*. A *trajectory* is a function which defines the state of the HA for every time moment. In the verification setting, we are interested in whether there exists a trajectory from the set *Init* to a set *Bad* which defines the *bad states* to be avoided.

Let $x(t) \in \mathbb{R}^n$ denote the values of the continuous variables at time t. We consider continuous dynamics *Flow* of the following two forms. If $\dot{x}(t) = f(x, t)$ where $f(x, t)$ is a multiaffine function, then the HA is called a *multiaffine hybrid automaton* (MHA). If $\dot{x}(t) \in P$ where P is a polytope, then the HA is called a *linear hybrid automaton* (LHA). We always consider *convex* polytopes and omit the dependence of f on t in what follows.

Genetic regulatory network. A genetic regulatory network [5] is defined by the dynamics of the following form:

$$\dot{x}_i = f_i(x, p) = \sum_{j \in P_i} \kappa_{ij} \, r_{ij}^P(x) - \sum_{j \in D_i} \gamma_{ij} \, r_{ij}^D(x) \, x_i, \quad i = 1, \ldots, n \qquad (1)$$

Here x_i is the i-th component of the state vector $x \in \mathcal{X} \subset \mathbb{R}^n$. P_i and D_i are sets of indices. κ_{ij} and γ_{ij} are production and degradation rate parameters, respectively. We assume that some parameters are uncertain, i.e., are defined on proper intervals. We denote the number of uncertain parameters by m. Therefore, the system is parametrized by the vector $p = (p_1, ..., p_m) \in \mathcal{D}$, where $\mathcal{D}$ is the hyper-rectangular domain of uncertain parameters.

The terms r_{ij} are continuous piecewise-multiaffine functions arising from products of ramp functions r^+ and r^- of the form shown in Fig. 1(a). Each r_{ij} captures the combined impact of several regulatory proteins in the sets P_i and D_i, respectively, on the control of the production or degradation of protein i. Assuming protein i does not regulate its own degradation, i.e., x_i does not occur in $r_{ij}^D(x)$ for $j \in D_i$, function $f = (f_1, \ldots, f_n)$ is multiaffine in x and affine in p.

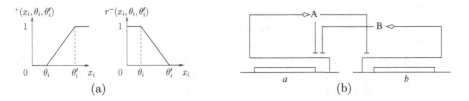

Fig. 1. (a) Ramp functions r^+ and r^-. (b) The two-genes network model.

We note that the ramp functions induce a partition of the state space $\mathcal{X}$ into a grid of hyper-rectangular regions H. The values of the separating hyperplanes are called *thresholds* θ. Let $\bar{\theta}_i$ be the number of thresholds in dimension i.

Definition 1. *Let* $\mathfrak{H} := \left\{ H_c \mid c = (c_1, \ldots, c_n), c_i \in \{1, \ldots, \bar{\theta}_i - 1\}, i = 1, \ldots, n \right\}$ *be the set of hyper-rectangles* H_c *with coordinates* c *in the grid. Furthermore, let* $coord : \mathfrak{H} \to \prod_{i=1}^{n} \{1, \ldots, \bar{\theta}_i - 1\}$ *map hyper-rectangle* H_c *to its coordinate* c.

Problem statement. A property φ specifies the desired system behavior. In this paper, we consider properties of the form $R_{Init} \to \neg \Diamond R_{Bad}$ where the region R_{Init} denotes the *initial* system states and the region R_{Bad} denotes the states to be avoided. Note that φ belongs to the class of *safety* properties. Our goal is to identify a subset of the parameter domain $\mathcal{D}$ which ensures that the property φ holds for a given MHA, i.e., R_{Bad} is avoided when starting in R_{Init}.

Note that an MHA provides a semantically equivalent representation of the dynamics (1). We consider an abstraction of a parametric MHA $M(p)$ to an infinite transition system.

Definition 2. *Let* H_x *be the hyper-rectangle strictly containing* x. *Given a parameter* p *and an MHA* $M(p)$, *the embedding transition system* $T_M(p)$ *is defined as follows. The states* $\mathcal{X}$ *are the same as the continuous states of* $M(p)$. *There is a transition* $x \to x'$ *iff: (1)* H_x *and* $H_{x'}$ *are either equal or adjacent. (2) There is a solution* ξ *of (1) and time points* $t_0 < t_1$ *such that* $\xi(t_0) = x$, $\xi(t_1) = x'$ *and for all* t *in* $[t_0, t_1]$, $\xi(t)$ *stays within* H_x *or* $H_{x'}$.

Almost all trajectories in $M(p)$ are represented in $T_M(p)$. The exception are trajectories not passing through a common facet of two hyper-rectangles. In what follows, we consider the representation of the system $T_M(p)$.

Example (two-genes network). In the following, we illustrate our approach on the *two-genes network* [6] (also called *toggle switch* or *cross-inhibition network*).

$$\dot{x}_a = \kappa_a \cdot r^-(x_a, \theta_a^4, \theta_a^5) \cdot r^-(x_b, \theta_b^2, \theta_b^3) - \gamma_a x_a \qquad \kappa_a \in [0, 30], \gamma_a = 1$$

$$\dot{x}_b = \kappa_b \cdot r^-(x_a, \theta_a^2, \theta_a^3) - \gamma_b x_b \qquad \kappa_b \in [0, 40], \gamma_b = 2$$

$$(\theta_a^1, \theta_a^2, \theta_a^3, \theta_a^4, \theta_a^5, \theta_a^6) = (0, 8, 12, 18, 22, 30) \qquad (\theta_b^1, \theta_b^2, \theta_b^3, \theta_b^4) = (0, 8, 12, 20)$$

Here x_a and x_b define the concentrations of the proteins A and B, respectively. The uncertain parameters κ_a and κ_b define the range of their production rates in the given intervals. As Fig. 1(b) shows, protein A inhibits the production of both proteins A and B, while protein B only inhibits the production of protein A. We are interested in checking whether the protein concentrations cannot reach some specific threshold values when starting in a given initial region.

In addition, we consider an extended version of the dynamics (1) which features a *stimulus*. The stimulus is a time-dependent function which models an external influence on the system.

Example (two-genes network with stimulus). We extend the previous example with the first equation now featuring some stimulus u:

$$\dot{x}_a = \kappa_a \cdot r^-(x_a, \theta_a^4, \theta_a^5) \cdot (1 - r^+(x_b, \theta_b^2, \theta_b^3) \cdot (1 - u)) - x_a$$

$$\dot{u} = r^-(t, t_2, t_3) \qquad (t_1, t_2, t_3, t_4) = (0, 0.29, 0.3, 1)$$

We use a stimulus which is 1 at the beginning up until 0.29 ms and then drops linearly to 0 within 0.01 ms, expressed by the ramp function of time $r^-(t, 0.29, 0.3)$. This stimulus regulates the production of the protein A together with the protein B. The term $(1 - r^+(x_b, \theta_b^1, \theta_b^2) \cdot (1 - u))$ encodes the logical formula $\neg(x_b \wedge \neg u)$, which is equivalent to $\neg x_b \vee u$. Thus, this term contributes to the production of the protein A whenever the protein B is absent or the stimulus is present. Since the stimulus is time-dependent and decreasing, this means that the inhibitory effect of the protein B is only relevant for the production of the protein A after 0.29 ms.

3 Abstraction of MHA

In this section, we first introduce an LHA $L_M(p)$ which overapproximates the behavior of the transition system $T_M(p)$ for a particular parameter value $p \in \mathcal{D}$. In order to provide efficient exploration of the parameter state space, we then lift this definition to parameter sets. We use the two-genes model as a running example throughout this section.

3.1   Pointwise LHA Abstraction

State space and invariants. We use the same continuous variables for $L_M(p)$ as in the MHA $M(p)$. Thresholds θ partition the continuous state space into a grid of hyper-rectangular regions, which naturally induces a discrete structure of the LHA and location invariants. In particular, we map every hyper-rectangular region to a location in the LHA and use the bounds on the regions as invariants.

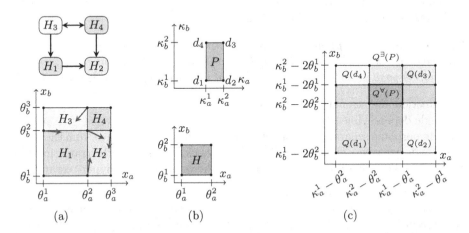

Fig. 2. (a) From state space partition to transition system. Example for $\kappa_a = 10$ and $\kappa_b = 15$ (arrows normalized). (b–c) Flow computation for $P = [8, 12] \times [15, 20]$ (Color figure online).

Example. In the two-genes example we get a 2D-partition by the planes at $x_a = \theta_a^i$ and $x_b = \theta_b^j$. Parts of the state space and the associated locations are shown in Fig. 2(a). The invariant of location H_3 is $\theta_a^1 \leq x_1 \leq \theta_a^2 \wedge \theta_b^2 \leq x_2 \leq \theta_b^3$.

Discrete transitions. We use the quotient of $T_M(p)$ with respect to the state space partition to define the discrete transitions.

Definition 3. *Let H_ℓ and $H_{\ell'}$ be the regions associated with the location ℓ and ℓ', respectively. $L_M(p)$ has a transition from location ℓ to ℓ' if*

– *ℓ and ℓ' are adjacent,*
– *there is a solution ξ of (1) and time points $t_0 < t_1 < t_2$ such that $\xi(t) \in Inv(\ell)$ for all t in $[t_0, t_1]$, and $\xi(t) \in Inv(\ell')$ for all t in $[t_1, t_2]$.*

We do not add any guards on the transitions as the chosen invariants already ensure that a transition between two locations can only be taken on the common facet of two adjacent regions H_ℓ and $H_{\ell'}$.

In order to effectively construct the transitions, we use the facts that the dynamics $f(x, p)$ are multiaffine in x and we consider only hyper-rectangular regions for the locations in $L_M(p)$. In the following, let *hull* denote the convex hull operator.

Theorem 1. *[7] Let $f : \mathbb{R}^n \to \mathbb{R}^n$ be a multiaffine function and $H \subset \mathbb{R}^n$ be a hyper-rectangle with corner set C_H. Then*

$$f(H) \subseteq hull(\{f(v) \mid v \in C_H\}).$$

Intuitively, this theorem says that the behavior of f inside a hyper-rectangle H is completely determined by the behavior of f in the corners of H. As a consequence, the following proposition along the lines of a similar proposition for Kripke structures [5] can be proven.

Proposition 1. *$L_M(p)$ has a transition from location ℓ to ℓ' associated with hyper-rectangles H_ℓ and $H_{\ell'}$ only if the projection of $f(x,p)$ on the $H_\ell \to H_{\ell'}$ direction is positive in at least one corner of the facet separating H_ℓ from $H_{\ell'}$.*

Direction and strength of the derivative $\dot{x}_i = f_i(x, p)$ in a corner v of a hyper-rectangle depends linearly on parameter vector p. As a consequence, $f_i(v, p) = 0$ is the hyperplane separating parameter values p where $\dot{x}_i$ is positive from the ones where $\dot{x}_i$ is negative. Thus, Proposition 1 allows us to construct the transitions of $L_M(p)$ based on the sign of the function f at the vertices of the hyper-rectangles.

Example. The transitions for the excerpt shown in Fig. 2(a) are determined by the direction of the derivatives in the corners (shown in blue). For instance, we add a transition from H_1 to H_2 because there is a corner, e.g., (θ_a^2, θ_b^1), which point to this direction, but there is no transition from H_2 to H_1.

Continuous flows. For computing the flows of the LHA we again use the multiaffine dependence of $f(x,p)$ on x and the affine dependence on p.

For a fixed hyper-rectangle H with corner set C_H and a fixed parameter vector p, by Theorem 1 we know that $f(x,p)$ is included in the convex hull of the hyper-rectangle corners $v \in C_H$. Therefore, we can bound the flow of $L_M(p)$ by a polytope, i.e., the dynamics can be represented in the form of differential inclusion.

Definition 4. *The flow of $L_M(p)$ is defined as $Q(p) := hull(\{f(v, p) \mid v \in C_H\})$.*

3.2 Set-Based LHA Abstraction

In order to handle infinite sets of parameters, we lift the pointwise definition of $L_M(p)$ to sets of parameters. In particular, given a parameter polytope P, we introduce an LHA $L_M^{\exists}(P)$ which overapproximates the behavior of $L_M(p)$ for all $p \in P$. Therefore, if $L_M^{\exists}(P)$ satisfies a property φ, we can conclude that P is a valid parameter set. Otherwise, we partition the parameter set P into two subsets P_1 and P_2 and proceed with their analysis. In order to prune the parts of the parameter space where our analysis will not provide any valid parameters, we introduce a further LHA called $L_M^{\vee}(P)$ which underapproximates the LHA $L_M(p)$ for the parameter class P. In the following, we assume a parameter $p \in P$.

State space and invariants. We use the same state space and invariants for both $L_M^{\exists}(P)$ and $L_M^{\vee}(P)$ as defined for $L_M(p)$.

Discrete transitions. The theorem below provides an effective way to compute the image of $f(v, p)$ for a particular state space corner v and a parameter vector $p \in P$.

Theorem 2. *[14] Let $f : \mathbb{R}^m \to \mathbb{R}^m$ be an affine function and $P \subset \mathbb{R}^m$ be a convex polytope with corner set C_P. Then*

$$f(P) = hull(\{f(d) \mid d \in C_P\}).$$

Now, $L_M^{\exists}(P)$ has a transition from location ℓ to ℓ' if there is a transition from ℓ to ℓ' in $L_M(p)$ for *some* $p \in P$. Analogously, $L_M^{\forall}(P)$ has a transition from location ℓ to ℓ' if there is a transition from ℓ to ℓ' in $L_M(p)$ for *all* $p \in P$.

Definition 5. *Let $c := coord(H)$ and $c' := coord(H')$ be the coordinates of two adjacent hyper-rectangles. Furthermore, let $V := C_H \cap C_{H'}$ be the corners on the separating facet and let ℓ and ℓ' be the locations associated to H and H', respectively.*
We define $g(\ell, \ell') := \bigcup_{v \in V} \{p \in P \mid f_i(v, p) \cdot (c'_i - c_i) > 0\}$, where $i \in \{1, \ldots, n\}$ such that $c'_i - c_i \neq 0$. A transition $\ell \to \ell'$ belongs to the LHA

- $L_M^{\exists}(P)$ *if $g(\ell, \ell') \neq \emptyset$, and to*
- $L_M^{\forall}(P)$ *if $g(\ell, \ell') = P$.*

Note that Theorem 2 allows us to construct the parameter set satisfying the constraint $f_i(v, p) \cdot (c'_i - c_i) > 0$ by only considering the vertices of P. The term $c'_i - c_i = \pm 1$ is used to express the direction of the transition. The construction uses the union operation and test for equality and emptiness for polytopes.

Continuous flows. For $L_M^{\exists}(P)$ to be an overapproximation of all $L_M(p)$ and $L_M^{\forall}(P)$ to be an underapproximation, the tightest definition we can find is the union and intersection of all $Q(p)$, respectively. Let $Q_{\exists}^*(P) := \bigcup_{p \in P} Q(p)$ and $Q_{\forall}^*(P) := \bigcap_{p \in P} Q(p)$. Computing $Q_{\exists}^*(P)$ and $Q_{\forall}^*(P)$ is, however, infeasible. Therefore, similarly to the transition construction, we propose an approximation which relies on the values of the derivatives in the corners of state space partitions H and parameter sets P.

Theorem 3. *Let $f(x, p) : \mathbb{R}^n \times \mathbb{R}^m \to \mathbb{R}^n$ with $x \in \mathbb{R}^n$ and $p \in \mathbb{R}^m$ be a multiaffine function which is affine in p, $H \subset \mathbb{R}^n$ be a hyper-rectangle with a corner set C_H and $P \subset \mathbb{R}^m$ be a convex polytope with a corner set C_P. Then the following holds:*

- $\bigcup_{p \in P} Q(p) \subseteq hull \left(\bigcup_{d \in C_P} Q(d) \right),$
- $\bigcap_{p \in P} Q(p) \subseteq \bigcap_{d \in C_P} Q(d).$

Note that the left-hand sides are $Q_{\exists}^*(P)$ and $Q_{\forall}^*(P)$, respectively. Based on this theorem, we define the flows in the following way.

Definition 6. *The flow of $L_M^{\exists}(P)$ is defined as $Q_{\exists}(P) := hull \left(\bigcup_{d \in C_P} Q(d) \right)$. The flow of $L_M^{\forall}(P)$ is defined as $Q_{\forall}(P) := \bigcap_{d \in C_P} Q(d)$.*

We obtain an algorithm for computing $Q_\exists(P)$ and $Q_\forall(P)$ by first traversing all vertices $v \in C_H$ and $d \in C_P$ and collecting $f(v,d)$ in order to compute the polytope $Q(d)$. In the end, we take the finite union and intersection of those polytopes. Note that similar to $L_M(p)$ we end up with LHA whose dynamics are defined by differential inclusions.

The following proposition relates the flow representations we have introduced.

Proposition 2. *The sets $Q(p)$, $Q_\exists^*(P)$, $Q_\forall^*(P)$, $Q_\exists(P)$ and $Q_\forall(P)$ are related as follows.*

- $Q_\forall^*(P) \subseteq Q_\forall(P)$.
- $Q_\forall^*(P) \subseteq Q(p) \subseteq Q_\exists^*(P) \subseteq Q_\exists(P)$ *for all $p \in P$.*

Thus, $Q_\exists(P)$ is indeed an overapproximation of $L_M(p)$ as required. However, while $Q_\forall^*(P)$ is an underapproximation of $L_M(p)$, $Q_\forall(P)$ is not necessarily an underapproximation of $L_M(p)$ for $p \in P$. We discuss this issue in the next section.

We define the automaton $L_M^{\exists*}(P)$ by replacing $Q_\exists(P)$ with $Q_\exists^*(P)$ in the continuous flow of the automaton $L_M^\exists(P)$. We derive $L_M^{\forall*}(P)$ from $L_M^\forall(P)$ in the analogous way, i.e., by replacing $Q_\forall(P)$ with $Q_\forall^*(P)$.

Example. Consider the state space rectangle H and the parameter space rectangle P in Fig. 2(b). Recall that the state equation $\dot{x} = f(x,p)$ is given as

$$\dot{x}_a = f_a(x,p) = \kappa_a - x_a \qquad \dot{x}_b = f_b(x,p) = \kappa_b - 2x_b.$$

Hence the dynamics $f(v,d)$, for v and d in the corner sets C_H and C_P of H and P, respectively, are of the form $(\kappa_a^i - \theta_a^j, \quad \kappa_b^k - 2\theta_b^\ell)$.

Let the corners of the parameter space rectangle P be denoted in anti-clockwise order as d_1, d_2, d_3 and d_4. Now construct the state space rectangles $Q(d_1)$, $Q(d_2)$, $Q(d_3)$ and $Q(d_4)$. The intersection of all these rectangles results in the rectangle $Q^\forall(P)$, while the union is the rectangle $Q^\exists(P)$. Since it is already convex, *hull* is the identity operation in this case. The results are visualized in Fig. 2(c).

We observe that, by construction, $L_M(p)$ is a conservative abstraction of $T_M(p)$, and $L_M^\exists(P)$ is a conservative abstraction of $L_M(p)$, i.e., if $L_M^\exists(P)$ satisfies a safety property, then so does $T_M(p)$. This fact ensures the soundness of our approach.

Proposition 3. $L_M^\exists(P)$ *is an overapproximation of $T_M(p)$ for any $p \in P$.*

4   Hierarchical Parameter Search

In this section, we first show that by using sampling techniques we can compute the automaton $L_M^{\forall*}(P)$ with arbitrary precision. Afterwards, in order to leverage different levels of abstractions during the parameter space exploration, we introduce a discrete abstraction of MHA. Finally, we describe an abstraction-based parameter search procedure which explores the parameter domain in a hierarchical fashion.

4.1 Computation of Underapproximative Abstractions

As outlined in the previous section, the role of the underapproximation $L_M^{\forall *}(P)$ is to detect parameter regions which our approach cannot classify as valid ones. The LHA $L_M^{\forall}(P)$, an overapproximated version of $L_M^{\forall *}(P)$, does not generally underapproximate $L_M(p)$ for all $p \in P$. The reason is that the flows $Q_\forall(P)$ do not necessarily underapproximate the flows $Q(p)$ of all $L_M(p)$. In particular, as we take an intersection only over corner points of a considered parameter set, there might exist some $p \in P$ such that $Q_\forall(P) \nsubseteq Q(p)$.

Note that as we only use $L_M^{\forall}(P)$ for pruning purposes, soundness of our approach is not affected by imprecision. We might at most ignore some parameter region which could have been classified as valid by our approach. Still, in order to improve the precision of $L_M^{\forall}(P)$, we can randomly sample parameter vectors $p \in P$ and consider the intersection of $Q(p)$ with $Q_\forall(P)$.

The following theorem describes the possible improvements by sampling. For notational convenience, let $\|\cdot\|$ denote the Euclidean norm, ∂S denote the border of a closed set S, $d(t, S) := \min_{s \in S} \|t - s\|$ denote the distance of t to the border of S, and $Ker_\epsilon(S) := \{s \in S \mid d(s, \partial S) \geq \epsilon\}$.

Theorem 4. *Let* $f(x, p) : \mathbb{R}^n \times \mathbb{R}^m \to \mathbb{R}^n$ *with* $x \in \mathbb{R}^n$ *and* $p \in \mathbb{R}^m$ *be a multiaffine function which is affine in* p, $H \subset \mathbb{R}^n$ *be a hyper-rectangle and* $P \subset \mathbb{R}^m$ *be a convex polytope. Then the following formulae hold:*

$$\forall p, p' \in P. \lim_{\|p - p'\| \to 0} Q(p) = Q(p') \tag{2}$$

$$\forall p \in P, \epsilon > 0. \exists \delta > 0. \forall p' \in P. \|p - p'\| < \delta \tag{3}$$
$$\implies Ker_{2\epsilon}(Q(p)) \subseteq Q(p) \cap Q(p') \wedge Ker_{2\epsilon}(Q(p')) \subseteq Q(p) \cap Q(p')$$

This theorem asserts that if we sample sufficiently many points in a uniform way in parameter space, then we can approximate $L_M^{\forall *}(P)$ infinitely closely for non-degenerate cases, i.e., when $Ker_{2\epsilon}(Q(p)) \neq \emptyset$ for all $p \in P$. However, for practical purposes, sampling can clearly shrink the overapproximation even in degenerate cases.

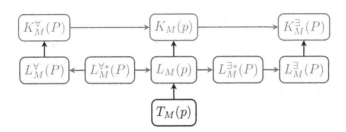

Fig. 3. Relations of the systems presented in this paper. Let $p \in P$. An arrow $S_1 \longrightarrow S_2$ indicates that S_2 is an overapproximation of S_1.

Figure 3 shows the relationship between the systems considered in this paper.

4.2   Discrete Abstraction of MHA

For later discussion, it is useful to define the induced Kripke structures (KS) of the LHA $L_M(p)$, $L_M^{\exists}(P)$ and $L_M^{\forall}(P)$. Basically, we drop the continuous behavior and map initial and bad states to the locations with non-empty intersection.

Definition 7. *Given an LHA $\mathcal{H}$ with set of locations Loc, let S be a set of discrete states with $|S| = |Loc|$ and let disc : Loc $\to S$ be a bijection which maps every location to a discrete state. In addition, let Bad be the bad states of $\mathcal{H}$.*

The pair $(\mathcal{H}, Bad)$ induces a Kripke structure $\mathcal{K} = (S, S_0, S_B, T)$, where $S = \{disc(\ell) \mid \ell \in Loc\}$ is the set of states, $S_0 = \{disc(\ell) \mid inv(\ell) \cap Init \neq \emptyset\}$ is the set of initial states, $S_B = \{disc(\ell) \mid inv(\ell) \cap Bad \neq \emptyset\}$ are the bad states, and $T = \{disc(\ell) \to_{\mathcal{K}} disc(\ell') \mid \ell \to_{\mathcal{H}} \ell' \in Trans\}$ is the set of transitions.

We denote by $K_M(p)$, $K_M^{\exists}(P)$, $K_M^{\forall}(P)$ the Kripke structures induced by $L_M(p)$, $L_M^{\exists}(P)$, $L_M^{\forall}(P)$, respectively. Clearly, the induced Kripke structure is a conservative abstraction of the LHA as it allows for additional trajectories to the bad states for two reasons. The behavior in the states is unconstrained due to the absence of flows, and the initial and bad states of the Kripke structure overapproximate their LHA counterparts.

Proposition 4. $K_M(p)$ $(K_M^{\exists}(P)$, $K_M^{\forall}(P)$, respectively) is an overapproximation of $L_M(p)$ $(L_M^{\exists}(P)$, $L_M^{\forall}(P)$, respectively) for any $p \in \mathcal{D}$ $(P \subseteq \mathcal{D}$, respectively).

We incorporate the Kripke structures into our approach in the following way. Whenever we analyze an LHA, we first analyze the respective KS. If the KS *satisfies* the given property, we skip the LHA analysis. This is justified because by Proposition 4 we know that the respective LHA will also satisfy the property. In this way, we improve analysis performance as the reachability problem for LHA is computationally harder to solve. We note that the construction of the KS does not impose any further computational efforts since we need to construct the locations and transitions for the LHA anyway.

4.3   Parameter Identification

Given an MHA M with $\dot{x} = f(x, p)$, a safety property φ and the domain of uncertain parameters $\mathcal{D}$, we explore the parameter space in a hierarchical way. Recall from the construction of the transitions that the constraints $f(x, p) = 0$ are the separating hyperplanes responsible for adding transitions. Based on those constraints, the instantiation of $f(x, p)$ in every corner v of the state space leads to a parameter space partition into polytopes.

We now explain the algorithm with the help of the pseudocode given in Fig. 4.

In a preprocessing step, the algorithm examines the corners of the state space partition and collects the constraints Ψ over the parameters in the function *CollectConstraintsList* (line 3) such that $f(x, p) = 0$.

```
1  ParameterIdentification (M, φ, D)
2  % M: MHA, φ: property, D: uncertain parameters
3    Ψ := CollectConstraintsList (M, D);
4    global V := ∅;
5    Explore (ε, Ψ, M, φ, D, ⊤); % start at root (ε = empty list)
6    return V; % found valid parameters
```

```
6   Explore (CL, Ψ, M, φ, D, b) % CL: list of current constraints
7     P := PolytopeFromConstraintsList (CL, D);
8     K_M^∃, K_M^∀, L_M^∃, L_M^∀ = ConstructSystems (M, P);
9     if (b ∧ ¬Reach (K_M^∃, φ))
10      V := V ∪ P; return; % valid set found by the KS analysis
11    elseif (¬Reach (L_M^∃, φ))
12      V := V ∪ P; return; % valid set found by the LHA analysis
13    elseif (¬b ∨ Reach (K_M^∀, φ))
14      b := ⊥; % no future valid sets for the KS analysis
15      if (Reach (L_M^∀, φ))
16        return; % no future valid sets for the LHA analysis
17    % partition P and descend to child nodes in the search tree
18    c := first (Ψ); Ψ := rest (Ψ);
19    Explore (concatenate (CL, c ≥ 0), Ψ, M, φ, D, b);
20    Explore (concatenate (CL, c ≤ 0), Ψ, M, φ, D, b);
```

Fig. 4. The algorithm in pseudocode.

Next, the algorithm moves on to the function **Explore** (line 5) which actually implements the search in the parameter space. This function successively builds a number of abstractions of the MHA for a considered parameter set in order to find valid subsets. It takes a list CL of constraints which encodes hyperplanes used to define the current parameter set. We initially call the function with $CL = \varepsilon$ as we first consider the whole parameter space. Now we look at the function **Explore** in more detail.

We start by calling the function **PolytopeFromConstraintsList** (line 7) which builds a parameter polytope P based on the provided list CL of constraints over parameters and the parameter space domain $\mathcal{D}$. In line 8 we compute the KS $K_M^\exists(P)$, $K_M^\forall(P)$ and the LHA $L_M^\exists(P)$, $L_M^\forall(P)$. Note that on the implementation level we compute them only *on demand*. The computed approximations are analyzed in the following way:

1. If the property φ holds for the KS $K_M^\exists(P)$ already (line 9), we conclude that the current parameter set P is valid. Therefore, we add P to the set of valid parameters V and stop considering the current branch in the search tree (line 10).
2. If the discrete abstraction $K_M^\exists(P)$ was too coarse to prove the validity of P, we continue with the finer analysis using $L_M^\exists(P)$ (line 11). Similar to step 1, in the case of property satisfaction we add P to the valid parameters (line 12).

3. If the parameter set validity has not been shown up to now, we proceed to the pruning phase by considering $K_M^\forall(P)$ and $L_M^\forall(P)$. If both of them *violate* the property φ, we prune the search tree as we expect that no valid parameter sets can be found for any subset of P.

   Note that due to efficiency reasons we first analyze $K_M^\forall(P)$ (line 13) and move on to $L_M^\forall(P)$ (line 15) only if the KS is not safe with respect to the property φ. If $L_M^\forall(P)$ is not safe either, we prune the current subtree. However, if $L_M^\forall(P)$ is safe, we continue with the search. In this case, we can omit the KS analysis for all nodes in the current subtree as it will always give the same result. We assume the conditions in lines 9 and 13 are evaluated in a lazy fashion and therefore we only use the KS analysis based on the value of the Boolean switch b.

4. If $K_M^\forall(P)$ or $L_M^\forall(P)$ are safe, we partition the parameter set P into two subsets by considering a further constraint from the list Ψ (line 18). Those two subsets correspond to the positive and negative values of the chosen constraint, respectively. We proceed by recursively analyzing both subsets (lines 19–20).

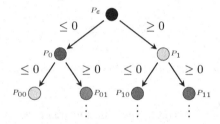

Fig. 5. Search tree in the parameter space. **yellow:** $L_M^\exists(P)$ satisfies the property φ while $K_M^\exists(P)$ violates it. **blue:** $L_M^\forall(P)$ satisfies the property φ while $K_M^\forall(P)$ violates it. **gray:** The node is only explored by the LHA analysis. **red:** The node is only explored by the KS analysis (Color figure online).

Search tree implications. In Fig. 5, we illustrate the potential impact of the LHA $L_M^\exists(P)$ and $L_M^\forall(P)$ on the structure of the search tree compared to an approach only using the KS analysis. We observe that $L_M^\exists(P)$ satisfies the property φ in the node P_1, whereas $K_M^\exists(P)$ violates the property. The LHA analysis benefits in two ways from this result. Firstly, it finds a large parameter set P_1, whereas the KS analysis can at most find valid sets in some of the child nodes, which are subsets of P_1. Secondly, the LHA analysis does not explore the children of P_1 in the search tree, which improves the algorithm performance. Moreover, $L_M^\forall(P)$ satisfies the property φ in the node P_0, whereas $K_M^\forall(P)$ violates the property. Therefore, the KS analysis prunes the subtree P_0, but a valid parameter set P_{00} can be found by the LHA analysis.

5   Evaluation

We have implemented the algorithm in MATLAB in the tool Hydentify. We use the library PPL [2] for the operations on polytopes and the SpaceEx model checker [11] for the analysis of the LHA. Note that the default version of SpaceEx does not stop immediately after having found a property violation. Therefore, we have modified the version of SpaceEx so that it stops as soon as a property violation has been detected. This adjustment lets us improve the analysis performance. We apply the PHAVer scenario of SpaceEx which uses constraint polytopes to represent reachable regions to precisely analyze LHA.

Batt *et al.* [5] have presented a parameter identification approach for multiaffine systems implemented in a tool called RoVerGeNe. They approximate the system on the level of the induced Kripke structures. In the following evaluation, we compare the parameter identification results of our approach and RoVerGeNe. The integration of the induced KS into our algorithm allows for both a qualitative and a quantitative comparison of the two approaches. The implementation and models we used for the evaluation are available online[1].

Two-genes network model. We evaluate our tool on a number of models from the class of genetic regulatory networks. The experiments have been performed on a notebook with an Intel Core 2 Duo @ 2.26 GHz processor and 4 GB RAM.

For the evaluation purpose, we consider two classes of the two-genes network model introduced in Sect. 2. The first model class is the original system, while the second class is augmented by a stimulus. Note that our LHA framework enables an easy modeling and analysis of models with time dependent stimuli. In particular, we model a stimulus as a ramp function of an auxiliary variable t defined by the differential equation $\dot{t} = 1$. For every model class, we present two model instances. We look for parameters which lead to the repression of a given protein. For every instance and parameter identification algorithm, we report the following data: the coverage of the parameter domain, the number of the valid parameter sets found, the number of nodes in the search tree considered, the number of KS and LHA analyzed, and the runtime in seconds. By the term *parameter coverage* we denote the relation of the volume of the found valid parameters to the volume of the whole parameter domain $\mathcal{D}$. The results are provided in Table 1. The instances 1–2 correspond to the model class without a stimulus, whereas the other two instances belong to the class with a stimulus.

We first observe that the valid parameter regions found by our algorithm are usually much larger than the ones found by RoVerGeNe for both the models with and without the stimulus. Instance 2 provides a particularly illustrative example for the difference. Here, RoVerGeNe does not find any valid parameters, whereas our approach discovers valid parameter regions covering 38 % of the whole parameter domain. This behavior can be justified as follows. On the one hand, RoVerGeNe reports that both $K_M^\exists(P)$ and $K_M^\forall(P)$ at the root level reach the bad states. This results in analysis termination of RoVerGeNe. On the other hand, our algorithm proceeds in-depth with the analysis of the parameter space and detects 5 valid parameter regions. In instance 3, we see similar impact of taking LHA into account. In particular, both approaches consider 5 $K_M^\forall(P)$. However, our approach additionally considers 3 $L_M^\forall(P)$ which allow to extra unfold the parameter space. In this way, our approach analyzes 15 nodes and

---

[1] http://swt.informatik.uni-freiburg.de/tool/spaceex/hydentify.

Table 1. model ID: 1–2: without stimulus; 3–4: with stimulus; **% valid**: percentage of parameter space verified; **# sets**: number of parameter sets found; **# nodes**: number of nodes in the search tree; **# ∃-KS/∃-LHA**: number of $K_M^{\exists}/L_M^{\exists}$ analyzed; **# ∀-KS/∀-LHA**: number of $K_M^{\forall}/L_M^{\forall}$ analyzed; **runtime**: runtime in seconds

model ID	% valid		# sets		# nodes		# ∃-KS/∃-LHA			# ∀-KS/∀-LHA			runtime [s]	
								Hydentify			Hydentify			
	RoVerGeNe	Hydentify	RoVerGeNe	Hydentify	RoVerGeNe	Hydentify	RoVerGeNe	KS	LHA	RoVerGeNe	KS	LHA	RoVerGeNe	Hydentify
1	60	85	7	5	23	23	23	9	21	16	5	10	11	32
2	0	38	0	5	1	79	1	1	79	1	1	62	2	95
3	65	73	3	5	9	15	9	9	12	5	5	3	6	22
4	60	84	4	3	13	9	13	7	7	9	4	1	8	18

finds 5 valid regions compared to 9 nodes and 3 valid regions for RoVerGeNe, respectively. At the same time, the refined precision of LHA can shrink the search space. For example, in instance 4, the new algorithm achieves the parameter coverage of 84 % vs. 60 % by RoVerGeNe having considered only 9 nodes vs. 13 nodes in case of RoVerGeNe. We note that the valid parameter sets which are near the search tree root lead to larger parameter coverage with only a few parameter sets. This fact is confirmed by instance 4 where our approach finds 3 valid sets which cover a bigger region than the 4 valid sets found by RoVerGeNe.

Myocyte model. A fundamental question in the treatment of cardiac disorders, such as tachycardia and fibrillation [8], is the identification of circumstances under which such a disorder arises. Cardiac contraction is electrically regulated by particular cells, known as myocytes. For each electric stimulus originating in the sino-atrial node of the heart (its natural pacemaking unit), the myocytes propagate this stimulus and enforce the contraction of the cardiac muscle, known as a heart beat. Grosu *et al.* [13] have identified an MHA model for human ventricular myocytes and recast the biological investigation of lack of excitability to a computational investigation of the parameter ranges for which the MHA accurately reproduces lack of excitability. We apply our algorithm to this model and compare its performance with RoVerGeNe. The model has 4 continuous variables and 4 parameters. In our setting, a valid parameter set ensures that the myocyte is not excited.

We remark that our parameter identification approach has a large potential with respect to *parallelization* as the LHA and KS can be analyzed independently. We made use of this property and utilized a parallel version of our implementation for the analysis of the myocyte model. The experiments have been run on a Linux cluster with 32 AMD @ 2.3 GHz cores and 256 GB RAM. The model behavior is analyzed within a biologically reasonable time span of 1 ms. We note that the stimulus and particularly its duration require a special treatment as it strongly impacts the myocyte behavior. The stimulus in our model starts with the value 1 and linearly drops to 0. We explore the impact of the stimulus length on the myocytes excitement.

Our approach empirically shows that the *whole* parameter domain is valid for *all* stimuli of length up to approximately 0.12 ms. In other words, we can provide a *lower bound* on the stimulus length which makes the myocyte model *excitable*. For this purpose, we have discretized the stimulus length with a step of 0.1 ms, i.e., we have considered stimuli of the length $0, 0.1, \ldots, 1$ ms. Having identified an interval of interest [0.1; 0.2], we have discretized it in a finer way with a step of 0.02 ms. The new analysis takes 187 s and detects that the *whole* parameter domain is valid for the stimulus of length 0.12 ms, whereas RoVerGeNe reports the coverage of 29 % after 48 s. The parameter coverage computed by our algorithm drops to 30 % for the stimulus length of 0.14 ms and the analysis takes 1785 s. We note that the coverage computed by RoVerGeNe stays the same for all stimulus lengths as it cannot reason about time. This is a conceptual improvement over RoVerGeNe.

6   Related Work

A number of approaches have been developed to solve the parameter identification problem for hybrid automata. First, as already outlined in the previous section, Batt *et al.* [5] presented a parameter identification approach based on the abstraction of MHA by Kripke structures. By using our LHA abstraction, we improve the abstraction precision and in this way find more valid parameters. Dang *et al.* [9] introduced a "sensitive barbarian" approach. Bartocci *et al.* [3] consider a modular version of this approach. The main idea is to combine *numerical* simulation with sensitivity analysis to reduce the considered parameter space. A crucial difference to our approach lies in the fact that we utilize a *symbolic* analysis of the reachable states. In a further approach, Dreossi *et al.* [10] provide a parameter synthesis algorithm for polynomial dynamical systems. Their synthesis technique uses the Bernstein polynomial representation and recasts the synthesis problem as a linear programming problem. Note that they consider only *discrete* time dynamical systems, whereas we treat time as a *continuous* entity. The work by Liu *et al.* [16] tackles the parameter synthesis problem using δ-complete decision procedures [12] for first-order logic (FOL) formulae to overcome undecidability issues. In this setting, a FOL formula describes the states reachable with a finite number of steps. Therefore, the parameter identification problem is reduced to finding a satisfying valuation of the parameters for this formula. This approach requires enumerating *all the discrete paths* of a particular length, which leads to performance degradation for large models. In our approach, we employ the *symbolic* model checker SpaceEx, which prunes the state space exploration by checking whether the currently considered states have already been visited.

7   Conclusion

We have presented a novel parameter identification algorithm for multiaffine hybrid automata. In our algorithm, we compute equivalence classes in the parameter space and explore them in a hierarchical way. The approximation of the system dynamics with linear hybrid automata lets us keep the timing information in our abstraction. This allows us to precisely treat time-dependent properties such as a stimulus.

Given a parameter polytope P, we compute an LHA which overapproximates the system behavior for P. Furthermore, we compute another LHA which enables us to prune the search tree. We have evaluated our approach on a model of a genetic regulatory network and a myocyte model and demonstrated its improvement over RoVerGeNe, a tool for parameter identification based on a purely discrete abstraction.

In the future, we plan to investigate the application of hybrid model checkers which support more expressive continuous dynamics. This enables approximating the parametrized system dynamics with a hybrid automaton class featuring dynamics beyond the ones of LHA.

Acknowledgments. This work was partly supported by the European Research Council (ERC) under grant 267989 (QUAREM), by the Austrian Science Fund (FWF) under grants S11402-N23, S11405-N23 and S11412-N23 (RiSE/SHiNE) and Z211-N23 (Wittgenstein Award), and by the German Research Foundation (DFG) as part of the Transregional Collaborative Research Center "Automatic Verification and Analysis of Complex Systems" (SFB/TR 14 AVACS, http://www.avacs.org/).

References

1. Alur, R., Courcoubetis, C., Halbwachs, N., Henzinger, T.A., Ho, P.-H., Nicollin, X., Olivero, A., Sifakis, J., Yovine, S.: The algorithmic analysis of hybrid systems. Theor. Comput. Sci. **138**(1), 3–34 (1995)
2. Bagnara, R., Hill, P.M., Zaffanella, E.: The parma polyhedra library: toward a complete set of numerical abstractions for the analysis and verification of hardware and software systems. Sci. Comput. Program. **72**(1), 3–21 (2008)
3. Bartocci, E., Bortolussi, L., Nenzi, L.: A temporal logic approach to modular design of synthetic biological circuits. In: Gupta, A., Henzinger, T.A. (eds.) CMSB 2013. LNCS, vol. 8130, pp. 164–177. Springer, Heidelberg (2013)
4. Bartocci, E., Corradini, F., Di Berardini, M.R., Entcheva, E., Smolka, S., Grosu, R.: Modeling and simulation of cardiac tissue using hybrid I/O automata. Theor. Comput. Sci. **410**(410), 3149–3165 (2009)
5. Batt, G., Belta, C., Weiss, R.: Temporal logic analysis of gene networks under parameter uncertainty. IEEE Trans. Autom. Control **53**, 215–229 (2008)
6. Batt, G., Yordanov, B., Weiss, R., Belta, C.: Robustness analysis and tuning of synthetic gene networks. Bioinformatics **23**(18), 2415–2422 (2007)
7. Belta, C., Habets, L.: Controlling a class of nonlinear systems on rectangles. IEEE Trans. Autom. Control **51**(11), 1749–1759 (2006)

8. Cherry, E.M., Fenton, F.H.: Visualization of spiral and scroll waves in simulated and experimental cardiac tissue. New J. Phys. **10**, 125016 (2008)
9. Dang, T., Donzé, A., Maler, O., Shalev, N.: Sensitive state-space exploration. In: CDC, pp. 4049–4054 (2008)
10. Dreossi, T., Dang, T.: Parameter synthesis for polynomial biological models. In: Proceedings of HSCC 2014: The 17th International Conference on Hybrid Systems: Computation and Control, HSCC 2014, pp. 233–242. ACM, New York, NY, USA (2014)
11. Frehse, G., Le Guernic, C., Donzé, A., Cotton, S., Ray, R., Lebeltel, O., Ripado, R., Girard, A., Dang, T., Maler, O.: SpaceEx: scalable verification of hybrid systems. In: Gopalakrishnan, G., Qadeer, S. (eds.) CAV 2011. LNCS, vol. 6806, pp. 379–395. Springer, Heidelberg (2011)
12. Gao, S., Avigad, J., Clarke, E.M.: δ-complete decision procedures for satisfiability over the reals. In: Gramlich, B., Miller, D., Sattler, U. (eds.) IJCAR 2012. LNCS, vol. 7364, pp. 286–300. Springer, Heidelberg (2012)
13. Grosu, R., Batt, G., Fenton, F.H., Glimm, J., Le Guernic, C., Smolka, S.A., Bartocci, E.: From cardiac cells to genetic regulatory networks. In: Gopalakrishnan, G., Qadeer, S. (eds.) CAV 2011. LNCS, vol. 6806, pp. 396–411. Springer, Heidelberg (2011)
14. Habets, L.C.G.J.M., Collins, P.J., van Schuppen, J.H.: Reachability and control synthesis for piecewise-affine hybrid systems on simplices. IEEE Trans. Autom. Control **51**(6), 938–948 (2006)
15. Kloetzer, M., Belta, C.: Reachability analysis of multi-affine systems. In: Hespanha, J.P., Tiwari, A. (eds.) HSCC 2006. LNCS, vol. 3927, pp. 348–362. Springer, Heidelberg (2006)
16. Liu, B., Kong, S., Gao, S., Zuliani, P., Clarke, E.M.: Parameter synthesis for cardiac cell hybrid models using delta-decisions. CoRR, abs/1407.1524 (2014)
17. Myers, C.J.: Engineering Genetic Circuits. Chapman and Hall/CRC (2010)

Tools

Combining Static and Dynamic Analyses for Vulnerability Detection: Illustration on Heartbleed

Balázs Kiss[1], Nikolai Kosmatov[2]([⊠]), Dillon Pariente[3], and Armand Puccetti[2]

[1] Search Lab, Budapest 1117, Hungary
balazs.kiss@search-lab.hu
[2] Software Reliability and Security Laboratory, CEA, LIST, PC 174,
91191 Gif-sur-Yvette, France
{nikolai.kosmatov,armand.puccetti}@cea.fr
[3] Dassault Aviation, 92552 Saint-Cloud, France
dillon.pariente@dassault-aviation.com

Abstract. Security of modern information and communication systems has become a major concern. This tool paper presents FLINDER-SCA, an original combined tool for vulnerability detection, implemented on top of FRAMA-C, a platform for collaborative verification of C programs, and Search Lab's FLINDER testing tool. FLINDER-SCA includes three steps. First, abstract interpretation and taint analysis are used to detect potential vulnerabilities (*alarms*), then program slicing is applied to reduce the initial program, and finally a testing step tries to confirm detected alarms by fuzzing on the reduced program. We describe the proposed approach and the tool, illustrate its application for the recent OpenSSL/Heart-Beat Heartbleed vulnerability, and discuss the benefits and industrial application perspectives of the proposed verification approach.

Keywords: Vulnerability detection · Static analysis · Program slicing · Fuzzing · Frama-C · Flinder · Heartbleed

1 Introduction

The recent Heartbleed bug [6] illustrated once again that critical security flaws can remain undetected by a static or a dynamic analysis technique alone [8]. This paper presents FLINDER-SCA, a novel verification tool for vulnerability detection using a *combination* of static and dynamic analyses, as well as a case study illustrating the capabilities of the proposed combined verification approach to detect recent vulnerabilities at the source code level with reasonable amounts of efforts and computing time. This work has been realized in the context of the STANCE project.

This work has been partially funded by the EU FP7 project STANCE (grant 317753).

The **STANCE project**[1] belongs to the European FP7 Research Program and proposes to design and implement validation and verification (V&V) tools to ensure security of industrial software in C, C++ or Java. STANCE builds on the FRAMA-C [7], FLINDER [10] and VERIFAST[2] toolkits and extends their capabilities to handle the aforementioned programming languages and perform security analyses. STANCE studies security properties of industrial applications provided by partners. These are related to an Aeronautic use case (from Dassault Aviation, France), Trusted Computing platforms for embedded systems based on the TPM[3] (from Infineon AG, Germany and TU Graz, Austria), and authentication software for complex distributed networks (from Thales COM, France). The vulnerabilities addressed by STANCE have been classified by using the CWE classification [1] and keeping those vulnerabilities that (1) can be detected in the source code, (2) are written in C, C++ or Java, and (3) are related to the considered application categories.

The original contributions of the present work include

- a new combined verification technique for detection of security vulnerabilities,
- its implementation, FLINDER-SCA, realized in the context of the STANCE project,
- an illustration of its application to the recent Heartbleed vulnerability, and
- a discussion of benefits and application perspectives of the proposed approach.

This paper is structured as follows. Section 2 describes the Heartbleed vulnerability. Section 3 provides on overview of the FLINDER-SCA tool and the associated methodology. Sections 4, 5 and 6 describe the tool components and illustrate them on the case study. Section 7 provides a short tool demo. Section 8 discusses the difficulties of detecting the Heartbleed vulnerability. Finally, Sect. 9 concludes with the benefits of the approach and some future work.

2   The Heartbleed Vulnerability

The Heartbleed bug [6] was discovered in 2014 in OpenSSL[4], the famous cryptographic library widely used to encrypt communications over the Internet. This bug was identified in the HeartBeat functionality, originally intended to check whether a given server is still alive and able to encipher TCP/IP packets with SSL techniques. How HeartBeat operates is straightforward: a client sends a "keep-alive" message containing a *payload* (a random array of bytes intended to be repeated) as well as the payload's size. In turn, if alive, the server is expected to send the very same payload back to the client. This ensures that the server is — at least — able to copy a message previously received and to forward it back to the sender.

---

[1] See http://www.stance-project.eu/.
[2] See http://people.cs.kuleuven.be/bart.jacobs/verifast.
[3] See http://www.trustedcomputinggroup.org.
[4] See https://www.openssl.org.

The security issue comes from the fact that the size of the payload is specified by the client, and this size is not checked by the server against the effective payload length — causing it to read past the end of the memory area allocated to hold the payload, which is a typical buffer over-read vulnerability [1]. For instance, if the client sends a 3-byte message and indicates *0xFFFF*(=65535) as the fake size, the server will send the following non-padding data back to the client: the message header and length (1+2 bytes), the 3-byte message itself, then 65532 bytes from the server's heap memory immediately following the payload at the time of processing. Since the memory area allocated to the payload changes with each request, an attacker can repeatedly send such a request and obtain data stored in many different areas of the heap. Unfortunately, such data may contain confidential data from other processes (e.g. Apache credentials) as well as any other compromising information, and most importantly the secret keys used by OpenSSL itself — which could then be used to impersonate or steal information from the server. Many commonly-used and important Internet sites and their services (such as Google, Youtube, Wikipedia, and Reuters) were compromised by this vulnerability.

The code snippet in Fig. 1, extracted from the OpenSSL/HeartBeat extension v1.0.1+, illustrates the Heartbleed bug. The buffer over-read vulnerability clearly stands in the memcpy call statement (line 7). The payload length variable payload is indeed specified by the client, possibly an attacker, and determines how many bytes from the payload pl will be copied into the buffer starting from buffer pointer bp. A few statements later, after adding additional padding bytes (line 10), the contents of the buffer variable are sent back to the client (line 11), potentially with a substantial part of the heap.

```
1 buffer = CRYPTO_malloc(1 + 2 + payload + padding);
2                                   /* normally payload=16, padding=18 */
3 bp = buffer;
4            /* Write response type, payload length and contents into buffer */
5 *bp++ = TLS1_HB_RESPONSE;         /* store 1-byte response header in buffer */
6 s2n(payload, bp);                 /* store 2-byte payload length in buffer */
7 memcpy(bp, pl, payload);          /* copy the payload contents into buffer */
8 bp += payload;
9            /* Create random padding to protect against traffic analysis */
10 RAND_pseudo_bytes(bp, padding);
11 r = ssl_write_bytes(s, TLS1_RT_HEARTBEAT, buffer, 3 + payload + padding);
```

Fig. 1. Extract from OpenSSL/HeartBeat source code (tls1_process_heartbeat function)

3 Overview of the FLINDER-SCA Tool

The FLINDER-SCA tool has been realized in the context of two V&V tools: the FRAMA-C code analysis platform [7], and the FLINDER security testing platform [10]. FRAMA-C provides a collection of scalable and interoperable tools for static and dynamic analyses of ISO C99 source code. It is based on a common kernel that hosts analyzers as collaborating plug-ins that share a common formal

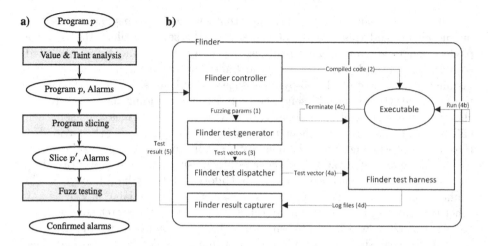

Fig. 2. (a) Overview of the proposed methodology, and **(b)** Architecture of the FLINDER tool

specification language. FRAMA-C includes plug-ins based on abstract interpretation, deductive verification and dynamic analysis, as well as a series of derived plug-ins which build elaborate analyses upon the former. In addition, the extensibility of the overall platform, and its open-source licensing, have fostered the development of an ecosystem of independent third-party plug-ins.

The proposed verification methodology is illustrated in Fig. 2a. First, a static analysis step relying on value and taint analyses (detailed in Sect. 4) is applied to detect *alarms* reporting potential vulnerabilities. Second, a program slicing step (described in Sect. 5) is used to reduce the initial program p and to produce a smaller one, p', called a *slice*. These two steps are realized by FRAMA-C plug-ins. Finally, the fuzz testing step (presented in Sect. 6) applies FLINDER on p' to confirm these alarms as actual vulnerabilities. This methodology enhances the SANTE approach [3] that combined value analysis, slicing and structural testing for detection of runtime errors, and makes it well-adapted for detection of security flaws. (For more related work, see [3]).

4   Detection of Alarms by Static Analysis

With FRAMA-C, potential runtime errors (*alarms*) can be detected and localized by the VALUE plug-in [7]. It implements an abstract interpretation based value analysis that computes (over-approximated) domains of possible values for program variables at each program location. For the memcpy call responsible for Heartbleed (cf. Fig. 1), VALUE generates the following assertions (slightly rewritten here for the sake of clarity):

```
//@ assert Alarm1: mem_access: \valid(bp[0 .. (payload-1)]);
//@ assert Alarm2: mem_access: \valid(pl[0 .. (payload-1)]);
```

These alarms indicate that the tool cannot ensure the validity of pointers bp and pl in the range of the payload size payload, and therefore dereferencing them may be dangerous.

As VALUE is a sound analyzer [7], it guarantees to generate alarms for all potential runtime errors. It may also generate spurious cases — false positives —, due to over-approximations, especially when users do not provide it with a sufficiently accurate initial state for the inputs. As a result, the alarms of interest with regard to Heartbleed might be raised among numerous other alarms, with no means — at first glance — to *distinguish* preeminent assertions. Of course, more precise analyses could be performed through additional efforts, for instance on the specification of the initial state, or additional annotations in the code to reduce non-conclusive over-approximations. These two workarounds imply a deeper understanding of the application under analysis, and may not be affordable in terms of required efforts or functional expertise in practice.

In this work, we use another approach based on taint analysis [5] to identify code variables and statements concerned with the propagation of *taintable,* i.e. potentially corrupted inputs. Taintable inputs may contain information controlled by an attacker, and therefore represent a high risk to introduce malicious behaviors. *Taint analysis* allows the user to distinguish which source code statements are concerned with the taintable input flow and are used by a potentially vulnerable function. Taintable data flows are propagated, for instance, in case of pointer aliasing, or copy of memory zones. The proposed taint analysis approach is based on static analysis results computed by VALUE. We have implemented it in an experimental FRAMA-C plug-in.

To apply it on the Heartbleed case, the user specifies the potentially taintable inputs (rrec.data, the major part of the HeartBeat message sent by the client), and the vulnerable functions (e.g. libc functions memcpy, strcpy, fgets,. . . that give rise to a significant number of vulnerabilities [4]). The tool reports that the assertions related to memcpy call handle the taintable input flow, and the memcpy statement is identified as vulnerable[5]. This permits to *distinguish security-related alarms* among all alarms generated by VALUE.

5   Simplification of the Program by Slicing

Program slicing [11,12] consists in computing the set of program instructions, called *program slice*, that may influence the program state at some point of interest, called *slicing criterion*. Slicing preserves the behaviors of the initial program at the selected criterion after removing irrelevant instructions. It relies on dependency analysis, that can in turn use the results of value analysis.

The SLICING plug-in [7] of FRAMA-C offers various ways to define slicing criteria, including program statements, function calls and returns, read and write accesses to selected variables, and logical annotations. SLICING is also able to handle a conjunction of atomic criteria: by construction, the slice will verify all criteria simultaneously.

---

[5] For convenience of the reader, taint analysis results are illustrated in Sect. 7.1.

In this work, we apply SLICING to simplify the code with respect to the set of alarms produced by static analysis (cf. Sect. 4). For the program with the Heartbleed vulnerability, initially containing 8 defined functions and 51 lines of code, using SLICING allows us to simplify the code and to keep only 2 defined functions and 38 lines in the slice used in the last step.

6 Confirmation of Alarms by Fuzz Testing

Fuzz testing consists of injecting faulty, erroneous or malformed input into a system under test, and monitoring the state of the system. Detecting an observable error state (such as a crash) indicates that the system cannot properly handle the input in question, confirming the existence of a bug in the code. To be more efficient, fuzzing must be able to generate *syntactically correct*, but *semantically invalid* input by modifying some (sets of) fields within it. The FLINDER fuzz testing framework [10] was originally developed to perform "smart", syntax-aware *black-box fuzzing*: the tester specified the exact format of the input being tested, provided a valid input sample, and defined which of the fields within the format should be modified.

Within STANCE, FLINDER plays a different role: it is used to determine whether a certain alarm identified by static analysis is an actual vulnerability. FLINDER accomplishes this via *white-box fuzzing:* a specific function inside a program becomes the system under test, and its parameters define individual input fields to be modified. The main white-box operation steps, labelled (1)– (5), are shown in Fig. 2b:

(1) Based on the previously-instrumented code (with the potentially vulnerable callsites detected by e.g. value analysis) and information about the particular variables to modify in a function (provided by e.g. taint analysis), FLINDER generates a list of fuzzing parameters for each variable to be modified, specifying what kind of values should be generated for them to look for certain kinds of vulnerabilities.
(2) The instrumented code is compiled and fed to the FLINDER test harness.
(3) Test vectors are generated according to the fuzzing parameters — e.g. strings of varying length for a string variable to identify buffer overflow problems, and very small and very large values for an integer variable to identify integer overflow and array overindexing issues.
(4) Each test vector is sent to the test harness (4a), where its values are used to replace the values in the variables targeted by the fuzzing at runtime (4b). The test harness observes the termination of the function (4c), detects anomalies thanks to the instrumentation, and logs the results (4d).
(5) Based on the presence of anomalies in the logs — such as invalid memory accesses or crashes — FLINDER decides whether the vulnerability is confirmed or not.

In the Heartbleed example, the static analysis step reports to FLINDER six potential bugs, while the slicing step reduces the code and the number of parameters of the function tls1_process_heartbeat. Next, the code is instrumented to be able to detect memory violation errors. Used in the white-box mode, FLINDER generates test cases for modifying each of the parameters in turn: 10 test cases for a different-size Heartbeat message buffer, and 32 test cases each for different Heartbeat message length and sequence number values. The first test case where the Heartbeat message length is larger than the buffer size causes an invalid memory read attempt. Captured by the test harness, this operation allows FLINDER to identify the specific FRAMA-C alarm connected to the test. FLINDER ultimately relays this information to FRAMA-C, which can then change the status of the corresponding alarms to *confirmed* (showing them in red in the FRAMA-C GUI)[6].

7 Tool Demonstration

7.1 Static Analysis Step Applied to the Heartbleed Vulnerability

Figure 3 provides a screenshot illustrating how the first step of FLINDER-SCA allows the verification engineer to detect potential vulnerabilities within the FRAMA-C toolset. The culprit memcpy statement is identified as vulnerable, because it manipulates a taintable data flow. We extended the original FRAMA-C GUI by some complementary columns to ease the localization of vulnerable statements in the source code. In the upper left panel, several columns identify functions comprising taintable data flows, vulnerable statements and alarms. The upper right panel shows the source code with the taintable data flows and vulnerable statements highlighted in orange and pink respectively. This provides the verification team with a user-friendly overview of taint analysis results on the code under review (especially thanks to the causality with taintable input parameters).

7.2 Fuzz Testing Step Applied to the Heartbleed Vulnerability

In this example, FLINDER is applied to the simplified version of the Heartbleed vulnerability (see Fig. 1). The static analysis step has identified six potential bugs in the tls1_process_heartbeat function, and the slicing step has simplified the program to reduce the size and complexity of the code. After appropriately instrumenting the sliced code at each alarm location where memory issues are suspected, FLINDER determines which fuzzing rules to apply — in this case, simple integer fuzzing is applied to the two integer parameters of the function tls1_process_heartbeat, and binary data fuzzing is applied to the string parameter (see Fig. 4). Fuzzing the first (string) parameter s_s3_rrec_data proves to be inconclusive: injecting modified values into the program does not result in crashes or other incorrect operation. Regardless, fuzzing buffers such as this is important — in many cases, they can contain important data that can affect the execution path of the application. Changing the second (integer) parameter s_s3_rrec_length to a value that is larger than the size of the buffer results in an invalid memory access, which is then detected by the test harness due to the hooks inserted

---

[6] For convenience of the reader, fuzzing results are illustrated in Sect. 7.2.

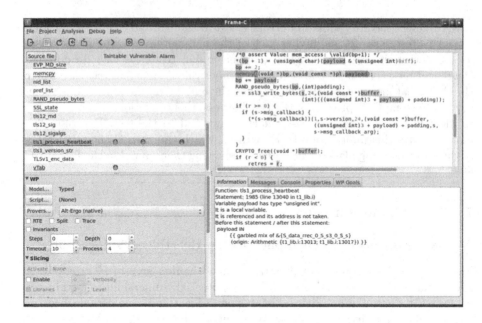

Fig. 3. Frama-C GUI after applying VALUE and taint analysis. (Color figure online)

into the code. This allows FLINDER to confirm the presence of the vulnerability. Finally, this information is sent back to FRAMA-C to set the status of the corresponding alarms as *confirmed* (in other words, the corresponding assertions are marked in red as invalid, see Fig. 5).

8   Discussion

According to [8], the main difficulties in detecting Heartbleed with static analysis tools were four-fold: the way data is stored and referenced, complexity of following the execution path, difficulty of identifying the specific parts in the storage structure that are misused, and resistance to taint analysis heuristics due to the difficulty of determining whether a specific part within a complex storage structure has become untainted.

Detecting the bug via dynamic analysis ran into another problem: the custom memory management used by OpenSSL would prevent dynamic testing frameworks such as VALGRIND [9] from being able to successfully detect a memory corruption or over-read problem. This — combined with encapsulation of the heartbeat length field within the payload — made its detection via fuzz testing infeasible.

In the end, Heartbleed was detected with two main approaches: Neel Mehta (Google) found it using manual code review[7], and Codenomicon found it through

---

[7]   as reported by Andrew Hintz, Google vulnerability analyst, see https://news.ycombinator.com/item?id=7558015.

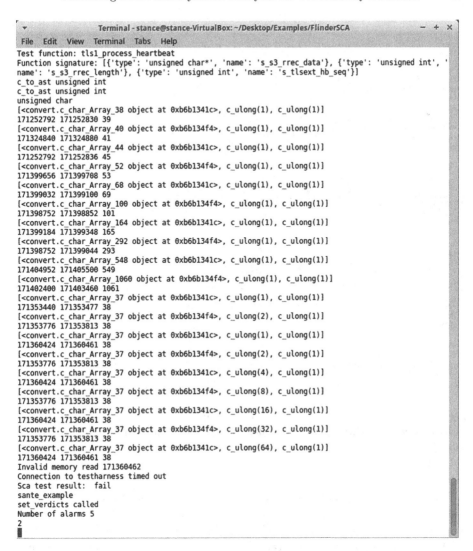

Fig. 4. The results produced by FLINDER after applying it to the Heartbleed vulnerability.

the use of a hybrid fuzzer/dynamic analyzer tool. The latter approach is very interesting from a tool standpoint: instead of relying purely on fuzzing, an additional mechanism was employed to detect when the output of a system was semantically incorrect in several ways (bypassing authentication, data leakage, amplification, and weak encryption) [2]. This approach requires additional manual work in the creation of additional information to describe the output, but this only needs to be done once for each interface.

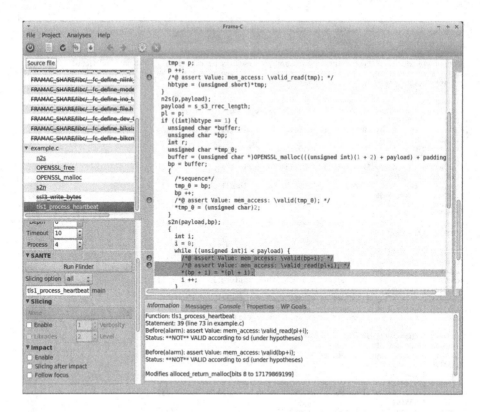

Fig. 5. The final results in the FRAMA-C GUI after applying FLINDER-SCA to the Heartbleed vulnerability. The last two alarms shown in red are real flaws. (Color figure online)

This trend of combining fuzz testing tools with other static and dynamic analysis techniques proves to be an important way of detecting complex and non-obvious security vulnerabilities, moving forward.

To summarize, complex vulnerabilities such as Heartbleed present significant challenges to state-of-the-art static and dynamic analysis tools. While manual code review can always be effective, it is not always a viable solution due to the sheer volume of source code to be inspected in some cases. Thus, new approaches — such as the one proposed in the present work — that combine existing methods are essential in their capacity to detect vulnerabilities automatically without requiring significant manual effort.

9   Conclusion and Future Work

The difficulties of detecting the Heartbleed vulnerability by a static or a dynamic analysis technique alone have been identified and discussed in [8]. To address such vulnerabilities, this work proposes an innovative *combined* approach whose different steps are *complementary* and offer a very promising *synergy*. First, value analysis reports potential errors as alarms, while taint analysis identifies a subset of alarms that are most likely to lead to attacks. Notice that static analysis alone reports several alarms and cannot precisely find the security flaw. Second, slicing reduces the source code by removing statements that are irrelevant w.r.t. the identified subset of alarms. In this case study, slicing reduced the program by 25 %, while in earlier experiments on runtime error detection with SANTE [3], the average rate of program reduction by slicing was about 32 %. These two steps help to focus on security-relevant alarms in the last step and avoid wasting time by analyzing safe or irrelevant statements. Finally, a fuzz testing step is applied on the reduced code in order to try to confirm the selected alarms. In the present case study, fuzz testing with FLINDER without a preliminary static analysis step could be applied only in a black-box manner and would not be able to find the Heartbleed bug either. Similarly, only using static analysis techniques could not confirm the validity of any identified alarms. Another important benefit for industrial applications of the method is its capacity to detect bugs with *reasonable efforts,* e.g. without the tester having to provide a detailed specification of the input state or additional annotations in the code.

We implemented this method in the Flinder-SCA tool, aiming to connect several new plug-ins developed on top of the Frama-C platform: a taint analysis tool, and a fuzz testing prototype currently being developed within the STANCE project. The originality of the present work with respect to SANTE [3] lies in using taint analysis for identifying the most security-relevant alarms, and fuzz testing for efficient detection of vulnerabilities. That enhances the SANTE method, adapts it to detection of security flaws and makes it effective for such subtle vulnerabilities as Heartbleed.

FLINDER-SCA is currently used to analyze other proprietary or open-source pieces of software, with negligible adaptations; however, it is important to note that much of the intended vulnerability detection functionality of FLINDER-SCA is still under active development within the STANCE project. Several improvements are planned to enlarge the scope of applications. This concerns in particular the FLINDER tool to address more types of vulnerabilities, and a better integration with taint analysis to be able to apply fuzzing techniques to any control point in the potentially vulnerable workflow under analysis and better identify which parts of the code are the best candidates for fuzzing.

Future improvements also include the investigation of complex input that cannot be represented by variable types — such as a string variable containing an entire SSL3 record consisting of several distinct pieces of data. This can be achieved by adapting Flinder's already existing structure-aware fuzz testing capabilities and employing static analysis methods to help users create the inner structure for such variables as necessary — or in some cases, generating it automatically.

These future developments will permit to apply the methods and tools discussed in this paper to several application candidates, sub-parts of the STANCE project use cases. They could range from basic Apache resource libraries, for which the feasibility can be considered as acquired, to more sophisticated functions (possibly from SingleSignOn software for instance). It is also expected to expand these applications to critical infrastructures in future projects, coupling dynamic and static approaches, in which fuzzing will remain one of the key techniques for verification of complex security properties in complement to classical static analysis methods.

Acknowledgment. We thank the FRAMA-C team for providing the tools and support, and the anonymous referees for many helpful comments.

References

1. CWE-126: Buffer Over-read. http://cwe.mitre.org/data/definitions/126.html
2. Carvalho, M., DeMott, J., Ford, R., Wheeler, D.A.: Heartbleed 101. IEEE Secur. Priv. **12**(4), 63–67 (2014)
3. Chebaro, O., Cuoq, P., Kosmatov, N., Marre, B., Pacalet, A., Williams, N., Yakobowski, B.: Behind the scenes in SANTE: a combination of static and dynamic analyses. Autom. Softw. Eng. **21**(1), 107–143 (2014)
4. Common Vulnerabilities and Exposures. https://cve.mitre.org
5. Denning, D.E.: A lattice model for secure information flow. Commun. ACM **19**, 236–243 (1976)
6. CVE-2014-0160.   https://cve.mitre.org/cgi-bin/cvename.cgi?name=CVE-2014-0160
7. Kirchner, F., Kosmatov, N., Prevosto, V., Signoles, J., Yakobowski, B.: Frama-C: a software analysis perspective. Formal Asp. Comput. **27**(3), 573–609 (2015)
8. Kupsch, J.A., Miller, B.P.: Why do software assurance tools have problems finding bugs like Heartbleed? Continuous Software Assurance Marketplace, April 2014
9. Nethercote, N., Seward, J.: Valgrind: a framework for heavyweight dynamic binary instrumentation. In: PLDI (2007)
10. Search Lab: Flinder security testing platform. http://www.flinder.hu
11. Tip, F.: A survey of program slicing techniques. J. Prog. Lang. **3**(3), 121–189 (1995)
12. Weiser, M.: Program slicing. In: ICSE 1981, pp. 439–449 (1981)

The Verification Cockpit – Creating the Dream Playground for Data Analytics over the Verification Process

Moab Arar[1], Michael Behm[2], Odellia Boni[1], Raviv Gal[1(✉)], Alex Goldin[1],
Maxim Ilyaev[1], Einat Kermany[1], John Reysa[2], Bilal Saleh[1],
Klaus-Dieter Schubert[3], Gil Shurek[1], and Avi Ziv[1]

[1] IBM Research, Haifa, Israel
{moab,odelliab,ravivg,alexgo,imaxim,
einatke,bilal,shurek,aziv}@il.ibm.com
[2] IBM Systems, Austin, TX, USA
{behm,reysa}@us.ibm.com
[3] IBM Systems, Boeblingen, Germany
kdschube@de.ibm.com

Abstract. The Verification Cockpit (VC) is a consolidated platform for planning, tracking, analysis, and optimization of large scale verification projects. Its prime role is to provide decision support from planning to on-going operations of the verification process. The heart of the VC is a holistic centralized data model for the arsenal of verification tools used in modern verification processes. This enables connection of the verification tools and provides rich reporting capabilities as well as hooks to advanced data analytics engines. This paper describes the concept of the Verification Cockpit, its architecture, and implementation. We also include examples of its use in the verification of a high-end processor, while highlighting the capabilities of the platform and the benefits of its use.

1 Introduction

Modern verification is a highly automated process in which an endless number of verification jobs are continuously being executed in verification farms [15]. The process involves many tools and subsystems that handle tasks such as: the documentation and management of the verification plan, tracking changes in the design and the verification environment, scheduling verification jobs, generating stimuli, simulating the design under verification (DUV), collecting coverage data, and more.

These verification tools, which we sometime refer to as data sources, produce a large amount of data that is essential for understanding the state and progress of the verification process. For example, simulation traces are needed for efficient debug. Another example is coverage analysis that is used to monitor the state of the verification process and identify areas that need more attention [1]. These examples use data from a single tool or data source. In many

N. Piterman (Ed.): HVC 2015, LNCS 9434, pp. 51–66, 2015.
DOI: 10.1007/978-3-319-26287-1_4

cases, cross-referencing data from several sources can provide additional insight into the verification process. For example, the correlation between coverage, bugs found, and new features in the DUV can help the verification team assess the quality of new features and identify holes in the verification and coverage plans.

Today, we are witnessing the growing complexity and size of the verification process on the one hand, and the availability of more and more verification tools that produce large amounts of data on the other. This combination is causing a shift in the verification domain from a world that contains little data, forcing verification engineers to fumble in the dark, to a world with too much data that can drown the verification team. This raises the challenge of using the data produced in the verification process to provide the verification team with decision support from planning to on-going operations. This requires extraction of useful concise information from data coming from a single source or combination of multiple sources. This, in turns, calls for an open platform that allows existing tools to feed data into it and analysis and reporting engines to consume and process the data.

Existing solutions can be categorized into three main types. The first type includes integrated verification platforms, such as Incisive from Cadence [18], VCS from Synopsys [20], and Questa from Mentor Graphics [19]. These platforms integrate several verification tools and engines, usually coming from the same vendor. They also provide some reporting and analysis capabilities. The disadvantage of these platforms is that they are relatively closed and do not allow the easy connection and integration of external tools. (The main exceptions are some external version control and bug tracking tools.) Another limitation of these platforms is their databases, which are usually designed as operational databases optimized for insertion and processing single entries; however, these are less efficient when it comes to retrieving and manipulating large amounts of records.

The second type of solutions are *product lifecycle management* (PLM) tools and platforms [14]. Life cycle management is geared towards providing connectivity between the various tools used in different phases of a product, such as design, development, and maintenance. This connectivity enables a holistic view of the data created by the different tools. Some forms of PLM, such as application lifecycle management (ALM) and collaborative lifecycle management (CLM), are used for applications and systems development in the software engineering and system engineering domains. To the best of our knowledge, an equivalent solution does not exist for the hardware verification domain.

An alternative solution lies in the form of standards, such as the Unified Coverage Interoperability Standard (UCIS) [24]. These standards provide an open interface that allows the connection of coverage producers and consumers, as well as several producers or consumers. The disadvantage of such standards is that they are not generic enough. For example, they do not address the connection of coverage data to other data sources such as bug tracking.

This paper introduces the *Verification Cockpit* (VC), a consolidated platform for planning, tracking, analysis, and optimization of large scale verification projects, such as the verification of IBM high-end systems. The VC is influenced by the Project Lifecycle Management concept, and its implementation is based in parts on IBM's CLM platform, which helps meet the requirements of an open platform. Specifically, the VC is based on the Jazz architecture [22] and OSLC protocol [23], which provide services that allow tools and data sources to publish their data schemas and actual data. This, in turn, allows other tools that are part of the platform to link to that data and connect it to their own data. For example, after the coverage collection tool publishes its data, the verification planning tool can add a link pointing to the coverage model for each item in the plan. In this way, when the user points to or hovers over the coverage model, the definition and current coverage status are displayed.

The Verification Cockpit uses the vast amount of data collected by the individual data sources for analysis and reporting. This type of usage requires processing and manipulating a large number of data records. This, in turn, calls for the use of a high-volume *data warehouse*. The data warehouse is fed with data from the various data sources using *Extract, Transform and Load* (ETL) processes. It organizes the data in a star schema that is efficient for data retrieval and creates the required connectivity between the data items from different sources. The data analysis components of the VC and its report engines use this repository as the source for their analyses.

To complete the Verification Cockpit picture, the tool uses the rich reporting capabilities of Rational Insight (Cognos) [21] to provide users with customizable reports on many aspects of the data sources connected. It is also connected to in-house analysis engines that mine the data produced by the verification process. As we show in later sections, one such example is the *Template Aware Coverage* (TAC) analysis engine, which explores the relations between test templates[1] and coverage.

With these components of the VC, it can provide the verification team decision support throughout the verification process from planning via on-going operations to tape-out decisions and beyond. In addition, it can be used to feed automation applications from end-to-end process optimization to single aspect services.

We are now in the initial phase of deploying the Verification Cockpit in the verification of the latest high-end processor developed at IBM. Part of the potential data sources, namely, the verification plan, the work plan, the batch test submitter and monitor, and the coverage database, are connected to the VC and through it to each other. A rich set of reports provides various views into each of these data sources individually and to combinations of the sources. Even with this limited connectivity, the VC proves that it can manage the volumes of data required, and, more importantly, provide the verification team with the means to easily dive into the data and extract useful information.

---

[1] Test templates are definitions provided to stimuli generators or test-benches for generation of random tests. Test templates are sometimes called test definitions or simply tests.

The rest of the paper is organized as follows. In Sect. 2, we provide the motivation for the Verification Cockpit project and its goals. Section 3 describes the architecture of the tool and its implementation. In Sect. 4, we present some examples that highlight the benefits of using the Verification Cockpit. We conclude the paper in Sect. 5.

2   Motivation and Goals

The verification process follows many tasks and steps from the initial plans to successful completion of its execution. To perform all these tasks, a typical modern verification environment comprises many tools originating from many vendors. In many cases a tool suite from one vendor provides most of the needs, but such suites are often augmented by tools from other vendors and in-house tools. The major components of the verification environment can be seen in Fig. 1.

The *Verification Plan* holds the features that need to be verified, the verification means (simulation, special checker, formal verification etc.), and the metrics (coverage or other). The *Work Plan* breaks down the features into tasks. The *Test Submission* system keeps the different random (and directed) test templates, and monitors their submission according to the current verification goals (new feature to verify, wide regression etc.). The *Failure Tracking* system provides the data required for triage, debug, and rerun of failures (the error message, the number of failures, the test template, etc.). The *Coverage Tracking* tool holds the definition and the status of the coverage events and models. The *Bug Tracking* tool provides status and information regarding the bugs found in the verification process. Finally, the *Design* and the *Test Bench* data can be provided by the version control (owner, number of rows, changes, etc.).

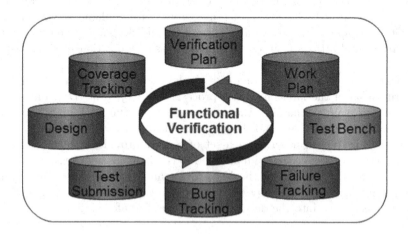

Fig. 1. Modern verification environment components

Each of the tools mentioned above, and many other tools omitted for lack of space, produces and stores data that is important for its operation. The data also helps in understanding the state and progress of the verification process. Many of the tools produce structured data that is kept in local databases, but some tools produce unstructured data, such as test logs and definition documents. Not all of the produced data is stored. Understanding the data produced by each of the verification tools alone and in combination with the data of other tools is an essential part of the day-to-day work done by each member of the verification team, starting from the project manager and going all the way to each of the team members. This task can be difficult, time consuming, as it requires expertise and experience. Therefore, any automatic assistance provided by analysis tools and engines can be a welcome relief for the verification team.

Data analytics, or the analysis of data, is the process of inspecting, cleaning, transforming, and modeling data with the goal of discovering useful information, suggesting conclusions, and supporting decision-making [17]. Data analytics combine techniques and algorithms from domains such as statistics, data mining, and machine learning to extract the essence of the input data [13]. In general, the information coming from data analysis can be classified into three main categories: descriptive, quantitatively describing the main features of a collection of data; predictive, analyzing current and historical facts to make predictions about the future; and prescriptive, making predictions and then suggesting decision options that take advantage of the predictions.

Data analytics has been used in the verification process for many years, mostly to support coverage analysis. Coverage hole analysis [1] is an example of descriptive analysis used to detect large uncovered areas and report these areas instead of reporting large lists of uncovered events. The work by Hajjar et al. [9] uses statistical models to predict coverage progress. In the domain of prescriptive analysis, the work by Copty et al. [5] proposed the use of probabilistic regression suites to improve the coverage progress in regression, and the work by Farkash et al. [6] showed how to efficiently target coverage around changes in the DUV. Coverage directed generation (CDG) [10] is another form of prescriptive analysis that closes the loop between coverage data and test templates, leading to the coverage of the requested events. Various methods that use techniques such as machine learning (e.g., [7]) and data mining (e.g., [4]) have been proposed to automatically construct test templates based on coverage information. Quality estimation and bug prediction is another area in which data analytics is often used. For example, Guo et al. [8] use machine learning to correlate design and bug characteristics, and predict bug distribution.

To enable widespread use of data analytics in the hardware functional domain, we need a platform that connects the various tools involved in the verification process and is capable of handling the vast amount of data created by these tools. The main requirements for such a platform are the following: The platform should be based on an open architecture so any verification tool can connect to the platform. Moreover, an existing standardized architecture is preferred because it could reduce the effort needed to define and implement the interfaces to the platform. The openness of the architecture should exist for both the connection of the verification tools as data sources and the analytics engines as consumers of the data.

The platform needs to provide a centralized data model that defines the relationship between data items coming from different data sources. For example, the data model needs to ensure that the same names are used for the hardware units by all the data sources. Alternatively, if different names are used, the mapping of the name used by the coverage collection tools should be mapped to the name used by the test job submission tool.

The open architecture provides the means for connecting the data sources, either directly or using a centralized meeting place. The data model is used to connect the relevant matching data items out of all the data items existing in the data sources.

The platform needs to handle the vast amount of data created by the verification process and allow the analysis engines efficient methods for accessing and manipulating the data. This includes the ability to process and store (some of) the structured data produced by the verification tools and process, but leave off some of the structured and unstructured *Big Data* [11] produced by these tools.

Finally, the platform should provide rich reporting capabilities that clearly show users the essence of the data collected. The reports can be created directly from the data or as the output of the data analysis engines that are part of the platform and/or are attached to it. The platform should support pre-defined reports and allow easy customization of the reports to fit the users' needs. In addition, the platform should provide support for alerts that warn users whenever anomalies are detected in the process.

3   Architecture and Implementation of the Verification Cockpit

3.1   Architecture of the Verification Cockpit

The basic approach of the Verification Cockpit, described in Fig. 2, borrows from the *Product Lifecycle Management* (PLM) concept. The interconnection between the different verification tools is illustrated by the circular line connecting the tools. The converging lines from the data sources into the data warehouse (or Big Data tool) represent a standard *Extract Transform and Load* (ETL) process extracting the data from the data source, transforming it to the coherent data model, and loading it into the target database. Data analytics in all levels – descriptive, predictive and descriptive – over the data in the data warehouse are then used to optimize directives over the verification process. The optimization directives can use reports and alerts to recommend actions. They can also directly activate actions, such as modifying the test submission policy to maximize the coverage rate of a feature in the DUV.

The *Verification Cockpit* architecture that implements this concept is based on the IBM Rational *Collaborative Lifecycle Management* (CLM) built on the

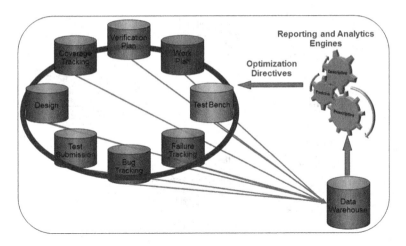

Fig. 2. Verification Cockpit concept

Jazz platform [22]. The IBM Rational CLM was originally designed for software development. The VC adjusts the platform for hardware functional verification. CLM brings together project planning and tracking (*Rational Team Concert - RTC*), requirements management and quality (testing) management, on a common unified platform. All the operational data from the CLM tools can be connected to *IBM Rational Insight* (Cognos), which provides rich level of reports and dashboards over this data. The IBM Rational CLM is an open solution. New tools can be connected to the system using the *Open Service for Lifecycle Collaboration* (OSLC) interface [23].

The Verification Cockpit architecture, described in Fig. 3, has three main components: RTC is used as both the verification plan and work plan tools; Rational Insight (Cognos) and DB2 are used for the data warehouse and the reports hub; and the VC server at the bottom hosts all the new VC components. The ETL engines job is to extract the data from the data source, transform it to the data warehouse model, and finally load it into the data warehouse. The OSLC bridges expose services to connect different data sources. The analytics engines perform the advanced analysis over the data in the data warehouse. Users access the VC by web browser since the Rational Insight dashboards and RTC are both web applications. Another access point is the interface of each analytics engine, where our preferred flow is to store the analysis results in the data warehouse and present it through Cognos reports.

3.2 The Data Model

We define a coherent data model for the data warehouse based on the star schema methodology [12]. There is a fundamental difference between the operational database usually managed by each tool and the star schema model used in the data warehouse. While the operational database is optimized for insert, update,

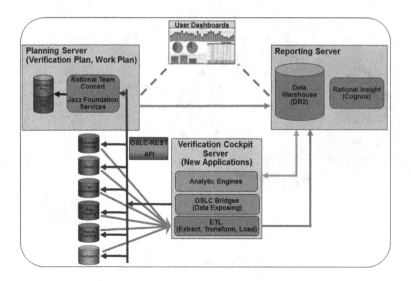

Fig. 3. Verification Cockpit architecture

and delete operations, the star schema model is optimized for data analytics, where the common operation would be data retrieval. A partial example of our star schema is presented in Fig. 4. The star schema is built from dimensions and metrics. While the metrics usually hold numeric values that can be aggregated, the dimensions define the "aggregate by" options. There are common dimensions like the date and the project name. There are also tool-specific dimensions such as the test template name for the test submission data, and the coverage model name for the coverage data. The VC keeps separate metric tables per data source, and they use the dimensions to generate the unique key in the table. The common dimensions are essential components to cross-reference data queries.

Clearly, as the tools were developed independently, their data does not follow this model directly. This is a known issue with data warehousing that is handled in the *Transform* step of the ETL process, where we select the data we want to load into the data warehouse and transform it to its data model. This includes, for example, data aggregation and renaming.

3.3 Implementation

We built the entire VC system, but connecting the data sources to the VC is an ongoing process. To date, we have connected three tools that serve four roles to the VC: RTC for the verification plan and the execution plan, the Test Submission tool, and the Coverage tool. While RTC is a natural player in the IBM Rational CLM solution, the last two are in-house tools that demonstrate what it takes to integrate such tools into the VC.

We developed an ETL for each tool to connect the test submission and coverage tools to the data warehouse. Since these are in-house tools that enable

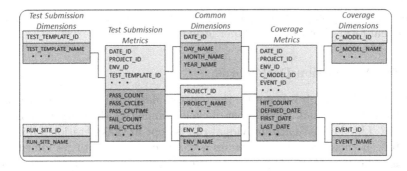

Fig. 4. Star schema data model for test submission and coverage data (partial)

direct access to their data, we developed the ETL in Java and JDBC. The ETLs update the data warehouse on a daily basis, and handle several million records within less than 30 min. Our data warehouse now holds around 400 GB of data, which covers Test Submission data for a couple of years, and Coverage summary data. The historic data provides the means for long term trends analysis.

IBM RTC was designed to support an agile software development flow. Since the RTC template can be configured, and there is a lot in common between SW development and HW verification, we extended the basic RTC template to support the verification teams flow. We defined *RTC-Feature*, a new work item type for a feature in the DUV needed to be verified. The RTC-Feature contains hardware verification specific attributes, such as the verification means (simulation, special checker, formal verification, etc.) It also contains a link to the coverage model that provides the metric for the feature. To provide this capability, we developed an OSLC bridge that exposes the coverage data and provides services that enable accessing through RTC.

We developed a rich layer of reports and dashboards over the data. While the majority of these reports are for a single data source, we already developed a few cross data reports and advanced analytics over the data.

4   Use Examples

The vision of the Verification Cockpit is to provide all levels of data analytics over the verification process data, whether descriptive, predictive, or prescriptive. Our use examples cover all three levels. Moreover, it covers the different actors in the verification team: the verification engineer, the team lead, and the verification manager. The examples described below are from the verification of the latest high-end processors in IBM.

The Verification Cockpit can display its reports in many forms. For example, many reports can be displayed as graphic plots (e.g., pie charts) that provide a clear visual qualitative view. For a quantitative view and for deeper digging, the reports can also be displayed as text tables. The reports shown in this section contain only one form. Moreover, some of the reports were slightly modified from their actual form to fit onto the paper format.

4.1 Test Submission Dashboards

For each simulation job we capture the test template used to generate the test, the resulting pass or fail, the number of cycles simulated, the simulation model, and more. The data for each individual run is kept in the operational database of the test submission tool. Later on users can query the tool to get information about specific runs. The VC provides aggregations and summaries of the simulated tests. To efficiently prepare the needed reports, the data is accumulated on a daily basis. We also aggregated the data at different levels and views, ranging from the test templates level, through the verification environment level, all the way up to the project level.

There are many potential uses for the test submission reports generated by the VC. Consider a verification engineer that developed a list of test templates intended to cover a certain feature. For this list of tests, the engineer uses a dashboard containing several charts and tables, and starts with a chart showing the daily pass rate for each of the templates as shown in Fig. 5. The figure shows that on July 15 and 16 many of the test templates suffered from a low pass rate.

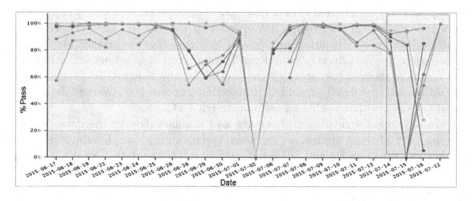

Fig. 5. Test submission - daily pass rate report. Each line represents a test template.

The next step in the investigation is to check if a broken model of the hardware was used during the days in question. This information can be detected in the report of Fig. 6, which displays the pass rate (the bars in the figure) and the number of tests (the line) for each hardware model. The report shows that indeed the model used on these dates (if_p910_105u02c) suffered from a low passing rate. Here, we do not show the report indicating when each model is used.

To reduce the workload of the verification engineer and save some analysis time, the VC can automatically perform some of the analyses and alert the engineer only when things go wrong or anomalies are detected. For example,

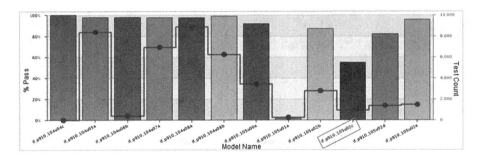

Fig. 6. Test submission - pass rate progress by model (x axis). The bars represent the pass rate and the dotted line represents the number of tests.

the verification engineer can specify that she wants to receive an alert if the success rate of her test template list drops below 80 %, in which case she wants to receive the reports of Fig. 5.

4.2 Coverage Dashboards

Coverage driven verification (CDV) [3] is the leading methodology for hardware verification today. The CDV methodology emphasizes the tight relationship between the verification plan and coverage. It does this using the coverage status and progress reports as the main measure for the state and progress of the verification process. The Verification Cockpit supports CDV in several ways. In general, the coverage reports and the connection between coverage and the verification plan follow the IBM flavor of CDV presented by Schubert et al. [16].

Our coverage collection tool stores the coverage data using a daily granularity. The VC coverage ETL takes this raw data for each verification environment and model, and loads it into the data warehouse, from which the VC provides classic and new analysis of the data.

The summary coverage report for the *Instruction Sequencing Unit* (ISU) is displayed in Fig. 7. The figure shows the coverage summary for each of the tags (coverage models) defined for the unit; it also compares the coverage in different environments, such as unit level, core level and system level simulation. The report is usually the first step in an attempt to analyze the coverage status of the unit. The next step is to drill down into one of the tags that requires special attention; an example would be the exceptions tag.

Figure 8 shows the summary report of this tag. For each coverage event in the tag, the report shows the status of the event in each environment. We distinguish between well and lightly covered events according to a hit threshold. We further divide the zero-hit events into those that were never hit and the ones that were previously hit but have been zero for some time (*aged-out*) [2]. The colors provide a quick view of the status of events; the data in the table allows deeper analysis.

One of the main advantages of using a data warehouse is that it allows trend analysis. We can analyze and present the historic trends of this coverage model

Tag Name	target: Unit										Core			System		
	Total #	Covered #	Covered %	Lightly Covered #	Lightly Covered %	Zero Hit #	Zero Hit %	Aged Out #	Never Hit #	Newly Hit #	Total #	Covered+Lightly #	Covered+Lightly %	Total #	Covered+Lightly #	Covered+Lightly %
notag	681	652	(95.7%)	0	(0%)	29	(4.3%)	0	29	0	669	646	(96.6%)	669	495	(74%)
unit	1,270	1,045	(82.3%)	34	(2.7%)	191	(15%)	52	140	6	1,270	1,068	(84.1%)	1,270	812	(63.9%)
exceptions	579	276	(47.7%)	42	(7.3%)	261	(45.1%)	10	251	5	579	263	(45.4%)	578	130	(22.6%)
sors	372	293	(78.8%)	9	(2.4%)	70	(18.8%)	3	67	3	372	196	(52.7%)	372	61	(16.4%)
threadpriority	83	32	(38.6%)	41	(49.4%)	10	(12%)	2	8	3	83	62	(74.7%)	83	16	(19.3%)
finish	52	48	(92.3%)	0	(0%)	4	(7.7%)	0	4	0	52	52	(100%)	52	52	(100%)

Fig. 7. Coverage summary for ISU

Zero only at Target	Covered	Lightly Covered		*Report target - in bold*
Zero at All Refs	Not Available	Aged Out	Never Hit	

Event Details			References - Hit Count			
Name	VAR_CLASS	Tags	Unit	Core	System	Total
all except nt bhrb unavail	exception	exceptions,facilityunavailable,	0	0	0	0
all except nt dscr unavail	exception	exceptions,facilityunavailable,	0	300	0	300
all except nt ebb unavail	exception	exceptions,facilityunavailable,	0	82	0	82
all except nt flipso	exception	exceptions,	6 K	148 K	318	154 K
all except nt foreign link l2abort twalk	exception	exceptions,	5 K	0	0	5 K
all except nt fp suppress	exception	exceptions,	90	234	6	330

Fig. 8. Detailed coverage for the exceptions tag in the ISU (Color figure online)

as shown in Fig. 9. This provides the verification engineer with a better means for understanding the coverage picture and detecting problems in the verification process. For example, identifying the time when events started to age-out can help find the change in the design or verification environment that caused it. A further drill down is possible to see the trend of each event.

4.3 Connecting Coverage to the Verification Plan

Another important aspect of the CDV methodology is the connection between the verification plan and the coverage status. To provide this connectivity, we developed an OSLC bridge that exposes the coverage data and provides services to access it from RTC. This allows users to define a bidirectional hyperlink between the RTC-Feature and the coverage model.

The first step in creating the connection is to add a coverage goal to an RTC-Feature. This is done by selecting the proper coverage model out of a list of models available for this project in the coverage database. Because the RTC-Feature can have more than one coverage model, and the coverage model can measure more than a single RTC-Feature, a many-to-many relation is allowed.

Once a link is established, the user can view the coverage model summary information by hovering over the link. The data presented is similar to the data for the given tag in the coverage summary report of Fig. 7. A link which leads to the detailed coverage report of this coverage model (Fig. 8) is also provided. Moreover, the coverage status is also used to color RTC-Features in the verification plan,

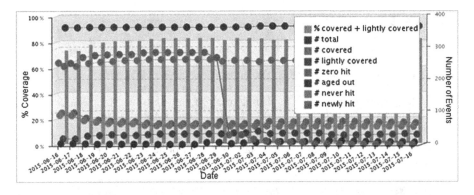

Fig. 9. Coverage model trend - last month

thus quickly pointing the verification lead (and anyone else looking at the plan) to weaknesses in the implementation and progress of the plan.

4.4 Template Aware Coverage

To further investigate the coverage state and devise actions that improve it, it is important to understand the relationship between coverage and test templates. Today, in high-volume verification environments, the simulation to coverage flow is template blind. That is, coverage accumulation is done for all tests, regardless of their origin test templates. The Verification Cockpit infrastructure that connects the test submission tool and the coverage collection tool lead the way to incorporating test-template information into the coverage data, thus enhancing the coverage information that is stored and analyzed. We use the term *Template Aware Coverage* (TAC) for the connection between the origin test template and the coverage it achieves.

Even with the capacity of the data warehouse, processing and maintaining the coverage data for the thousands to millions of coverage events and hundreds to thousands of test templates can be tough. Our solution is to use the Big Data approach, processing the coverage data on the fly and keeping only a summary of it for the deep analysis. Specifically, the VC keeps only the probability of each test template to hit each coverage event.

This information can be used in many ways. Descriptive reports using TAC data can extend the understanding of the coverage and provide hooks for improvement. For example, the test template developer can be given feedback on how well the template is doing its job and hitting the events targeted. Another example is presented in Fig. 10, where we wish to find the best test templates to cover a coverage model. Given a test template, we can learn how it performs, by looking at the different coverage models (features) that are hit by tests generated from this template; this can be seen in Fig. 11.

A prescriptive analytic usage of the TAC matrix is to find an optimized test policy for a given set of verification goals, as defined by a coverage space.

Test Temp. Name	Hit Events		Uniquely Hit Events	Hard to Hit Events		Easy to Hit Events		# Inst. to Run	Should Hit Tag by Plan
t₁	1,692	(90.5%)	13	501	(26.8%)	1,191	(63.7%)	471	Yes
t₂	1,658	(88.7%)	1	246	(13.2%)	1,412	(75.6%)	226	Yes
t₃	729	(39.0%)	0	216	(11.6%)	513	(27.5%)	286	Yes
t₄	1,377	(73.7%)	1	366	(19.6%)	1,011	(54.1%)	364	No
t₅	1,548	(82.8%)	1	430	(23.0%)	1,118	(59.8%)	362	No
t₆	1,497	(80.1%)	0	477	(25.5%)	1,020	(54.6%)	1,119	No

Fig. 10. Coverage model - best test templates (number of instances to run to get mean hit percent of 95 %)

Tag Name	Hit Events		Uniquely Hit Events	Hard to Hit Events		Easy to Hit Events		# Inst. to Run
T₁	1,692	(90.5%)	13	501	(26.8%)	1,191	(63.7%)	471
T₂	3,739	(48.0%)	0	897	(11.52%)	2,842	(36.5%)	658
T₄	6,292	(74.0%)	0	4,959	(58.29%)	1,333	(15.7%)	1014
T₈	1,172	(19.9%)	32	477	(7.6%)	725	(12.3%)	936
All	85,068	(40.9%)	180	22,292	(10.7%)	62,776	(30.2%)	649

Fig. 11. Test template - best coverage models

Given the coverage goals, we use optimization algorithms [5] to find an optimized policy, minimizing the total number of tests needed to cover the coverage space. A policy is a weighted list of test templates, in which the weight is the number of times we need to run a test of this template. The optimization engine can be used, for example, to find an optimized wide-regression set close to tapeout. A common use case in any verification team is finding a *light regression* to verify that a new model is not dead on arrival. Another important usage can follow a bug fix to run regression for this feature. In this case, we define the coverage space by the coverage models connected to this feature.

5 Conclusions

This paper presented the concept, architecture, and implementation of the Verification Cockpit (VC), a platform that connects verification tools to a holistic centralized data model and hooks them to rich reporting and data analytics engines. With these connections and hooks, the VC allows deep mining of useful information that is sometimes hidden deep in the vast amount of data produced by the verification tools. In that sense, the VC is a dream playground that allows data analytics applications to analyze and improve the verification process.

The Verification Cockpit is based on the open Jazz architecture that allows any verification tool to connect to it and through it to other tools and reporting/analysis engines. It utilizes a high-end data warehouse that can handle the data produced by the verification tools. The data warehouse and the star schema at its base provide the reporting and analysis engines with an efficient way to retrieve and manipulate the data.

The VC is now in its initial state of deployment with a small number of tools connected to it. Nevertheless, we can already see the benefits of the centralized data model and the connectivity between verification tools that enable enrichment of the information extracted from the data.

We are continuing to develop the Verification Cockpit and extend its capabilities as well as its use in the field. In general, our development effort follows three main directions. First, we are continuing to connect more tools and data sources to the VC. Second, we are adding more analysis and reports to our arsenal of engines. For example, we are now investigating the automatic detection of anomalies in bug finding rates. Finally, we are working to enhance our Big Data and unstructured data analysis capabilities. In addition to the Template Aware Coverage presented in the paper, we are exploring the relations between bugs and coverage to assist in the triage process.

References

1. Azatchi, H., Fournier, L., Marcus, E., Ur, S., Ziv, A., Zohar, K.: Advanced analysis techniques for cross-product coverage. IEEE Trans. Comput. **55**(11), 1367–1379 (2006)
2. Birnbaum, A., Fournier, L., Mittermaier, S., Ziv, A.: Reverse coverage analysis. In: Eder, K., Lourenço, J., Shehory, O. (eds.) HVC 2011. LNCS, vol. 7261, pp. 190–202. Springer, Heidelberg (2012)
3. Carter, H.B., Hemmady, S.G.: Metric Driven Design Verification: An Engineer's and Executive's Guide to First Pass Success. Springer, New York (2007)
4. Chen, W., Wang, L.C., Bhadra, J., Abadir, M.: Simulation knowledge extraction and reuse in constrained random processor verification. In: Proceedings of the 50th Annual Design Automation Conference, DAC 2013, pp. 120:1–120:6, June 2013
5. Copty, S., Fine, S., Ur, S., Yom-Tov, E., Ziv, A.: A probabilistic alternative to regression suites. Theor. Comput. Sci. **404**(3), 219–234 (2008)
6. Farkash, M., Hickerson, B., Behm, M.: Coverage learned targeted validation for incremental HW changes. In: Proceedings of the 51st Annual Design Automation Conference on Design Automation Conference, pp. 57:1–57:6, June 2014
7. Fine, S., Ziv, A.: Coverage directed test generation for functional verification using Bayesian networks. In: Proceedings of the 40th Design Automation Conference, pp. 286–291, June 2003
8. Guo, Q., Chen, T., Chen, Y., Wang, R., Chen, H., Hu, W., Chen, G.: Pre-silicon bug forecast. IEEE Trans. Comput. Aided Des. Integr. Circuits Syst. **33**(3), 451–463 (2014)
9. Hajjar, A., Chen, T., Munn, I., Andrews, A., Bjorkman, M.: High quality behavioral verification using statistical stopping criteria. In: Proceedings of the 2001 Design, Automation and Test in Europe Conference, pp. 411–418, March 2001
10. Ioannides, C., Barrett, G., Eder, K.: Feedback-based coverage directed test generation: an industrial evaluation. In: Barner, S., Harris, I., Kroening, D., Raz, O. (eds.) HVC 2010. LNCS, vol. 6504, pp. 112–128. Springer, Heidelberg (2010)
11. Marz, N., Warren, J.: Big Data: Principles and Best Practices of Scalable Realtime Data Systems. Manning Publications, Westampton (2015)
12. Ponniah, P.: Data Warehousing Fundamentals for IT Professionals, 2nd edn. Wiley, Hoboken (2010)

13. Runkler, T.A.: Data Analytics - Models and Algorithms for Intelligent Data Analysis. Springer, Wiesbaden (2012)
14. Saaksvuori, A., Immonen, A.: Product Lifecycle Management, 3rd edn. Springer, Heidelberg (2010)
15. Schubert, K.D., et al.: Solutions to IBM POWER8 verification challenges. IBM J. Res. Dev. **59**(1), 1–17 (2015)
16. Schubert, K.D., et al.: Functional verification of the IBM POWER7 microprocessor and POWER7 multiprocessor systems. IBM J. Res. Dev. **55**(3), 308–324 (2011)
17. Wikipedia: Data analysis – Wikipedia, the free encyclopedia (2014). http://en.wikipedia.org/wiki/Data_analysis. Accessed 29 October 2014
18. Incisive enterprise manager. http://www.cadence.com/products/sd/enterprise-manager/pages/default.aspx. Accessed 19 July 2015
19. Questa verification management. http://www.mentor.com/products/fv/questa-verification-management/. Accessed 19 July 2015
20. VCS. http://www.synopsys.com/Tools/Verification/FunctionalVerification/Pages/VCS.aspx. Accessed 19 July 2015
21. IBM - rational insight. http://www-03.ibm.com/software/products/en/rtl-insight. Accessed 21 July 2015
22. The people, places, history, and ideas behind Jazz. https://jazz.net/story/about/. Accessed 19 July 2015
23. What is OSLC? http://open-services.net/resources/tutorials/oslc-primer/what-is-oslc/. Accessed 19 July 2015
24. Unified coverage interoperability standard (UCIS). http://accellera.org/images/downloads/standards/ucis/UCIS_Version_1.0_Final_June-2012.pdf. Accessed 19 July 2015

Verification of Robotics

Coverage-Driven Verification —
An Approach to Verify Code for Robots that Directly Interact with Humans

Dejanira Araiza-Illan[1], David Western[1], Anthony Pipe[2], and Kerstin Eder[1(✉)]

[1] Department of Computer Science and Bristol Robotics Laboratory,
University of Bristol, Bristol, UK
{dejanira.araizaillan,david.western,kerstin.eder}@bristol.ac.uk
[2] Faculty of Engineering Technology and Bristol Robotics Laboratory,
University of the West of England, Bristol, UK
tony.pipe@brl.ac.uk

Abstract. Collaborative robots could transform several industries, such as manufacturing and healthcare, but they present a significant challenge to verification. The complex nature of their working environment necessitates testing in realistic detail under a broad range of circumstances. We propose the use of Coverage-Driven Verification (CDV) to meet this challenge. By automating the simulation-based testing process as far as possible, CDV provides an efficient route to coverage closure. We discuss the need, practical considerations, and potential benefits of transferring this approach from microelectronic design verification to the field of human-robot interaction. We demonstrate the validity and feasibility of the proposed approach by constructing a custom CDV testbench and applying it to the verification of an object handover task.

1 Introduction

Human-Robot Interaction (HRI) is a rapidly advancing sector within the field of robotics. Robotic assistants that engage in collaborative physical tasks with humans are increasingly being developed for use in industrial and domestic settings. However, for these technologies to translate into commercially viable products, they must be demonstrably safe and functionally sound, and they must be deemed trustworthy by their intended users [7]. In existing industrial robotics, safety is achieved predominantly by physical separation or through limiting the robot's physical capabilities (e.g., speed, force) to thresholds, according to predefined interaction zones. To fully realize the potential of collaborative robots, the correctness of the software with respect to safety and functional (liveness) requirements needs to be verified.

HRI systems present a substantial challenge for software verification — the process used to gain confidence in the correctness of an implementation, i.e. the robot's code, with respect to the requirements. *The robot responds to an environment that is multifaceted and highly unpredictable.* This is especially true for robots involved in direct interaction with humans, whether this is in an

© Springer International Publishing Switzerland 2015
N. Piterman (Ed.): HVC 2015, LNCS 9434, pp. 69–84, 2015.
DOI: 10.1007/978-3-319-26287-1_5

unstructured home environment or in the more structured setting of collaborative manufacturing. We require a verification methodology that is sufficiently realistic (models the system with sufficient detail) while thoroughly exploring the range of possible outcomes, without exceeding resource constraints.

Prior work [3,6,14,19,20,25] has explored the use of formal methods to verify HRI. Formal methods can achieve full coverage of a highly abstracted model of the interactions, but are limited in the level of detail that can practically be modelled. *Sensors, motion and actuation in a continuous world present a challenge for models and requirement formulation in formal verification.* Physical experiments or simulation-based testing may be used to achieve greater realism, and to allow a larger set of requirements to be verified over the real robot's code. However, neither of these can be performed exhaustively in practice.

Robotic code is typically characterised by a high level of concurrency between the communicating modules (e.g., nodes and topics used in the Robot Operating System, ROS[1]) that control and monitor the robots sensors and actuators, and its decision making. Parallels can be drawn here to the design of microelectronics hardware, which consists of many interacting functional blocks, all active at the same time. Hence it is natural to ask: 'Can techniques from the microelectronics field be employed to achieve comprehensive verification of HRI systems?'

In this paper, we present the use of Coverage-Driven Verification (CDV) for the high-level control code of robotic assistants, in simulation-based testing. CDV is widely used in functional verification of hardware designs, and its adoption in the HRI domain is an innovative response to the challenge of verifying code for robotic assistants. CDV is a systematic approach that promotes achieving coverage closure efficiently, i.e. generation of effective tests to explore a System Under Test (SUT), efficient coverage data collection, and consequently efficient verification of the SUT with respect to the requirements. The resulting efficiency is critical in our application, given the challenge of achieving comprehensive verification with limited resources.

The extension of CDV to HRI requires the development of practical tools that are compatible with established robotics tools and methods. The microelectronics industry benefits from the availability of hardware description languages, which streamline the application of systematic V&V techniques. No practical verification tool exists for Python or C++, common languages for robotics code [24]. A novel contribution of this paper is the development of a CDV testbench specifically for HRI; this implementation makes use of established open-source tools where possible, while custom tools have been created as necessary to complete and connect the testbench components (Test Generator, Driver, Checker and Coverage Collector). Additionally, we outline the relevant background to ensure robust implementation of CDV.

To demonstrate the feasibility and potential benefits of the method, we applied CDV to an object-handover task, a critical component of a cooperative manufacture scenario, implemented as a ROS and Gazebo[2] based simulator.

---

[1] http://www.ros.org/.

[2] http://gazebosim.org/.

Our automated testbench conveniently allows the actual robot code to be used in the simulation. Model-based and constrained pseudorandom test generation strategies form the Test Generator. A Driver applies the tests to the simulation components. The Checker comprises assertion monitors, collecting requirement coverage. The Coverage Collector, besides requirement, includes code coverage.

We verified selected safety and liveness (functional) requirements of the handover task to showcase the potential of CDV in the HRI domain.

The paper proceeds with an overview of the CDV testbench components and verification methodology in Sect. 2. The handover scenario is introduced in Sect. 3, where we then present the CDV testbench we used to verify the code that implements the robot's part of the handover task. Section 4 discusses the verification and coverage results for this example. Conclusions and future work are given in Sect. 5.

2   Coverage-Driven Verification

2.1   Structure of a CDV Testbench

In CDV, a verification plan must be constructed before the testing process begins [23]. This plan includes the aspects of the SUT that need to be verified, e.g. a requirements list or a functional description of the SUT, and a coverage strategy. The coverage strategy indicates how to achieve effective coverage, i.e. the exploration of the SUT and advancement of the verification progress, through the design of the testbench components, especially the Test Generator, the Checker and the Coverage Collector. The coverage strategy also specifies how to measure the coverage, e.g. a requirements model or a functional model to traverse.

In Testing, the SUT is placed into a test environment, a *testbench*. The testbench represents (a model of) the universe, or of its target environment. The process of testing is realised using the following four core components in a testbench, as shown in Fig. 1:

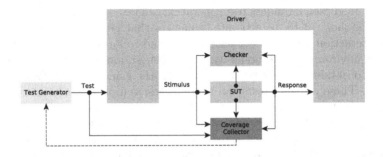

Fig. 1. Structure of a basic CDV testbench

- the **Test Generator** is the component that generates stimulus for the SUT;
- the **Driver** is the component that takes a test, potentially at a high level of abstraction, translates it into the level of abstraction used in the simulation, and drives it to stimulate the SUT;
- the **Checker** is the component that checks the response of the SUT to the stimulus and detects failures;
- the **Coverage Collector** is the component that records the quality of the generated tests with respect to a set of complementing coverage models.

A key objective in the design of a CDV testbench is to achieve a fully autonomous environment, so that verification engineers can concentrate on areas requiring intelligent input, namely efficient and effective test generation, bug detection, reliable tracking of progress and timely completion.

In the following sections we describe each testbench component in more detail, explaining how they can be used for verification in robotics.

2.2   Test Generator

The test generator aims to exercise the SUT for verification (activation of faults), while working towards full coverage. Test generators in CDV make use of pseudorandom generation techniques. Using pseudorandom as opposed to random generation allows repeatability of the tests. The generated tests must be valid (realistic, like a sensor input that reflects a valid scene). An effective set of tests includes a good variety that explores unexpected conditions and addresses the scenarios of interest as per the requirements list. An efficient set of tests maximises the coverage and verification progress, whilst minimizing the number of tests needed. To achieve the former while allowing for the latter, pseudorandom test generation can be biased using constraints. These constraints can be derived from the SUT's functional requirements or from the verification plan [23]. However, supplying effective constraints requires significant engineering skill and application knowledge. It is particularly difficult to generate meaningful sequences of actions, whether these are transactions on the interface of a system-on-chip, or interactions between humans and robots.

Constrained pseudorandom test generation can be complemented with model-based techniques [10,16] to generate sequences that address specific use cases, such as interaction protocols between human and robot in a collaborative manufacturing environment. In model-based test generation, a model is explored or traversed to obtain abstract tests, i.e. tests at the same level of abstraction as the model. These abstract tests can serve as test templates, or constraints, for tests that target specific behaviours [15,21]. For this, a model needs to be implemented, e.g. one that captures the intended behaviours of the robot when interacting with humans and/or its environment. In robotics, the degree of abstraction between such a model and the simulation often differs significantly compared to that observed in microelectronics [22]. Many low-level implementation details such as motion control, sensing models or path planning are abstracted from (e.g., as in [25]) to keep these models within manageable size. For model-based testing to be credible and effective, the correctness of the behavioural model with respect to the robot's code needs to be established. However, this is beyond the scope of this paper.

2.3 Driver

The Driver is a fully automated component that translates a (potentially high-level) description of a test into signal-level stimulus that can be applied to the interfaces of the SUT in order to expose the SUT to the situation prescribed by the test. The Driver may comprise an interacting network of modules corresponding to the distinct interfaces of the SUT. The SUT reacts to the stimuli provided on its interfaces. The Driver runs in parallel with the SUT and responds to it, if necessary; i.e., the Driver can be reactive. The automation of the Driver makes it feasible to execute batches of abstract tests, to accelerate testing.

In HRI, the Driver comprises a model of the human, a physics model, and communication channels to represent any interactions that do not require detailed physical simulation. For example, if the human element in the simulator is driving the robot's code, the Driver would execute the corresponding high-level action sequence, one item at a time, by translating it into the respective sequence of input signals, potentially passing through the physics model before exposing the signals to the robot's input channels.

2.4 Checker

The automation of test generation prompts the need for automatic and test independent checkers, i.e. self-checking testbenches. Assertion-based verification [8] allows locating checkers, in the form of assertion monitors, close to the code that is being observed.

Requirements to verify can be expressed as Temporal Logic properties. Assertion monitors can be derived automatically from these properties [12], in an automata-based form. Since the simulations are time bound, some safety properties defined over infinite traces (e.g., using an `always` Temporal Logic operator) are bound over the duration of a simulation run. Relevant work in [2] mentions the advantages of the automatic generation of monitors as automata, including the reduction of errors caused by manual translation.

For requirements about the low-level continuous behaviour of the SUT (e.g., trajectories computed by the motion planning), the monitoring can be performed in a quasi-continuous manner, considering computational limitations. Otherwise, over-approximations or interpolation can be performed to predict events at instants of time between computations, such as the overlapping of regions in the 3D space for collision avoidance.

2.5 Coverage Collector

Automatic test generation necessitates monitoring the quality of the tests to gain an understanding of the verification progress. To achieve this, statistics can be collected on the tests, the driven stimulus (external events), the SUT's response, and the SUT's internal state, including assertion monitors. In general, we distinguish between *code* coverage models and *functional* coverage models. A comprehensive account on coverage can be found in [23].

The collected coverage data provides information on unexplored (coverage "holes") or lightly covered areas. *Coverage closure* is the process of identifying coverage holes and creating new tests that address these holes. This introduces a feedback loop from coverage collection/analysis to test generation, termed Coverage Directed test Generation (CDG) [23]. Attempts have been made to automate CDG using machine learning techniques [13]. However, CDG remains a difficult challenge in practice.

In principle, coverage collection and analysis techniques can be transferred directly into the domain of robotics verification. In fact, it is interesting to note that functional coverage in the form of "cross-product" coverage [26], as widely used in hardware design verification, has recently been proposed (independently) for the verification of autonomous robots in [1], where it is termed *situation* coverage and includes combinations of external events only.

2.6   CDV Methodology

In CDV, an iterative process of test generation, execution, coverage collection and analysis is used to achieve coverage closure over several cycles. In practice, engineering input is required to interpret the data and to guide test generation towards closing coverage holes. This is either achieved simply by allowing further pseudorandom tests to be generated, by adding constraints to bias test generation, by employing model-based test generation or, as a last resort, by directed testing. If model-based test generation has already been applied, modifications to the formal model may yield new tests.

It is important to note that further test generation is not always the only appropriate response to a coverage hole or a requirement violation. The following options should also be considered: (1) the SUT has a bug, to be referred to the design team; (2) modifications to one or more of the requirements models (e.g. assertions or formal properties) are needed to more accurately reflect the actual requirements and/or design of the SUT; and/or (3) modifications to one or more of the testbench components are needed. This third decision may be reached if the tests and requirements models are deemed appropriate but the testbench does not allow the SUT's full range of functions to be exercised and observed.

3   CDV Implementation

A case study from a collaborative manufacture scenario is presented. We demonstrate the transferability of CDV into the HRI domain by constructing a CDV testbench for this case study using a combination of established open-source tools and custom components. Our implementation showcases the potential of CDV to verify robotic code used in HRI.

3.1   Case Study: Robot to Human Object Handover Task

Our case study is an object handover, a critical subtask in a broader scenario where a robot (BERT2 [17]) and a person work together to assemble a table. The handover starts with an activation signal from the person to the robot. The robot then picks up an object, and holds it near the person. The robot indicates it is ready for the person to receive the object. Then, the person is expected to hold the object simultaneously, moving closer if necessary, and to look at it — indicating readiness of the person. The robot collects data through two different sensing systems: "pressure", sensors that determine whether just the robot, or simultaneously the robot and the person, are holding the object; and "location" and "gaze" sensors, an 'EgoSphere' system that tracks whether the human hand is close to the object and whether the human head is directed towards the object [17]. Based on the sensors, the robot determines whether the release condition is satisfied, and decides on a course of action: the robot will release the object and allow the person to take it, if the human was ready; if not, the robot will not release the object. The robot or human may disengage from the task (look or move away). The sensors are considered perfect.

According to the handover task's interaction protocol, a robot ROS 'node' was developed in Python, comprising 209 code statements. This node was structured as a state machine, using the SMACH modules [4], to facilitate modularity. The states, with their transitions, can be enumerated as shown below. Each state transitions to the next in sequence, except where indicated otherwise. The code is also depicted as a flow chart in Fig. 5.

1. `reset` - The robot moves to its starting position, with gripper open.
2. `receive_signal` - Read signals. If 'startRobot' is received, transition to `move`; elseif timeout, transition to `done`; else, loop back to present state.
3. `move` - Plan trajectory of hand to piece. Move arm. Close gripper. Plan trajectory of hand to human. Move arm.
4. `send_signal` - Send signal to inform human of handover start.
5. `receive_signal` - Read signals. If 'humanIsReady' is received, transition to `sense`; elseif timeout, transition to `done`; else loop back to present state.
6. `sense` - Read sensors. If timeout, transition to `done`; elseif not all signals available, loop back to present state; else, transition to `decide`.
7. `decide` - If all sensors are satisfied, transition to `release`; else, transition to `done` (without releasing).
8. `release` - Open the gripper. Wait for 2 s.
9. `done` - End of sequence.

3.2   Requirements

Requirements were derived from ISO 13482:2014 and desired functionality of the robot in the interaction [9]:

1. If the gaze, pressure and location are sensed as correct, then the object shall be released.

2. If the gaze, pressure or location are sensed as incorrect, then the object shall not be released.
3. The robot shall make a decision before a threshold of time.
4. The robot shall always either time out, decide to release the object, or decide not to release the object.
5. The robot shall not close the gripper when the human is too close.

Requirements 1 to 4 refer to sequences of high-level events over time, whereas Requirement 5 refers to a lower-level safety requirement of the continuous state space of the robot in the HRI. Thus, the former can be both targeted with model-based techniques and implemented as assertion monitors, whereas the latter is only suitable for implementation as an assertion monitor.

3.3 CDV Testbench Implementation

ROS is a widely used open-source platform for the design of code for robots in C++ and/or Python. ROS allows interfacing directly with robots. Gazebo is a robot simulation tool designed for compatibility with ROS, that is able to emulate the physics of our world. Thus, the combination ROS-Gazebo provides a means of developing a robotic simulator, as shown in Fig. 2.

Fig. 2. BERT2 robot and a human, and the simulator in ROS-Gazebo

Figure 3 shows the structure of our CDV testbench implementation, incorporating the robot's high-level control code. The Driver incorporates the Gazebo physics simulator and the MoveIt![3] packages for path-planning and inverse kinematics of the robot's motion. The human is embodied as a floating head and hand for simplicity; in future, this representation can be replaced by one that is anatomically accurate. The implementation in ROS ensures that assertion monitors and coverage collection can access parameters internal to the robot code as well as the external physics model and other interfaces, such as signals. Observability of the external behaviour allows validating the robot's actions. In real life experiments, this is equivalent to observing the robot's physical behaviour to see if its responses are as expected.

---

[3] http://moveit.ros.org/.

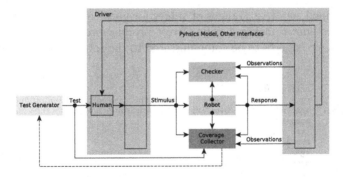

Fig. 3. Testbench and simulator elements in ROS-Gazebo

3.4   Test Generator and Driver

Tests were generated pseudorandomly, by concatenating randomly selected elements from the set of high-level actions belonging to the handover workflow, forming random action sequences and instantiating relevant parameters. These randomized sequences represent environmental settings that do not necessarily comply with the interaction protocol. Thus, pseudorandom action sequence generation produces stimulus that correspond to unexpected behaviours that were not previously considered in the requirements. Posteriorly, constraints were introduced to bias the pseudorandom generation to obtain tests that do comply with the interaction protocol (e.g., enforcing particular sequences of actions).

The handover interaction protocol was formalized as a set of six automata, in particular Probabilistic-Timed Automata (PTA) [11], comprising the robot, the workflow, the gaze, the location, the pressure, and the sensors. Behaviours of the different elements (e.g., protocol compliant actions to activate the robot through signals) were abstracted in terms of state transitions and variable assignments. The structure of the robot's code guided the abstraction process, and the abstraction was verified via bisimulation analysis [18].

Model-based test templates were obtained from witness traces (examples or counterexamples) produced by model checking the product automaton [21]. These witnesses contain combined sequences of states from the different automata. Requirements 1 to 4 (Sect. 3.2) were used to derive model-based test templates that would trigger corresponding assertion monitors. We employed UPPAAL[4], a model checker for PTA that produces witnesses automatically. Projections over these traces with respect to the workflow, gaze, location, pressure and sensors automata remove the elements that correspond to the robot's activities, to form a test template. Based on these test templates, tests were generated pseudorandomly.

A test template for our simulator consists of a sequence of high-level actions (workflow) to activate the robot expressed as a state machine. A test comprises, besides the high-level actions, the pseudorandom instantiation of parameters,

---

[4] http://www.uppaal.org/.

from well defined sets (e.g., ranges of values for gaze correct or gaze incorrect). An example is shown in Fig. 4. The Driver produces responses in the physical model in Gazebo, signals to be communicated to the robot, and sensor readings.

1	sendsignal	activateRobot
2	setparam	time = 40
3	receivesignal	informHumanOfHandoverStart
4	sendsignal	humanIsReady
5	setparam	time = 10
6	setparam	honTask = true
7	setparam	hgazeOk = true
8	setparam	hpressureOk = true
9	setparam	hlocationOk = true

This time instantiation produces a waiting time of 40 × 0.05 seconds.

Gaze instantiation for true: choosing offset, distance and angle, from ranges $\{[0.1, 0.2],$ $[0.5, 0.6], [15, 40]\}$, e.g., $(0.1, 0.5, 30)$

Fig. 4. Example test from a test template, comprising high-level actions and some parameter instantiations (time and gaze)

An example of a constraint for constrained pseudorandom generation is the enforcement of the sequence of actions in lines 1 to 4 of Fig. 4, followed by any other action sequence. This constraint ensures the immediate activation of the robot, when a simulation starts.

An added benefit from the development of a formal model for test generation is that this allows formal verification through model checking [5]. Formal verification can thus complement CDV. However, properties that hold for abstract models must still be verified at the code level. Model checkers for code (e.g., CBMC[5], Java PathFinder[6]) target runtime bugs in general, such as arrays out of bounds or unbounded loop executions. These are, however, at a different level than the complex functional behaviours we aim to verify. In [25], the runtime detail is abstracted, giving way to high-level behaviour models where functional requirements can be verified with respect to the model only.

3.5   Checker

Assertion monitors were implemented for all the requirements in Sect. 3.2. Requirements 1 to 4 were translated first into CTL properties, and then automata-based assertion monitors were generated manually. This process will be automated in the future. For example, Requirement 1 corresponds to the property:

$$E <> sgazeOk \wedge spressureOk \wedge slocationOk \wedge releasedTrue.$$

The resulting monitor is triggered when reading a sensors signal indicating the gaze, pressure and location are correct. Then, the automaton transitions when receiving a signal of the object's release. If the latter signal event happens within a time threshold (3 s), a True result is reported. Finally, the automaton returns to the initial state.

---

[5] http://www.cprover.org/cbmc/.

[6] http://javapathfinder.sourceforge.net/.

Requirement 2 corresponds to the CTL property:

$$E <> (sgazeNotOk \lor spressureNotOk \lor slocationNotOk) \land releasedFalse.$$

This monitor is triggered when any of the gaze, pressure or location are incorrect in a sensing signal. Then, the automaton transitions to either a **False** result when receiving a signal of the object's release, or a **True** result if some time has elapsed (2 s) and no release signal has been received. Finally, the automaton returns to the initial state.

Requirement 5 refers to physical space details abstracted from our PTA model, and it cannot be expressed as a Temporal Logic property. Hence, it was directly implemented as an automaton-based assertion monitor. When the robot grabs the object, it needs to make sure the human's hand (or any other body part) is at a distance. The monitor is triggered every time the code invokes the **hand(close)** function, which causes the motion of the robot's hand joints. The location of the human hand is then read from the Gazebo model (the head is ignored, since the model is abstracted to a head and a hand). If this location is close to the robot's hand (within a 0.05 m distance of both mass centres), the monitor registers a **False** result, or otherwise **True**.

The monitors automatically generate report files, indicating their activation time, and the result of the checks if completed.

3.6 Coverage Collector

We implemented two coverage models: code (statement) coverage and functional coverage in the form of requirements (assertion) coverage. The statement coverage was implemented through the 'coverage'[7] module for Python. For each test run, statistics on the number of executed code statements are gathered. The assertion coverage is obtained by recording which assertion monitors are triggered by each test. If all the assertions are triggered at the end of the test runs, the testbench has achieved 100 % requirements coverage.

4 Experiments and Verification Results

The CDV testbench described in Sect. 3 was used *(a)* to demonstrate the benefits of CDV in the context of HRI; *(b)* to obtain an insight into the verification results, including unexpected behaviours or requirement violations; and *(c)* to explore options to achieve coverage closure (from Sect. 2.6).

The requirements mentioned in Sect. 3.1 were verified using a CDV testbench in ROS (version Indigo) and Gazebo (2.2.5), and through model checking in UPPAAL (version 4.0.14), using the model we developed for model-based test generation. We used a PC with Intel i5-3230M 2.60 GHz CPU, 8 GB of RAM, running Ubuntu 14.04.

---

[7] http://nedbatchelder.com/code/coverage/.

Table 1 presents the assertion coverage for the handover, and the verification results from model checking. In model checking, the requirements were verified as true (T) or false (F). Through model checking, we were only able to cover Requirements 1 to 4. From each of the model checking witnesses (test templates) of Requirements 1 to 4, we generated a test (model-based generation). We also generated 100 pseudorandom (unconstrained) tests, and 100 constrained pseudorandom tests that enforced the activation of the robot as explained in Sect. 3. We verified Requirements 1 to 5 in simulation, and recorded the results of the assertion monitors: Pass (P), Fail (F), Not Triggered (NT), or Inconclusive (U) when the monitor was triggered but the check was not completed within the simulation run. The same setup was used to compute both assertion and statement coverage, allowing the comparison of the test generation strategies in terms of coverage efficiency.

Table 1. Requirements (assertion) coverage and model checking results

Req.	Model checking	Simulation-based testing											
		Pseudorandom				Constrained-pseudorandom				Model-based			
		P	F	NT	I	P	F	NT	I	P	F	NT	I
1	T	0/100	0/100	100/100	0/100	0/100	0/100	100/100	0/100	3/4	0/4	1/4	0/4
2	T	33/100	0/100	67/100	0/100	87/100	0/100	13/100	0/100	1/4	0/4	3/4	0/4
3	T	33/100	0/100	67/100	0/100	87/100	0/100	13/100	0/100	4/4	0/4	0/4	0/4
4	T	98/100	0/100	0/100	2/100	98/100	0/100	0/100	2/100	4/4	0/4	0/4	0/4
5	-	46/100	0/100	54/100	0/100	93/100	0/100	7/100	0/100	4/4	0/4	0/4	0/4

The results in Table 1 confirm our expectations for the different test generation strategies. For assertion-based functional coverage, pseudorandom and constrained-pseudorandom test generation are less efficient than model-based test generation, which triggered all five assertions with just four tests. Requirement 1 was not covered by either the pseudorandom or the constrained pseudorandom strategy. If either of these strategies was used alone, the coverage hole could potentially be closed by adding further constraints or by using a more sophisticated test generation strategy such as model-based test generation.

The assertion monitor checks for Requirement 4 were inconclusive for some of the pseudorandom and constrained-pseudorandom generated tests. This occurs because in these tests the robot is activated long after the start of the handover task (when the robot is reset and proceeds to wait for a signal). These tests do not comply with the protocol which requires to activate the robot at the start and within a given time threshold.

This coverage result could trigger different actions, e.g. the assertion monitor could be modified to choose either pass or fail at the end of the simulation; the Driver could be modified such that the simulation duration is extended; or, the inconclusive checks could be dismissed as trivial, in which case the efficiency of any further tests could be improved by directing them away from such cases. As noted in Sect. 2.6, further test generation is not always the sole appropriate response to a coverage hole. It is worth noting that this scenario was exposed only by pseudorandom and constrained-pseudorandom test generation, demonstrating the unique benefit of these approaches; by exploring the SUT's behaviour beyond the assumptions of the verification engineer, they provide a useful complement to the more directed approach of model-based test generation.

Figure 5 illustrates the code coverage (statements) achieved with each test generation strategy over 206 statements (the actual percentages may vary ±2% due to decision branches with 1 or 2 lines of code each). The lines of code are grouped using the state machine structure in the Python module, to facilitate visualization. The block of code corresponding to the "release" state is not covered by the pseudorandom and constrained pseudorandom generated tests, hence it is shown in white. This coverage hole could be closed by applying the test template produced by model-based test generation for Requirement 1.

Because our code is structured as a finite state machine (FSM), it would be appropriate to also incorporate structural coverage models in the future. A comprehensive test suite would include tests that visit all states, trigger all possible state transitions, and traverse all paths.

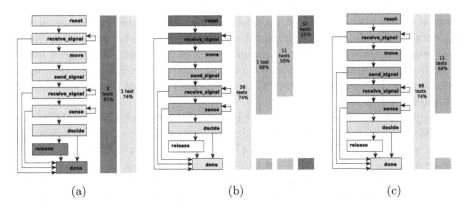

(a)   (b)   (c)

Fig. 5. Code coverage (percent values) obtained in simulation with (a) model-based (4 tests), (b) pseudorandom (100 tests), and (c) constrained-pseudorandom test generation (100 tests)

The generation of effective tests, that target both the exploration of the SUT and the verification progress, is fundamental to maximising the efficiency of a CDV testbench reaching for coverage closure. From the overall results, it can be seen that the three test generation approaches applied have complementary strengths that overcome their respective weaknesses in terms of coverage. While model-based test generation ensures that the requirements are covered in an efficient manner, pseudorandom test generation can construct scenarios that the verification engineer has not foreseen. Such cases are useful for exposing flawed or missing assumptions in the design of the testbench or the requirements.

5   Conclusions

We advocated the use of CDV for robot code in the context of HRI. By promoting automation, CDV can provide a faster route to coverage closure, compared with manually directed testing. CDV is typically used in Software-in-the-Loop simulations, but it can also be used in conjunction with Hardware-in-the-Loop simulation, Human-in-the-Loop simulation or with emulation. The flexibility of CDV with regard to the levels of abstraction used in both the requirements models and the SUT makes it particularly well suited to verification of HRI.

The principal drawback of CDV, compared with directed testing, is the overhead effort associated with building an automated testbench. Directed testing produces early results, but CDV significantly accelerates the approach towards coverage closure once the testbench is in place. Hence CDV is an appropriate choice for systems in which complete coverage is difficult to achieve due to a broad and varied state space that includes rare but important events, as is typically the case for HRI.

We proposed implementations of four automatic testbench components, the Test Generator, the Driver, the Checker and the Coverage Collector, that suit the HRI domain. Different test generation strategies were considered: pseudorandom, constrained pseudorandom and model-based to complement each other in the quest for meaningful tests and exploration of unexpected behaviours. Assertions were proposed for the Checker, accommodating requirements at different levels of abstraction, an important feature for HRI. Different coverage models were proposed for the Coverage Collector: requirements (assertion), code statements, and cross-product.

The potential for CDG (Coverage-Driven test Generation), through the implementation of automated feedback loops, has been considered. Nevertheless, we believe a great part of the feedback work needs to be performed by the verification engineer, since CDG is difficult to implement in practice.

A handover example demonstrated the feasibility of implementing the CDV testbench as a ROS-Gazebo based simulator. The results show the relative merits of our proposed testbench components, and indicate how feedback loops in the testbench can be explored to seek coverage closure. Several key observations can be noted from these results. Pseudorandom test generation allows a degree of unpredictability in the environment, so that unexpected behaviours of the SUT may be exposed. Model-based test generation usefully complements this technique by systematically directing tests according to the requirements of the SUT. This requires the development of a formal model of the system, which additionally enables exhaustive verification through formal methods, as explored by previous authors for HRI [3,6,14,19,20,25].

If the requirements are translated into Temporal Logic properties for model checking, assertion monitors can be derived automatically. In future work, we will be exploring generation of monitors for different levels of abstraction in the simulation (e.g., events-based, or checked at every clock cycle) in a more formal manner. We will further explore the use of bisimulation analysis to ensure equivalence between a robot's high-level control code and any associated formal models. We intend to incorporate probabilistic models of the human, the environment and other elements in the simulator, to enable more varied stimulation of an SUT. We also intend to verify a more comprehensive set of requirements for the handover task, e.g., according to the safety standard ISO 15066 (currently under development) for collaborative industrial robots.

Our approach is scalable, as more complex systems can be verified using the same CDV approach, for the actual system's code. We are confident CDV can be used for the verification and validation of autonomous systems in general. Open source platforms and established tools can serve to create simulators and models at different abstraction levels for the same SUT.

Acknowledgments. This work was supported by the EPSRC grants EP/K006320/1 and EP/K006223/1 "Trustworthy Robotic Assistants".

We are grateful for the productive discussions with Yoav Hollander, Yaron Kashai, Ziv Binyamini and Mike Bartley.

References

1. Alexander, R., Hawkins, H., Rae, D.: Situation Coverage - A Coverage Criterion for Testing Autonomous Robots. Department of Computer Science, University of York, Technical Report (2015)
2. Armoni, R., Korchemny, D., Tiemeyer, A., Vardi, M.Y., Zbar, Y.: Deterministic dynamic monitors for linear-time assertions. In: Havelund, K., Núñez, M., Roşu, G., Wolff, B. (eds.) FATES 2006 and RV 2006. LNCS, vol. 4262, pp. 163–177. Springer, Heidelberg (2006)
3. Bordini, R.H., Fisher, M., Sierhuis, M.: Formal verification of human-robot teamwork. In: Proceedings of ACM/IEEE HRI, pp. 267–268 (2009)
4. Boren, J., Cousins, S.: The SMACH high-level executive. IEEE Robot. Autom. Mag. **17**(4), 18–20 (2010)
5. Clarke, E.M., Grumberg, O., Peled, D.A.: Model Checking. MIT Press, Cambridge (1999)
6. Cowley, A., Taylor, C.J.: Towards language-based verification of robot behaviors. In: Proceedings of IEEE/RSJ International Conference on Intelligent Robots and Systems (IROS), pp. 4776–4782. IEEE (2011)
7. Eder, K., Harper, C., Leonards, U.: Towards the safety of human-in-the-loop robotics: challenges and opportunities for safety assurance of robotic co-workers. In: Proceedings of IEEE ROMAN, pp. 660–665 (2014)
8. Foster, H.D., Krolnik, A.C., Lacey, D.J.: Assertion-Based Design, 2nd edn. Springer, Heidelberg (2004)
9. Grigore, E.C., Eder, K., Lenz, A., Skachek, S., Pipe, A.G., Melhuish, C.: Towards safe human-robot interaction. In: Groß, R., Alboul, L., Melhuish, C., Witkowski, M., Prescott, T.J., Penders, J. (eds.) TAROS 2011. LNCS, vol. 6856, pp. 323–335. Springer, Heidelberg (2011)
10. Haedicke, F., Le, H., Grosse, D., Drechsler, R.: CRAVE: an advanced constrained random verification environment for System C. In: Proceedings of SoC, pp. 1–7 (2012)
11. Hartmanns, A., Hermanns, H.: A modest approach to checking probabilistic timed automata. In: Proceedings of QEST, pp. 187–196 (2009)

12. Havelund, K., Roşu, G.: Synthesizing monitors for safety properties. In: Katoen, J.-P., Stevens, P. (eds.) TACAS 2002. LNCS, vol. 2280, pp. 342–356. Springer, Heidelberg (2002)
13. Ioannides, C., Eder, K.I.: Coverage-directed test generation automated by machine learning - a review. ACM Trans. Des. Autom. Electron. Syst. **17**(1), 7:1–7:21 (2012)
14. Kouskoulas, Y., Renshaw, D.W., Platzer, A., Kazanzides, P.: Certifying the safe design of a virtual fixture control algorithm for a surgical robot. In: Belta, C., Ivancic, F. (eds.) Proceedings of Hybrid Systems: Computation and Control (HSCC), pp. 263–272. ACM (2013)
15. Lackner, H., Schlingloff, B.: Modeling for automated test generation a comparison. In: Proceedings of MBEES Workshop (2012)
16. Lakhotia, K., McMinn, P., Harman, M.: Automated test data generation for coverage: haven't we solved this problem yet? In: Proceedings TAIC (2009)
17. Lenz, A., Skachek, S., Hamann, K., Steinwender, J., Pipe, A., Melhuish, C.: The BERT2 infrastructure: an integrated system for the study of human-robot interaction. In: Proceedings of IEEE-RAS Humanoids, pp. 346–351 (2010)
18. Milner, R.: A Calculus of Communicating Systems. LNCS. Springer, Heidelberg (1980)
19. Mohammed, A., Furbach, U., Stolzenburg, F.: Multi-robot systems: modeling, specification, and model checking. In: Robot Soccer, pp. 241–265 (2010)
20. Muradore, R., Bresolin, D., Geretti, L., Fiorini, P., Villa, T.: Robotic surgery. IEEE Robot. Autom. Mag. **18**(3), 24–32 (2011)
21. Nielsen, B., Skou, A.: Automated test generation from timed automata. Int. J. Softw. Tools Technol. Transfer **5**, 59–77 (2003)
22. Nielsen, B.: Towards a method for combined model-based testing and analysis. In: Proceedings of MODELSWARD, pp. 609–618 (2014)
23. Piziali, A.: Functional Verification Coverage Measurement and Analysis. Kluwer Academic, Boston (2004)
24. Trojanek, P., Eder, K.: Verification and testing of mobile robot navigation algorithms: a case study in SPARK. In: Proceedings of IROS, pp. 1489–1494 (2014)
25. Webster, M., Dixon, C., Fisher, M., Salem, M., Saunders, J., Koay, K.L., Dautenhahn, K.: Formal verification of an autonomous personal robotic assistant. In: Proceedings of AAAI FVHMS 2014, pp. 74–79 (2014)
26. Wile, B., Goss, J.C., Roesner, W.: Comprehensive Functional Verification. Morgan Kaufmann, San Francisco (2005)

Symbolic Execution

PANDA: Simultaneous Predicate Abstraction and Concrete Execution

Jakub Daniel and Pavel Parízek[✉]

Department of Distributed and Dependable Systems,
Faculty of Mathematics and Physics,
Charles University in Prague, Prague, Czech Republic
{daniel,parizek}@d3s.mff.cuni.cz

Abstract. We present a new verification algorithm, PANDA, that combines predicate abstraction with concrete execution and dynamic analysis. Both the concrete and abstract state spaces of an input program are traversed simultaneously, guiding each other through on-the-fly mutual interaction. PANDA performs dynamic on-the-fly pruning of those branches in the abstract state space that diverge from the corresponding concrete trace. If the abstract branch is actually feasible for a different concrete trace, PANDA discovers the covering trace by exploring different data choices. Candidate spurious errors may also arise, for example, due to over-approximation of the points-to relation between heap objects. We eliminate all the spurious errors using the well-known approach based on lazy abstraction refinement with interpolants. Results of experiments with our prototype implementation show that PANDA can successfully verify programs that feature loops, recursion, and manipulation with objects and arrays. It has a competitive performance and does not report any spurious error for our benchmarks.

1 Introduction

Program verification techniques based on predicate abstraction and iterative refinement have been the subject of extensive research. The set of popular approaches includes counterexample-guided abstraction refinement (CEGAR) [11] and lazy abstraction with interpolants [1,16,18], which are implemented in tools such as BLAST [6] and CPACHECKER [8]. Although these approaches are successful in verifying programs with predominantly acyclic control-flow, programs containing loops with many iterations and programs with arrays pose a challenge to them. The initial abstraction is usually too coarse to capture only the feasible executions of a loop. Therefore, these kinds of approaches are forced to repeatedly refine the abstraction and effectively unroll the loop. Many of the unrollings are incomplete, and the corresponding traces are spurious because they exit the loop prematurely.

Each step of abstraction refinement is considerably costly because it usually involves expensive SMT calls, and therefore use of refinement makes a verification procedure rather inefficient in this setting. More recent techniques (e.g., SMASH [14]) complement the abstraction refinement with some kind of under-approximating analysis (e.g., testing) in order to rule out spurious traces and

© Springer International Publishing Switzerland 2015
N. Piterman (Ed.): HVC 2015, LNCS 9434, pp. 87–103, 2015.
DOI: 10.1007/978-3-319-26287-1_6

to focus directly on the complete unrollings with proper number of loop iterations. Some of the recent approaches, such as DASH [5] implemented in the tool
YOGI [20], in fact alternate between predicate abstraction and concrete execution. Tests always explore a feasible number of loop iterations, and therefore
spurious traces that would otherwise cause refinement are avoided, saving many
calls to SMT. In general, the combination of abstraction with testing preserves
the benefits of each approach while mitigating their respective weaknesses.

Example 1. Consider the small example program in Fig. 1. The function find-
Greater searches the array a of integer values and returns the index of the first
value that is greater than t. If no such value is present in a, then the length of the
array is returned instead. The program further contains a procedure main that
asserts the correct behavior of findGreater. The function loadUnknownArray creates
an array of arbitrary integer values with a statically given length and stores it
into the variable a. After the call of findGreater(a, 10), the procedure main asserts
the desired property of the returned value.

```
1   void main(String[] args) {
2       int[] a = loadUnknownArray();
3       int i = findGreater(a, 10);
4       assert i == a.length || a[i] > 10;
5   }
6
7   int findGreater(int[] a, t) {
8       for (int j = 0; j < a.length; j++) {
9           if (a[j] > t) return j;
10      }
11      return a.length;
12  }
```

Fig. 1. Example program

Both CEGAR and lazy abstraction, as implemented for example in BLAST [6],
would struggle analyzing the loop at lines 8–10 in Fig. 1 provided the array
was large enough. They would iteratively discover spurious traces that exit the
loop prematurely, and rule out the traces one by one in separate refinement
steps by deriving predicates that relate j to a specific constant. On the other
hand, approaches like DASH employ testing in order to find the correct number
of loop iterations. A run of a test always represents a feasible execution and
thus never yields spurious behavior. Furthermore, concrete execution is typically
cheap because it does not use expensive SMT calls.

Based on the same observations, we introduce a new technique that combines
predicate abstraction with concrete execution. We propose a verification algorithm PANDA, which performs abstract state space traversal that is augmented
with simultaneous concrete execution in order to eliminate spurious abstract
traces on-the-fly. The predicate abstraction and the concrete execution guide

each other during the traversal. Usage of concrete execution enables PANDA to faithfully capture the behavior of programs written in mainstream object-oriented languages, and to support features of such programs that are hard to model with abstraction predicates. It also allows PANDA to prune infeasible abstract traces that arise due to the overapproximating predicate abstraction, and thus greatly reduces the number of necessary refinement steps.

The state space is constructed on-the-fly during the systematic traversal by unrolling the control-flow graph of the program. In each state, all possible outgoing transitions are determined using the overapproximate abstract information, and then every transition is explored using both concrete and abstract execution. The complete reachable state space of a given program is covered in this way.

Although pruning based on concrete execution eliminates some spurious traces, it may not prune everything for two reasons: (1) consistency between abstract and concrete executions is checked only locally, and (2) concrete execution still allows for non-determinism (see Sect. 3). Therefore, the state space traversal procedure may still report a spurious error. To address this problem, PANDA uses the well-known approach of lazy abstraction with iterative refinement that is based on inter-polants computed for the spurious counterexample [16].

In the case of our example program, PANDA eliminates the traces that are spurious due to an infeasible number of the loop body unrollings (at line 8) without resorting to iterative refinement. The algorithm explores all the feasible traces — more specifically, one trace returning from the function findGreater at line 9 for every value of the index j between 0 and the length of the array a, and one trace returning from findGreater through line 11.

We implemented the PANDA approach in a tool with the same name. Unlike most of the tools we target Java and not C. PANDA builds on concrete state space traversal provided by Java Pathfinder [25], and simultaneously computes predicate abstraction in such a way that the systematic exploration of a concrete state space and the predicate abstraction can interact. We also performed experimental evaluation of PANDA on small examples from our previous work [21] and benchmarks taken from the Competition on Software Verification [26], and compared its performance with other tools. Results show that the proposed approach is promising — our prototype implementation has a competitive performance and does not report spurious errors.

2 Preliminaries

Here we define more formally basic concepts that are used in the rest of this paper, and the important terminology.

Program. We model programs using control-flow automata (CFA). A *program* P is a tuple $(\mathcal{C}, l_{init}, l_{err})$, where $\mathcal{C}$ is a set of control-flow automata representing individual methods in the program, l_{init} is the initial location of the whole program, and l_{err} is the error location. The *control-flow automaton* C for a method m is a tuple (L, A, l_{en}) that encodes a directed graph with a single root node and labeled edges. Nodes of the graph correspond to the set L of program locations in the method m, and edges correspond to the set A of actions between locations. An action $a \in A$ from the location l to the location l', written as (l, a, l'), is represented by a graph edge that is labeled with the program statement corresponding to a. The location $l_{en} \in L$ is the *entry point* of the method m. We use the symbol $vars(C)$ to denote the set of local variables that appear in statements that correspond to actions of the control-flow automaton C.

The initial location l_{init} of the whole program corresponds to the entry point l_{en} of some method m_{init}, which is modeled by $C_{init} \in \mathcal{C}$. Any two distinct CFA's may have only the error location l_{err} in common. It is the destination location of every action that triggers a possible runtime error.

A program statement can be either an assume, an assignment, a procedure call, or a return from the current procedure. The assume statements are used to model the intra-procedural control flow, such as branching and loops. If there are more actions defined at one location, they all have to be assume statements. We allow only variables (fields, array elements) of an integer type and references to heap objects.

Abstraction. The symbol abs denotes a global mapping from program locations to sets of abstraction predicates. For a given location l, the set $abs(l)$ contains all predicates associated with the location l, i.e. the set of predicates whose scope includes l.

States. A *program state* s is a pair $(\mathcal{H}, \mathcal{S})$, where $\mathcal{H}$ denotes the heap and $\mathcal{S}$ is the call stack. The heap $\mathcal{H}$ is a directed graph. Inner nodes of the graph represent objects, classes, and arrays. Leaf nodes are associated with the concrete values of object fields and array elements that have an integer type. In general, edges in the graph capture the points-to relation between heap objects, and associate objects with values of their fields, respectively arrays with values of their elements. An edge (o, f, v) connects a node that represents a heap object o with a node that represents the possible value v of the field f. Similarly, an edge (o, n, v) connects a node that represents an array object o with a node that represents the value v of an element with the index n.

The call stack is a sequence of tuples (l_i, σ_i, Φ_i) that represent method frames. The symbol l_i denotes the current program location within the corresponding method, σ_i is the assignment of values to all local variables, and Φ_i is the valuation of all abstraction predicates in $abs(l_i)$. Possible values of each predicate are $\bot$, $\top$, and $*$ representing *false*, *true*, and *unknown*, respectively.

We assume that a program P has a single initial concrete state, and reads input from the environment during its execution. The initial state s_0 has an empty heap and stack with a single frame. This frame contains the initial location l_{init} where the program execution starts, initial values σ_{init} of local variables in the scope of the entry CFA, and the initial valuation Φ_{init} of abstraction predicates (i.e., *unknown*). More formally, $\sigma_{init} = \{v \mapsto 0 \mid v \in vars(C_{init})\}$ and $\Phi_{init} = \{p \mapsto * \mid p \in abs(l_{init})\}$.

Reachability Graph. We use reachability graphs, defined over the set S of program states and the set T of transitions between states, to model the program behavior and state space. A *reachability graph* $R(P)$ for the program P is a possibly infinite directed graph $R = (S, T)$. A transition $\tau \in T$ is an edge (s, a, s') labeled with action a in some CFA. We use a single monolithic reachability graph for the whole program P. It is constructed inductively as fixpoint of a monotonic sequence $R_i, i \geq 0$ of finite approximations, which starts in $R_0 = (\{s_0\}, \{\})$. An approximation R_{k+1} extends R_k with a new state s' and a transition $\tau = (s, a, s')$ such that s is a state already present in R_k but unexpanded and a is the action executed by τ. The order of state expansions can be arbitrary, although we use only the depth-first order in this paper for simplicity.

Note that $R(P)$ is always specific to a given set of abstraction predicates. The sets S and T, and therefore also the shape of the reachability graph, are changed upon refinement. For brevity, we use the symbol R to denote a finite approximation of $R(P)$ in the rest of the paper.

Alternative Interpretations. Each statement of an input program P is executed both concretely and abstractly. The abstract execution of a single statement may give rise to multiple *alternative interpretations*.

The symbol $alt(R, s, a)$ denotes the set $\{s' \mid (s, a, s') \in R\}$ of all alternative interpretations for an action a in the state s in R. The set contains all the already explored transitions from s. Note that although in general there may be infinitely many alternative interpretations of an action in any given state in the entire $R(P)$, e.g. interpretations of x = unknown(), the set $alt(R, s, a)$ is always finite for a given approximation R and it is initially empty.

The symbol alt^* denotes the set of potential alternative interpretations that will be expanded later (in future); it is initially defined as:

$$alt^*(s, a) = \begin{cases} \emptyset & a \text{ is not an action at the current location of } s \text{ in } \mathcal{C} \\ \{s'\} & a \text{ is } \boxed{\text{x = unknown()}}; s' \text{is successor for } \boxed{\text{x = 0}} \\ \{s'_1, \ldots, s'_n\} & a \text{ is } \boxed{\text{x = e}}; s'_i \text{ are successors for valuations of } \boxed{\text{e}} \\ \{s'\} & a \text{ is } \boxed{\text{m(x)}}, \text{ or } \boxed{\text{return x}}; s' \text{ is the only successor} \\ \emptyset \text{ or } \{s'\} & a \text{ is } \boxed{\text{assume c}}; s' \text{ augments } s \text{ with the condition } c \end{cases}$$

There are no interpretations defined for actions that are not enabled in the given state. The initial interpretation of x = unknown() is such that x is assigned the value 0. The interpretation of a regular assignment may not be deterministic due to heap abstraction, e.g. in the case of x = a[i], and therefore we consider the set of alternative interpretations to contain all the choices. Interpretation of procedure calls and returns is straightforward and affects the call stack component of a program state. The interpretation of an assume statement depends on the valuation of the assumed condition c in the state s. If the fact is satisfiable there is one interpretation s', otherwise there is none.

The new alternatives to be expanded later are discovered on-demand, and in the majority of cases only a small finite subset of alternatives needs to be expanded. An expansion of an action a in s effectively moves the corresponding interpretation s' from $alt^*(s, a)$ to $alt(R \oplus (s, a, s'), s, a)$. For convenience, we define a set $unexp(s) = \{a \mid alt^*(s, a) \neq \emptyset\}$ of actions that are not completely expanded. We assume the presence of a special unique state s_{end}, for which the set $unexp(s_{end})$ is always empty.

Traces. An *execution trace* tr of the program P is a finite path in the reachability graph $R(P)$ that starts in s_0 and can be viewed as an alternating sequence of states and actions $(s_0, a_1, s_1, \ldots, a_n, s_n)$. Every such trace tr is associated with a *trace formula* φ_{tr} that captures the execution of the program P along the trace. The trace formula φ_{tr} is a conjunction of constraints that express the semantics and effects of all executed statements (corresponding to actions $a_1, \ldots, a_n$). Each constraint is defined using the static-single-assignment form. We say that an execution trace tr is *feasible* if the corresponding trace formula φ_{tr} is satisfiable. A trace tr that reaches the error state s_{err} is called an *error trace* or a *counterexample*.

3   Panda Algorithm

We describe the core PANDA algorithm in the first part of this section, and then we provide more details on selected aspects in the following subsections.

The core algorithm is shown in Fig. 2. It takes a program $P = (\mathcal{C}, l_{init}, l_{err})$ and the initial map abs as input, and constructs the monolithic reachability graph R for P through iterative unrolling of control-flow graphs in the set $\mathcal{C}$. Note that the map abs is usually empty at the start, but the user can provide some predicates for specific locations in this way. The reachability graph R is iteratively unrolled in the function UNROLL by means of an overloaded function *advance* and a dual function *backtrack* that carry out key steps of the search. When the error location l_{err} is reached by the last transition τ', the PANDA algorithm checks feasibility of the counterexample cex. If the error is real then it is reported to the user; otherwise PANDA performs abstraction refinement in order to eliminate the spurious counterexample and then restarts the state space traversal. The verification of a program terminates when all the reachable states are processed. This happens when PANDA backtracks over the initial state s_0 and the current trace tr becomes empty (line 4). Note also that the verification algorithm does not perform state matching. Our definition of the verification algorithm in Fig. 2 contains several other auxiliary functions (*scopes*, *locs*, and *itp*) that are described later in this section, and also the function TRANS that we first explain as a black box and then provide more details in Sect. 3.1.

The function TRANS(R, tr, s, a) performs simultaneous concrete and abstract execution of a given action a in the state s at the end of the trace tr in R. It returns some transition $\tau' = (s, a, s')$ for some candidate successor state $s' \in alt^*(s, a)$. There is always at least one successor state, otherwise $a \notin unexp(s)$. See Sect. 3.1 for more details on the selection of s'. New valuation of abstraction predicates in s' after the execution of the action a is computed using the standard approach based on weakest preconditions and decision procedures. In addition, the abstract interpreter uses knowledge of the abstract heap to determine more precise valuation of predicates that capture aliasing between reference variables. However, predicates that help maintain the aliasing relation among variables

```
 1: function PANDA(P, abs)                  20: function UNROLL(P, R, tr)
 2:     R ← ({s₀}, {})                       21:     (C, l_init, l_err) ← P
 3:     tr ← (s₀)                            22:     cex ← ⊥
 4:     while tr ≠ () do                     23:     s ← last state of tr
 5:         (R, tr, cex) ← UNROLL(P, R, tr)  24:     if ∃a ∈ unexp(s) then
 6:         if cex ≠ ⊥ then                  25:         τ' ← TRANS(R, tr, s, a)
 7:             if REAL(cex) then return cex 26:         R ← advance(R, τ')
 8:             abs ← REFINE(P, abs, cex)    27:         tr ← advance(tr, τ')
 9:             (R, tr) ← RESET(R, tr, cex)  28:     else
10:     return safe                          29:         tr ← backtrack(tr)
                                             30:     if tr reaches l_err then
11: function REFINE(P, abs, cex)             31:         cex ← tr
12:     (C, l_init, l_err) ← P               32:     return (R, tr, cex)
13:     for φ_scp ∈ scopes(φ_cex) do
14:         L_scp ← locs(cex, φ_scp, C)      33: function REAL(cex)
15:         for l ∈ L_scp do                 34:     return is φ_cex satisfiable?
16:             p ← itp(φ_scp, φ_cex, l)
17:             if p ∉ abs(l) then           35: function RESET(R, tr, cex)
18:                 abs(l) ← abs(l) ∪ {p}    36:     return (({s₀}, {}), (s₀))
19:     return abs
```

Fig. 2. PANDA algorithm

still have to be introduced through refinement. Effects of the action a on the concrete part of the program state s are determined by concrete semantics of the statement corresponding to a.

A non-deterministic choice in the state space is created when the result of abstract execution of a given action a cannot be determined precisely using information from the program state. Possible sources of non-determinism include especially predicate valuations at branching statements (e.g., when the condition is *unknown*) and overapproximating points-to relation due to weak update. The effect of an assignment to a reference variable is modeled by weak update whenever the destination cannot be determined precisely, and in that case the variable may point to multiple heap objects. When processing an access to array, PANDA can make choices at two levels to consider all the possibly affected elements and values — first it has to determine all concrete indices that satisfy constraints encoded by abstraction predicates, and then for each index it has to find all the array element values based on the points-to relation.

When executing a procedure call, PANDA computes initial valuation of abstraction predicates of the new stack frame (i.e., in the callee scope) using predicates over the actual arguments of the call. Upon return, valuation of abstraction predicates in the scope of the caller procedure is updated using valuation of predicates over the actual arguments of a reference type and predicates over the returned value.

New abstraction predicates are derived from a spurious counterexample cex in the function REFINE by the means of interpolation. We use a variant of the standard approach based on computing an interpolation-sequence [23] over the trace formula φ_{cex}. The trace formula is obtained as a conjunction of clauses that encode individual statements, heap manipulation (via read and write), and the non-deterministic choices made during their execution (e.g., choice of a concrete array index when processing statements like $x = a[i]$). In our case, interpolants are generated separately for each method call in φ_{cex}. To ensure a proper scope of interpolants within each individual method call on the given trace, PANDA uses a procedure similar to *nested interpolants* [15]. The function *scopes* divides the whole trace formula φ_{cex} into many fragments, where each of them corresponds to the scope of execution of some method call. The function *locs* returns a list L_{scp} of locations that appear in the given fragment of the trace formula, i.e. in the corresponding scope. Note that if a method m is executed several times in cex, then the function *scopes* will return a separate fragment φ_{scp} for each execution of m, and similarly a location can appear multiple times in L_{scp} (e.g., due to a loop in the code). Actual interpolants for every fragment φ_{scp} are computed by the function $itp(\varphi_{scp}, \varphi_{cex}, l)$, which calls an interpolating solver. This approach respects method call boundaries and variable scopes. In particular, interpolants generated for locations inside a method m contain only symbols that represent local variables of m.

3.1   Dynamic Pruning and Discovery of Feasible Covering Paths

A consequence of the simultaneous concrete and abstract execution is that a transition may reach an inconsistent combined state. This situation occurs when an action a allows for non-deterministic expansion, i.e. when the abstract pre-state s induces multiple alternative interpretations in $alt^*(s, a)$, while there is usually a single successor in the concrete state space. In such a case, the concrete successor is consistent only with one of the abstract successors.

Figure 3 illustrates *dynamic pruning and discovery of feasible covering paths*, the strategy that we propose for resolving such situations. The function TRANS$_{pruning}$ is the implementation of TRANS from Sect. 3. First, at line 2, it selects and executes one interpretation of action a in the state s (there must be at least one due to the check at line 24 in Fig. 2) and marks it as processed at line 4. Further, if the abstract part of s' overapproximates the concrete part, i.e. when there are no inconsistencies, the function returns a transition leading to s'. Otherwise, PANDA is bound to prune the current trace by returning transition to s_{end} at line 10, because the currently analyzed interpretation is not consistent. Then the main algorithm is forced to backtrack in the next iteration, i.e. in the next call to UNROLL. However, there may still exist a concrete trace that captures different values returned by the unknown statements and conforms to the same abstract trace. Its existence is checked at lines 6 and 7 by means of generating a model for the related trace formula, and the corresponding branch will be explored by PANDA under a different combined trace in R. Although we omit this from the pseudocode of TRANS in Fig. 3, when PANDA searches for the

```
1: function TRANS_pruning(R, tr, s, a)
2:     s' ← any successor in alt*(s, a)
3:     τ ← (s, a, s')
4:     remove s' from alt*(s, a)
5:     if s' is consistent then return τ
6:     M ← model of φ_tr⊕τ
7:     if M ≠ ⊥ then
8:         for all (s₁, b, s₂) ∈ tr and b is | x = unknown() | do
9:             augment alt*(s₁, b) with s₂[x ← M(x)]
10:    return (s, a, s_end)
```

Fig. 3. The implementation of TRANS within PANDA

alternative concrete trace, it first tries to reuse the already discovered values that were returned in statements x = unknown() (in order to minimize backtracking) and only then it explores new models. PANDA extracts new interpretations (i.e., new values of all unknown statements) from the model and adds them into respective sets alt^*, so that they are explored later (line 9). Here the operator $\cdot [x \leftarrow e]$ produces a state that differs from its operand only in valuation of the variable x, which is fixed to the value e. Note that a single value returned by some unknown may prevent further execution of a trace in combination with specific values of other unknown statements along the trace, and it may permit the execution in combination with different values.

Example 2. Now consider the situation depicted in Fig. 4 that illustrate the whole process. On the left, there is a short code snippet, which first stores a non-deterministic value into the variable x and then compares this variable with the constant 1. The rest of the figure shows combined concrete and abstract traces that are explored by PANDA during analysis of the code snippet. Dashed circles represent abstract states, solid dots represent concrete states, tubes depict abstract transitions, and finally solid arrows stand for concrete transitions. Each state label always applies to both the concrete and abstract part of a state, and the same is true for transitions.

The process of pruning inconsistent traces and discovering feasible alternative traces that cover the pruned behavior is divided into three phases. Each of the phases is illustrated with a subfigure to the right of the code snippet in Fig. 4.

Phase 1. PANDA expanded the action b corresponding to x = unknown() in state s_1 to produce the transition τ_1 and reach the state s_2. The default interpretation of b is equivalent to x = 0 (recall the definition of alt^*). At this point, the *then*-branch is selected first and TRANS$(R, tr, s_2, \boxed{\text{assume } x > 1})$ yields the state s', which is not consistent because the abstract state satisfies $x > 1$ while the concrete state assigns 0 to x. This is the reason why the solid dot is not included in the dashed circle for the state s', and therefore the solid arrow leaves the tube — representing the inconsistency between concrete and abstract interpretation of

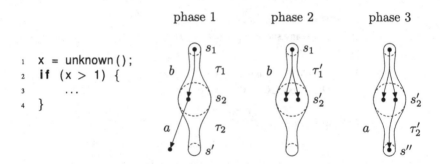

Fig. 4. On-the-fly discovery of feasible covering paths

the action a in the state s_2. However, a different interpretation of b in s_1 exists that would produce a consistent transition. It is extracted from the model of $\varphi_{(s_1,b,s_2,a,s')}$. We suppose, for the purpose of the example, that the discovered interpretation of b is equivalent to $x = 2$, although many other integer values could be returned from unknown(). The new interpretation is added to the set $alt^*(s_1, b)$ before TRANS returns s_{end} and forces PANDA to backtrack to s_1.

Phase 2. After the backtrack, $b \in unexp(s_1)$ as it was reintroduced in the previous phase, and so it is selected for expansion. In the middle subfigure, the alternative interpretation s'_2 of the action b is expanded by PANDA in TRANS(R, tr, s_1, b). As a result, the state s'_2 is added to the reachability graph R.

Phase 3. The search now continues from s'_2. In the right-most subfigure, TRANS explores the interpretation of a in state s'_2. This time, it is consistent and yields the transition τ'_2 and the state s''. Thus the abstractly reachable *then*-branch is covered also by the concrete execution, although first it has been discovered with a concrete trace that had no feasible extension entering the branch.

In general, dynamic pruning eliminates many infeasible traces from the abstract state space based on the knowledge of concrete states. That is an important benefit of the simultaneous concrete and abstract execution. Note, however, that usage of pruning does not guarantee that all the infeasible abstract branches are eliminated, because it handles only choices introduced by actions that read non-deterministic values. Although only the feasible concrete execution traces will be explored for many input programs, iterative abstraction refinement still may be necessary in the case of choices caused by non-determinism of other kinds (e.g., imprecise heap abstraction).

3.2   Soundness and Termination

In this section, we discuss soundness of the proposed PANDA algorithm, and why it may not terminate in general. We show that dynamic pruning and discovery of feasible covering paths is sufficient to guarantee exploration of all the feasible behaviors of the given program.

We say that a reachability graph R is *complete* if every reachable state of the program P is directly contained in R, and that R is *precise* if it does not contain a spurious trace reaching s_{err}.

The proof of soundness of our verification procedure PANDA is based on the following theorem.

Theorem 1. *The program P is safe if and only if the error state s_{err} is not contained in a complete and precise reachability graph R constructed for P.*

Proof. We show the two directions of the equivalence separately for some complete precise reachability graph R for P.

$\Leftarrow$) The state s_{err} is not in R, and since R is complete it contains all the reachable states of P. Therefore, s_{err} is not reachable in P and by definition P is safe.

$\Rightarrow$) Assume that P is safe. Then, s_{err} is unreachable in any execution of P, and any abstract trace reaching s_{err} is spurious. Because the given R is precise, it cannot contain spurious abstract trace reaching s_{err} and thus s_{err} is excluded from R.   □

What remains to be shown is that when PANDA does not report an error in P, it either terminates with a complete precise reachability graph $R(P)$ or does not terminate at all. Precision of R follows from the abstraction refinement step of the main algorithm. PANDA either does not terminate or there are finitely many refinement steps, and thus the resulting reachability graph may not contain spurious error traces and it is precise.

Now assume that PANDA terminates on P and the reachability graph R is not complete, i.e. there is a reachable state s of P that is not contained in R. In that case, there must be a trace tr from s_0 to s and a state $\overset{\bullet}{s}$ that is the first state on that trace not contained in R. Let $(\overset{\bullet}{s}, a, \overset{\circ}{s})$ be the transition reaching $\overset{\circ}{s}$ on the trace tr for the first time, which means that $\overset{\bullet}{s} \in R$. The only reason for a consistent reachable state $\overset{\circ}{s}$ to be excluded from R is that it was never included in $alt^*(\overset{\bullet}{s}, a)$. Since the heap abstraction and computation of abstract successors are overapproximating, the sets of alternative interpretations for assignment statements, branching, looping, function calls, and returns are overapproximating as well, and they never exclude any abstractly reachable successor unless it is pruned. Every abstract successor that is being pruned is analyzed (lines 6–9 in Fig. 4) for feasibility and appropriate enabling interpretations of actions along the trace are added to alt^*, so that they can be explored later. Consequently, if the algorithm terminated without processing the alternative that reaches $\overset{\circ}{s}$, it could not have been feasible and R is, in fact, complete.

Theorem 2. PANDA *soundly verifies safety of programs.*

Proof. Follows directly from the discussion above.   □

The whole PANDA algorithm may not terminate. The reachability graph may be infinite due to unbounded loops and recursion that admit infinite number of concrete traces of different lengths. Also, the abstraction refinement loop may diverge for input programs with possibly infinite state spaces [16].

4   Implementation

We implemented the proposed verification algorithm in the tool called PANDA, which is built upon Java Pathfinder (JPF) [25] and accepts programs in Java. JPF is responsible for concrete execution of Java bytecode instructions and systematic traversal of the concrete state space, and it also provides concrete values taken from dynamic program states. Predicate abstraction and lazy refinement are performed with the help of SMT solvers. The current version of PANDA uses CVC4 [4] and Z3 [19]. The complete source code of our implementation, including examples and benchmark programs, is available at https://github.com/d3sformal/panda.

In the rest of this section, we describe several optimizations of the core algorithm in Fig. 2 that apply to the restart of state space traveral after refinement.

The basic variant of the function RESET backtracks to the initial state, and drops all information about the state space fragment explored before the spurious error was hit. However, in this case PANDA would explore again the fragment of the program state space that has already been proven safe. A more efficient approach, heavily inspired by lazy abstraction [16] used in BLAST [6], is the following: (1) determine which locations and states on the spurious error trace are affected by the refinement, (2) backtrack only to the last state of the longest unaffected prefix of the error trace, and (3) then resume state space exploration from that point with the refined abstraction. Location l is affected by the refinement when new predicates were added to $abs(l)$.

Another limitation of the basic PANDA algorithm is repeated exploration of certain safe fragments of the program state space. We designed an optimization that is based on recording information about explored state space branches. During the traversal, PANDA remembers all safe branches for each choice on the current trace, and when the traversal resumes with the more precise abstraction it skips the recorded branches.

5   Evaluation

We performed experiments on three groups of Java programs in order to evaluate PANDA. A brief description of each group of benchmarks follows.

The first group contains 7 benchmarks from the categories *loops* and *arrays* of the Competition on Software Verification (SV-COMP) [26]. Four benchmarks in this group (Array, Invert String, Password, and Reverse Array) use arrays whose content is based on non-deterministic input, Eureka 01 computes aggregate properties of data structures based on the values of corresponding elements of multiple arrays, TREX 03 involves loops with a possibly large number of iterations but without a single explicit control variable, and the benchmark Two Indices maintains a relation over array elements at different indices. We had to translate all of them from C into Java, and we also reduced the sizes of arrays in both language variants, because the current version of PANDA is not yet optimized for programs with large arrays.

The second group contains 4 example programs that we used in previous work [21], namely Data-flow Analysis, Cycling Race, Image Rendering, and Scheduler. These benchmark programs are more realistic; they involve manipulation with arrays (sorting), field accesses on heap objects, and loops.

The third group contains variants of two benchmarks from the CTC repository [24]: Alarm Clock and Producer-Consumer. We translated the original concurrent programs into sequential programs using an approach similar to context-bounded reduction [22].

As the benchmark programs in the second and third group are relatively larger, we used them to find whether PANDA is competitive in terms of scalability. Note also that source code of all the programs contains assertions but the corresponding error states are not reachable.

We ran PANDA and selected other tools – namely BLAST [6], CPACHECKER [8], UFO [1], and WOLVERINE [17] – on all the benchmark programs in order to find whether our proposed approach is competitive with respect to the ability of verifying program safety and the running time. We used CPACHECKER in the version from SV-COMP'15, BLAST and UFO in the versions from SV-COMP'14, and WOLVERINE from the year 2012. Table 1 contains results of the experiments.

For PANDA, we report the total running time (t), size of the reachable state space ($|S|$), number of refinement steps, maximum number of abstraction predicates at some location, and the total number of satisfiability queries executed by PANDA. For the other tools, we report only the total running time in case the respective tool provided a correct answer. Other possible outcomes are expressed by specific symbols. We use the symbol ✗ to denote that a tool reported a spurious error (i.e., a wrong answer), the symbol ? to indicate that a tool says "don't

Table 1. Experimental results and comparison with other tools

Benchmark	PANDA					BLAST	CPA	UFO	WOLVERINE
	t	$|S|$	#ref	$|abs|$	#sat				
Array	4 s	38	0	7	1802	2 s	2 s	1 s	1 s
Eureka 01	23 s	741	0	53	11462	✗	?	✗	timeout
TREX 03	21 s	1425	0	9	14371	✗	✗	1 s	1 s
Invert String	6 s	126	0	18	2728	✗	6 s	✗	9 s
Password	22 s	870	0	19	12837	23 s	3 s	✗	4 s
Reverse Array	5 s	135	0	18	2358	✗	3 s	✗	3 s
Two Indices	4 s	55	0	15	1921	✗	2 s	✗	1 s
Data-flow Analysis	379 s	508	0	64	8159	?	?	✗	✗
Cycling Race	5 s	87	0	28	2151	6 s	3 s	2 s	2 s
Image Rendering	timeout					-	44 s	-	✗
Scheduler	5 s	108	0	35	2185	?	4 s	✗	4 s
Alarm Clock	970 s	21200	0	20	87628	?	✗	✗	-
Producer-Consumer	timeout					?	✗	-	✗

know", and the character "-" when a tool fails for some other reason (e.g., missing support for a particular language feature). We put the limit of two hours on the running time for all experiments.

The results show that PANDA did not have to perform abstraction refinement in the case of all our benchmarks for which verification finished before the time limit. In addition, PANDA did not report a spurious error for any benchmark program, unlike some of the other tools. This observation supports our claim that simultaneous abstract and concrete execution is very precise and avoids spurious behaviors.

Regarding performance, the results are mixed — PANDA is faster than other tools for some of the programs and slower in other cases, but its running times are competitive for all the benchmarks. Data for the benchmarks Alarm Clock, Image Rendering, and Producer-Consumer show that PANDA has limited scalability, but the other tools failed on these benchmarks with the exception of CPACHECKER on Image Rendering. By manual inspection of execution logs, we found the following main reasons for the long running times and state explosion in the case of these three programs.

1. Each trace contains many non-deterministic data choices (unknown statements) for which multiple concrete values have to be explored.
2. Some of the more complex SMT queries executed by PANDA, in particular those used to derive new return values for unknown statements, take a very long time to answer — for example, even up to 200 seconds in the case of Image Rendering.

On the other hand, PANDA successfully verified the programs Alarm Clock, Dataflow Analysis, and Eureka 01, for which all the other tools failed or reported a wrong answer.

6   Related Work

Many verification techniques based on the CEGAR principle [11] have been proposed in the past. However, we are not aware of any existing approach that combines abstraction with concrete execution in the same way as PANDA does. We provide details about selected techniques and highlight the main differences.

The PANDA algorithm extends the approach to lazy predicate abstraction, which was originally proposed by Henzinger et al. [16] and implemented in BLAST [6]. Simultaneous combination of abstraction with concrete execution allows PANDA to prune many infeasible execution paths and spurious errors on-the-fly during the state space traversal, thus avoiding many expensive steps of abstraction refinement. In the more recent work of McMillan [18] and Alberti et al. [3], lazy abstraction is done using only interpolants without predicate abstraction, but in this case it is more difficult to check whether a given state was already covered during traversal. UFO [1] is another verification technique that combines abstraction, unrolling of a control flow graph, and interpolants. It captures multiple error traces with a single formula in order to reduce the number of necessary refinement steps.

CPACHECKER [8] is a tool that performs multiple custom analyses simultaneously, using the framework proposed by Beyer et al. [7]. For example, it enables users to combine predicate abstraction with shape analysis. The definition of each program analysis consists of an abstract domain, transfer relation, merge operator, and an operator that performs the covering check. It might be possible to implement the PANDA algorithm in CPACHECKER, assuming that different analyses can exchange the necessary information during a run of the tool. Concrete execution would have to be expressed as one of the analyses.

Charlton [9] proposed another framework that supports combination of multiple analyses and verification techniques. The analyses are executed in steps by the overall worklist algorithm. In each iteration, they exchange computed facts about the program behavior using logic formulas, and they can also query each other.

The DASH algorithm [5] combines testing with abstraction in an iterative manner to achieve better precision and performance. In each iteration, it explores the current abstract state space in order to search for a possible error trace. Then, if there is an abstract error trace, DASH attempts to find a corresponding concrete trace by creating and running new tests. Based on their results, it can either confirm the presence of a real error or extend the current forest of tests. Only when such a test cannot be found, the abstraction is refined by predicates that are derived from the first infeasible transition on the given error trace. Like in the case of PANDA, use of concrete execution (testing) saves many refinement steps and helps to avoid many SMT queries, especially if the input program contains loops with many iterations. The main difference is that DASH performs the individual phases, i.e. concrete execution and changes of the abstraction, consecutively (in turns), while PANDA unrolls the reachability graph on-the-fly using both concrete execution and predicate abstraction simultaneously (in tandem). This enables PANDA to refine multiple regions of the abstraction in each iteration, achieving faster convergence.

SMASH [14] combines may analysis (abstraction) with must analysis (concrete execution in the form of dynamic test generation) using a compositional approach based on procedure summaries. In each step, it can update either the may summary of some procedure or the must summary, but not both of them simultaneously. The key feature of SMASH is the alternation (interplay) of testing and abstraction such that intermediate analysis results are exchanged between the two. Both the DASH and SMASH algorithms are implemented in the YOGI tool [20].

PANDA resembles also mixed symbolic and concrete execution, implemented in tools such as DART [13] and KLEE [10]. However, in PANDA the concrete execution and predicate abstraction are performed simultaneously in such a way that they guide each other, while in DART, for example, they do not interact during the traversal of one path. In addition, PANDA uses predicates that are more expressive than path constraints in DART, because it generates new predicates by applying interpolation to trace formulas (i.e. not just by extraction from the program code). It is also more efficient because it can prune several infeasible paths in one step. The main practical limitation of symbolic execution is that users must put a bound on the number of explored paths and their depth. Tools based on this approach are therefore used mainly for dynamic test generation and bug hunting, while PANDA can explore all paths in the reachability graph of a given program to check whether it is safe.

Some work has been done also on combining symbolic execution with predicate abstraction and iterative refinement. The approach proposed by Albarghouthi et al. [2] uses symbolic execution to explore the underapproximation of a program behavior, and in each iteration checks whether the abstract model created by symbolic execution is also an overapproximation of the concrete state space. Abstraction refinement is performed to add new predicates that would enable the verification procedure to cover more feasible execution paths.

7 Conclusion

In this paper we presented the PANDA algorithm that combines predicate abstraction with simultaneous concrete execution. Dynamic pruning, the method that we proposed for solving inconsistencies between concrete and abstract execution, eliminates many spurious execution paths on-the-fly. A consequence of this combination is a higher analysis precision that allows PANDA to keep the number of necessary refinement steps to a minimum. Specifically, PANDA did not have to perform abstraction refinement for any of the benchmark programs that we used in our experiments.

In future, we plan to optimize our prototype implementation and we would also like to use a different abstract representation of the program heap. Our long term goals include support for data containers, concurrency, and predicates over data shared between threads, most probably through adaptation of some already known techniques [12,21].

Acknowledgements. This work was partially supported by the Grant Agency of the Czech Republic project 13-12121P and by Charles University institutional funding SVV-2015-260222.

References

1. Albarghouthi, A., Gurfinkel, A., Chechik, M.: From under-approximations to over-approximations and back. In: Flanagan, C., König, B. (eds.) TACAS 2012. LNCS, vol. 7214, pp. 157–172. Springer, Heidelberg (2012)
2. Albarghouthi, A., Gurfinkel, A., Wei, O., Chechik, M.: Abstract analysis of symbolic executions. In: Touili, T., Cook, B., Jackson, P. (eds.) CAV 2010. LNCS, vol. 6174, pp. 495–510. Springer, Heidelberg (2010)
3. Alberti, F., Bruttomesso, R., Ghilardi, S., Ranise, S., Sharygina, N.: Lazy abstraction with interpolants for arrays. In: Bjørner, N., Voronkov, A. (eds.) LPAR-18 2012. LNCS, vol. 7180, pp. 46–61. Springer, Heidelberg (2012)
4. Barrett, C., Conway, C.L., Deters, M., Hadarean, L., Jovanović, D., King, T., Reynolds, A., Tinelli, C.: CVC4. In: Gopalakrishnan, G., Qadeer, S. (eds.) CAV 2011. LNCS, vol. 6806, pp. 171–177. Springer, Heidelberg (2011)
5. Beckman, N.E., Nori, A.V., Rajamani, S.K., Simmons, R.J.: Proofs from tests. In: Proceedings of ISSTA. ACM (2008)

6. Beyer, D., Henzinger, T.A., Jhala, R., Majumdar, R.: The software model checker BLAST. STTT **9**(5–6), 505–525 (2007)
7. Beyer, D., Henzinger, T.A., Théoduloz, G.: Configurable software verification: concretizing the convergence of model checking and program analysis. In: Damm, W., Hermanns, H. (eds.) CAV 2007. LNCS, vol. 4590, pp. 504–518. Springer, Heidelberg (2007)
8. Beyer, D., Keremoglu, M.E.: CPACHECKER: a tool for configurable software verification. In: Gopalakrishnan, G., Qadeer, S. (eds.) CAV 2011. LNCS, vol. 6806, pp. 184–190. Springer, Heidelberg (2011)
9. Charlton, N.: Program verification with interacting analysis plugins. Form. Aspects Comput. **19**(3), 375–399 (2007)
10. Cadar, C., Dunbar, D., Engler, D.: KLEE: unassisted and automatic generation of high-coverage tests for complex systems programs. In: Proceedings of OSDI. USENIX (2008)
11. Clarke, E.M., Grumberg, O., Jha, S., Lu, Y., Veith, H.: Counterexample-guided abstraction. In: Emerson, E.A., Sistla, A.P. (eds.) CAV 2000. LNCS, vol. 1855, pp. 154–169. Springer, Heidelberg (2000)
12. Donaldson, A., Kaiser, A., Kroening, D., Wahl, T.: Symmetry-aware predicate abstraction for shared-variable concurrent programs. In: Gopalakrishnan, G., Qadeer, S. (eds.) CAV 2011. LNCS, vol. 6806, pp. 356–371. Springer, Heidelberg (2011)
13. Godefroid, P., Klarlund, N., Sen, K.: DART: directed automated random testing. In: Proceedings of PLDI. ACM (2005)
14. Godefroid, P., Nori, A., Rajamani, S.K., Tetali, S.: Compositional may-must program analysis: unleashing the power of alternation. In: Proceedings of POPL. ACM (2010)
15. Heizmann, M., Hoenicke, J., Podelski, A.: Nested interpolants. In: Proceedings of POPL. ACM (2010)
16. Henzinger, T.A., Jhala, R., Majumdar, R., Sutre, G.: Lazy abstraction. In: Proceedings of POPL. ACM (2002)
17. Kroening, D., Weissenbacher, G.: Interpolation-based software verification with WOLVERINE. In: Gopalakrishnan, G., Qadeer, S. (eds.) CAV 2011. LNCS, vol. 6806, pp. 573–578. Springer, Heidelberg (2011)
18. McMillan, K.L.: Lazy abstraction with interpolants. In: Ball, T., Jones, R.B. (eds.) CAV 2006. LNCS, vol. 4144, pp. 123–136. Springer, Heidelberg (2006)
19. de Moura, L., Bjørner, N.S.: Z3: an efficient SMT solver. In: Ramakrishnan, C.R., Rehof, J. (eds.) TACAS 2008. LNCS, vol. 4963, pp. 337–340. Springer, Heidelberg (2008)
20. Nori, A.V., Rajamani, S.K., Tetali, S.D., Thakur, A.V.: The YOGI project: software property checking via static analysis and testing. In: Kowalewski, S., Philippou, A. (eds.) TACAS 2009. LNCS, vol. 5505, pp. 178–181. Springer, Heidelberg (2009)
21. Parizek, P., Lhotak, O.: Predicate abstraction of java programs with collections. In: Proceedings of OOPSLA. ACM (2012)
22. Qadeer, S., Wu, D.: KISS: keep it simple and sequential. In: Proceedings of PLDI. ACM (2004)
23. Vizel, Y., Grumberg, O.: Interpolation-sequence based model checking. In: Proceedings of FMCAD. IEEE (2009)
24. Concurrency Tool Comparison. https://facwiki.cs.byu.edu/vv-lab/index.php/Concurrency_Tool_Comparison
25. Java Pathfinder. http://babelfish.arc.nasa.gov/trac/jpf
26. Competition on Software Verification. http://sv-comp.sosy-lab.org/2015/

TSO to SC via Symbolic Execution

Heike Wehrheim and Oleg Travkin[(⊠)]

Institut für Informatik, Universität Paderborn, 33098 Paderborn, Germany
{wehrheim,oleg82}@uni-paderborn.de

Abstract. Modern multi-core processors equipped with weak memory models like TSO exhibit executions which – due to store buffers – seemingly reorder program operations. Thus, they deviate from the commonly assumed *sequential consistency* (SC) semantics. Analysis techniques for concurrent programs consequently need to take reorderings into account. For TSO, this is often accomplished by explicitly modelling store buffers.

In this paper, we present an approach for reducing TSO-verification of concurrent programs (with fenced or write-free loops) to SC-verification, thereby being able to reuse standard verification tools. To this end, we transform a given program P into a new program P' whose SC-semantics is (bisimulation-) equivalent to the TSO-semantics of P. The transformation proceeds via a symbolic execution of P, however, only with respect to store buffer contents. Out of the thus obtained abstraction of P, we generate the SC program P' which can then be the target of standard analysis tools.

1 Introduction

With the advent of multi-core processors we recently see new types of bugs in concurrent programs coming up[1]. These bugs are due to the weak memory semantics of multi-core processors, which in their architectures are streamlined towards high performance. In executions of concurrent programs, weak memory causes program statements to seemingly be executed in an order different from the given program order. TSO (total store order) is one such weak memory model (of the x86 processors [18]), incorporating characteristics common to a lot of other weak memory models. On the contrary, concurrent executions adhering to program order are said to be *sequentially consistent* (SC) [14].

As concurrent programs are today executed on multi-cores, analysis techniques for concurrent software need to be based on weak memory semantics. This is often accomplished by an explicit modelling of store buffers, which are the cause of statement reordering. Store buffers are attached to cores, and values of variables shared among processes are first written to the corresponding store buffer before being flushed to main memory. Thereby, a read operation following a write may seem to overtake it from the point of view of other process. Analysis techniques employing store buffer modelling are for instance model checking

---

[1] See e.g. T. Lane. Yes, waitlatch is vulnerable to weak-memory-ordering bugs, http://www.postgresql.org/message-id/24241.1312739269@sss.pgh.pa.us, 2011.

© Springer International Publishing Switzerland 2015
N. Piterman (Ed.): HVC 2015, LNCS 9434, pp. 104–119, 2015.
DOI: 10.1007/978-3-319-26287-1_7

approaches [19,23], predicate abstraction [11], or interactive proving [20]. The modelling of store buffers does, however, impose a non-neglectable overhead on the analysis, might it be automatic, supported by theorem provers or manual.

In this paper, we propose an approach for reducing TSO analysis (i.e., analysis of concurrent programs taking the TSO semantics into account) to SC analysis. The technique is applicable to all programs with *fenced* or *write-free* loops, i.e., programs in which all loops contain at least one fence operation (memory barrier), or alternatively have no write operations in loops. While this seems rather restrictive, a lot of concurrent algorithms already possess this property, e.g., concurrent data structures using compare-and-swap operations (acting as fences) in loop conditions. Our approach proceeds by translating a program P into a program P' such that P's TSO semantics is bisimilar to P''s SC semantics. Like [5], the approach closest to ours, the additional condition (fenced or write-free loops) guarantee finite (though a priori unknown) store buffer sizes during execution. Unlike [5], we however only need few additional program variables in the constructed program P', and these are furthermore all local to processes. As a result, our technique is *compositional* in that it separately translates the programs of processes in a parallel composition.

The translation proceeds via a sort of symbolic execution of P [17] which constructs an abstraction of P symbolically tracking store buffer contents. This abstraction is transformed into a new program P' (by an approach for program generation out of abstract reachability graphs [22]). For the generated program we can afterwards re-use established analysis techniques and tools for SC. To show the practicability of our approach, we apply the technique to four mutual exclusion algorithms and two concurrent data structures, which we translate into an SC version and give to the model checker SPIN [13]. In almost all cases, it can be seen that the number of states generated by SPIN is reduced when going from a TSO version with explicit store buffer modelling to our SC version.

The paper is structured as follows. We start with a short introduction to weak memory models and the reorderings they generate. We will then proceed with defining the syntax and semantics of single processes, both for TSO and SC. On the semantic domain, we define our notion of equivalence (of programs viz. their executions). Sections 4 and 5 explain the transformation of a program into an SC form. We report on experimental results in Sect. 6 and discuss related work in Sect. 7. Section 8 concludes.

2   Weak Memory Reorderings

Weak memory models describe the semantics of concurrent programs when executed on multi-core machines. In general, the execution of memory instructions on the TSO memory model involves the usage of store buffers local to processes. A write operation on a shared variable thus first puts its written value into the store buffer. The contents of store buffers are occasionally *flushed* into main memory. Memory barriers (fences) can be used to enforce flushing, because fence operations can only be executed when the store buffer is empty. All read operations on shared variables will first examine the contents of the process' store buffer: if there is a value for the variable in the store buffer, the read will take the most recent one, otherwise it reads from main memory.

This usage of store-buffers leads to two kinds of reorderings on TSO: write-read reorderings and early-reads. These effects can best be understood on examples. Such small examples exhibiting certain interesting behaviours of multi-processors are known as *litmus tests*. Figures 1 and 2 give two such litmus tests. The first example is a write-read reordering. Both processes first write on a shared variable and then read from another shared variable into local registers. Since both writes might first be placed into the local store buffers, both reads can still see the initial values of x and y, and hence $r1 = 0 \land r2 = 0$ is a possible final state. It looks as though the writes and reads have changed position.

Initially : $x = 0 \land y = 0$

Process 1	Process 2
1 : $write(x, 1)$;	1 : $write(y, 1)$;
2 : $read(y, r1)$;	2 : $read(x, r2)$;
3 :	3 :

$r1 = 0 \land r2 = 0$ possible

Fig. 1. Litmus test for write-read reordering

Initially : $x = 0 \land y = 0$

Process 1	Process 2
1 : $write(x, 1)$;	1 : $write(y, 1)$;
2 : $read(x, r1)$;	2 : $read(y, r3)$;
3 : $read(y, r2)$;	3 : $read(x, r4)$;
4 :	4 :

$r1 = r3 = 1 \land r2 = r4 = 0$ possible

Fig. 2. Litmus test for early reads

The litmus test in Fig. 2 exemplifies the phenomenon of early reads (or inter-processor forwarding). The possible outcome $r1 = 1 \land r2 = 0 \land r3 = 1 \land r4 = 0$ occurs when both reads from lines 2 read from the process' own written value in the store buffer, and thus at the end the processes observe different orders of writes. It looks as though the reads on lines 3 have happened before both writes.

The basic idea of our approach is now to make these reorderings explicit in a new version of the program, and give this new version to standard SC verification tools for analysis.

3   Processes and Their Parallel Composition

Reorderings are being made explicit by transforming – in a concurrent program $[P_1 || \ldots || P_n]$ – the programs P_i of single processes into a form P_i' such that the following holds: execution of P_i on TSO is "equivalent" to execution of P_i' on SC. We can then use standard SC verification tools for checking properties on $[P_1' || \ldots || P_n']$. In this section, we will first of all explain how programs look like, and what we mean by "equivalent". The equivalence should in particular guarantee that other processes running in parallel cannot distinguish equivalent programs. We will thus base our equivalence on a notion of bisimulation [16].

As a consequence, our transformation need not be defined on the whole parallel program, but can transform programs of single processes in isolation: our technique is *compositional*.

For programs, we assume a set *Reg* of registers local to processes and a set of variables *Var*, shared by processes. For simplicity, both take as values just natural numbers. Thus the local state of a program is - among others - represented by a function $reg : Reg \to \mathbb{N}$, and the global state by a function $mem : Var \to \mathbb{N}$. We use the notation $mem[x \mapsto n]$ to stand for the function mem' which agrees with mem up to x which is mapped to n (and similar for other functions). Processes use local *store buffers*, i.e., FIFO queues, into which values for shared variables are first written before being flushed to main memory. A store buffer $sb \in (Var \times \mathbb{N})^*$ is a sequence of (variable and value) pairs. We write $x \in sb$ to state that there is a pair $(x, \cdot)$ in the store buffer sb. Program statements are labelled with *locations* out of some set L. A variable pc taking values $\ell \in L$ determines the statements that can be executed next. Thus, the local state s of some process is characterised by a tuple (ℓ, reg, sb).

We describe the programs of processes by *predicates*, one predicate stating conditions on the initial state and a set of predicates for operations (indexed by $i \in I$). Thus a *program* P of a process is given as $(Init, (COp^i)_{i \in I})$, where $Init$ is a predicate on pc, reg and sb. Each COp^i is a predicate over $pc, pc', reg, reg',$ sb, sb' and mem, mem' in which the primed versions refer to the state after executing the operation. We assume $Init$ to specify $sb = \langle \rangle$ (empty sequence).

Processes are allowed to interact with the memory using pre-defined operations from the set $\{write, read, fence, flush\}$. The latter two are only meaningful in a TSO context. In TSO, their semantics is defined by the following predicates.

Write: Writing the value of a register or a constant to a variable x:
$$write(x, n) \mathrel{\widehat{=}} sb' = sb \frown \langle (x, n) \rangle, \text{ writing constant } n$$
$$write(x, r) \mathrel{\widehat{=}} sb' = sb \frown \langle (x, reg(r)) \rangle, \text{ writing value from register } r$$
Read: Reading the value of a variable x into register r:
$$read(x, r) \mathrel{\widehat{=}} (x \notin sb \land read_{mem}(x, r)) \lor (x \in sb \land read_{loc}(x, r)) \text{ where}$$
$$read_{mem}(x, r) \mathrel{\widehat{=}} reg' = reg[r \mapsto mem(x)]$$
$$read_{loc}(x, r) \mathrel{\widehat{=}} reg' = reg[r \mapsto latest(x, sb)]$$
$$latest(x, sb) = n \mathrel{\widehat{=}} \exists sb_{pre}, sb_{suf} : sb = sb_{pre} \frown \langle (x, n) \rangle \frown sb_{suf} \land x \notin sb_{suf}$$

Fence: Memory barrier blocking until store buffer is empty:
$$fence \mathrel{\widehat{=}} sb = \langle \rangle$$
Flush: Flushing single store buffer entries to main memory:
$$flush \mathrel{\widehat{=}} \exists (x, v) \in (Var \times \mathbb{N}) : sb = \langle (x, v) \rangle \frown sb' \land mem' = mem[x \mapsto v]$$

The operation *read* has two cases: Reads might be *early*, reading from the contents of the store buffer ($read_{loc}$) or - if the store buffer contains no entry for the variable - read from main memory ($read_{mem}$). In addition to the above operations we have thread-local operations *LocOp*, i.e., operations of the form $r := expr$ (semantics $reg' = reg[r \mapsto reg(expr)]$), where *expr* is an expression build out of constants and register names using e.g. arithmetic operations, or boolean conditions over registers and constants.

We assume all operations (predicates) to have the following form (or equivalent):

$$COp \cong pc = \ell \wedge pc' = \ell' \wedge op$$

where op is either a memory operation or a local operation, e.g., $op = read(x, r)$.

We define $op(COp) \cong op$ to state the operational part of COp (similar for $Init$), without the part referring to program locations, and $pc(COp)$ to be the part of the predicate referring to the program counter. When executed on TSO, we implicitly add the operation $COp^f \cong flush$ to each process. This is the only operation without location predicates. We let $def(op)$ be the set of registers assigned to (changed) in an operation op and $use(op)$ to be the registers used. Process 1 of Fig. 1 would be specified as follows:

$$Init \cong pc = 1 \wedge r1 = 0 \wedge sb = \langle \rangle$$
$$COp^1 \cong pc = 1 \wedge pc' = 2 \wedge write(x, 1)$$
$$COp^2 \cong pc = 2 \wedge pc' = 3 \wedge read(y, r1)$$
$$COp^f \cong flush$$

The semantics of programs is given by labelled transition systems. For being able to compare the semantics of programs run under TSO with those run on SC, we define a *common* set of labels:

$$Lab = \{skip, r := expr, bexpr, wr(x, n), rd(x, r) \mid$$
$$x \text{ variable}, r \text{ register}, n \in \mathbb{N}\}$$

For the semantics, we use the convention that all entities (registers, pc, ...) which are not mentioned in the operation formula keep their values. For pairs of (global) states (g, g'), $g = (\ell, reg, sb, mem)$, $g' = (\ell', reg', sb', mem')$ we write $(g, g') \models COp$ to say that the predicate COp is satisfied by states g and g'. Similarly, for predicates p on unprimed variables only and states g, we write $g \models p$ to say that the predicate p is valid in the state g.

For single processes, we next define an *open* semantics. It is open in the sense that we assume other processes, possibly running in parallel, to arbitrary change shared memory, and thus incorporate into the semantics all steps the process can do with *arbitrary* values of mem.

Definition 1. *The* process-local TSO transition system *of a program* $P = (Init, (COp^i)_{i \in I})$, $[\![P]\!]_{tso}$, *is* $(S, \rightarrow, S_0)$ *with*

- $S_0 = \{s = (\ell, reg, sb) \mid s \models Init\}$,
- $s \xrightarrow{lab} s'$ *with* $s = (\ell, reg, sb)$ *and* $s' = (\ell', reg', sb')$ *iff* $\exists COp^i, \exists mem, mem'$ *s.t.* $((mem, s), (mem', s')) \models COp^i$, *and the label* lab *is*
  - $r := reg(expr)$ *if* $op(COp^i) = (r := expr)$,
  - $reg(bexpr)$ *if* $op(COp^i) = bexpr$,

- $skip$ if $op(COp^i) \in \{fence, write(x, n), write(x, r), skip\}$,
- $wr(x, n)$ if $op(COp^i) = flush$ and $sb = \langle(x, n)\rangle \frown sb'$,
- $rd(x, r)$ if $op(COp^i) = read(x, r)$ and $x \notin sb$, and
- $r := n$ if $op(COp^i) = read(x, r)$, $x \in sb$ and $n = latest(x, sb)$.

For such transitions we use the notation $s \xrightarrow{lab}_{mem, mem'} s'$.
- S is the set of all states reachable from S_0 by transitions.

The choice of labels reflects what is visible to the environment (i.e., other processes): a local write to a store buffer looks to the outside as if nothing happens, hence gets a *skip* label; a local read from store buffer looks like an assignment to a register, and hence gets an assignment label; finally, a flush operation looks to the outside like a proper write on shared memory and thus is labelled as write. This idea of *relabelling* transitions according to what effects are visible to the outside is also the basic principle of our TSO to SC transformation.

For the SC semantics of programs, we slightly restrict the set of operations. In SC, programs cannot (and do not) have fence operations, and furthermore their write and read predicates have a different semantics.

Write: Writing the value of a register or a constant to a variable x:
$write_{sc}(x, n) \triangleq mem' = mem[x \mapsto n]$, writing constant n
$write_{sc}(x, r) \triangleq mem' = mem[x \mapsto reg(r)]$, writing value from register r
Read: Reading the value of a variable x into register r:
$read_{sc}(x, r) \triangleq reg' = reg[r \mapsto mem(x)]$

As we see now, none of the operation predicates is refering to the store buffer. The local states of the SC transition system are thus of the form (ℓ, reg). Note that in this case we do not implicity add a flush operation to the set of program operations.

Definition 2. *The* process-local SC transition system *of a program* $P = (Init, (COp^i)_{i \in I})$, $[\![P]\!]_{sc}$, *is* $(Q, \rightarrow, Q_0)$ *with* $Q_0 = \{q = (\ell, reg) \mid q \models Init\}$ *and* $q \xrightarrow{lab} q'$ *with* $q = (\ell, reg)$ *and* $q' = (\ell', reg')$ *iff* $\exists COp^i, \exists mem, mem' : ((mem, q), (mem', q')) \models COp^i$ *and the label lab is*

- $r := reg(expr)$ *if* $op(COp^i) = (r := expr)$,
- $reg(bexpr)$ *if* $op(COp^i) = bexpr$,
- $skip$ *if* $op(COp^i) = skip$,
- $wr(x, n)$ *if* $op(COp^i) \in \{write_{sc}(x, n), write_{sc}(x, r)$ *and* $reg(r) = n\}$,
- $rd(x, r)$ *if* $op(COp^i) = read_{sc}(x, r)$.

Again, Q is the set of all reachable states.

Processes typically run in parallel with other processes. The semantics for parallel compositions of processes is now a *closed* semantics already incorporating all relevant components. We just define it for two processes here; a generalisation to larger numbers of components is straightforward.

Definition 3. *Let* $P_j = (Init_j, (COp_j^i)_{i \in I})$, $j \in \{1, 2\}$, *be two processes, Init an additional predicate on mem, and let* $(S_j, \rightarrow_j, S_{0,j})$, *be their process local (i.e., open) semantics (TSO or SC).*

The closed TSO or SC semantics, *respectively, of* $P_1 \|_{Init} P_2$ *is the labelled transition system* $(S, \rightarrow, S_0)$ *with* $S \subseteq \{(mem, s_1, s_2) \mid s_1 \in S_1, s_2 \in S_2\}$, $S_0 = \{s \in S \mid s \models Init_1 \wedge Init_2 \wedge Init\}$, *and* $s = (mem, s_1, s_2) \xrightarrow{lab} s' = (mem', s_1', s_2')$ *when* $(s_1 \xrightarrow{lab}_{mem, mem'} s_1' \wedge s_2 = s_2')$ *or* $(s_2 \xrightarrow{lab}_{mem, mem'} s_2' \wedge s_1 = s_1')$.

Due to the open semantics for processes, we have thus been able to give a *compositional* semantics for parallel composition.

Ultimately, we will be interested in comparing the TSO semantics of one program with the SC semantics of another. Our notion of equality is based on bisimulation equivalence [16]. Our definition of bisimulation compares transition systems with respect to their *labels* on transitions as well as their local *states*.

Definition 4. *Let* $T_1 = (S, \rightarrow_{tso}, S_0)$ *be a TSO and* $T_2 = (Q, \rightarrow_{sc}, Q_0)$ *an SC transition system.*

Transition systems T_1 *and* T_2 *are* locally bisimilar, $T_1 \approx_\ell T_2$, *if there is a bisimulation relation* $\mathcal{R} \subseteq S \times Q$ *such that the following holds:*

1. *Local state equality:*
   $\forall (s, q) \in \mathcal{R}, s = (\ell_1, reg_1, sb), q = (\ell_2, reg_2), \forall r \in Reg: reg_1(r) = reg_2(r).$
2. *Matching on initial states:*
   $\forall s_0 \in S \exists q_0 \in Q_0$ *s.t.* $(s_0, q_0) \in \mathcal{R}$, *and reversely* $\forall q_0 \in Q_0 \exists s_0 \in S_0$ *s.t.* $(s_0, q_0) \in \mathcal{R}.$
3. *Mutual simulation of steps:*
   if $(s_1, q_1) \in \mathcal{R}$ *and* $s_1 \xrightarrow{lab}_{tso} s_2$ *then* $\exists q_2$ *such that* $q_1 \xrightarrow{lab}_{sc} q_2$ *and* $(s_2, q_2) \in \mathcal{R}$, *and reversely, if* $(s_1, q_1) \in \mathcal{R}$ *and* $q_1 \xrightarrow{lab}_{sc} q_2$ *then* $\exists s_2$ *such that* $s_1 \xrightarrow{lab}_{tso} s_2$ *and* $(s_2, q_2) \in \mathcal{R}.$

Similarly, one can define *global bisimilarity* for the closed semantics of a parallel composition, in addition requiring equality of shared memory *mem*. We use the notation $\approx_g$ to denote global bisimilarity. This lets us state our first result: Local bisimilarity of processes implies global bisimilarity of their parallel compositions.

Theorem 1. *Let* P_1, P_1', P_2, P_2' *be processes such that* $\llbracket P_1 \rrbracket_{tso} \approx_\ell \llbracket P_1' \rrbracket_{sc}$ *and* $\llbracket P_2 \rrbracket_{tso} \approx_l \llbracket P_2' \rrbracket_{sc}$ *and let Init be a predicate on mem. Then*

$$\llbracket P_1 \|_{Init} P_2 \rrbracket_{tso} \approx_g \llbracket P_1' \|_{Init} P_2' \rrbracket_{sc}.$$

Proof idea: Let $\mathcal{R}_i$ be the bisimulation relations showing $\llbracket P_i \rrbracket_{tso} \approx_\ell \llbracket P_i' \rrbracket_{sc}$. Then

$$\mathcal{R} := \{((mem, s_1, s_2), (mem, s_1', s_2')) \mid (s_1, s_1') \in \mathcal{R}_1 \wedge (s_2, s_2') \in \mathcal{R}_2\}$$

is the relation showing global bisimilarity.   □

This result enables us to carry out the transformation from TSO to SC *locally*, i.e., transform the programs of processes individually and after that combine their SC versions in parallel.

4   Symbolic Store-Buffer Graphs

The basic principle behind our verification technique is to transform every program P into a program P' such that $[\![P]\!]_{tso}$ is locally bisimilar to $[\![P']\!]_{sc}$. The construction of P' proceeds by symbolic execution of P and out of the thus constructed symbolic states generation of P'. The symbolic execution tracks - besides the operations being executed and the program locations reached - store buffer contents *only*, and only in a symbolic form. The symbolic form stores variable names together with either values of $\mathbb{N}$ (in case a constant was used in the *write*), or register *names* (in case a register was used). A symbolic store buffer content might thus for instance look like this: $\langle (x, 3), (y, r_1), (x, r_2), (z, 5) \rangle$. The symbolic execution thereby generates a symbolic reachability graph, called store-buffer graph.

Definition 5. *A store-buffer (or sb-)graph $G = (V, E, v_0)$ consists of a set of nodes $V \subseteq (L \times (Var \times (Reg \cup \mathbb{N}))^*)$, edges $E \subseteq V \times Lab_{tso} \times V$ and initial node $v_0 \in V$ where $Lab_{tso} = \{write(x, r), write(x, n), read(x, r), flush, fence\} \cup LocOp$.*

The store-buffer graph for a program P is constructed by a form of symbolic execution, executing program operations step by step without constructing the concrete states of registers. We let $tail(list)$ of a nonempty sequence $list$ denote the sequence without its first element.

Definition 6. *Let $P = (Init, (COp^i)_{i \in I})$ be the program of a process. The sb-graph of P, $sg(P)$, is inductively defined as follows:*

1. $v_0 := (\ell_0, \langle \rangle)$ with $Init \Rightarrow pc = \ell_0$,
2. if $(\ell, ssb) \in V$, we add a node (ℓ', ssb') and
   – an edge $(\ell, ssb) \xrightarrow{lab} (\ell', ssb')$ if $\exists COp^i$ with $op(COp^i) = lab$ and
     • $lab = flush$, $\ell = \ell'$ and $ssb \neq \langle \rangle$ and $ssb' = tail(ssb)$, or $pc(COp^i) = (pc = \ell \wedge pc' = \ell')$ and
       ∗ $lab \in LocOp$ and $ssb' = ssb$, or
       ∗ $lab = write(x, r)$ and $ssb' = ssb \frown \langle (x, r) \rangle$, or
       ∗ $lab = write(x, n)$ and $ssb' = ssb \frown \langle (x, n) \rangle$, or
       ∗ $lab = fence$ and $ssb = ssb' = \langle \rangle$, or
   – an edge $(\ell, ssb) \xrightarrow{read_{mem}(x, r)} (\ell', ssb')$ and a node (ℓ', ssb') if $\exists COp^i = (read(x, r) \wedge pc = \ell \wedge pc' = \ell')$ and $ssb' = ssb \wedge x \notin ssb$, or
   – an edge $(\ell, ssb) \xrightarrow{read_{loc}(x, r)} (\ell', ssb')$ and a node (ℓ', ssb') if $\exists COp^i = (read(x, r) \wedge pc = \ell \wedge pc' = \ell')$ and $ssb' = ssb \wedge x \in ssb$.

As an example, Figs. 3 and 4 show the store-buffer graphs of process 1 from Fig. 1 and of process 1 in Fig. 2, respectively. On them, we directly see when the effects of writes take place in main memory, namely when the corresponding flush happens. On the left graph, right branch, we thus see the read of y happening before the "real" write of x (flush) to memory. On the right graph, right branch, we see the read of x taking place before the write to x (flush). Later we will

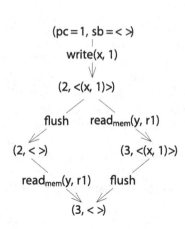

Fig. 3. Store buffer graph representing the reachable store buffer states of process 1 in Fig. 1.

Fig. 4. Store buffer graph representing the reachable store buffer states of process 2 in Fig. 2.

see that all such early reads still read correct values in the SC version of the program.

Note that store-buffer graphs need not necessarily be finite. They are infinite if a program has loops with write operations, but no fences in order to enforce flushing of store buffer content. Since this finiteness of the store buffer graph is key to our technique, we next define our only restriction on the class of programs considered: all loops have to be *fenced* or *write-free*.

We first define loops. A (syntactically possible) path of a program P is a sequence $\ell_1, \ell_2, ..., \ell_n$ of locations such that there are operations $COp^1, ..., COp^{n-1}$ such that $pc(COp^i) = (pc = \ell_i \wedge pc' = \ell_{i+1})$. We also write paths like this: $\ell_1 \xrightarrow{COp^1} \ell_2 \xrightarrow{COp^2} ... \xrightarrow{COp^{n-1}} \ell_n$. A *loop* is a path $\ell_1, \ell_2, ..., \ell_n$ such that $n > 1$ and $\ell_1 = \ell_n$. A loop is *write-free* if none of the operations on the loop is a write. A loop is *fenced*, if at least one of the operations on the loop is a fence. We furthermore assume that all process programs are in *SSA-form* (static single assignment [10]), meaning that all the registers are (statically) assigned to only once, i.e., for every register r there is at most one operation op with $r \in def(op)$. We furthermore assume that registers are never used before defined. Both, this and the SSA-form is guaranteed by modern compilers, e.g., the LLVM-framework[2] which we use for our approach only generates intermediate code in this form.

Proposition 1. *Let P be a process program in which every loop is fenced or write-free. Then $sg(P)$ is finite.*

---

[2] http://www.llvm.org.

In the generation of a new program out of an sb-graph we transform every edge of the graph into an operation (predicate). In this, a flush operation in the sb-graph, flushing a symbolic store buffer content (x, r) (r being a register name), becomes a $write_{sc}(x, r)$ operation. For this to be sound (w.r.t. the intended equivalence of old and new program), we need to make sure that the content of register r at a flush is still the same as the one at the time of writing the pair (x, r) into the (symbolic) store buffer. This is not necessarily the case. A path $\ell_1 \xrightarrow{COp^1} \ell_2 \xrightarrow{COp^2} \ldots \xrightarrow{COp^{n-1}} \ell_n$ is a $write$-def chain (wd-chain) if there is an $r \in Reg$ such that $op(COp^1) = write(., r)$ and $r \in def(COp^{n-1})$. A wd-chain is $fenced$, if one of the operations in between the write and the definition of the register is a fence. If this is guaranteed, we know that a register occuring with its name in the symbolic store buffer still has the same value as of the corresponding write.

Proposition 2. *Let P be the program of a process in SSA form with fenced write-def chains only. Let $s = (\ell, reg, sb)$ be a state of $[\![P]\!]_{tso}$ such that sb contains an entry $(x, n), n \in \mathbb{N}$. If this value has been put into the store buffer by an operation $write(x, r), r \in Reg$, then $reg(r) = n$.*

Proof: By the definition of wd-chains: after $write(x, r)$ there is no further operation defining r before the next fence operation. A fence, however, needs an empty store buffer in order to execute. □

As this property is key to our transformation, we next define a way of changing every program into an equivalent one with fenced wd-chains only. We first determine all write operations causing unfenced wd-chains, e.g. by a simple dataflow analysis. Let W be the set of all such *write sources* of wd-chains, and $Rg(W) \subseteq Reg$ be the set of registers participating in such writes. For every register $r \in Rg(W)$ we now introduce a new register r_{aux} and add it to Reg (thereby giving a set Reg_{aux}). Note that this is the only point in our program transformation where new variables or registers are introduced. The registers r_{aux} act as auxiliary variables in the programs. Every write $COp \in W, COp = (pc = \ell \wedge write(x, r) \wedge pc' = \ell)$ is now transformed into a new operation $COp_{aux} \widehat{=} (pc = \ell \wedge write_{aux}(x, r) \wedge pc' = \ell)$ where

$$write_{aux}(x, r) \widehat{=} write(x, r) \wedge reg' = reg[r_{aux} \mapsto reg(r)]$$

We let P' denote the program P with all such changes.

Proposition 3. *The program P' has no unfenced wd-chains.*

The label of this new operation $write_{aux}$ in the TSO semantics is $r_{aux} := n$ for $n = reg(r)$ (see Definition 1). Note that the number of new registers needed is bounded by the number of registers used in loops. For each COp_{aux} operation, we add an edge $(\ell, ssb) \xrightarrow{lab} (\ell', ssb')$ to the sb-graph, where $lab = write(x, r_{aux}) \wedge reg' = reg[r_{aux} \mapsto reg(r)]$ and $ssb' = ssb \frown \langle (x, r_{aux}) \rangle$. Note that we use r_{aux} in the symbolic store buffer, although the value of r is used in the transition system.

5   SC Program Generation

The store-buffer graph presents an *abstraction* of the actual TSO transition system of a program. The basic idea behind the generation of new programs out of store-buffer graphs is now to take the store-buffer graph as the control flow graph of the new program. We do so by using the nodes in the sb-graph as new program locations, i.e., program locations become pairs of (location, symbolic store buffer contents). If we would simply take the operations on edges as they are, we would arrive at a new program P' which is equivalent to P w.r.t. the TSO semantics. However, instead of using the operations as they are written on the edges, we make changes analogous to the relabelling used in the TSO semantics: The generated operation in the SC program should reflect the visible effect of an TSO operation, e.g. flush operations become writes and local reads become local assignments. For the latter, we use the fact that the symbolic store buffer contents contains *names* of registers, not just their values.

Definition 7. *Let $G = (V, E, v_0)$ be an sb-graph of a program P with init predicate Init. The new SC program of G, $prog(G)$, $(Init', (COp^i)_{i \in I'})$ is defined as follows:*

– *We use $Init' \stackrel{\frown}{=} pc = v_0 \wedge op(Init)$,*
– *for every edge $v \xrightarrow{lab} v'$, we define an operation $COp^i \stackrel{\frown}{=} pc = v \wedge pc' = v' \wedge op^{sc}(lab)$, where op^{sc} maps the edges of the sb-graph to the behaviorally equivalent steps in an SC setting:*

$$op^{sc}(lab) \stackrel{\frown}{=} skip \text{ iff } lab \in \{fence, write(x, r), write(x, n)\}$$
$$op^{sc}(lab) \stackrel{\frown}{=} write_{sc}(x, r) \text{ iff } lab = flush \wedge v = (\ell, ssb)$$
$$\wedge \, ssb = \langle (x, r) \rangle \frown tail(ssb)$$
$$op^{sc}(lab) \stackrel{\frown}{=} r_{aux} := r \text{ iff } lab = (write(x, r_{aux})$$
$$\wedge \, reg' = reg[r_{aux} \mapsto reg(r)])$$
$$op^{sc}(lab) \stackrel{\frown}{=} read_{sc}(x, r) \text{ iff } lab = read_{mem}(x, r)$$
$$op^{sc}(lab) \stackrel{\frown}{=} r := r_{src} \text{ iff } lab = read_{loc}(x, r) \wedge v = (\ell, ssb)$$
$$\wedge \, r_{src} = latest(x, ssb)$$
$$op^{sc}(lab) \stackrel{\frown}{=} lab \qquad else$$

The transformation of a program into its SC form is then defined as

$$tso2sc(P) \stackrel{\frown}{=} prog(sg(P))$$

As a preparatory step to this, we might need to bring P into a form without unfenced wd-chains as described in the previous section. For process 1 of Fig. 1 and its store buffer graph in Fig. 3, its SC version is the following:

$$Init \stackrel{\frown}{=} pc = (1, \langle \rangle)$$
$$COp^1 \stackrel{\frown}{=} pc = (1, \langle \rangle) \wedge pc' = (2, \langle (x, 1) \rangle) \wedge \, skip$$

$$COp^2 \cong pc = (2, \langle(x,1)\rangle) \wedge pc' = (2, \langle\rangle) \wedge \; write_{sc}(x,1)$$
$$COp^3 \cong pc = (2, \langle\rangle) \wedge pc' = (3, \langle\rangle) \wedge \; read_{sc}(y, r1)$$
$$COp^4 \cong pc = (2, \langle(x,1)\rangle) \wedge pc' = (3, \langle(x,1)\rangle) \wedge \; read_{sc}(y, r1)$$
$$COp^5 \cong pc = (3, \langle(x,1)\rangle) \wedge pc' = (3, \langle\rangle) \wedge \; write_{sc}(x,1)$$

In parallel with the SC version of process 2, this can then be given to standard SC verification tools. Our approach is *compositional*: transformations of processes can be done without considering other parallel processes (see Theorem 1); we can reuse transformation results when processes are combined in different ways.

Our main result showing the soundness of this approach is the equivalence of P and $tso2sc(P)$ with respect to local bisimulation.

Theorem 2. *Let P be a program with fenced or write-free loops only and with no unfenced wd-chains. Then*

$$[\![P]\!]_{tso} \approx_\ell [\![tso2sc(P)]\!]_{sc}.$$

Proof sketch: The proof proceeds by defining a relation on the states of $[\![P]\!]_{tso}$ and $[\![tso2sc(P)]\!]_{sc}$. For this, we need some concretisation function for symbolic store buffer contents, concretising the value of a symbolic store buffer ssb with respect to the current state s:

$$conc_s(\langle\rangle) = \langle\rangle$$
$$conc_s(\langle(x,n)\rangle \frown ssb) = \langle(x,n)\rangle \frown conc_s(ssb) \text{ for } n \in \mathbb{N}$$
$$conc_s(\langle(x,r)\rangle \frown ssb) = \langle(x, s(reg)(r))\rangle \frown conc_s(ssb) \text{ for } r \in Reg$$

The relation proving bisimilarity is then:

$$\mathcal{R} = \{(s,q) \mid \; first(q(pc)) = s(pc)$$
$$\wedge conc_s(second(q(pc))) = s(sb)$$
$$\wedge \forall r \in Reg : s(reg)(r) = q(reg)(r)\}$$

where $first((\ell, ssb)) = \ell$ and $second((\ell, ssb)) = ssb$.   □

This result allows us to re-use standard verification techniques for SC programs, might these be automatic or interactive.

6   Experimental Results

In our experiments we wanted to see whether the possibility of using standard SC tools for verification, opened up by our transformation technique, might now have to be paid by an increase in time and space usage of the tools. Our experimental setup was as follows. We used SPIN [13] as model checking tool, both for the SC semantics and for the TSO semantics. SC semantics are provided by SPIN. For TSO, we manually enhanced programs with store buffers and flush and fence operations, mimicking the TSO semantics (see [19] for details). The experiments all started with a C or C++ program which was compiled to an intermediate representation (IR) with the LLVM compiler. The IR code was then translated to Promela code (input to SPIN) with store buffers. Furthermore, we constructed the sb-graph automatically and out of this the transformed SC program, manually. Implementations of manual steps are on the way. The transformation is linear in the size of the sb-graph and hence, negligible compared to the actual verification effort. The latter depends on a model checker's ability to explore state space or the program complexity in case of a formal proof.

For our experiments we considered a number of mutual exclusion algorithms with two processes each (Dekker, Peterson, Lamport Bakery, Szymanski) and two concurrent data structures, a work-stealing queue by Arora et al. [3] and a stack implementation by Treiber [21]. The latter two allow for different instances in which the processes execute different operations. An instance $UO\|TT$ e.g. describes two processes, one doing operations $pushBottom$ followed by $popBottom$ and the other executing two $popTop$ operations. The mutual exclusion algorithms are known to be incorrect under weak memory models and hence, we used both the original unfenced and the correct fenced version. Only one of the examples did not fall into the category of programs with fenced or write-free loops (the unfenced version of Dekker's algorithm). The other examples either just have reading loops, or have implicit fence operations. An implicit fence is for instance generated by a CAS instruction (an atomic compare and swap), which is often used as the only synchronisation primitive in otherwise lock-free data structures. All tests were performed on a virtual machine, Ubuntu Linux, Intel Core i5, 2.53 GHz and 3 GB dedicated to SPIN 6.2.3. All models used for the verification can be found in our repositories at Github[3].

Table 1 provides our verification results giving verification time and number of states generated by SPIN for both the TSO and transformed SC programs. It also gives the number of nodes in the store buffer graph (for the processes viz. operations in the program). The experiments show that our transformation can in a lot of cases actually reduce the state space and verification time. Besides being able to use an SC tool, we can thus furthermore gain time and space when applying the TSO to SC transformation. Compared to the work of [5], who also used a transformation technique and in their experiments looked at these mutual exclusion algorithms, we can moreover state that the runtime of our approach is significantly smaller. The results are, however, not directly comparable since they used different verification tools.

In our previous work [20], we proved linearizability [12] of the Burns mutual exclusion algorithm [8] under TSO using an interactive theorem prover. Particularly, we compared the proof effort of (1) a program encoding TSO with explicit store buffers against (2) a transformed program version using SC semantics (based on the idea that we formalized in this paper). For the Burns mutex, the transformation reduced complexity (invariant size) and proof effort (number of proof steps) approximately by half. Our transformation technique can thus also be helpful in interactive proving.

---

[3] https://github.com/oleg82upb.

Table 1. Verification results for case studies.

Algorithm	TSO Model		Transformed SC Program		
(each for 2 processes)	states	time [s]	states	time [s]	nodes#
Dekker (fenced)	655	≈ 0	147	≈ 0	17
Dekker (unfenced)	540	≈ 0	unfenced writing loop		
Peterson (fenced)	709	≈ 0	270	≈ 0	14
Peterson (unfenced)	805	≈ 0	1,271	0.01	28
Lamport Bakery (fenced)	2,907	0.01	405	0.01	24
Lamport Bakery (unfenced)	16,087	0.17	163	≈ 0	75
Szymanski (fenced)	2,778	0.01	1,741	≈ 0	30/32
Szymanski (unfenced)	923	0.01	171	≈ 0	55
Work-Stealing Queue (fenced) UOUOUOU‖TTT	73,703	0.32	86,566	0.23	13/46/18
$\,\widehat{=}\,$ pushBottom, O $\,\widehat{=}\,$ popBottom, T $\,\widehat{=}\,$ popTop (stealing process)					
Treiber-Stack UUUOOO ‖ OOOUUU U $\,\widehat{=}\,$ push, O $\,\widehat{=}\,$ pop	1,913,313	8.93	1,821,426	4.68	29/15

7   Related Work

In the last years, several approaches were proposed in order to deal with software verification under the influence of weak memory models, ranging from theoretical results to practical techniques.

Atig et al. [4] have shown that the reachability problem for programs in a TSO or PSO environment is decidable via reduction to lossy channel machines. However, for other relaxed memory models like RMO, the problem is undecidable. Bouajjani et al. [7] determined the complexity (PSPACE) of deciding robustness of programs against TSO. Two recent approaches [1,6] provide underapproximating techniques for checking program correctness under TSO.

Several approaches [2,5,9,15] propose reduction techniques, which allow for a reuse of verification techniques developed for SC. The approach closest to us is the one by Atig et al. [5]. Similar to us, they provide a translation from a TSO program to an equivalent SC program, but assuming an age bound k. The bound k stems from the observation that store buffer entries can stay for at most k steps in the store buffer until they are eventually flushed to the memory. Their approach is, thus, to model the store buffer behavior as part of the new SC program by introducing k vectors of shared variable copies as part of the local state. Hence, rather than getting rid of the complexity of store buffers, store buffers are replaced with auxiliary vectors in the SC program. The bound results in some sort of bounded verification; if the program exceeds the bound (e.g., in case of loops without fences), the bound needs to be increased and verification restarted.

In our approach (auxiliary) variable copies are only used if they are indeed required, i.e., when the symbolic store buffer entry of a write source of a wd-chain can be redefined between write and flush. We have at most one new variable per register in the program. This is enough since we consider a restricted class of programs (fenced loops only) for which we can then carry out a (non-bounded) verification. In summary, our approach works for a restricted class of programs, but for this carries out a full verification, whereas Atig et al.'s technique works for all programs, however, sometimes only with an underapproximating analysis. For the class of programs with fenced-loops our approach furthermore generates fewer auxiliary variables, and – as the experiments show – may speed up verification. We thus see our approach as an excellent alternative to Atig et al.'s, in case the program falls into our category of fenced-loop programs.

8   Conclusion

In this paper, we have presented a simple and practical reduction of program verification under the influence of TSO to an SC setting via program transformation. Consequently, the transformed program can be verified using common techniques assuming a sequential consistent memory model.

Our transformation exploits that most of the non-determinism inherent to TSO can be computed statically, which is captured by a store buffer graph in our approach. By encoding the store buffer graph into an equivalent SC program, we completely get rid of store buffers and the burden of reasoning about them. Our experiments show that the transformation can even simplify verification (using a model checker and a theorem prover) of programs under TSO.

Our approach is restricted to programs with at least one fence in loops containing writes. The reason to restrict ourselves to this class of programs is that they can be represented by a finite store buffer graph. We could extend our approach to also deal with unfenced writing loops in a setting of bounded store buffers. However, we would then have to introduce multiple copies of register variables in the new program corresponding to different loop iterations in the original program. In principle, we would then arrive at a technique similar to [5].

References

1. Abdulla, P.A., Aronis, S., Atig, M.F., Jonsson, B., Leonardsson, C., Sagonas, K.: Stateless model checking for TSO and PSO. In: Baier, C., Tinelli, C. (eds.) TACAS 2015. LNCS, vol. 9035, pp. 353–367. Springer, Heidelberg (2015)
2. Alglave, J., Kroening, D., Nimal, V., Tautschnig, M.: Software verification for weak memory via program transformation. In: Felleisen, M., Gardner, P. (eds.) ESOP 2013. LNCS, vol. 7792, pp. 512–532. Springer, Heidelberg (2013)
3. Arora, N.S., Blumofe, R.D., Plaxton, C.G.: Thread scheduling for multiprogrammed multiprocessors. Theor. Comput. Syst. 34(2), 115–144 (2001)
4. Atig, M.F., Bouajjani, A., Burckhardt, S., Musuvathi, M.: On the verification problem for weak memory models. In: Hermenegildo, M.V., Palsberg, J. (eds.) POPL 2010, pp. 7–18. ACM (2010)
5. Atig, M.F., Bouajjani, A., Parlato, G.: Getting rid of store-buffers in TSO analysis. In: Gopalakrishnan, G., Qadeer, S. (eds.) CAV 2011. LNCS, vol. 6806, pp. 99–115. Springer, Heidelberg (2011)

6. Bouajjani, A., Calin, G., Derevenetc, E., Meyer, R.: Lazy TSO reachability. In: Egyed, A., Schaefer, I. (eds.) FASE 2015. LNCS, vol. 9033, pp. 267–282. Springer, Heidelberg (2015)

7. Bouajjani, A., Meyer, R., Möhlmann, E.: Deciding robustness against total store ordering. In: Aceto, L., Henzinger, M., Sgall, J. (eds.) ICALP 2011, Part II. LNCS, vol. 6756, pp. 428–440. Springer, Heidelberg (2011)

8. Burns, J., Lynch, N.A.: Mutual exclusion using indivisible reads and writes. In: 18th Allerton Conference on Communication, Control, and Computing, pp. 833–842 (1980)

9. Cohen, E., Schirmer, B.: From total store order to sequential consistency: a practical reduction theorem. In: Kaufmann, M., Paulson, L.C. (eds.) ITP 2010. LNCS, vol. 6172, pp. 403–418. Springer, Heidelberg (2010)

10. Cytron, R., Ferrante, J., Rosen, B.K., Wegman, M.N., Zadeck, F.K.: Efficiently computing static single assignment form and the control dependence graph. ACM Trans. Program. Lang. Syst. 13(4), 451–490 (1991)

11. Dan, A.M., Meshman, Y., Vechev, M., Yahav, E.: Predicate abstraction for relaxed memory models. In: Logozzo, F., Fähndrich, M. (eds.) Static Analysis. LNCS, vol. 7935, pp. 84–104. Springer, Heidelberg (2013)

12. Herlihy, M., Wing, J.M.: Linearizability: a correctness condition for concurrent objects. ACM Trans. Program. Lang. Syst. 12(3), 463–492 (1990)

13. Holzmann, G.J.: The SPIN Model Checker - Primer and Reference Manual. Addison-Wesley, Boston (2004)

14. Lamport, L.: How to make a multiprocessor computer that correctly executes multiprocess programs. IEEE Trans. Comput. 28(9), 690–691 (1979)

15. Linden, A., Wolper, P.: An automata-based symbolic approach for verifying programs on relaxed memory models. In: van de Pol, J., Weber, M. (eds.) Model Checking Software. LNCS, vol. 6349, pp. 212–226. Springer, Heidelberg (2010)

16. Milner, R. (ed.): A Calculus of Communicating Systems. Springer, Heidelberg (1980)

17. Pasareanu, C.S., Visser, W.: A survey of new trends in symbolic execution for software testing and analysis. STTT 11(4), 339–353 (2009)

18. Sewell, P., Sarkar, S., Owens, S., Nardelli, F.Z., Myreen, M.O.: x86-TSO: a rigorous and usable programmer's model for x86 multiprocessors. Commun. ACM 53(7), 89–97 (2010)

19. Travkin, O., Mütze, A., Wehrheim, H.: SPIN as a linearizability checker under weak memory models. In: Bertacco, V., Legay, A. (eds.) HVC 2013. LNCS, vol. 8244, pp. 311–326. Springer, Heidelberg (2013)

20. Travkin, O., Wehrheim, H.: Handling TSO in mechanized linearizability proofs. In: Yahav, E. (ed.) HVC 2014. LNCS, vol. 8855, pp. 132–147. Springer, Heidelberg (2014)

21. Treiber, R.K.: Systems programming: coping with parallelism. Technical report RJ 5118, IBM Almaden Res. Ctr. (1986)

22. Wonisch, D., Schremmer, A., Wehrheim, H.: Programs from proofs – a PCC alternative. In: Sharygina, N., Veith, H. (eds.) CAV 2013. LNCS, vol. 8044, pp. 912–927. Springer, Heidelberg (2013)

23. Yang, Y., Gopalakrishnan, G., Lindstrom, G.: UMM: an operational memory model specification framework with integrated model checking capability. Concurrency Comput. Pract. Experience 17(5-6), 465–487 (2005)

Parallel Symbolic Execution: Merging In-Flight Requests

Martin Nowack[✉], Katja Tietze,
and Christof Fetzer

Technische Universität Dresden, Dresden, Germany
martin_nowack@tu-dresden.de

Abstract. The strength of symbolic execution is the systematic analysis and validation of all possible control flow paths of a program and their respective properties, which is done by use of a solver component. Thus, it can be used for program testing in many different domains, e.g. test generation, fault discovery, information leakage detection, or energy consumption analysis. But major challenges remain, notably the huge (up to infinite) number of possible paths and the high computation costs generated by the solver to check the satisfiability of the constraints imposed by the paths. To tackle these challenges, researchers proposed the parallelization of symbolic execution by dividing the state space and handling the parts independently. Although this approach scales out well, we can further improve it by proposing a thread-based parallelized approach. It allows us to reuse shared resources like caches more efficiently – a vital part to reduce the solving costs. More importantly, this architecture enables us to use a new technique, which merges parallel incoming solver requests, leveraging incremental solving capabilities provided by modern solvers. Our results show a reduction of the solver time up to 50 % over the multi-threaded execution.

1 Introduction

Symbolic Execution [12] is a method to automatically and thoroughly test software and generate test cases. Lately it has also received attention in other domains like estimation of power consumption [10], analysis of mobile applications [1,14], security, and taint tracking [3,8]. Despite these advances, two major problems remain: the state space explosion problem and high solver times.

To tackle these issues, researchers introduced *process-based parallelization* [4,7,11,18] to symbolic execution engines in order to scale to multiple cores, multiple machines, and cloud environments [7]. However, this approach typically involves higher communication costs between concurrent components, e.g., using Java Remote Method Invocation (RMI) [18] or communicating with the manager process [4], which distributes and load-balances the single jobs of the symbolic execution. To reduce these costs, the search space is partitioned, so that the individual components work independently. But this way, partial solutions (e.g., previously solved path constraints that apply to multiple paths) are less likely

© Springer International Publishing Switzerland 2015
N. Piterman (Ed.): HVC 2015, LNCS 9434, pp. 120–135, 2015.
DOI: 10.1007/978-3-319-26287-1_8

to be reused, which results in re-execution, and thus, in redundant solver calls. Additionally, the partitioning itself imposes communication overhead for the manager process to find the best search space segmentation.

Still, solving costs are one major part of the computational expenses - i.e. as high as 40 % [16] or more of the execution time. Reducing them allows symbolic execution to explore more of the state space.

In this paper, we propose to use *thread-based parallelization* as an orthogonal approach to existing solutions. We introduce techniques like batching of parallel-running solver requests to minimize the number of solver calls and merging of solver requests to avoid redundant constraint analysis. Consequently, our approach reduces the overall solving time.

Our major contributions are:

- A multi-threaded implementation of a symbolic execution engine (we modified KLEE [5]); and
- An extension, which allows combining multiple solver calls, thus reducing the average time spent per solver request.

The remainder of this paper is structured as follows: We describe symbolic execution in Sect. 2, extending single threaded execution to our multi-threaded solution. In Sect. 3 we continue with the approach to batch and merge solver requests. We detail our implementation based on KLEE in Sect. 4, continue with the evaluation of our approach in Sect. 5, and finish with related work and a conclusion in Sects. 6 and 7.

2 Multi-threaded Symbolic Execution

In this section, first we introduce the standard single-threaded symbolic execution and point out challenges regarding the current use of process-based parallelization. Next we will present our approach to improve parallelization by applying a thread-based approach.

2.1 Symbolic Execution

Symbolic execution systematically executes a program by assuming arbitrary values for input parameters. By observing the behavior of a specific program path, it collects logic formulas (*constraints, C*) that describe this path. The collected path constraints ($PC = C_1 \wedge \cdots \wedge C_n$) are sent to a solver: (a) if the program reaches a conditional control flow statement (e.g., an if(cond) statement) or (b) to check a property of the current program state (e.g., if the following memory access can be a null pointer, if no out-of-bounds access or overflow occurs). In both cases, the constraint (C_{cond}) or its negation ($\neg C_{cond}$) is checked combined with the other path constraints. For the conditional control flow, if both outcomes are possible, the program state is duplicated with C_{cond} added to one state and $\neg C_{cond}$ to the other; further work on the states is done independently. If the set of constraints is impossible to fulfill the state can be removed. For the second case (to check properties), the solver can find possible input values for the program that trigger the condition to be true or false. This greatly helps a programmer, e.g., for debugging, by providing him with a concrete input that can be used to follow a particular path, possibly to reach a bug. However, even for small non-trivial applications (e.g., containing endless-loops) this approach can lead to a huge or infinite number of paths, the so-called state space explosion problem. Besides, checking satisfiability by the solver is computationally expensive, accounting for the major part of the runtime costs.

2.2   Single-Threaded Symbolic Execution

We based our prototype on KLEE [5], a state-of-the-art implementation of symbolic execution. Other implementations are structured similarly, so our findings will be easy to transfer. The main work flow of a symbolic execution engine is depicted in Fig. 1. First, an execution unit selects a state from the pool of available states (*state selection*). The execution engine uses the state and interprets its next instructions (*interpretation*) until: (i) a final instruction of the interpreted program is reached and the state is terminated; (ii) a bug is found, so the state must be terminated prematurely; or (iii) another state is selected. When path constraints must be solved or conditions need to be checked, the interpreter invokes the solver (*solving*).

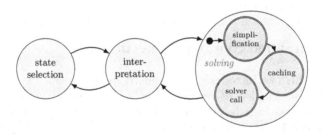

Fig. 1. The basic symbolic execution flow: First, a state is selected and then interpreted. If needed, collected constraints during interpretation are solved. To reduce the solver overhead, several optimizations like simplification and caching are done before the actual solver call.

The solver is a major, computationally expensive part of the symbolic execution. The feasibility of formulas has to be calculated, which is typically NP complete. Hence, a chain of additional optimizations (*simplification*, like independence optimization or *caching* [5]) is executed before the solver is called.

Symbolic execution engines like KLEE typically use existing solvers [9,16]. But these can suffer from issues like segmentation faults or memory leakage. To improve the reliability, KLEE forks and runs the solver in the child process from where it returns the result through shared memory. As expected, the forking imposes non-negligible overhead as we show in the evaluation.

2.3   Going Multi-Threaded

A major challenge of parallelizing symbolic execution is to efficiently partition and search the execution tree without knowing in the first place which parts are costly. First, if a leaf node is explored, the size of the subtree it expands is typically unknown. For example, if only a few expansions are possible, the subtree will be terminated earlier than if it must be expanded repeatedly. Second, the individual cost of exploring each node of a subtree is highly dependent on the costs of solving the path constraints, which are not easy to predict.

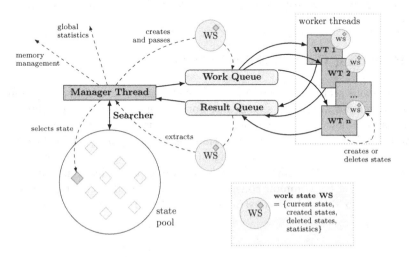

Fig. 2. Basic general architecture of a multi-threaded symbolic execution. A manager thread prioritizes states and puts them in a working queue. Worker threads select states from the queue and work independently on them, each calls the solver individually.

We propose the architecture depicted in Fig. 2. It resembles the steps from Sect. 2.2 Fig. 1 and assigns them to different threads. A *manager thread* is decoupled from a group of *worker threads* by using two queues. While the *work queue* buffers the states that are to be handled by the workers, the *result queue* is filled with states returned by the workers. The manager selects the states from the state pool and puts them in the work queue. With the order in which states get inserted, the managing thread can steer the exploration process. This selection is based on the statistics that are maintained by symbolic execution engines. They include information about the code checked during operation, e.g., which lines of code were already covered. The manager further extracts finished states from the result queue and updates the global statistics. In case not enough memory is available, e.g., due to state space explosion, the manager deletes the least important states (e.g., the state furthest away from uncovered instructions. Each worker takes a state from the work queue and runs the symbolic execution by iterating over the code. In case the solver is called, the worker executes it in a forked process.

The *current state* to be worked on is wrapped in a *worker state* used by only one worker at a time and is thread local. Workers add new states (which were found by their current exploration) to it, mark states as deleted, and update local statistics. Later, these information are used by the manager thread to update the state pool and global statistics. This way, workers manage their updates locally which improves their access time and reduces pressure on the CPU cache.

The major advantage of our thread-based approach is an improved utilization of the CPU cores while additional communication costs between different processes are avoided. At the same time, components like caches are shared. New solutions found by the solver are added to the cache which avoids solving them again.

3   Reducing Overall Solver Costs

In the previous section, we explained how we use more cores for solving, but the overall solver costs are still significant. Fortunately, our multi-threading architecture allows new ways of combining solver requests to reduce the number of solver calls. For our approach we distinguish between *unique constraints* and *common constraints* as depicted in Fig. 3(a). While unique constraints are state specific (i.e., request specific), common constraints are true for multiple states. Hence, solutions for common constraints can be reused without recalculation. The figure also shows how constraints are gathered along a path of the code tree.

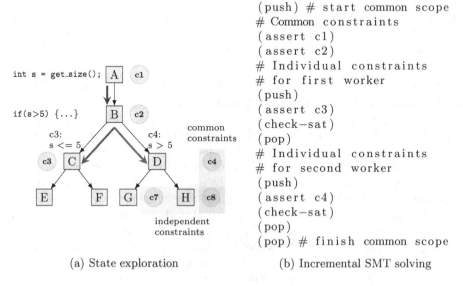

(a) State exploration   (b) Incremental SMT solving

Fig. 3. Example of state exploration (a) and incremental solving using push/pop (b). If two workers work on C and D independently, they still share a common path. In that case, to expand C respectively D, the solver can reuse solutions.

We leverage two key observations (i) the likelihood that two or more requests are worked on in parallel is quite high; and (ii) requests from different paths can share a common history, hence they are likely to share common path constraints. More precisely, we address the first observation by batching requests and the second by reusing the partial solutions for common constraints, as we explain in Sects. 3.1 and 3.2.

For the second option, we leverage the feature of recent SMT solvers to *incrementally* find a solution to solver requests (e.g. [6,15]). Instead of solving all requests independently, we first start a new scope (**push**) and put all common constraints in it (Fig. 3(b)). After that, for the remaining constraints, we open a new scope (**push**) for each individual request, solve the constraint (**check-sat**) and close the scope again (**pop**). This way, specific lemmas learned get removed, common lemmas are kept (e.g. for value forward propagation).

3.1 Batching Solver Requests

We enable a rendezvous of solver requests by a new layer in the solver chain as depicted in Fig. 4. The *waiting barrier* (before the solver call) consists of a set of slots, each describing a possible rendezvous point.

Our waiting barrier is a ring buffer with multiple slots. Each slot can gather a number of queries. All requests in one slot will be combined to be handled by one solver request, instead of each provoking a solver call individually. This batching reduces the number of solver calls, thus reducing the overall costs.

Apart from the set of queries, each slot contains a *busy flag*, which indicates whether a solving process is currently running for the queries gathered in the slot. A global *open slot pointer* indicates the next open slot in the ring. Open means that the solving process for the queries in this slot has not yet started, so other workers are still allowed to add their query to the slot.

We distinguish worker threads and, along them, one *primary* worker thread per slot, which acts as a master and manages the solving process. The course of a solving process is depicted in Fig. 5. The first thread to enter an open slot will become the primary. Then it starts spinning until a *waiting timeout* has

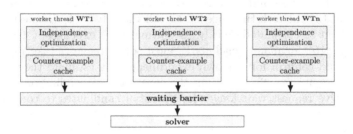

Fig. 4. Additional rendezvous layer: Instead of every worker calling the solver individually, each thread waits briefly at a waiting barrier for potential other workers to call the solver. In case a worker arrives in the meanwhile, their requests are combined.

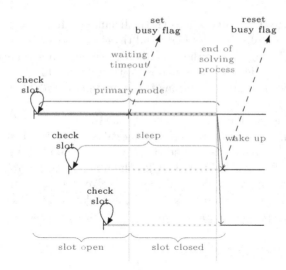

Fig. 5. Temporal course of the solving process. The first worker to arrive at a slot becomes primary and waits for others. Later arriving workers, enqueue their solver request in the same slot and sleep. After a timeout, the first thread closes the slot, solves all queries, returns the result to all sleeping workers, and wakes them up.

exceeded. Subsequently it sets the busy flag, increments the open slot pointer, and triggers the solving process.

Every worker thread that enters a slot with an existing primary goes to sleep immediately. When the solving process is finished, the primary wakes up the other workers, hands them their solver results, and all threads leave the slot, thus leaving the waiting barrier.

Currently, our matching is trivial: as long as the current slot is still open, new requests can be matched to others in this slot. However, for future work we plan to improve this and follow a multiple lane approach, in which we use multiple ring buffers and assign threads to slots based on the complexity of the request ("slow track" vs. "fast track"). For this refinement the waiting time depends on (i) the simplicity of the request and, therefore, the benefit of waiting for another request to arrive and (ii) the fork time needed to call the solver. If a request is simple its solution can be calculated quickly, so waiting is too expensive ("fast track"). As shown by [16], for many benchmarks most solver requests take 1 ms or less, which we could confirm for our own experiments. We estimate the complexity of requests resembling [18]: we weight the constraints depending on their costs. More expensive request wait longer for potential candidates to combine them with ("slow track").

3.2 Merging and Solving Requests

Once the primary worker's timeout has exceeded, it sets the busy flag (to prevent other workers from entering the slot) and start the solving process. It consists of two steps, which facilitate the capabilities of incremental solvers. First, it calculates the intersection of all constraints, thus determining the *common constraints*, which are shared by all queries. The solver will cache this solution for the common constraints to subsequently reuse it for solving all queries without recalculation. Second, the requests of all worker threads are handled iteratively: for each worker, the primary pushes the unique constraints on the working stack, solves the request, and combines it with the previously calculated solution for the common constraints.

Once the primary finished solving all worker requests, it wakes the sleeping worker threads of this batch and passes them their respective results. The threads leave the slot, thus splitting up again.

Currently we only determine the common constraints of all requests. However, in future work we plan to extend on this and also calculate subsets of constraints that are shared by multiple (but not all) workers in a slot. This way, solver time could be reduced further.

3.3   Merging vs. Caching

One could argue that a global cache to store common constraints and their solutions should be sufficient and simpler in comparison to our proposed solution. A major challenge we see is the identification of common constraints. One cannot know easily upfront the number of common constraints for two or more requests. Therefore, to make a global cache efficient, one has to save subsets of constraints for requests. This poses two challenges, first to subsequently match, the subset should not contain specific constraints otherwise subsequent hits are less likely; second, choosing the right size of a subset influences the number of entries in the cache and its hit rate. The smaller entries should be, the larger the cache has to be. Otherwise, entries might get evicted too often.

4   Implementation

Our prototype is based on the current version of KLEE [5][1]. As a symbolic execution engine for running C and C++ programs, KLEE is built on top of LLVM [13] (a tool chain for building compilers and interpreters) and uses STP [9] as a solver for quantifier-free first order logic with support for bit-vectors and arrays.

We parallelized KLEE by implementing the architecture described in Sect. 2.3. By converting KLEE to C++11, it enabled us to leverage support for multi-threading (e.g. using `std::shared_ptr`, `std::atomics`).

Based on the basic architecture, we added our waiting barrier as an additional stage before the final solver as depicted in Fig. 4. Precisely, the waiting barrier is a ring buffer with a number of slots whose contents consist of a set of queries and a busy flag. The total number of slots in the ring buffer is equal to the number

---

[1] https://github.com/klee/klee.

of CPUs, so every worker thread running in parallel is guaranteed to fit into a slot.

Once a thread enters an open slot, it will be assigned one of two roles. The first thread to enter runs in *primary* mode, thus following a separate code path and executing primary tasks. All threads that enter a slot with an existing primary become *secondaries*.

Flexible waiting timeout: Previously, we explained that threads are matched to each other by being assigned to the same slot in the waiting barrier. While our concept allows for different approaches of a waiting timeout, our prototype implements the following batching process: Every time the primary detects a newly arrived secondary, it will decrease the waiting timeout by interval I, with N being the number of possible parallel threads (i.e., the number of CPUs) and T_w being the length of the waiting timeout: $I = T_w/N$. Hence, the new waiting timeout T'_w is $T'_w = T_w - I$.

This flexible waiting timeout allows to include multiple threads in the batching while reducing the overall idle time. However, in the meantime between the end of the waiting timeout and the slot actually being closed, other threads can still enter the slot.

In future work, we will focus on a more sophisticated batching process. First, we intend to experiment with varying waiting timeouts and matching approaches. Second, we will implement a multiple lane approach to allow different complexity tracks as described in Sect. 3.2.

Resetting the busy flag: When the solving process is finished, the primary wakes up the secondaries and passes them their respective solutions. To avoid unnecessary delays of single threads and additional overhead, the primary gives up its role right afterwards. The last thread to leave the barrier resets the busy flag and, thus, opens the slot again.

Limitations to the approach and the prototype: Calls to external libraries have to be synchronized. Our implementation resembles the original KLEE, e.g., if a worker calls an external function (e.g. to print to screen), all memory objects contained in the current state will be written to the real process memory, the external call will be executed, and changes will be written back. If other workers also need to execute external calls they will be stalled.

5 Evaluation

For our experiments we used an Intel E5405 2 GHz with 8 cores and 8 GB of RAM running Ubuntu 14.04.02. To evaluate our approach, we used Coreutils suite[2] 6.10 as our benchmark suite, the same version as in [4,5,16]. Coreutils contains around 90 basic utilities for text, file, and shell manipulation and are part of most Linux-based systems. Written in C, the utilities often have system interactions

---

[2] https://www.gnu.org/software/coreutils/.

and contain low-level bit manipulations. We used the same input parameters for KLEE as in [5] as far as they are available in the current unmodified KLEE version. The major difference of our experiment setup is that we run the 64 bit version of the test applications, our KLEE-based implementation builds on top of LLVM 3.4, and we limit the maximum memory to use to 4 GB. We allow a solver request to take up to a maximum of 30 s to execute.

Each of the test tools from the benchmark suite was run 3 times and up to 1h each for every version of our implementation.

5.1   Time Spent by the Solver

To be able to show the improvement of the solving time, we first need to have a closer look at the solving time spent in the case of the single-threaded execution. We ran the Coreutils benchmark with the original version of KLEE and recorded the generated solver requests and the time it took (t_{klee}). In a second step, we used the solver independently of KLEE and re-ran each request individually using the solver front end KLEAVER. We disabled the forking mechanism or any other optimization happened before the solver call, and recorded the solving time (t_{real}). To our surprise, the solving times varied vastly ($t_{diff} = t_{klee} - t_{real}$).

One example run is depicted in Fig. 6 for csplit. The graph depicts solver request and their execution time over finished instructions made during 1 h. The green dots depict the real solving time (t_{real}). The blue dots depict the additional time (t_{diff}) spent for a request. The solving time is measured in seconds with maximum of 21.89 s. The allocated memory (red points) is depicted in the same graph as well. We normalized the measured values to a 0–1 range with 1 being equivalent to a 4 GB allocation.

As one can see, the real solver time is distributed in three lanes. The major part of requests is below 10 ms with a slight concentration in the 1st third of the time; followed by up to 100 ms quite equally distributed over time; with only minor number of requests above more concentrated during the last two third of the execution.

As one can see, the solver time difference (t_{diff}) increase over time highly correlates with the total size of allocated memory (red points). The higher the allocation, the higher is t_{diff}.

We could reproduce similar behavior with a very simple toy program executed natively that has two phases: first, it allocates an amount of memory and writes into it, and in the second phase, a few thousand forks() are executed. The average time a fork takes increases linearly with the amount of allocated memory. If multiple threads run in parallel in the second phase, the fork time will not change significantly over the single-threaded execution.

In essence, the less often we need to fork, especially under memory pressure (e.g. due to state space explosion), the more time can be spent in solving. Therefore, if many solver requests can be merged and combined to one, the overall time spent in forking can be reduced.

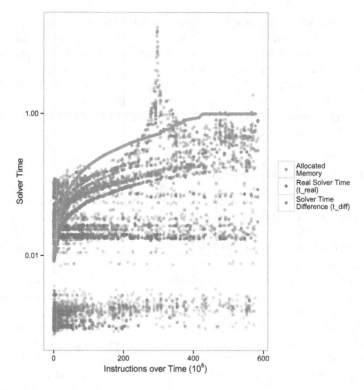

Fig. 6. Example of one run for `csplit` and the time spent for solving the requests (Color figure online).

5.2   Thread-Based Parallel Symbolic Execution

Our major contribution is combining in-flight solver requests which is built on top of a multi-threaded implementation of a symbolic execution engine. Before we evaluate the combining, we evaluated the thread-based symbolic execution.

To show the effectiveness of our multi-threaded implementation, we need to compare it with the single-threaded execution. To do so, we use two metrics: the *achieved line coverage* and the *instructions executed*.

Multi-threading adds a big source of randomness, which makes it hard to compare single-threaded and multi-threaded runs. Already for original single-threaded KLEE, its behavior is highly random, making it hard to repeat experiments. We took similar measures as [16] to disable random influences (e.g., deactivate address space random layout). To show the effectiveness (e.g. using line coverage criterion) of our multi-threaded implementation, we could not use non-random searchers like depth-first search or breadth-first search. It would be a disadvantage for single-threaded implementations, as already with a second worker thread covering an additional path, a multi-threaded implementation has an advantage over a single threaded implementation. We used a searcher which selects states randomly from the state space but prefers states close to an uncovered instruction.

Our results for the coverage show that for the group of applications of Core-utils, which can be fully covered during the execution of 1 h, the multi-threaded execution achieves the full coverage in most of the runs earlier up to 6.7x faster for 8 threads. For the second group of applications, for which full coverage cannot be achieved during 1 h, the multi-threaded implementation achieved on average a higher coverage faster in comparison to the single-threaded execution. Still, the coverage metric is highly influenced by selecting the right states to explore as early as possible. Using *instructions executed* as a metric is also fragile. If a taken path covers instructions for which the constraints are hard to solve, less instructions can be executed. In contrast, if constraints can be solved fast, more instructions can be executed. Still our experiments show an improvement for 14 out of 40 experiments executing at least 2 billion more instructions and up to 5 billions more at most (e.g. md5sum).

5.3   Batching and Merging Parallel Requests

The success of our method depends highly on how many requests can be batched. Obviously, this depends on the time a thread in primary mode is waiting at the barrier for other threads to arrive and the average time it takes to solve a request. The second is often specific to the application under test (Sect. 3.1). In our tests, we varied the waiting time between 1 ms and 100 ms. As a result, different applications were favored depending on the timeout of the waiting barrier.

How often are solver requests batched and how many together? We run all the Coreutils suite with our implementation of merging in-flight requests. We recorded the solver requests which have been made. The experiments generated 7.8 million queries per different waiting configuration. Figure 7(a) shows the distribution of combined queries. For every observed number of queries involved for batching (x axis - 1 to 8), we depict the number of how often this happened. Our testing machines has 8 cores and up to 8 queries were batched, therefore up to 8 threads arrived at the waiting barrier and used the same slot at one time. The majority of requests do not execute in parallel (57 %). For the remaining requests, two threads share requests most often. It is an order of magnitude less for 3, down to a couple of hundreds for 8.

How many constraints did batched requests have in common? The number of shared constraints for batched requests varied highly. Figure 7(b) shows the distribution over the number of common constraints. It varies between 0 and 246 in the example of the Coreutils experiment. On average, requests had 69.9 constraints in common. This indicates a good applicability of our method. Reason why the graph has the ragged shape are the way a program is explored. Our used searcher prefers states close to uncovered instructions. If instructions from a code region are uncovered, branch points in the code enable different workers to work on similar states. This makes it more likely to have common constraints. Also loops in code containing switches make it more likely that several workers work on different switch cases but still sharing common constraints.

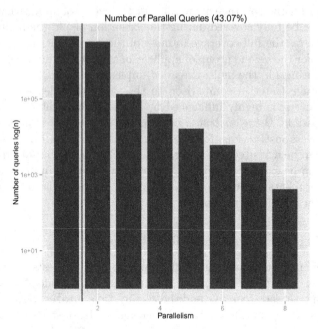

(a) Distribution of combined queries encountered.

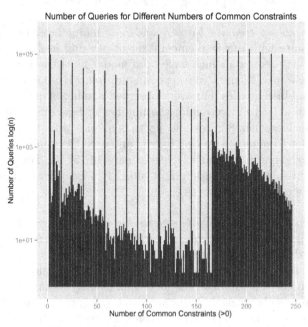

(b) Distribution of common constraints for combined queries.

Fig. 7. Results for Coreutils having a barrier waiting time of up to 10 ms. Total number of queries: 7.8 million.

Results show a saving of solver costs up to 50 % over the multi-threaded only version, which is almost 7 h in case of the time spent for solver requests on Coreutils.

5.4   Prototype Limitations

External Calls Calling external functions (i.e. system calls) is essential for testing system applications like the ones in Coreutils The problem is that changes made by calls to external libraries (i.e. modifications of the memory) cannot be observed by KLEE. Therefore, the current implementation of KLEE works around the issue by, first, writing all memory associated to the execution state to their native positions, second, executing the external call, and last, writing back all changes from the native memory to the execution state. For our prototype, to avoid inconsistencies, we made calling external calls mutual exclusive. This has an impact on the execution time of the application, we measured waiting costs up to 8 % of the total execution time for each thread (i.e. for md5sum). On average it was 1.8 % per application and thread.

5.5   Threats to Validity

We verified our implementation and experiment setup to the best of our knowledge. Still it is hard to cope with inherent randomness of symbolic execution plus the multi-threaded implementation. We tried to mitigate the problem by running the experiments multiple times and calculating the average. We validated our approach comparing the code coverage of the checked applications, which is similar or better.

6   Related Work

To the best of our knowledge, no existing solutions follow a thread-based approach as proposed by us. All solutions we know build on a process-based approach to utilize multiple cores for symbolic execution.

Staats et al. [18] propose an extension to parallelize the symbolic execution part of Java Pathfinder [2]. They partition the search tree statically upfront. First, they perform a symbolic search with iterative deepening to depth n and collect the sets of constraints. Second, they reassemble the constraints according to complexity and use them to split the domains of the input variables in independent pieces. In a third step, they assign these pieces to different workers, which work on them separately to reduce costs. Bucur et al. [4] propose a dynamic approach named Cloud 9. The search tree is split dynamically and a load balancer observes the workers. As soon as a worker is over-utilized, its search tree is split and parts of the tree are transfered to the load balancer, which distributes them to under-utilized nodes. Our approach can be combined with both solutions to help each worker accelerate its progress, thus allowing a better overall throughput. Additionally, our thread-based parallelization can also enhance the light-weight symbolic execution proposed by Staats et al. [18].

An interesting alternative is using a portfolio solver as proposed by Palikareva et al. [16]. A request is sent to different SMT solvers in parallel and the fastest and/or best solution will be used. This can efficiently utilize multiple cores available on the same machine. We see our work as an orthogonal approach.

Our solution for merging solver requests is based on similar ideas (see Pötzl et al. [17]) for solver preprocessing, e.g., Push/Pop Encoding.

7 Conclusion

We presented a new way to combine solver requests in symbolic execution: We leverage multi-threaded execution and merge parallel occurring solver requests. Our prototype shows a reduction of the solver time by up to 50 %. We consider our work a viable extension of existing approaches for parallelized symbolic execution.

Acknowledgment. We thank the anonymous reviewers for their insightful comments. This work was partially founded by the German Research Foundation (DFG) under grant FE 1035/1-2.

References

1. Anand, S., Naik, M., Harrold, M.J., Yang, H.: Automated concolic testing of smartphone apps. In: Proceedings of the ACM SIGSOFT 20th International Symposium on the Foundations of Software Engineering, FSE 2012, pp. 59:1–59:11. ACM, New York (2012). http://doi.acm.org/10.1145/2393596.2393666
2. Anand, S., Păsăreanu, C.S., Visser, W.: JPF–SE: a symbolic execution extension to Java PathFinder. In: Grumberg, O., Huth, M. (eds.) TACAS 2007. LNCS, vol. 4424, pp. 134–138. Springer, Heidelberg (2007)
3. Avancini, A., Ceccato, M.: Comparison and integration of genetic algorithms and dynamic symbolic execution for security testing of cross-site scripting vulnerabilities. Inf. Softw. Tech. **55**(12), 2209–2222 (2013). http://dx.doi.org/10.1016/j.infsof.2013.08.001
4. Bucur, S., Ureche, V., Zamfir, C., Candea, G.: Parallel symbolic execution for automated real-world software testing. In: EuroSys 2011: Proceedings of the Sixth Conference on Computer Systems, pp. 183–198. ACM Request Permissions, New York, April 2011. http://portal.acm.org/citation.cfm?doid=1966445.1966463
5. Cadar, C., Dunbar, D., Engler, D.: Klee: unassisted and automatic generation of high-coverage tests for complex systems programs. In: Proceedings of the 8th USENIX Conference on Operating Systems Design and Implementation, OSDI 2008, pp. 209–224. USENIX Association, Berkeley (2008). http://dl.acm.org/citation.cfm?id=1855741.1855756
6. Cimatti, A., Griggio, A., Schaafsma, B.J., Sebastiani, R.: The MathSAT5 SMT solver. In: Piterman, N., Smolka, S.A. (eds.) TACAS 2013. LNCS, vol. 7795, pp. 93–107. Springer, Heidelberg (2013)

7. Ciortea, L., Zamfir, C., Bucur, S., Chipounov, V., Candea, G.: Cloud9: a software testing service. ACM SIGOPS Operat. Syst. Rev. **43**(4), 5–10 (2010). http://dl.acm.org/citation.cfm?id=1713254.1713257
8. Corin, R., Manzano, F.A.: Taint analysis of security code in the KLEE symbolic execution engine. In: Chim, T.W., Yuen, T.H. (eds.) ICICS 2012. LNCS, vol. 7618, pp. 264–275. Springer, Heidelberg (2012)
9. Ganesh, V., Dill, D.L.: A decision procedure for bit-vectors and arrays. In: Damm, W., Hermanns, H. (eds.) CAV 2007. LNCS, vol. 4590, pp. 519–531. Springer, Heidelberg (2007)
10. Hönig, T., Eibel, C., Kapitza, R., Schröder-Preikschat, W.: SEEP: exploiting symbolic execution for energy-aware programming. Operat. Syst. Rev. **45**(3), 58–62 (2011). http://doi.acm.org/10.1145/2094091.2094106
11. King, A.: Distributed Parallel Symbolic Execution. Master's thesis, August 2009
12. King, J.C.: Symbolic execution and program testing. Commun. ACM **19**(7), 385–394 (1976). http://doi.acm.org/10.1145/360248.360252
13. Lattner, C., Adve, V.: LLVM: a compilation framework for lifelong program analysis & transformation. In: CGO 2004: Proceedings of the International Symposium on Code Generation and Optimization: Feedback-Directed and Runtime Optimization. pp. 75–86. IEEE Computer Society, March 2004. http://ieeexplore.ieee.org/lpdocs/epic03/wrapper.htm?arnumber=1281665
14. Mirzaei, N., Malek, S., Pasareanu, C.S., Esfahani, N., Mahmood, R.: Testing android apps through symbolic execution. ACM SIGSOFT Softw. Eng. Not. **37**(6), 1–5 (2012). http://doi.acm.org/10.1145/2382756.2382798
15. de Moura, L., Bjørner, N.S.: Z3: an efficient smt solver. In: Ramakrishnan, C.R., Rehof, J. (eds.) TACAS 2008. LNCS, vol. 4963, pp. 337–340. Springer, Heidelberg (2008)
16. Palikareva, H., Cadar, C.: Multi-solver support in symbolic execution. In: Sharygina, N., Veith, H. (eds.) CAV 2013. LNCS, vol. 8044, pp. 53–68. Springer, Heidelberg (2013)
17. Pötzl, D., Holzer, A.: Solving constraints for generational search. In: Veanes, M., Viganò, L. (eds.) TAP 2013. LNCS, vol. 7942, pp. 197–213. Springer, Heidelberg (2013)
18. Staats, M., Păsăreanu, C.: Parallel symbolic execution for structural test generation. In: The 19th International Symposium, p. 183. ACM Press, New York (2010). http://portal.acm.org/citation.cfm?doid=1831708.1831732

Model Checking

Limited Mobility, Eventual Stability

Lenore D. Zuck[1] and Sanjiva Prasad[2]([⊠])

[1] University of Illinois at Chicago, Chicago, USA
lenore@cs.uic.edu
[2] IIT Delhi, New Delhi, India
sanjivap@cse.iitd.ac.in

Abstract. The IPv6 Mobility protocol, an archetypal system for supporting communication amongst mobile devices, presents challenging verification problems. While model-checking techniques have been used to illustrate subtle oversights and flaws in the informal specifications previously, the more difficult question — whether it is possible to verify the correctness of the core architecture by checking properties on a small model — has not been adequately examined. In this paper we present a novel technique combining ideas from verification of parameterised systems, abstraction, model-checking of temporal logic properties and simulation relations found in process algebras. The technique relies on the fact that the system can be considered to eventually stabilise to a form more amenable to techniques used for model-checking parameterised systems, allowing the checking of arbitrary LTL properties.

Keywords: Parameterised verification · Abstraction · Simulation · IPv6 mobility

1 Introduction

The IPv6 mobility protocol [14] is designed to allow mobile nodes (MNs) to remain reachable while moving around from one network to another, while maintaining a permanent IP address (thus facilitating uninterrupted functioning of transport and application protocols). It is a *proxy-based architecture* and uses a small set of control messages to let correspondent nodes know one another's current locations. The protocol assigns to each node a permanent identifying address and a *home agent* router (HA) in its default home network, which is responsible for recording its current location and forwarding messages addressed to it when it moves. When it moves to a different subnet, a MN is associated with a care-of address (CoA), which it conveys to its HA and also (optionally) to correspondent nodes (CNs) via a *foreign agent*. By letting CNs *cache the current location* of a MN, Mobile IPv6 avoids having messages "dog-leg" via the home network of the target MN, though this is the default path for CNs who are unaware of the MN's location. This solution also avoids the vulnerabilities

---

This research was supported in part by NSF grant CNS-1228697.

N. Piterman (Ed.): HVC 2015, LNCS 9434, pp. 139–154, 2015.
DOI: 10.1007/978-3-319-26287-1_9

of having all messages go via the home router, such as increased traffic, node failure, denial of service, congestion etc.

Mobile IP is an archetypal *distributed* framework for supporting communication between MNs. With the explosive growth in the number of mobile devices, verifying the correctness of this protocol is important. Its correct functioning depends on maintaining a global property across the forwarding tables in a distributed system of routers, and reestablishing it, via coordinated local changes at different routers, when it is disrupted by the mobility of MNs. The basic correctness ty required of the protocol is that even with mobility, messages to a MN eventually get delivered[1]. Clearly if a restless peripatetic node moves very frequently, a message addressed to it may forever be chasing it without ever catching up with it. The correctness of the protocol may therefore be informally phrased as: *if a MN stays "long enough" at a place, a message addressed to it will eventually be delivered to it*. We posit that establishing the essential correctness of the protocol does not require explicitly modelling time, but that a temporal ordering suffices to characterise its properties (which we do in LTL).

There have been several attempts at formally specifying and verifying the IP mobility model, using a variety of techniques (see Sect. 1.1). The different approaches have focussed on modelling the protocol at various degrees of detail, sometimes focussing on different issues (security, lifetime of cache entries, basic invariants, etc.). Model-checking tools have been used to detect (usually minor) errors in the design of the system. The common characteristic of these efforts is that the systems modelled have a very small number of mobile nodes and routers (usually 2 or 3 of each), and have been plagued by an extremely large state space. While the presence of a property violation in such a limited model provides a trace identifying an error in the design, the absence of errors in the model does not vouch for the correctness of the protocol.

In this paper, we show the correctness of (the essence of) the IP mobility infrastructure by verifying the basic correctness property in a small model (comprising one message, one mobile node and three routers). We argue that checking for correctness on this model is adequate in establishing the correctness of much larger systems with many more routers, messages and mobile nodes. Our work uses a novel methodology for verifying systems such as these, using ideas from parameterised verification, abstraction, model-checking and a form of fair simulation.

Note that the correctness requirement is a liveness property. Moreover, the system that we are modelling has inconvenient data structures that render traditional parameterised verification techniques unsuitable. However, the system we study enjoys an exploitable property: *it is guaranteed to eventually reach, and remain in, a state* where the unwieldy data structures can be dispensed with. We are thus able to propose a proof rule that focuses on such "good" states,

---

[1] IP only promises a best effort at datagram delivery; there are the usual reasons for non-delivery of messages: node failure, link failure, noisy traffic, inadequate buffer space at congested nodes, etc. The question thus is whether mobility adduces any additional reasons for non-deliverability of messages.

where the data structures can be replaced with simpler ones. The system being parameterised, it can be reduced to a (small) finite instance amenable to efficient model-checking. We use TLV to model and verify the system.

Thus, faced with a parameterised system with non-trivial data structures and a liveness property, we can reduce the problem to that of model-checking a small system with simpler data structures. Small model theorems have been used before in parameterised verification. For example, [7] proposes such for a restricted class of systems where everything is universal, and the method of invisible invariants (e.g., [9]) uses a small model theorem for the proof obligation of the premises of proof rules. While parts of our method resemble the latter approach, our method is fundamentally different: the small model theorem of invisible invariants is used to generate invariants on small instances, while here we verify the property directly on the small instance.

Paper Structure. The rest of the paper is structured as follows. This introduction concludes with a review of previous work on verifying mobile IP. In Sect. 2, we present our computational model, and the method used for verification. Section 3 overviews the IP mobility architecture, and presents a finite model of the core Mobile IP system in TLV which can be model-checked. In Sect. 4, we present *two different proof techniques* for establishing the required correctness of the message delivery property. Both techniques rely on the fact that the system reaches a *stable* state which is more amenable to efficient analysis. The first technique is based on transforming the stable suffix of the original system into a new one and converting the liveness property into a bounded liveness property using techniques based on the "method of invisible invariants" (see [2,15,17]) adapted to bounded liveness [8]. The other technique (manually) establishes the existence of a small model using simulation and then directly model checks the behavior of that small model. We conclude in Sect. 5, highlighting the novelty of the method presented.

1.1   Related Work on Verifying Mobile IP

McCann and Roman [13] present a specification of IP mobility in the Mobile UNITY notation and proof logic, in which they prove several properties of the system including real-time ones. Their specification is parameterised, comprising mobile nodes, home and foreign routers and the network, and involves explicit modelling of clocks and their synchronization. Jackson *et al.* [11] used the lightweight formal tool Nitpick to model the protocol, concentrating on time and time-stamping of messages to analyse the lifetimes of cache bindings. They detected certain anomalies in the informal protocol specification, identifying circumstances in which messages may traverse cycles, and how a cycle may form in the forwarding tables. Our work shows that the protocol may work correctly even if such forwarding cycles form temporarily. Dang and Kemmerer [6] use the ASTRAL model-checking tool to model the system in great detail, including message formats, physical locations and time. They perform a bounded-time explicit state space exploration, leading to a huge state space explosion (10^8) for even a very small number of mobile nodes, and home and foreign routers (2 of each). However, their analysis also focuses on security properties of the protocol, which they correctly argue are intimately connected to the correctness of the cache updates. Amadio and Prasad [1] model the protocol in a process calculus framework, and identify essential invariant properties that the protocol should maintain, such as the absence of forwarding table cycles and the need for buffering messages at previously visited nodes. They posit that the correctness of the protocol architecture does not depend on explicit time (time-stamping, lifetimes etc.) but on the temporal order of certain control messages, and prove that the protocol is behaviourally equivalent to IP without mobility. While their analysis is exhaustive, the process calculus setting results in some "over-modelling" and no automated techniques are presented. The authors, however, do report an attempt to model-check a small finite version of the protocol using SPIN, which required state space in excess of the tool's capabilities. Rodrigues *et al.* [16] report the use of an object-oriented Petri Net based tool to verify the protocol. However, one of the properties they claim is that every data message goes through the home router, which is not true of Mobile IPv6.

2   The Formal Framework

2.1   Just Discrete Systems

Our computational model is a *just discrete system* (JDS) $\mathcal{S} = \langle V, \Theta, \rho, \mathcal{J}, \rangle$, where

- V is a set of *system variables*. A *state* of $\mathcal{S}$ provides a type-consistent interpretation of the variables V. For state s and variable $v \in V$, we denote by $s[v]$ the value assigned to v by the state s. Let Σ denote the set of all states over V.
- Θ is the *initial condition*: An assertion (state formula) characterising the initial states.
- $\rho(V, V')$ is the *transition relation*: An assertion, relating the values V of the variables in state $s \in \Sigma$ to the values V' in an $\mathcal{S}$-successor state $s' \in \Sigma$.
- $\mathcal{J}$ is a set of *justice* (*weak fairness*) requirements (assertions). A computation must include infinitely many states satisfying each of the justice requirements.

    For an assertion ψ, we say that $s \in \Sigma$ is a ψ-state if $s \models \psi$.

    A *computation* of an JDS $\mathcal{S}$ is an infinite sequence of states $\sigma : s_0, s_1, s_2, ...$, satisfying the requirements:

- *Initiality*: s_0 is initial, i.e., $s_0 \models \Theta$.
- *Consecution*: For each $\ell = 0, 1, ...$, the state $s_{\ell+1}$ is an $\mathcal{S}$-successor of s_ℓ. That is, $\langle s_\ell, s_{\ell+1} \rangle \models \rho(V, V')$ where, for each $v \in V$, we interpret v as $s_\ell[v]$ and v' as $s_{\ell+1}[v]$.
- *Justice*: For every $J \in \mathcal{J}$, σ contains infinitely many occurrences of J-states.

    We say that a temporal property φ is *valid over* $\mathcal{S}$, denoted by $\mathcal{S} \models \varphi$, if for every computation σ of $\mathcal{S}$, $\sigma \models \varphi$.

2.2   Finitary Abstraction

We now give an overview of (a somewhat simplified version of) the material in [12], to which the reader may refer for details.

An *abstraction* is a mapping $\alpha \colon \Sigma \to \Sigma_A$ for some set Σ_A of *abstract states*. The abstraction α is *finitary* if the set of abstract states Σ_A is finite. We focus on abstractions that can be represented by a set of equations of the form $u_i = E_i(V)$, $i = 1, \ldots, n$, where the E_i's are expressions over the concrete variables V and $\{u_1, \ldots, u_n\}$ is the set of *abstract variables*, denoted by V_A. Alternatively, α can be written as a system of equations $V_A = \mathcal{E}_\alpha(V)$.

For an assertion $p(V)$, we define its abstraction by:

$$\alpha(p) \colon \quad \exists V.(V_A = \mathcal{E}_A(V) \, \wedge \, p(V))$$

The semantics of $\alpha(p)$ is the set of abstract states given by $||\alpha(p)|| = \{\alpha(s) \mid s \in ||p||\}$. Note that $||\alpha(p)||$ is, in general, an over-approximation – an abstract state is in $||\alpha(p)||$ iff *there exists* some concrete p-state that is abstracted into it. An assertion $p(V, V')$ over both primed and unprimed variables is abstracted by:

$$\alpha(p) \colon \quad \exists V, V'.(V_A = \mathcal{E}_A(V) \wedge V_A' = \mathcal{E}_A(V') \, \wedge \, p(V, V'))$$

The assertion p is said to be *precise with respect to the abstraction* α if $||p|| = \alpha^{-1}(||\alpha(p)||)$, i.e., if two concrete states are abstracted into the same abstract state, they are either both p-states, or they are both $\neg p$-states. For a temporal formula ψ in positive normal form (where negation is applied only to state assertions), ψ^α is the formula obtained by replacing every maximal state sub-formula p in ψ by $\alpha(p)$. The formula ψ is said to be *precise with respect to* α if each of its maximal state sub-formulas is precise with respect to α.

In all cases discussed in this paper, the formulae are precise with respect to the relevant abstractions. Hence, we can restrict to the over-approximation semantics.

2.3   Partial System Abstraction

Let S be a JDS as above, and let $S_a = \langle V_a, \Theta_a, \rho_a, \mathcal{J}_a, \rangle$. The following theorem, whose proof follows a similar proof in [12], is the basis of our method that allows a partial abstraction of a system.

Theorem 1. *Let $S \subset \Sigma$ and let $\alpha \colon S \to \Sigma_a$ be an abstraction mapping. Then if the following all hold:*

1. $\Diamond \, \Box \, S$ *is valid over S;*
2. *all $\alpha(S)$ states are S_a reachable from Θ_a;*
3. $\bigcup_{J \in \mathcal{J}} \alpha(J) \subseteq \bigcup_{J' \in \mathcal{J}_a} J'$

Then for every state assertion ϕ,

$$S_a \models \Diamond \Box \, \phi^\alpha \quad \implies \quad S \models \Diamond \Box \phi$$

For $S : \langle V, \Theta, \rho, \mathcal{J}, \rangle$ and $S_a : \langle V_a, \Theta_a, \rho_a, \mathcal{J}_a, \rangle$
   set of states $S \subseteq \Sigma$,
   abstraction mapping $\alpha \colon S \to \Sigma_a$
   and property $\Diamond \square \varphi$ that is precise with respect to α,
S1. $S \models \Diamond \square S$
S2. $\bigcup_{J \in \mathcal{J}} \alpha(J) \subseteq \bigcup_{J' \in \mathcal{J}_a} J'$
S3. For every $s_1, s_2 \in S$, if $(s_1, s_2) \in \rho$ then $(\alpha(s_1), \alpha(s_2)) \in \rho_a$;
S4. For every $s \in \alpha(S)$ there is a S_a computation that reaches s;
S5. $S_a \models \Diamond \square \varphi^\alpha$

$$S \models \Diamond \square \varphi$$

Fig. 1. Verification by Partial Abstraction

Based on Theorem 1, we propose the following proof methodology outlined in Fig. 1.

Step 1 requires that S is guaranteed to eventually remain in S-states. Step 2 requires that the abstraction of the S's justice requirements is a subset of S_a's justice requirements. Note that this does not imply that every J-state of S maps to a J-state of S_a, but rather that if all S's justice requirements are met then so are all of S_a's requirements. Step 3 requires each S transition among S-states α-maps into a S_a transition. Since the partial abstraction may not be defined for some of S's states, Step 4 requires that every $\alpha(S)$ state is S_a-reachable. Finally, Step 5 requires that the desired property is valid over S_a.

Note that the S1–S4 may be mechanically verified. The only obviously manual step in the proof rule is the identification of S and the construction of α. In fact, this is just a case of fair simulations [10] for a restricted set of states. As to Step 5, if S_a is finite-state, or possibly in some other cases, it may be possible to verify the condition. In the example we outline next, when applying the proof rule, S_a is a finite (and small) system and we can model check any temporal property on it.

3 Modelling Mobility

In this section we present an abstraction of the protocol which allows us to prove its main properties. This can be used as a reference specification for many lower level protocols that implement it. The model is parametric in the number of routers, but (without loss of generality, we believe) we focus on the possible behaviours given just one MN to which a message is addressed.

3.1 IPv6 Mobility Basics

IPv6 support for mobility is based on a proxy architecture, where a mobile node B is associated with

– its *identifying* IP address n_B;
– its home router, denoted H_B, which never changes;

– its current location, denoted h_B, which may change over time. At any point in time, B is "hosted by" at most one router.

In a stable state of the network, a sender sends a message to a mobile node B by either

1. tunnelling it to B's home router H_B (B's default location); (a) if B is at home ($h_B = H_B$), the message will be delivered to B. (b) if B is away ($h_B \neq H_B$), H_B tunnels it to h_B, which H_B presumably knows.
2. alternatively, if the sender knows h_B, it may tunnel the message to h_B.

However, when B moves, we cannot assume that the new h_B will be known to nodes wishing to communicate with it, in particular to H_B. The IPv6 mobility protocol achieves correct forwarding of messages with a small number of *control messages* that eventually lead to (re)establishing correct forwarding tables. We focus here on the effects that the control messages have on the forwarding tables.

Let B be a mobile node. We assume that each node i has a table indicating how to forward each message according to its addressee. For simplicity, since we focus only on one node (B), we assume that $nextB[i]$ is i's routing information for B, i.e., when i receives a message intended for B, if $i \neq h_B$, then i sends the message to $nextB[i]$. Initially, for every node i, $nextB[i] = H_B$. Moreover, at any time, if nodes $i, j \neq H_B, h_B$ and $nextB[i] = j$, $nextB[i]$ can be reset to H_B. The only possible other $nextB[i]$ changes are triggered by B's moves, with the associated updates summarised in Fig. 2. These changes are *not synchronous – they can happen at any time and in any order*. In fact, if B moves fast enough, some of the changes may never take place. Allowing such partial changes in the forwarding table correctly captures the mechanism used in the IPv6 protocol where mobile nodes ask to be registered at the foreign hosts, requests that may time out before the mobile node seeks another host.

B **Move**	**Updates**
H_B to $j \neq H_B$	$nextB[H_B] = j$,
	$nextB[i] = \{H_B \text{ or } j\}$ (For all $i \neq H_B$)
$j \neq H_B$ to H_B	$nextB[i] = H_B$ (for all i)
j_1 to $j_2, j_1, j_2 \neq H_B$	$nextB[H_B] = j_2$,
	$nextB[i] = \{H_B \text{ or } j_2\}$ (For all $i \neq H_B$)

Fig. 2. $nextB$ updating on moves

The main property of IPv6 is that messages get correctly forwarded, hence we need to model messages and their handling. We choose not to focus on the precise modelling of messages and their traversal of the network. For a message with addressee B, we record the node where the message resides. (We also assume, for simplicity, that all messages are intended for B, although we can easily clutter the model and allow multiple messages to multiple recipients. However, the single message single recipient case is simpler and extremely easy to generalise.) Assume that some message was generated and addressed to B. We let msg denote the current location of the message. Consequently, our goal is to verify that $\Diamond\, msg = h_B$

Since B is mobile, we cannot assume that the node generating the message has its $nextB$ set to h_B, or even to H_B (or that $nextB[H_B] = h_B$. Moreover, if B keeps changing hosts, it is possible that the changes happen frequently enough so that the forwarding tables cannot keep up with it. We can thus only expect the message to be delivered (reach h_B) if B stays put at some location long enough so that all updates to the tables can take place. In LTL, this can be expressed by

$$\exists i.\, \Box (h_B = i) \;\longrightarrow\; \Diamond (msg = h_B)$$

As in all liveness properties, this property can only be met under certain fairness assumptions. We formulate those below, when we describe how the system can be modelled.

3.2   The System

The system corresponding to the protocol above can be expressed as an asynchronous composition

$$Move||Node_0||\ldots||Node_N||Messenger||M_0||\ldots||M_N$$

where:

- *Move* controls B moves in the network;
- 0 denotes H_B;
- each $Node_i$ ($i \in [0..N]$) is the process at the ith node to update its routing table for B;
- *Messenger* is the process that generates a message (once) at some nondeterministically selected node; and
- each M_i is the process that forwards or consumes the message when it reaches node i.

The variables in the system are:

1. $h_B \in [0..N]$ that denotes B's current host; It is set by the process *Move* and can be read by any of the processes;
2. $msg \in [0..N]$ that denotes the current location of message;
3. $status \in \{never, transit, delivered\}$ that denotes whether a message is ever generated, is in transit, or is delivered. The process *Messenger* can set it to *transit* if its status is *never*, and consequently each process M_i can forward the message to $nextB[i]$ if it is at node $i \neq h_B$, or set *status* to *delivered* if it is at node $i = h_B$;
4. *stay_long* is a boolean that is non-deterministically set (once) by process *Move* and is read by no other process — its only purpose is to indicate B remains at some node "long enough";

5. *lastB* is an array that stores the last location at which a node "saw" B. That is, $lastB[i] = j$ indicates that when node i was last scheduled, B was in j. For every i, $lastB[i]$ is read/written by $Node_i$;
6. *nextB* is the routing table; $nextB[i]$ is written by $Node_i$ and read by *Messenger*.

Initially $h_B = 0$ indicating B is at home, *status* = *never* indicating that the message wasn't sent, *stay_long* = False indicating the B hasn't yet settled, and all the *nextB* pointers lead to home (0).

Process Move: The process may update either h_B (nondeterministically) or *stay_long* (to True) if $\neg stay\_long$. It can be described by:

Process *Move* ::
$$\left[\begin{array}{l} \textbf{loop forever do} \\ \left[\begin{array}{ll} \textbf{if } \neg stay\_long \textbf{ then } & h_B := \{0, 1, \ldots, N\} \\ \textbf{if } \neg stay\_long \textbf{ then } & stay\_long := \{\mathsf{True}, \mathsf{False}\} \end{array} \right] \end{array} \right]$$

where *stay_long* := {True, False} denotes a non-deterministic assignment of *stay_long*. The justice property associated with this process is *stay_long* = True, indicating that eventually *stay_long* has to be set to True.

Process $Node_i$: The code for $Node_i$ is described in Fig. 3. The assignment $nextB := \{0, h_B\}$ denotes a non-deterministic choice between 0 which denotes B's permanent home and the variable h_B which denotes B's current host. The process loops forever and when it realises that B has moved since its last update, assigns *nextB* accordingly. The justice condition is that the module is scheduled infinitely many times. This can be achieved, e.g., by adding a boolean variable that flips whenever the module is scheduled, and to require that it infinitely many times equals 1 and infinitely many times equals 0.

Process $Node_i(h_B, nextB[i])$ ::
    local *lastB* **natural in** $[0..N]$ **init** 0
    loop forever do
$$\left[\begin{array}{l} \textbf{if } h_B \neq lastB \textbf{ then} \\ \quad \textbf{if } i = 0 \textbf{ then } nextB[i] := h_B \textbf{ else } nextB := \{0, h_B\} \\ \quad lastB := h_B \end{array} \right]$$

Fig. 3. A Node Process to update Forwarding Table

Process Messenger: This process generates a message if none was generated. It does so by assigning *status* to *transit* and non-deterministically choosing a location for the message in $[0..N]$. This process can be described by:

Process Messenger ::
    loop forever do
$$\left[\begin{array}{l} \textbf{if } status := never \textbf{ then} \\ \quad status := \{never, transit\} \\ \quad \textbf{if } status := transit \textbf{ then } msg := \{0, \ldots, N\} \end{array} \right]$$

There is no justice condition associated with this process.

Process M_i: This process forwards a transiting message at node i to B if i is B's host, and then it sets *status* to *delivered*, or it forwards the message to node *nextB* and leaves *status* intact. The process can be described by:

Process M_i ::
  loop forever do
$$\left[\begin{array}{l} \textbf{if } \; status := transit \; \wedge \; msg = i \; \textbf{then} \\ \quad \textbf{if } \; h_B = i \; \textbf{then } status := delivered \\ \quad \textbf{else } \; msg := nextB[i] \end{array} \right]$$

The justice property here is that the module is scheduled infinitely many times.

3.3   Properties

Usually one proves several properties on IPv6: that messages are present at their senders and at prior hosts of B (including its home); that the *nextB* pointers don't form any cycles; and more. From these properties one establishes the main property we are interested in, namely

$$(status = transit \; \wedge \; stay\_long) \Longrightarrow (status = delivered)$$

(in LTL, $p \Longrightarrow q$ abbreviates $\square (p \rightarrow \Diamond q)$, i.e., that it is always the case that a p is eventually followed by a q.) This property states that if a message is in transit while B stays put at one host, then the message will be delivered.

In all previous work on the correctness of IP, a lot of effort was invested in showing the absence of forwarding cycles[2]. However, the correctness of IPv6 relies on a weaker property. While model-checking, we discovered that it is in fact possible for cycles to be formed in the forwarding tables, as is illustrated by the following scenario.

From the initial state, node B moves to node 1. This is first observed by node 2 (in IPv6 that could be because B sends node 2 a message before completing its registration at node 1) and *nextB*[2] is set to 1 while all the other *nextB* pointers still lead to 0. At this point the node migrates to 2, and the first to observe this change is node 1 that sets *nextB*[1] = 2. Until further changes, this creates a forwarding cycle between nodes 1 and 2. As we show in the next section, if B remains long enough at node 2 then eventually it will be registered there and the cycle will be broken. Of course, if B fails to register at node 2, it will move on to another host, which may create another cycle, but then again, such a cycle will be broken once B finds an "accommodating" host.

However, *message deliverability still holds if such cycles are eventually broken.* For this to occur, all that is required is that the home router eventually has a pointer to B's current location, and that by default other nodes revert their tables to point to B's home router if they do not know B's current location.

---

[2] In fact, some of the published works incorrectly claim that messages do not traverse cycles.

Of course, for efficiency, implementations may choose to enforce stronger properties such as avoiding forwarding cycle formation to prevent extra traffic and to ensure timely delivery, or carefully time-stamping binding caches to better manage resources. However, as with all candidate optimising transformations, there is a chance of inadvertently breaking this essential resilience property by not buffering messages long enough or not managing the caches correctly.

4   Formal Verification of the System

We formally verify the protocol using notions of simulation and model checking. The system is a prime candidate for parameterized verification.

The $nextB$ array poses some difficulty for "traditional" parameterized model checking, since it can contain pointer chains in the forwarding graph, which, as noted earlier, may contain cycles. Such structures are notoriously difficult for parameterised systems [3–5]. However, it is not hard to establish that once $stay\_long$ is set, then eventually all $nextB$ links lead to 0 or to h_B. Thus, the $nextB$ array entries don't form a chain, and in fact there can point to only these two nodes (0 and h_B) once $stay\_long$ is set.

We first establish the existence of the stable forwarding tables and then present two different proof techniques for establishing the required correctness of the message delivery property. One technique is based on the "method of invisible invariants" (see [2,15,17]) adapted to bounded liveness ([8]). The other technique (manually) establishes the existence of a small model using simulation and then directly model checks the system on that small model.

4.1   Proving Eventual Stable Routing

We show that once $stay\_long$ is set (indicating that B stays put in h_B), eventually all $nextB$ pointers stabilise, leading either to its permanent host h_B or to its home 0. Moreover, $nextB[0]$ will always lead to h_B, and $nextB[h_B]$ will lead to itself.

Lemma 1.

$$\Box(stay\_long \Longrightarrow \exists v \in [0..N].\forall i \in [0..N].\exists i_j \in \{0, v\}.$$
$$\Box(h_B = v \ \land \ nextB[v] = v \ \land \ nextB[i] = i_j)$$

Proof. Let σ be a computation, and assume $\sigma \models stay\_long$. The only module that can change the value of h_B is *Move*. However, no changes to h_B are enabled once $stay\_long = \mathsf{True}$. It follows that for some $v \in [0..N]$, $\sigma \models \Box(h_B = v)$.

Let i be a node in $[0..N]$. The only module that updates $nextB[i]$ is $Node_i$. From $Node_i$'s fairness guarantee it is scheduled at least twice in σ, and since $\sigma \models \Box(h_B = v)$, it follows that after the first scheduling of $Node_i$ $lastB[i] = v$, and remains so. Consequently, after $Node_i$ is scheduled at most twice in σ, $nextB[i] \in \{0, v\}$ and remains so.

Furthermore, it follows from the code of $Node_0$ that after $Node_0$ and $Node_v$ are scheduled at most twice, $nextB[0] = nextB[v] = v$ and remain so.

The fairness assumptions on module *Move* imply that every fair computation satisfies $\Diamond$ *stay_long*. We can thus conclude:

Lemma 2. *Let* stable *be the state assertion:*

$$stay\_long \;\land\; status \neq never \;\land\; \exists v \in [0..N].h_B = nextB[0] = nextB[v] = v$$
$$\land \;\; \forall i \in [0..N].\exists i_j \in \{0, v\}.nextB[i] = i_j$$

describing the stable states as in Lemma 1. Then we have:

$$\Diamond \,\square\; stable$$

4.2   Method I: From Stability to Safety

In the following we transform the system into a new one that is initialised according to the stable part of a computation of the original system and convert the original liveness property into a bounded liveness property (as per [8]). We can then verify the bounded liveness property on the small ($N = 2$) instantiation, and conclude that the original system satisfies the original liveness property. See [8] for details on soundness.

Fix a computation σ. We now construct a new system which is similar to the original one, only it is initialised to start with the stable prefix. That is, the new system satisfies $\square$ *stable*.

Since in the new system moves of B as well as updates are disabled, we ignore the *stay_long* variable as well as the modules *Move* and the *Node$_i$*'s (and, consequently, the *lastB* array), and initialise the system as follows:

1. *stay_long* is initialised to True;
2. h_B is initialised to $\sigma[h_B]$;
3. for every i, $nextB[i]$ is initialised to $\sigma[nextB[i]]$;

We can go further and replace the internal **if** in process M_i with the statement:

$$\left[\begin{array}{l} \textbf{if } status{:=}transit \;\land\; msg = i \textbf{ then} \\ \quad \textbf{if } h_B = i \textbf{ then } status := delivered \\ \quad \textbf{elseif } nextB[i] = 0 \textbf{ then } msg{:=}0 \textbf{ else } msg := h_B \end{array}\right]$$

The advantage of reformulating the above statement is that the new version avoids mention of an $[0..N] \mapsto [0..N]$ array and explicitly refers to a 2-valued array. In the terminology of [9], this allows defining *nextB* as a variable of type **index** $\mapsto$ **data** rather than as one of type **index** $\mapsto$ **index**.

Next, we observe that every message can be delivered now within at most two hops: possibly one to home, and then to h_B. We can thus combine all the M_i modules together, and, once a message is initiated (*transit* is set), initiate a counter to 2, and decrease it whenever the message reaches a new location (the fairness properties on the M_i's guarantee that the message will be routed infinitely many times if not delivered). All we have to verify now is that in the new system it is always the case that when the (message) counter reaches 0 the message is delivered.

Following the *small model theorem* used in invisible invariants, it suffices to model check it for $N = 2$. The resulting TLV code is in Fig. 4, and for which we verified $\Box((counter = 0) \rightarrow msg = h_B)$.

```
MODULE main
VAR
    h_B:      0..2;
    msg:      0..3;   -- msg=3 denotes message was not yet sent
    step:     0..2;
    counter:  0..2;
    nextB : array 0..3 of 0..2; -- nextB[3] is used to avoid
                                -- syntax error at line -1
    BGN: process BGN(h_B, nextB, msg, step);
    MSG: process Msg(msg, h_B, nextB, counter);
ASSIGN
    init(step)    := 0;
    init(counter) := 2;
    init(msg)     := 3;

MODULE BGN(h_B,nextB, msg, step)
ASSIGN
    next(B)        := (step=0 ? {0,1,2} : h_B);
    next(nextB[0]) := h_B;
    next(nextB[B]) := h_B;
    next(nextB[1]) := (step = 1 & h_B != 1 ? {0,h_B}    : nextB[1]);
    next(nextB[2]) := (step = 1 & h_B != 2 ? {0,h_B}    : nextB[2]);
    next(msg)      := (step = 1          ? {0,1,2} : msg);
    next(step)     := (step < 2          ? step + 1 : step);

MODULE Msg(msg, h_B, nextB, counter)
ASSIGN
    next(msg)     := (msg!= h_B & msg < 3   ? nextB[msg]  : msg);
    next(counter) := (msg < 3 & counter > 0 ? counter - 1 : counter);
```

Fig. 4. A TLV code to test for bounded liveness

4.3   Method II

We apply the method of Subsect. method taking S_N to be the system instantiated on $N > 2$ nodes and S_2 to be the system instantiated on 2 nodes. Let S be the *stable* states of S's system, i.e., $S = \Sigma_N \cap stable$. For every $s \in S$, we define a state $\alpha(s) \in \Sigma_2$ as follows. We use v to denote S_N variable $(s[v])$, and v' to denote S_2 variable (i.e., $\alpha(s)[v]$).

The constant range variables, *stay_long* and *status*, remain the same in $\alpha(s)$. We next define h'_B, msg', and $nextB'$, and let $lastB' = nextB'$. The assignment of the other $\alpha(s)$ values is summarised in the following table, in which for each row, we assume that none of the conditions in the first column of the earlier rows hold:

Condition	h'_B	msg'	$(nextB[0])'$	$(nextB[1])'$	$(nextB[2])'$
$h_B = msg = 0$	0	0	0	0	0
$h_B = 0 \neq msg$	0	1	0	0	0
$msg = h_B$	1	1	1	1	1
$nextB[msg] = 0$	1	2	1	1	0
$(nextB[msg] \neq 0)$	1	2	1	1	1

We next establish S2–S5 of the proof rule. S2 is obvious since $\mathcal{J}_N \supseteq \mathcal{J}_2$. S3 is also trivial, since it is easy to (manually or automatically) verify that for every $s_1, s_2 \in S$, if $(s_1, s_2) \in \rho_N$ then $(\alpha(s_1), \alpha(s_2)) \in \rho_2$. As for S4, there are 10 cases here (depending on *status*); for each case, let p be the assertion that the conditions of the case hold, and model check $\Box \neg p$ on $\mathcal{S}_2$. When all checks fail, it follows that every state in $\alpha(S)$ is $\mathcal{S}_2$-reachable. Similarly, S5 is model-checked directly on $\mathcal{S}_2$.

In fact, S3–S5 can be (and were) model checked in TLV.

5   Conclusions

The verification described in this paper follows the general lines of parameterised verification. Such verification is usually notoriously hard: with a few exceptions (e.g., [8,9]), they all deal with only safety properties. The system and correctness property studied here is not amenable to such methods since it encompasses a data structure that rules out most of these methods, and all those that handle liveness directly.

However, our system enjoys a pleasant property which we exploit: it is guaranteed to eventually reach, and remain in, a state where the unwieldy data structures are no more necessary. We then propose a proof rule that focuses on these "good" states, those whose data structures are equivalent to others that are (more) amenable for verification. The system is still parameterised, and so we resort to parameterised techniques, mainly, the reduction to a finite (and small) instantiation on which we can model check the required property.

Thus, faced with a parameterised system with non-trivial data structures and a liveness property, we can reduce the problem to that of model checking a small system with simple data structures without pointer chains. While parts of the method resemble the small model theorem of the method of invisible invariants, this method is fundamentally different: the small model theorem of invisible invariants is used to generate invariants on small instantiations, while here we verify the property directly on the small instantiation. Moreover, both the original and the small system allow for prefixes of computations that do not correspond to one another. Also, while parts of the method are inspired by fair simulation (similar to [10]), it is not such since we do not (and cannot) require simulation between all states, just between states in the "good" suffix.

Thus, we have a new simulation-based proof methodology that combines model checking and process algebraic ideas, and allows showing one system simulates another at the limit, for which we can derive some (infinitary) properties. While the IPv6 protocol provides a useful instance of this technique of directly model-checking a system that simulates an "eventually stable" system, we conjecture that this technique may be applicable to other systems.

Our work also results in some interesting observations about Mobile IPv6 from which protocol designers may benefit. The most important one is that the basic design of mobile IP, that of ensuring the home agent (HA) of a mobile node (MN) eventually learns its current location, provides the protocol a very high degree of resilience and efficiency. The formation of temporary forwarding cycles, usually viewed as a bug, may not cause incorrect behavior provided these cycles are eventually broken. For the HA to eventually know the location of a MN requires reliable and authenticated communication of a binding update between the MN (or a FA on its behalf) and the HA, and allowing the HA and corresponding nodes ignore out-of-date messages. This can be achieved by ordering these control messages using sequence numbers, rather than more complicated methods using time-stamping of the messages. The "timing out" of bindings and binding updates, and defaulting to routing via the home router are an important factor in the correctness of the protocol. This feature ensures that "in the limit", messages from any correspondent node will reach the HA, whence they can be delivered (so, delivery takes at most 2 hops). Thus, by freezing mobility, the behavior of the system very closely resembles IP without mobility. Efficiency considerations may suggest that forwarding cycles should be avoided, and obsolete cache entries retired, but sometimes it may be important to buffer messages to nodes in motion long enough that they can be delivered when they settle. It is *not* a good idea for a HA to set up a binding for a MN *prior to* its registering at a foreign network (in anticipation), since there is no guarantee that the MN will actually settle there. Nor is it a good idea for correspondent nodes to infer the location of a MN from header information in a data message, unless its header indicates it is also a binding update that is reliably communicated and authenticated, both for correctness and also for security reasons (replay attacks). Inferring the location of a MN from a data message will also require more complex recording of time-stamps of each data message received from each correspondent node, so that out-of-order messages do not cause incorrect updates to the caches. Finally, checking the integrity and authenticity of binding updates is essential.

References

1. Amadio, R.M., Prasad, S.: Modelling IP mobility. Formal Methods Syst. Design **17**(1), 61–99 (2000)
2. Arons, T., Pnueli, A., Ruah, S., Xu, J., Zuck, L.D.: Parameterized verification with automatically computed inductive assertions. In: Berry, G., Comon, H., Finkel, A. (eds.) CAV 2001. LNCS, vol. 2102, p. 221. Springer, Heidelberg (2001)
3. Balaban, I., Pnueli, A., Sa'ar, Y., Zuck, L.D.: Verification of multi-linked heaps. J. Comput. Syst. Sci. **78**(3), 853–876 (2012)
4. Balaban, I., Pnueli, A., Zuck, L.D.: Invisible safety of distributed protocols. In: Bugliesi, M., Preneel, B., Sassone, V., Wegener, I. (eds.) ICALP 2006. LNCS, vol. 4052, pp. 528–539. Springer, Heidelberg (2006)
5. Balaban, I., Pnueli, A., Zuck, L.D.: Shape analysis of single-parent heaps. In: Cook, B., Podelski, A. (eds.) VMCAI 2007. LNCS, vol. 4349, pp. 91–105. Springer, Heidelberg (2007)
6. Dang, Z., Kemmerer, R.A.: Using the ASTRAL model checker to analyze mobile IP. In: Proceedings of the 1999 International Conference on Software Engineering, ICSE 1999, Los Angeles, 16–22 May 1999, pp. 132–142 (1999)

7. Emerson, E.A., Kahlon, V.: Reducing model checking of the many to the few. In: Proceedings Automated Deduction - CADE-17, 17th International Conference on Automated Deduction, Pittsburgh, 17–20 June 2000, pp. 236–254 (2000)
8. Fang, Y., McMillan, K.L., Pnueli, A., Zuck, L.D.: Liveness by invisible invariants. In: Najm, E., Pradat-Peyre, J.-F., Donzeau-Gouge, V.V. (eds.) FORTE 2006. LNCS, vol. 4229, pp. 356–371. Springer, Heidelberg (2006)
9. Fang, Y., Piterman, N., Pnueli, A., Zuck, L.D.: Liveness with invisible ranking. STTT 8(3), 261–279 (2006)
10. Henzinger, T.A., Kupferman, O., Rajamani, S.K.: Fair simulation. Inf. Comput. 173(1), 64–81 (2002)
11. Jackson, D., Ng, Y.-C., Wing, J.M.: A nitpick analysis of mobile IPv6. Formal Aspects Comput. 11(6), 591–615 (1999)
12. Kesten, Y., Pnueli, A.: Verification by augmented finitary abstraction. Inf. Comput. 163(1), 203–243 (2000)
13. McCann, P.J., Roman, G.-C.: Modeling mobile IP in mobile unity. ACM Trans. Softw. Eng. Methodol. 8(2), 115–146 (1999)
14. Perkins, C., Johnson, D., Arkko, J.: Mobility Support in IPv6. RFC 6275 (Proposed Standard), July 2011
15. Pnueli, A., Ruah, S., Zuck, L.D.: Automatic deductive verification with invisible invariants. In: Margaria, T., Yi, W. (eds.) TACAS 2001. LNCS, vol. 2031, p. 82. Springer, Heidelberg (2001)
16. Rodrigues, C.L., Guerra, F.V., de Figueiredo, J.C.A., Guerrero, D.D.S., Morais, T.S.: Modeling and verification of mobility issues using object-oriented petri nets. In: Proceedings of 3rd International Information and Telecommunication Technologies Symposium (I2TS2004) (2004)
17. Zuck, L.D., Pnueli, A.: Model checking and abstraction to the aid of parameterized systems (a survey). Comput. Lang. Syst. Struct. 30(3–4), 139–169 (2004)

A New Refinement Strategy for CEGAR-Based Industrial Model Checking

Martin Leucker[1], Grigory Markin[1(✉)], and Martin R. Neuhäußer[2]

[1] University of Lübeck, Lübeck, Germany
{leucker,markin}@isp.uni-luebeck.de
[2] Siemens AG, Nuremberg, Germany
martin.neuhaeusser@siemens.com

Abstract. This paper presents a novel refinement strategy in the setting of counterexample-guided abstraction refinement (CEGAR)-based model checking. More specifically, the approach shown builds on lazy abstraction in the context of predicate abstraction. While the concept of interpolants is typically used for refinement, this paper employs unsatisfiability cores together with weakest preconditions. The new refinement technique is especially applicable in the setting where interpolants are hard to compute, such as for McCarthy's theory of arrays or for the theory of fixed-width bit vectors. It is implemented within a model-checking tool developed for the verification of industrial-critical systems and outperforms current refinement strategies on several examples.

1 Introduction

Today's industrial systems are increasingly controlled by software. When these systems are interconnected and control each other, they often form so-called cyber-physical systems acting in our physical environment. For such systems, verification is of major interest as safety and security concerns abound.

In this paper, we are concerned with the verification of industrial software by means of model checking [1]. To this end, we have developed a model checking tool for verifying code for programmable logical controllers (PLC code), which takes a PLC program as well as a reachability property characterizing error states as input and checks whether an error state can be reached from an initial state of our program. For testing and comparison, our model checker also accepts a subset of C programs as input.

As typically no single model checking approach acts as a silver bullet, our model checker comes with different algorithms. In [2], the last author reports about a technique following the idea of IC3 [3]. The current paper, however, describes an approach following the counterexample-guided abstraction refinement (CEGAR) paradigm [4]. Within CEGAR, an abstraction for the system to verify is continuously checked with respect to a correctness property. When the a bstract system satisfies the correctness property, the underlying system is correct as well, while in the case of a counterexample this might be spurious. If so, the counterexample is used to refine the abstract system and the CEGAR

© Springer International Publishing Switzerland 2015
N. Piterman (Ed.): HVC 2015, LNCS 9434, pp. 155–170, 2015.
DOI: 10.1007/978-3-319-26287-1_10

loop is continued. Eventually, the underlying system is either verified as correct or a non-spurious counterexample is found.

Lazy abstraction [5] builds on this scheme, yet refines the abstraction *on demand at locations* for which the current abstraction yields a spurious counterexample. In this way, the overall performance of the model checking process is improved. In [5], the concept of lazy abstraction is introduced in a general setting. In our model checker, we use predicate abstraction [6] as abstract domain. All (symbolic) computations are considered with respect to a given first-order theory, and we use the concept of strongest postconditions as well as that of weakest preconditions to give (partial) semantics to operations, in a way that is suitable for our approach. We assume the availability of a corresponding SMT solver allowing to check formulas in the given theory for satisfiability. In fact, our tool runs with both Microsoft Z3 [7] as well as MathSat [8] as back-end and the theory of fixed-width bit vectors.

One of the most interesting questions when realizing a lazy abstraction approach with predicate abstraction is how to refine the set of predicates when a (non-feasible) counterexample is found. In the original work by Henzinger [5], (negations of) weakest preconditions were used as one example to rule out a counterexample. Another typical approach is to use *interpolants* [9–11].

In this paper, we make use of the intermediate results available from the underlying SMT solver. Whenever a program path is witnessed as spurious, the encoding of the path as an SMT formula is unsatisfiable. We take a subset of the clauses of the formula that is already unsatisfiable. Such a subformula is also called an *unsatisfiability core*, or unsat core, for short. Actually, we take a sequence of unsat cores obtained via the infeasible program path and derive new predicates in this way, forming a new operator called *UCB-refinement operator*. Our approach can, in a way, be understood as an improvement of the original weakest precondition-based approach.

[12–14] also make use of unsat cores in the context of verification, yet none of the approaches uses unsat core-based techniques to improve lazy abstraction.

We have proven our approach as correct, i.e. that the underlying lazy abstraction algorithm always terminates with a correct answer when the underlying theory is bounded. Moreover, we have implemented our model checker and evaluated the performance of our UCB-refinement operator relative to the interpolation-based refinement strategy. Additionally, we evaluated the performance of the Lazy Abstraction algorithm in combination with UCB-predicates and interpolants relative to an implementation of the IC3 model-checking algorithm recently presented in [2]. It turns out that our UCB-refinement strategy is often comparable to the interpolation-based one and in a number of cases, it allows to solve the verification problems which could not be solved by using the interpolation-based approach. The Lazy Abstraction algorithm in combination with UCB-refinement operator typically outperforms the IC3 algorithm and can solve more problems than the latter. As such, the UCB refinement operator is valuable as more verification problems can be solved than before. More importantly, it allows the easy realization of the CEGAR approach for theories and

SMT solvers not supporting interpolants. However, using other theories in our model checker than fixed-width bit vectors is future work.

2   Preliminaries

In this section, we give the gist of the standard concepts of logical theories. For details, we refer the reader to [15].

Throughout this paper let V be a countable set of variables defined over a non-empty domain. The set of all assignments of elements to variables of the underlying domain forms the set of all *data states*, in the following denoted by S. In our setting the set of variables V comes with an associated first-order *theory* T, i.e., a set of closed first-order formulas. We denote by $T(V)$ the set of formulas that may contain *free* variables from V. We denote by $\top$ and $\bot$ the logical values *true* and *false* respectively. When concerned with satisfiability, we consider such variables as implicitly existentially quantified.

For the rest of this paper, we assume the theory T to be decidable, in practice by means of an SMT solver. We use the standard definition of *conjunctive normal form* (CNF) and we silently assume that every formula is in conjunctive normal form. We denote the set of all clauses of a CNF formula φ as $cl(\varphi)$ and use formulas in CNF and sets of clauses interchangeably. An *unsatisfiable core* of an unsatisfiable CNF formula φ is a non-empty subset of clauses of φ that is unsatisfiable. A *minimal unsatisfiable core* is an unsatisfiability core such that removing any one of its elements makes the remaining set of clauses satisfiable. The set of all unsatisfiability cores of φ is denoted by $UC(\varphi)$.

An *ascending chain* is a sequence of formulas $\varphi_1, \ldots$ such that for all $0 \leq i < j$, $\varphi_j \not\Rightarrow \varphi_i$. The ascending chain is called *finite*, if the sequence is finite. A theory T is called *bounded* if all ascending chains from T are finite.

This paper addresses the verification of imperative programs, ranging over program locations from a set L and performing operations from some given set *Ops*. For the sake of generality, we assume the *concrete semantics* of an operation $op \in Ops$ to be given by its *strongest postcondition* [16] $sp(\varphi, op) \in T(V)$ for a given precondition $\varphi \in T(V)$. In practice, we assume the availability of an *sp*-operator that computes for a given precondition φ, denoting a set of current states, the set of successor states. We denote by $wp(\varphi, op)$ the *weakest liberal precondition* [16,17] of φ with respect to op, representing the largest set of states from which φ is reachable by executing op, if it terminates. Similarly, we assume the existence of a *wp*-operator computing the set of predecessor states for a given φ. More specifically we also assume that corresponding sets of successor and predecessor states can be expressed by formulas of $T(V)$. See [16–18] for details on weakest preconditions and [9,19,20] for the use of strongest post- and weakest preconditions in model checking.

Throughout this paper, we follow [11] and use the concept of *control flow automata* (CFA) for encoding imperative programs. Hereby, a CFA A is a directed connected graph where the set of vertices L represents the program locations and the set of edges $E \subseteq L \times Ops \times L$ models the execution of operations from the set *Ops* (see Fig. 1a for an example).

We focus on the verification of *reachability properties* of programs. Hence, we assume a program to be given by its control flow automaton, together with an initial location and an error location. More precisely, a $\mathcal{T}$-*program* is tuple $\mathcal{P} = (V, A, l_I, l_e)$, where assignments of the variables V form the set of data states S, $A = (L, E)$ is a CFA that models the control flow of the program and $l_I, l_e \in L$ model the initial and the error locations, respectively.

A set of data states is called a *data region* and we restrict to data regions that can be encoded by a formula $\varphi \in \mathcal{T}(V)$ as a set of all data states $s \in S$ that entail φ. A *concrete state* of a program is a pair (l, s), where $l \in L$ is a program location and $s \in S$ is a data state. A *region* (l, φ) is a set of concrete states $\{(l, s) \mid s \in S\}$ such that $s \models \varphi$.

A *program path* π is a sequence of program operations $\pi = l_0 \xrightarrow{op_1} l_1 \xrightarrow{op_2} \cdots \xrightarrow{op_n} l_n$, where $l_i \in L$, $i \in \{0, \ldots, n\}$ and $op_i \in Ops$, $i \in [n]$, where $[n]$ is a shorthand for $\{1, \ldots, n\}$. The *concrete semantics for a program path* π is defined as $sp(\varphi, \pi) = sp(sp_{n-1}, op_n)$ where $sp_i = sp(sp_{i-1}, op_i)$ and $sp_0 = \varphi$. A program path π is *feasible* when starting from a data region φ if $sp(\varphi, \pi)$ is satisfiable, otherwise it is *infeasible*. For brevity, we sometimes only talk of a (in)feasible program path when the starting region is clear from the context.

Throughout the paper, let $\{\top, \bot\} \subseteq P \subseteq \mathcal{T}(V)$ be a finite set of predicates. A conjunction over the set of predicates P, denoted by $\bigwedge P$, is the conjunction of all predicates from P. The conjunction over an empty set $\bigwedge \emptyset$ is identified by $\top$. The *Cartesian abstraction* [21] of a formula $\varphi \in \mathcal{T}(V)$ with respect to P, denoted by φ^P, is the conjunction of all predicates from P that are (individually) implied by φ, i.e. $\varphi^P = \bigwedge\{p \mid p \in P, \varphi \rightarrow p\}$. We also denote by $C(P)$ a conjunction of predicates that arises from an element of the power set of P. An *abstract state* is a region (l, φ^P) computed by the Cartesian abstraction for a region (l, φ) with respect to a set of predicates P.

We define the *abstract semantics* of an operation $op \in Ops$ by the *abstract strongest postoperator* sp^P defined as $sp^P(\varphi, op) = (sp(\varphi, op))^P$. Similar to previously, we extend the abstract semantics to program paths by $sp^P(\varphi, \pi) = sp^P(sp^P_{n-1}, op_n)$ where $sp^P_i = sp^P(sp^P_{i-1}, op_i)$ and $sp^P_0 = \varphi$.

In our work we also use the concept of an *abstract reachability tree* (ART) to encode abstract models of programs. An ART is a rooted directed tree whose nodes are labeled by triples (l, φ, P) where the set of concrete states (l, φ) represents an abstract state and the set of predicates P is the local *precision*. For each ART node (l, φ, P), the child nodes are labeled with the abstraction precision P' and successor abstract nodes, computed according to the abstract strongest postoperator sp^P. A node $n = (l, \varphi, P)$ is called *covered* if there is a node $n' = (l, \varphi', P')$ such that $\varphi \Rightarrow \varphi'$. An ART tree is called *complete* if every leaf node is either covered or all possible abstract successor states are present in the ART as children of the node. In simple words, an ART is the unwinding of the CFA. If it is complete, the ART comprises a symbolic representation of all reachable states of the underlying program.

Algorithm 1. LAZYABSTRACTION($\mathcal{P}, \Phi$)

Require: A program $\mathcal{P} = (V, A, l_I, l_e)$ with a CFA $A = (L, E)$ and a refinement
   operator $\Phi : \mathcal{T}(V) \times E^+ \rightarrow 2^{\mathcal{T}(V)}$.
1: create an ART with a root node $n_0 = (l_0, \top, \{\top, \bot\})$
2: **while** there are unmarked nodes in ART **do**
3:     pick an unmarked node $n = (l, \varphi, P)$
4:     **if** $l = l_e$ **then**
5:         let $n' = (l', \varphi', P')$ be the oldest ancestor of n s.t.
              $n' \xrightarrow{\sigma} n$ and $wp(\top, \sigma) \wedge \varphi' \not\equiv \bot$
6:         **if** $l' = l_I$ **then**
7:             **return** "error trace" σ
8:         **else**
9:             let $n'' = (l'', \varphi'', P'')$ s.t. $(l'', op, l') \in E$
10:             let τ denote the time stamp of n''
11:             relabel n'' by $w = (l'', \varphi'', P'' \cup \Phi(\varphi'', op \cdot \sigma))$
12:             remove the sub-trees starting from n''
13:             **for all** covered leaf m that was marked after τ **do**
14:                 unmark m
15:     **else if** there exists $m = (l, \varphi', P')$ s.t. $\varphi \rightarrow \varphi'$ **then**
16:         mark m as *covered*
17:     **else**
18:         **for all** $l' \in L$ s.t. $(l, op, l') \in E$ **do**
19:             $\varphi' \leftarrow sp^P(\varphi, op)$
20:             **if** $\varphi' \not\models \bot$ **then**
21:                 add a child node $n' = (l', \varphi', P)$ to the ART
22:         mark n as *uncovered*
23: **return** ART

---

3   Lazy Abstraction

The traditional flow for CEGAR-based model checking [4] consists of the following steps: building an abstract model of the program using a chosen set of predicates; verification of the abstract model; checking the feasibility of the abstract counterexample, i.e. whether it can be executed in the original program; counterexample-driven refinement of the set of predicates. All steps are repeated until either no counterexample can be found in the abstract model, i.e. the original program is error-free, or an abstract counterexample is feasible, i.e. an error state is reachable from an initial state.

As the explicit construction of an abstract model and its verification are generally time-consuming operations, the *lazy abstraction* approach optimizes the CEGAR loop in that it continuously constructs an abstract model and checks whether an error state is reachable at the same time.

In our work, we consider the lazy abstraction algorithm (Algorithm 1), which is a slightly modified version of the one originally presented by Henzinger et al. in [5]. The algorithm constructs an ART which either is complete or contains a feasible abstract counter example. To this end, it starts by creating a new reachability tree containing one node: a root node corresponding to the initial node in the CFA. At any time, each node of the tree is either unmarked, i.e. not processed, or is marked as *covered* or *uncovered*. After the initialization step, the algorithm iteratively picks an unmarked node and checks whether it is labeled by an error location. If this is not the case, then the algorithm checks whether there is already another node that represents a superset of the data region represented by the current node. If so, it marks the node as covered, and, if not, it marks it as uncovered and adds its children into the tree.

If the picked node is labeled by an error location, then the algorithm checks whether this node is reachable from the initial node (in the concrete program). If the node is reachable, then an error trace is found and the algorithm terminates. Otherwise the algorithm searches backwards for the node, which abstracts concrete states from which an error state can be reached but which are unreachable from all concrete initial states. Such a node is also called a *pivot node* (n'' on line 9). In this refinement step (line 11) the algorithm uses a refinement operator, denoted by Φ, to increase the abstraction precision of the pivot node by adding further predicates. After that, the sub-tree rooted at the pivot node is discarded and all nodes that were covered after processing the pivot node are unmarked, so that it will (potentially) be reconstructed using the enriched set of predicates in later steps of the algorithm.

If an error trace is found or if the constructed ART is complete, i.e. all leaf nodes are covered, the algorithm terminates.

Our version of the algorithm is in fact a concretization of the more generic one given in [5]. Henzinger's algorithm operates on so-called *symbolic abstraction structures*, which comprise abstract domains and corresponding abstract operations (see [5] for details). These operations allow computation of abstract successor states, and predecessors of concrete data regions.

In our setting, we use predicate abstraction as abstract domain and the abstract strongest postoperator to compute abstract states. We use the weakest precondition operator to compute sets of concrete states that are reachable from a given region. As these operators and the abstract domain are built into the program, our algorithm only takes a program $\mathcal{P}$ and the refinement operator Φ as its input rather than a symbolic abstraction structure.[1]

In our version of the algorithm we also always remove the sub-tree rooted at the pivot node after the refinement step. The original algorithm uses an additional heuristic to determine whether the sub-tree can be kept. The heuristic does not affect the correctness but it may affect termination. And because, we

---

[1] Actually, a symbolic abstraction structure also contains an operator for computation of abstract states that can reach a given abstract state and an operator for computation of concrete states reachable from a given concrete state. These operators are required for a backward search, i.e. when the lazy abstraction algorithm constructs an ART starting from the error region and iteratively checks whether an initial region is reachable. In this paper we only consider lazy abstraction in combination with the forward search (Algorithm 1) and refer the reader to [5] for more details on the use of lazy abstraction in combination with backward search.

are interested in refinement techniques toward termination, we always discard the sub-tree rooted at a pivot node, to be on the safe side.

It was shown in [5] that the algorithm terminates with a correct result for finite-state systems, or, more generally, when (i) the language $\mathcal{T}(V)$ is bounded, i.e. does not contain infinite ascending chains, and (ii) the refinement step yields semantically equivalent data regions (see explanation below) as well as a superset of predicates, and (iii) the set of predicates returned in the refinement step is precise enough to rule out the path's suffix starting from the pivot node. The second constraint on the refinement step is needed for correctness. It means, that the region in node n'' (line 9), given by φ'', is not changed by the refinement step. This is clear in our setting, as the new node keeps φ'' (line 11) without any modification. Hence, correctness is immediate, regardless of which refinement operator is considered.[2] The first and last constraint entail termination of the algorithm.

The main objective of this paper is to introduce a new refinement operator. Hence, we concentrate in the next section on refinement methods and their properties toward termination of the algorithm LAZYABSTRACTION($\mathcal{P}, \Phi$) shown in Algorithm 1. More precisely, we introduce the notion of a progressive refinement operator and show the termination of the algorithm when applied with such an operator. We then introduce our concept of an unsatisfiability-core-based refinement operator and show that it is progressive and hence assure termination of the lazy abstraction algorithm.

4 Abstraction Refinement

When Algorithm 1 hits an error node, it checks whether the path from the initial node to the error node represents a valid counterexample, i.e. the path is feasible. If this is not the case, Algorithm 1 searches for the pivot node along that path that is the furthermost node from the initial node, representing a set of concrete states reachable from the set of initial states. As the path is an infeasible path, no error state is reachable from any concrete state represented by the pivot node. The algorithm constructs such path in the ART, however, due to the low abstraction precision of the pivot node. Hence, the goal of the refinement step is to increase the abstraction precision of the pivot node by adding new predicates in such a way that the algorithm will not be able to construct the same path's suffix leading to the error node in the next iteration.

We introduce the notion of *abstract infeasibility* of program paths to indicate whether a path can be constructed by the algorithm.

Definition 1 (Abstract (in)feasibility). *Let π be a program path that is infeasible when starting from a region φ. The program path π is* abstractly infeasible *with respect to a set of predicates P when starting from φ if $sp^P(\varphi, \pi)$ is unsatisfiable. Otherwise π is called* abstractly feasible.

---

[2] Due to page limitations, we refrain from formulating the correctness criteria precisely here but refer the reader to [5] for more details.

When Algorithm 1 constructs an infeasible program path, it is divided by the pivot node $n = (l, \varphi, P)$ into the feasible path prefix (feasible when starting from $\top$) and the path suffix that is infeasible when starting from the data region φ represented by the pivot node. The path suffix is, however, abstractly feasible with respect to the abstraction precision P when starting from φ. Thus, in order to avoid discovering the same path's suffix by the algorithm again, the goal for the refinement operator is to find a set of predicates P' such that the path suffix becomes abstractly infeasible with respect to P' when starting from φ.

Definition 2 (Progressive refinement operator). *Given a refinement operator $\Phi : \mathcal{T}(V) \times E^+ \to 2^{\mathcal{T}(V)}$. We call the refinement operator Φ progressive if for every program path π which is infeasible when starting from a data region φ, π is abstractly infeasible with respect to $\Phi(\varphi, \pi)$ when starting from φ.*

Definitions 1 and 2 reflect the constraint on the refinement step as it relates to the termination of the lazy abstraction algorithm presented in [5]. Lemma 1 formally states this condition in term of the progressive refinement.

Lemma 1 (Termination with progressive refinement operator). *Let $\mathcal{P} = (V, A, l_I, l_e)$ be a $\mathcal{T}$-program with a CFA $A = (L, E)$ and let $\Phi : \mathcal{T}(V) \times E^+ \to 2^{\mathcal{T}(V)}$ be a refinement operator. The execution of LAZYABSTRACTION($\mathcal{P}, \Phi$) terminates if $\mathcal{T}(V)$ is bounded and Φ is progressive.*

The proof is, on one hand, immediate from the developments in [5], as the concepts introduced so far are just an instantiation of Henzinger's more general approach. Nevertheless, termination can also be shown in a straightforward fashion, using König's lemma: The algorithm cannot produce an infinite tree in the limit, as a finitely-branching, infinite tree would contain an infinite path (according to König's lemma), which would be an infinite ascending chain violating the boundedness of $\mathcal{T}(V)$. Progressiveness ensures that the algorithm does not end up in an infinite loop producing the very same ART again and again.

For each ART node, Algorithm 1 computes a corresponding data region using the abstract strongest postoperator. If we consider a path in the ART, then the data regions represented by the nodes along that path form a sequence. In the following we introduce the notions of an *approximating sequence* and an *infeasibility witness* for a path, which are sequences of data regions of the path's length, where each element over-approximates the corresponding data region computed by the algorithm. The idea behind it is that if a refinement operator constructs a sequence of data regions for an infeasible path such that it is also an infeasibility witness, then the elements of that sequence can be used as new predicates and it will guarantee abstract infeasibility of that path.

Definition 3 (Approximating sequence and infeasibility witness). *Given a program path $\pi = l_0 \xrightarrow{op_1} l_1 \xrightarrow{op_2} \cdots \xrightarrow{op_n} l_n$, a data region φ_0 and a set of predicates P, we call a sequence of formulas $\varphi_1, \ldots, \varphi_n$, $\varphi_i \in C(P)$ for $i \in [n]$, a P-approximating sequence for π if $sp(\varphi_{i-1}, op_i) \models \varphi_i$ for all $i \in [n]$. We call a P-approximating sequence a P-infeasibility witness if $\varphi_n \equiv \bot$.*

As is evident, an approximating sequence for a path forms a sequence of data regions such that each data region φ_i over-approximates a data region that is reachable from the predecessor data region φ_{i-1} by executing the operation op_i. The first element of each sequence over-approximates the data region that is reachable from the given data region φ_0 by executing the first operation of the path. If the last data region of the sequence is empty, i.e. $\varphi_n \equiv \bot$, the approximating sequence forms an infeasibility witness.

We define an approximating sequence and an infeasibility witness with respect to a set of predicates P in order to determine whether a set of predicates is precise enough to show that a path is abstractly infeasible.

First we show that each element of a P-approximating sequence for a path over-approximates the corresponding data region constructed by Algorithm 1.

Lemma 2. *Given a program path* $\pi = l_0 \xrightarrow{op_1} l_1 \xrightarrow{op_2} \cdots \xrightarrow{op_n} l_n$, *a data region* φ_0 *and a set of predicates* P. *For every* P-*approximating sequence* $\varphi_1, \ldots, \varphi_n$ *it holds that* $sp^P(\varphi_0, op_1 \ldots op_i) \models \varphi_i$ *for all* $i \in [n]$.

Now we prove the necessary and sufficient condition of abstract infeasibility of an infeasible program path with respect to a set of predicates in terms of an infeasibility witness.

Lemma 3. *Given a set of predicates* P *and a program path* π, *which is infeasible when starting from a data region* φ. *The program path* π *is abstractly infeasible with respect to* P *when starting from* φ *iff there is a* P-*infeasibility witness for* π.

Corollary 1 (Termination and infeasibility witness). *Given a* $\mathcal{T}$-*program* $\mathcal{P}$ *and a refinement operator* Φ, *whereby* $\mathcal{T}$ *is bounded. If, for every program path* π *that is infeasible when starting from a data region* φ, *the refinement operator* Φ *yields an infeasibility witness, then* LAZYABSTRACTION$(\mathcal{P}, \Phi)$ *terminates.*

One of the examples of a set of predicates that forms an infeasibility witness for an infeasible path is the set of negated weakest preconditions computed on that path. Consider a path $\pi = l_0 \xrightarrow{op_1} l_1 \xrightarrow{op_2} \cdots \xrightarrow{op_n} l_n$, which is infeasible when starting from a data region φ. Let $wp_i = wp(\top, op_{i+1} \ldots op_n)$, $i \in [n]$ and $wp_n = \top$ to denote a weakest precondition for location l_i. Each wp_i represents the largest data region from which an error state can be reached by executing $op_{i+1} \ldots op_n$. But as the considered path is infeasible when starting from φ, wp_i cannot be reached from φ by executing $op_1, \ldots, op_{i-1}$. Thus, each $\neg wp_i$ represents the largest data region from which no error state can be reached by executing $op_1, \ldots, op_{i-1}$. Moreover, $\neg wp_1$ is reachable from φ and each $\neg wp_i$ is reachable from $\neg wp_{i-1}$ by executing op_1 and op_i respectively. It follows that the sequence $W = (\neg wp_1, \ldots, \neg wp_{n-1}, \neg wp_n = \bot)$ is a W-infeasibility witness. Hence, a refinement operator yielding weakest preconditions for an infeasible path would be progressive and would fulfill the termination criterion for refinement operators.

Weakest preconditions are used for the refinement operator in the original work to lazy abstraction [5]. Though the use of weakest preconditions are sufficient to guarantee the termination of the algorithm, they often encode too much information and hence are represented by quite complex formulas. Each formula encoding a weakest precondition would contain all variables from a path suffix, regardless of whether a variable has any impact on infeasibility of that path.

In the following, we present a novel method for computation of new predicates from infeasible paths. It is also based on weakest preconditions but tries to discard as much information as possible that does not affect infeasibility. It results in much simpler formulas as well as, in some cases, in generation smaller number of predicates needed to prove or disprove a property using lazy abstraction algorithm. All these can significantly improve overall performance of the lazy abstraction algorithm. The computation of new predicates makes use of unsatisfiability cores and weakest preconditions.

Definition 4 (Unsat-core-based (UCB) predicates). *Let* $\pi = l_0 \xrightarrow{op_1} l_1 \xrightarrow{op_2} \ldots \xrightarrow{op_n} l_n$ *be a program path that is infeasible with respect to a data region* φ. *We call a sequence of predicates* $p_1, \ldots, p_n$ *unsat-core based predicates if* $p_i = \neg(\varphi_i \setminus cl(\psi_i))$ *where* $\varphi_i \in UC(\psi_i \wedge wp_i)$, $\psi_i = sp\,(p_{i-1}, op_i)$, $p_0 = \varphi$, *and* $wp_n = \top$ *and* $wp_i = wp(\top, op_{i+1} \ldots op_n)$).

Definition 4 can be seen as an algorithm for computing new predicates. In the first pass, the algorithm computes the weakest preconditions $wp_1, \ldots, wp_n$ for program locations $l_1, \ldots, l_n$. Then, starting from the location l_1, it iteratively computes for each location l_i the data region ψ_i that is reachable from the data region p_{i-1} by executing corresponding operation op_i. The data region ψ_i over-approximates the set of states that are reachable from φ, and thus has no common states with the weakest precondition because the given path is infeasible with respect to φ. Using this fact, we compute an unsatisfiability core of the conjunction of ψ_i and wp_i and select all clauses from the unsatisfiability core that are only included in the weakest precondition. The resulting formula over-approximates the weakest precondition wp_i, which represents the largest set of states from which an error state can be reached by executing the path's suffix $op_i \ldots op_n$. Hence, we take the negation of that formula as a new predicate p_i, which represents an under-approximation of $\neg wp_i$, which is the largest set of states from which no error state can be reached by executing the path's suffix. At the same time, p_i represents an over-approximation of the data region that is reachable from the given data region φ by executing the path's prefix $op_1 \ldots op_{i-1}$.

Intuitively, the properties of UCB predicates described above allow us to use them for the abstraction refinement. Though each UCB predicate p_i represents in general a smaller data region than the corresponding $\neg wp_i$, they contain much more precise information about the reason of unsatisfiability than the corresponding weakest precondition.

Let us sketch how to prove that the use of UCB predicates computed according to Definition 4 in the refinement step guarantees termination of Algorithm 1.

First one shows that each UCB-predicate p_i as well as ψ_i represent the sets of states that are disjointed from the set of states represented by wp_i. As wp_i represents the set of all states from which the path suffix $op_{i+1} \ldots op_n$ can be

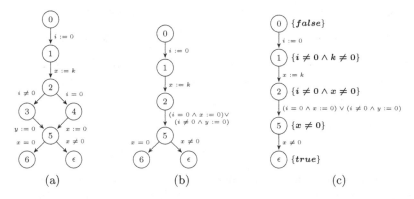

Fig. 1. A CFA of a simple imperative program (a). The optimized CFA (b) after merging "if-then-else" block. An infeasible path (c) from the optimized CFA, where nodes are labeled by the corresponding weakest preconditions (curly brackets).

executed, we show that p_i and ψ_i under-approximate the set of states represented by $\neg wp_i$: (i) $p_i \rightarrow \neg wp_i$ and $\psi_i \rightarrow \neg wp_i$ for all $i \in [n]$. Now we show that p_i over-approximates the data region reachable from p_{i-1}, which we use to show that the sequence $p_1, \ldots, p_n$ forms an approximating sequence: (ii) $sp(p_{i-1}, op_i) \rightarrow p_i$ for all $i \in [n]$. Now we can show that a sequence of UCB predicates computed according to Definition 4 forms an infeasibility witness. (iii) Given a path π that is infeasible when starting from a data region φ then a sequence of UCB predicates U computed for π is an U-infeasibility witness for π.

We sum up our developments with the following theorem, which follows easily from the items (i)–(iii) stated above.

Theorem 1 (Termination with UCB predicates). *Let $\mathcal{P}$ be a $\mathcal{T}$-program and let Φ be the refinement operator yielding the UCB predicates for an infeasible path. If $\mathcal{T}$ is bounded, then* LAZYABSTRACTION$(\mathcal{P}, \Phi)$ *terminates.*

4.1   Path Projection

One of the commonly used techniques to simplify the refinement based on unsatisfiability cores, is the refinement of a path formula based on an unsatisfiability core and the following predicate extraction on the refined path. As a path formula of an infeasible path is unsatisfiable, one can construct a path "projection", which will only contain the information included in the unsatisfiability core and then apply some predicate extraction technique, e.g. weakest precondition-based or interpolation-based techniques, on that path. The path projection is achieved by removing clauses from the encoding of program operations that are not included in the unsatisfiability core.

Unfortunately, the choice of the predicate extraction techniques in such approach strongly depends on the encoding of program operations as well as on other components of the Lazy Abstraction algorithm, such as the abstract post-operator.

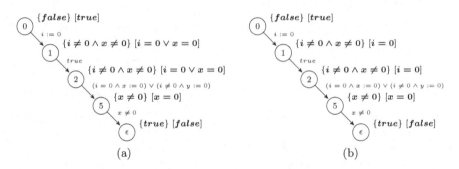

Fig. 2. The projected paths, where nodes are labeled by weakest preconditions (curly brackets) as well as by extracted predicates (square brackets): negated weakest preconditions (a) and UCB predicates (b).

In our model-checking tool we use the large-block encoding (LBE) technique [22] and Cartesian abstraction as the abstract postoperator. In the following we show by means of an example that in our configuration the combination of the weakest precondition-based predicate extraction and path projection does not guarantee termination of the Lazy Abstraction algorithm.

Consider a CFA (Fig. 1a) of a simple imperative program assigning a value to either variable x or y according to the value of the variable i assigned in the first step. Figure 1b presents the CFA after applying the optimization step that merges the "if-then-else" block into one transition. If we start the algorithm with an empty set of predicates, it will find a counterexample (Fig. 1c) in the first iteration, which is obviously infeasible. Due to infeasibility, one can simplify it using an unsatisfiability core. The example of such projection is presented in Fig. 2a and b. After simplification step, we can apply a predicate extraction algorithm. Figures 2a and b show the predicates that were constructed by negating the corresponding weakest preconditions (Fig. 2a) and by computing UCB predicates (Fig. 2b) as described in Definition 4. Unfortunately, the predicates, which were constructed using negation of weakest preconditions, do not form an approximating sequence for the original path and thus, do not fulfill the necessary condition for termination of the algorithm. The problem lies on the simplified transition between nodes 1 and 2. On one hand, the transition was simplified by removing the superfluous assignment $x := k$ but on the other hand, the variable x still appears in the predicate. This leads to the problem at program location 2, namely, there is no predicate, which under-approximates the negated weakest precondition $i = 0 \lor k = 0$ from the original path, which represents the largest set of states from which the error state is unreachable. As one can see, there is no such problem when using the UCB predicates, as all superfluous variables are removed from predicates as well.

We have to note that in order to use the UCB predicates in such configuration, one has to ensure that only minimal unsatisfiability cores are used in the computation of UCB predicates. The reason for that is that by applying path projection it is necessary that no superfluous variables will remain in the resulting predicate, which can be guaranteed by using minimal unsatisfiability cores. Also note, that the interpolation-based technique to predicate construction also has this property and hence can be used in combination with projection. We also consider successfully such an additional projection in our setting (see Sect. 5 (Results)). A formal proof of the previous remarks require a precise definitions of the notion of projection etc. and is, due to space constraints, left to a full version of the paper.

5   Implementation and Experimental Results

Implementation. We implemented the Lazy Abstraction algorithm in combination with the UCB-based as well as the interpolation-based refinement strategies on top of an existing proprietary model-checking framework. This framework makes use of LLVM project to parse C programs and translate them into the intermediate representation (IR). We apply some static analysis and optimization techniques on this IR, e.g. Steensgaard's pointer analysis and model minimization [23–25], as well large block encoding [22]. We use the bit-precise memory model that supports limited pointer operations including array-element and record-field addressing. While the Lazy Abstraction algorithm in combination with the UCB-based refinement strategy is fully theory unaware and can be used for infinite-domain theories, such as linear real arithmetic (LRA) we use the finite-domain theory of bit vectors. Our tool supports the Z3 and MathSAT SMT solvers, but as the Z3 solver does not support computation of interpolants for the theory of interest we executed all benchmarks using the MathSAT solver.

Besides the refinement algorithms we implemented and evaluated two optimizations which may improve performance of the Lazy Abstraction algorithm in some cases. The first one is the path projection described in the previous section and the second one is the limitation of number of extracted predicates. The intention behind it is that the fewer predicates are extracted the less SMT queries has to be done by the abstract postoperator and in some cases not all predicates extracted from an infeasible path are necessary to prove or disprove a property. It does not affect the correctness, as in the worst case, the algorithm will need to refine paths multiple times.

We additionally compared our implementation to an improvement of the IC3 model-checking approach that is currently one of the most actively studied model-checking algorithms. The improved version of the IC3 algorithm was recently presented in [2] and is implemented within the same model-checking framework. Hence, all preprocessing and optimization steps are identical to our implementation.

Experiments. We have evaluated our algorithms on 178 C programs taken from the SV competition and enriched by some of our own programs. For 89 programs, none of the algorithms has terminated within the given time or memory bound. In the following, we discuss the behavior of the algorithms on the remaining 89 examples, for which at least configuration of one algorithm terminated.

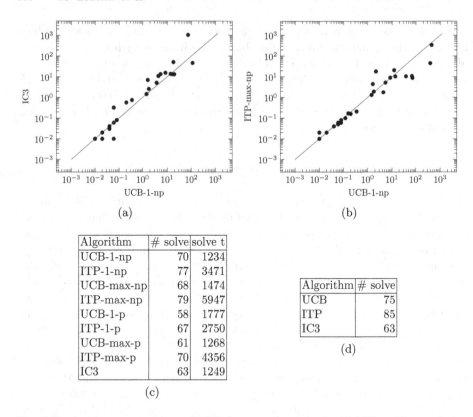

(a)   (b)

Algorithm	# solve	solve t
UCB-1-np	70	1234
ITP-1-np	77	3471
UCB-max-np	68	1474
ITP-max-np	79	5947
UCB-1-p	58	1777
ITP-1-p	67	2750
UCB-max-p	61	1268
ITP-max-p	70	4356
IC3	63	1249

(c)

Algorithm	# solve
UCB	75
ITP	85
IC3	63

(d)

Fig. 3. Performance comparison of UCB (best configuration) with IC3 and interpolants (best configuration) (a), (b). Number of solved problems by each algorithm in each configuration (1/max denotes the number of extracted predicates and p/np whether the path projection is applied (p) or not (np)) (c). Number of solved problems by algorithms for all configurations (d).

All experiments have been executed on a cluster using a single core running at 2.1 GHz, a memory limit of 4GB per file and a timeout of 3600 s.

We briefly compare the performance of the Lazy Abstraction algorithm in combination with UCB-based and interpolation-based refinement in its best configurations (w.r.t number of solved problems) as well the IC3 implementation from [2]. We also compare the number of solved problems by different approaches.

Results. From the results in Fig. 3 we can come to the following conclusions. First, the best configuration of the interpolation-based approach solved more problems out of 89 than others (Fig. 3c). At the same time, our results which are not presented in tables, shows that there are 4 problems which could only be solved by the UCB-based and IC3 algorithms. The best configuration of the UCB-based algorithm solved 8 problems more than the IC3 algorithm and the latter solved one problem which the best of UCBs could not solve. The best configuration of the interpolation-based approach solved 15 problems more than the best configuration of UCBs but at the same time the latter solved 6 problems which the best interpolation-based could not solve.

Second, application of the path projection and limitation of the number of predicates allow to solve problems which can not be solved otherwise, increasing thereby the total number of solved problems (Fig. 3c) and thus, also play an important role in Lazy Abstraction approach. While interpolation-based approach solved the most problems without any optimization, the UCB-based approach was most efficient by only taking one predicate during the refinement. The difference arises from the fact that for the computation of all UCB-predicates one needs to make as many SMT queries as the path's length, while an SMT-solver computes all interpolants from one query. At the same time, applying path projection may simplify the consequent queries but as we can see, in many cases it introduces the superfluous computation which decreases the overall performance.

Finally, the best configuration of the UCB-based approach outperforms the IC3 approach in most cases (Fig. 3a) and is comparable to the best configuration of the interpolation-based approach (Fig. 3b).

Summarizing our results we can conclude that the best results in our current setting can be achieved by combining the UCB-based and interpolation-based approaches for example by running them in parallel.

6   Conclusion

This paper studied a new refinement technique within the CEGAR-based approach to model checking. More specifically, we build on lazy abstraction, where the refinement step is usually carried out using weakest preconditions on program paths or using techniques like interpolants.

As interpolants are sometimes not available by the underlying SMT solver, we have developed a new refinement step that makes use of unsatisfiable cores to improve refinement and which can be used with any SMT solver (that can compute unsatisfiability cores). We have shown that our refinement step is progressive in the sense that the lazy abstraction approach terminates when verifying finite state systems. Moreover, we have implemented the strategy within our own model-checking tool. We have shown that UCB-based refinement nearly always outperforms one of the implementation of IC3 model-checking algorithms in our setting. Regarding interpolation-based refinement, UCB-based is often comparable but also allows to verify programs which can not be solved by using interpolants. As such, the papers presents a new valuable refinement strategy.

References

1. Baier, C., Katoen, J.: Principles of Model Checking. MIT Press, Cambridge (2008)
2. Lange, T., Neuhäußer, M.R., Noll, T.: IC3 software model checking on control flow automata. In: Formal Methods in Computer-Aided Design, FMCAD 2015 (2015)
3. Bradley, A.R.: SAT-based model checking without unrolling. In: Jhala, R., Schmidt, D. (eds.) VMCAI 2011. LNCS, vol. 6538, pp. 70–87. Springer, Heidelberg (2011)

4. Clarke, E., Grumberg, O., Jha, S., Lu, Y., Veith, H.: Counterexample-guided abstraction refinement. In: Emerson, E.A., Sistla, A.P. (eds.) CAV 2000. LNCS, vol. 1855, pp. 154–169. Springer, Heidelberg (2000)

5. Henzinger, T.A., Jhala, R., Majumdar, R., Sutre, G.: Lazy abstraction. ACM SIGPLAN Not. **37**, 58–70 (2002). ACM

6. Graf, S., Saïdi, H.: Construction of abstract state graphs with PVS. In: Grumberg, O. (ed.) CAV 1997. LNCS, vol. 1254, pp. 72–83. Springer, Heidelberg (1997)

7. de Moura, L., Bjørner, N.: Z3: an efficient SMT solver. In: Ramakrishnan, C.R., Rehof, J. (eds.) TACAS 2008. LNCS, vol. 4963, pp. 337–340. Springer, Heidelberg (2008)

8. Cimatti, A., Griggio, A., Schaafsma, B.J., Sebastiani, R.: The MathSAT5 SMT solver. In: Piterman, N., Smolka, S.A. (eds.) TACAS 2013. LNCS, vol. 7795, pp. 93–107. Springer, Heidelberg (2013)

9. Henzinger, T., Jhala, R., Majumdar, R., McMillan, K.: Abstractions from proofs. ACM SIGPLAN Not. **39**(1), 232–244 (2004)

10. McMillan, K.L.: Lazy abstraction with interpolants. In: Ball, T., Jones, R.B. (eds.) CAV 2006. LNCS, vol. 4144, pp. 123–136. Springer, Heidelberg (2006)

11. Beyer, D., Henzinger, T.A., Jhala, R., Majumdar, R.: The software model checker BLAST. Int. J. Softw. Tools Technol. Transf. (STTT) **9**(5), 505–525 (2007)

12. Jain, H., Kroening, D., Sharygina, N., Clarke, E.M.: Word-level predicate-abstraction and refinement techniques for verifying RTL Verilog. IEEE Trans. Comput. Aided Des. Integr. Circ. Syst. **27**(2), 366–379 (2008)

13. Andraus, Z.S., Liffiton, M.H., Sakallah, K.A.: Cegar-based formal hardware verification: a case study. Ann Arbor **2007**, 48109–2122 (1001)

14. Yang, Z., Al-Rawi, B., Sakallah, K., Huang, X., Smolka, S., Grosu, R.: Dynamic path reduction for software model checking. In: Leuschel, M., Wehrheim, H. (eds.) IFM 2009. LNCS, vol. 5423, pp. 322–336. Springer, Heidelberg (2009)

15. Kroening, D., Strichman, O.: Decision Procedures, vol. 5. Springer, New York (2008)

16. Gries, D.: The Science of Programming. Springer, Heidelberg (1981)

17. Dijkstra, E.W.: A Discipline of Programming, vol. 1. Prentice-Hall, Englewood Cliffs (1976)

18. Dijkstra, E.W.: Guarded commands, nondeterminacy and formal derivation of programs. Commun. ACM **18**(8), 453–457 (1975)

19. Jager, I., Brumley, D.: Efficient directionless weakest preconditions. Technical report, CMU-CyLab-10-002, Carnegie Mellon University, CyLab (2010)

20. Leino, K.R.M.: Efficient weakest preconditions. Inf. Process. Lett. **93**(6), 281–288 (2005)

21. Ball, T., Podelski, A., Rajamani, S.K.: Boolean and cartesian abstraction for model checking C programs. In: Margaria, T., Yi, W. (eds.) TACAS 2001. LNCS, vol. 2031, pp. 268–283. Springer, Heidelberg (2001)

22. Beyer, D., Cimatti, A., Griggio, A., Keremoglu, M.E., Sebastiani, R.: Software model checking via large-block encoding. In: Formal Methods in Computer-Aided Design, FMCAD 2009, pp. 25–32. IEEE (2009)

23. Weiser, M.: Program slicing. IEEE Trans. Softw. Eng. **10**(4), 352–357 (1984)

24. Lange, T., Neuhäußer, M.R., Noll, T.: Speeding up the safety verification of programmable logic controller code. In: Bertacco, V., Legay, A. (eds.) HVC 2013. LNCS, vol. 8244, pp. 44–60. Springer, Heidelberg (2013)

25. Nielson, F., Nielson, H.R., Hankin, C.: Principles of Program Analysis. Springer, New York (1999)

Timed Systems

Quasi-equal Clock Reduction:
Eliminating Assumptions on Networks

Christian Herrera and Bernd Westphal$^{(\boxtimes)}$

Albert-Ludwigs-Universität Freiburg, 79110 Freiburg, Germany
{salazars,westphal}@informatik.uni-freiburg.de

Abstract. Quasi-equal clock reduction for networks of timed automata replaces clocks in equivalence classes by representative clocks. An existing approach which reduces quasi-equal clocks and does not constrain the support of properties of networks, yields significant reductions of the overall verification time of properties. However, this approach requires strong assumptions on networks in order to soundly apply the reduction of clocks. In this work we propose a transformation which does not require assumptions on networks, and does not constrain the support of properties of networks. We demonstrate that the cost of verifying properties is much lower in transformed networks than in their original counterparts with quasi-equal clocks.

1 Introduction

Real-time systems can be modelled and verified using *networks of timed automata* [1]. Often the local timing behaviour and synchronisation activity of distributed components in a network are modelled by (local) clocks. If the valuations of those clocks only differ in points in time in which those clocks are reset, then we call them *quasi-equal* clocks [2]. Quasi-equality of clocks induces *equivalence classes* in networks of timed automata.

In systems using quasi-equal clocks, those clocks are often reset one by one at a given point in time. For instance, in TDMA [3] protocols, automata interleave when they reset quasi-equal clocks at the end of each communication phase. This interleaving induces sets of reachable intermediate configurations. These sets grow exponentially in the number of quasi-equal clocks in equivalence classes. Model checking tools like *Uppaal* [4] explore those configurations when a property being verified queries them. However, this exploration may also increase the memory consumption and verification time for properties which do not query those intermediate configurations.

In [5] a technique that reduces the number of quasi-equal clocks is presented. This technique can yield savings in the overall memory consumption and verification time of properties in transformed networks for two reasons. The first reason is that by using only the representative clock of each equivalence class, we reduce the size of the *Difference Bound Matrices (DBMs)* that Uppaal uses to represent *zones* [6]. The size of a DBM is determined by the size of the set of clocks

CONACYT (Mexico) and DAAD (Germany) sponsor the work of the first author.

N. Piterman (Ed.): HVC 2015, LNCS 9434, pp. 173–189, 2015.
DOI: 10.1007/978-3-319-26287-1_11

in a given system. A more compact DBM can be more efficiently represented, stored and accessed in memory. The second reason is that Uppaal explores less configurations when checking a property, since we eliminate intermediate configurations if and only if those configurations are reachable by taking edges which exclusively reset quasi-equal clocks.

In order to soundly reduce quasi-equal clocks, strong assumptions are required for networks in [5]. One of those assumptions states that there must be a delay greater than zero time units in the origin location of an edge resetting a quasi-equal clock. In networks which model the Foundation Fieldbus Data Link Layer protocol (FDLL) [7], there are edges resetting quasi-equal clocks which can be taken at any time, even without delaying at the origin locations of those edges. Hence we cannot transform those networks by using the technique from [5].

In this work we revisit the quasi-equal clock reduction approach, and we present an approach that does not require assumptions on networks with quasi-equal clocks. We now enforce a strong distinction of edges that reset quasi-equal clocks. Namely, edges which exclusively reset one quasi-equal clock, have no synchronisation with other edges, and are taken after a delay greater than zero time units, are called *simple edges*. All other edges resetting quasi-equal clocks are called *complex edges*. In general our approach allows us to yield savings related to having a more compact DBM in memory. Furthermore, for simple edges we also provide savings related to eliminating intermediate configurations.

As in [5] we delegate the reset of representative clocks to newly added *resetter* automata. Now automata with transformed simple or complex edges indicate resetters when to execute that reset which is part of a mechanism that, reduces the number of configurations reachable by taking transformed simple edges, and preserves all configurations reachable by taking transformed complex edges. Similar to [5], for those configurations that we eliminate, properties are restated in terms of an existing dedicated location in each resetter which encodes all the information about those configurations.

In this work we extend the applicability of the quasi-equal clock reduction approach by eliminating the assumptions on networks presented in [5]. Now we can transform any network with sets of quasi-equal clocks. Our new approach allows us to include three new case studies *FB* [7], *TA* [8] and *PG* [9], which cannot be transformed by the technique from [5]. In general, the cost of verifying properties is much lower in networks transformed with our new approach than in their original counterparts with quasi-equal clocks. Furthermore, our new approach allows us to prove in a much simpler and more elegant way that transformed networks are weakly bisimilar to their original counterparts. We show that properties wrt. an original network are fully reflected in the transformed network, i.e. the transformed network satisfies a transformed property if and only if the original network satisfies the original property. We evaluate our approach on nine real world examples, three of them new.

Related Work. The methods in [10,11] detect and reduce *equal* and *active* clocks by using static analysis over single timed automata and networks of timed automata, respectively. Two clocks are equal in a location if both are reset by the same incoming edge, so just one clock for each set of equal clocks is necessary to determine the future behavior of the system. A clock is active at a certain location if this clock appears in the invariant of that location, or in the guard of an outgoing edge of such a location, or another active clock takes its value when taking an outgoing edge. Non-active clocks play no role in the future evolution of the system and therefore can be eliminated. Our benchmarks use at most one clock per component which is always active, hence the equal and active approach is not applicable on them.

The work in [12,13] uses *observers*, i.e. single components encoding properties of a system, to reduce clocks in systems. For each location of the observer, the technique can deactivate clocks if they do not play a role in the future evolution of this observer. Processing our benchmarks in order to encode properties as per the observers approach may be more expensive than our method (one observer per property), and may not guarantee the preservation of information from intermediate configurations as required for our benchmark [14].

In sequential timed automata [15], one set of quasi-equal clocks is syntactically declared. Those quasi-equal clocks are implicitly reduced by applying the sequential composition operator. The approach in [16] detects quasi-equal clocks in networks of timed automata. Interestingly, the authors demonstrate the feasibility of their approach in benchmarks that we also use in this paper.

2   Preliminaries

Following the presentation in [17], we here recall the following definitions.

Let $\mathcal{X}$ be a set of *clocks*. The set $\Phi(\mathcal{X})$ of *simple clock constraints* over $\mathcal{X}$ is defined by the grammar $\varphi ::= x \sim c \mid x - y \sim c \mid \varphi_1 \wedge \varphi_2$ where $x, y \in \mathcal{X}$, $c \in \mathbb{Q}_{\geq 0}$, and $\sim \in \{<, \leq, \geq, >\}$. Let $\Phi(\mathcal{V})$ be a set of *integer constraints* over *variables* $\mathcal{V}$. The set $\Phi(\mathcal{X}, \mathcal{V})$ of *constraints* comprises $\Phi(\mathcal{X})$, $\Phi(\mathcal{V})$, and conjunctions of clock and integer constraints. We use $clocks(\varphi)$ and $vars(\varphi)$ to respectively denote the set of clocks and variables occurring in a constraint φ. We assume the canonical satisfaction relation "$\models$" between *valuations* $\nu :$ $\mathcal{X} \cup \mathcal{V} \rightarrow Time \cup \mathbb{Z}$ and constraints, with $Time = \mathbb{R}_{\geq 0}$. A timed automaton $\mathcal{A}$ is a tuple $(L, B, \mathcal{X}, \mathcal{V}, I, E, \ell_{ini})$, which consists of a finite set of *locations* L, where $\ell_{ini} \in L$ is the initial location, a finite set B of *actions* comprising the *internal action* τ, finite sets $\mathcal{X}$ and $\mathcal{V}$ of clocks and variables, a mapping $I : L \rightarrow \Phi(\mathcal{X})$, that assigns to each location a *clock constraint*, and a set of *edges* $E \subseteq L \times B \times \Phi(\mathcal{X}, \mathcal{V}) \times \mathcal{R}(\mathcal{X}, \mathcal{V}) \times L$. An edge $e = (\ell, \alpha, \varphi, \vec{r}, \ell') \in E$ from location ℓ to ℓ' involves an action $\alpha \in B$, a *guard* $\varphi \in \Phi(\mathcal{X}, \mathcal{V})$, and a *reset vector* $\vec{r} \in \mathcal{R}(\mathcal{X}, \mathcal{V})$. A reset vector is a finite, possibly empty sequence of *clock resets* $x := 0$, $x \in \mathcal{X}$, and *assignments* $v := \psi_{int}$, where $v \in \mathcal{V}$ and ψ_{int} is an integer expression over $\mathcal{V}$. We use $L^u, L^c \subseteq L$ to denote the set of urgent and committed locations in L, respectively. We write $\mathcal{X}(\mathcal{A})$, $\ell_{ini}(\mathcal{A})$, etc., to denote the set of clocks, the initial location, etc., of $\mathcal{A}$ and; $clocks(\vec{r})$ and $vars(\vec{r})$ to denote the sets of clocks and variables occurring in $\vec{r}$, respectively.

A *network* $\mathcal{N}$ (*of timed automata*) consists of a finite set $\mathcal{A}_1, \ldots, \mathcal{A}_N$ of timed automata with pairwise disjoint sets of clocks and sets $\mathcal{B}^r, \mathcal{B}^b, \mathcal{B}^u \subseteq \bigcup_{i=1}^{N} B(\mathcal{A}_i)$

of *rendez-vous, broadcast* and *urgent channels*, respectively. We write $\mathcal{A} \in \mathcal{N}$ if and only if $\mathcal{A} \in \{\mathcal{A}_1, \ldots, \mathcal{A}_N\}$.

The operational semantics of the network $\mathcal{N}$ is the labelled transition system $\mathcal{T}(\mathcal{N}) = (Conf(\mathcal{N}), Time \cup \{\tau\}, \{\xrightarrow{\lambda} \mid \lambda \in Time \cup \{\tau\}\}, \mathcal{C}_{ini})$. The set of configurations $Conf(\mathcal{N})$ consists of pairs of *location vectors* $\langle \ell_1, \ldots, \ell_N \rangle$ from $\times_{i=1}^{N} L(\mathcal{A}_i)$ and valuations of $\bigcup_{1 \leq i \leq N} \mathcal{X}(\mathcal{A}_i) \cup \mathcal{V}(\mathcal{A}_i)$ which satisfy the constraint $\bigwedge_{i=1}^{N} I(\ell_i)$. We write $\ell_{s,i}$, $1 \leq i \leq N$, to denote the location which automaton $\mathcal{A}_i$ assumes in configuration $s = \langle \boldsymbol{\ell}_s, \nu_s \rangle$ and $\nu_{s,i}$ to denote $\nu_s|_{\mathcal{V}(\mathcal{A}_i) \cup \mathcal{X}(\mathcal{A}_i)}$. Between two configurations $s, s' \in Conf(\mathcal{N})$ there can be four kinds of transitions. There is a *delay transition* $\langle \boldsymbol{\ell}_s, \nu_s \rangle \xrightarrow{t} \langle \boldsymbol{\ell}_s, \nu_s + t \rangle$ if for all $t' \in [0, t]$ and for all $1 \leq i \neq j \leq N$, $\nu_s + t' \models \bigwedge_{k=1}^{N} I_k(\ell_{s,k})$ (where $\nu_s + t'$ denotes the valuation obtained from ν_s by time shift t'), and (1) $\ell_{s,i} \notin L^u \cup L^c$, and (2) $\nu_s + t' \not\models \varphi(e)$, $e \in E(\mathcal{A})$, such that $\alpha(e) = b!$, $b \in \mathcal{B}^u \cap \mathcal{B}^b$ and $\ell_{s,i} = \ell(e)$; and (3) $\nu_s + t' \not\models \varphi(e_i) \wedge \varphi(e_j)$, with $e_i \in E(\mathcal{A}_i)$ and $e_j \in E(\mathcal{A}_j)$, such that $\alpha(e_i) = u!, \alpha(e_j) = u?, u \in \mathcal{B}^u(\mathcal{N}) \cap \mathcal{B}^r(\mathcal{N})$, $\ell_{s,i} = \ell(e_i)$ and $\ell_{s,j} = \ell(e_j)$. There is a *local transition* $\langle \boldsymbol{\ell}_s, \nu_s \rangle \xrightarrow{\tau} \langle \boldsymbol{\ell}_{s'}, \nu_{s'} \rangle$ if there is an edge $(\ell_{s,i}, \tau, \varphi, \vec{r}, \ell_{s',i}) \in E(\mathcal{A}_i)$, $1 \leq i \leq N$, such that $\boldsymbol{\ell}_{s'} = \boldsymbol{\ell}_s[\ell_{s,i} := \ell_{s',i}]$, $\nu_s \models \varphi$, $\nu_{s'} = \nu_s[\vec{r}]$, and $\nu_{s'} \models I_i(\ell_{s',i})$, and if $\ell_{s,k} \in L^c$ for some $1 \leq k \leq N$ then $\ell_{s,i} \in L^c$. There is a *synchronization transition* $\langle \boldsymbol{\ell}_s, \nu_s \rangle \xrightarrow{\tau} \langle \boldsymbol{\ell}_{s'}, \nu_{s'} \rangle$ if there are $1 \leq i \neq j \leq N$, and edges $(\ell_{s,i}, b!, \varphi_i, \vec{r}_i, \ell_{s',i}) \in E(\mathcal{A}_i)$ and $(\ell_{s,j}, b?, \varphi_j, \vec{r}_j, \ell_{s',j}) \in E(\mathcal{A}_j)$ such that $\boldsymbol{\ell}_{s'} = \boldsymbol{\ell}_s[\ell_{s,i} := \ell_{s',i}][\ell_{s,j} := \ell_{s',j}]$, $\nu_s \models \varphi_i \wedge \varphi_j$, $\nu_{s'} = \nu_s[\vec{r}_i][\vec{r}_j]$, and $\nu_{s'} \models I_i(\ell_{s',i}) \wedge I_j(\ell_{s',j})$, and if $\ell_{s,k} \in L^c$ for some $1 \leq k \leq N$ then $\ell_{s,i} \in L^c$ or $\ell_{s,j} \in L^c$. Let $b \in \mathcal{B}$ be a broadcast channel and $1 \leq i_0 \leq N$ such that $(\ell_{s,i_0}, b!, \varphi_{i_0}, \vec{r}_{i_0}, \ell_{s',i_0}) \in E(\mathcal{A}_{i_0})$. Let $1 \leq i_1, \ldots, i_k \leq N$, $k \geq 0$, be those indices different from i_0 such that there is an edge $(\ell_{s,i_j}, b?, \varphi_{i_j}, \vec{r}_{i_j}, \ell_{s',i_j}) \in E(\mathcal{A}_{i_j})$. There is a *broadcast transition* $\langle \boldsymbol{\ell}_s, \nu_s \rangle \xrightarrow{\tau} \langle \boldsymbol{\ell}_{s'}, \nu_{s'} \rangle$ in $\mathcal{T}(\mathcal{N})$ if $\boldsymbol{\ell}_{s'} = \boldsymbol{\ell}_s[\ell_{s,i_0} := \ell_{s',i_0}] \cdots [\ell_{s,i_k} := \ell_{s',i_k}]$, $\nu_s \models \bigwedge_{j=0}^{k} \varphi_{i_j}$, $\nu_{s'} = \nu_s[\vec{r}_{i_0}] \cdots [\vec{r}_{i_k}]$, and $\nu_{s'} \models \bigwedge_{j=0}^{k} I_{i_j}(\ell_{s',i_j})$, and if $\ell_{s,\hat{k}} \in L^c$ for some $\hat{k}, \bar{k} \in \{i_0, i_1, \ldots, i_k\}$ then $\ell_{s,\bar{k}} \in L^c$. $\mathcal{C}_{ini} = \{\langle \boldsymbol{\ell}_{ini}, \nu_{ini} \rangle\} \cap Conf(\mathcal{N})$, where $\boldsymbol{\ell}_{ini} = \langle \ell_{ini,1}, \ldots, \ell_{ini,N} \rangle$, $\nu_{ini}(x) = 0$ for each $x \in \mathcal{X}(\mathcal{A}_i)$, and $1 \leq i \leq N$. A finite or infinite sequence $\sigma = s_0 \xrightarrow{\lambda_1} s_1 \xrightarrow{\lambda_2} s_2 \cdots$ of configurations is called *transition sequence* (starting in $s_0 \in \mathcal{C}_{ini}$) of $\mathcal{N}$. Sequence σ is called *computation* of $\mathcal{N}$ if and only if it is finite and $s_0 \in \mathcal{C}_{ini}$. We denote the set of all computations of $\mathcal{N}$ by $\Pi(\mathcal{N})$. A configuration s is called *reachable* (in $\mathcal{T}(\mathcal{N})$) if and only if there exists a computation $\sigma \in \Pi(\mathcal{N})$ such that s occurs in σ.

The set of *basic formulae* over $\mathcal{N}$ is given by the grammar $\beta :: = \ell \mid \varphi$ where $\ell \in L(\mathcal{A}_i)$, $1 \leq i \leq n$, and $\varphi \in \Phi(\mathcal{X}, \mathcal{V})$. Basic formula β is satisfied by configuration $s \in Conf(\mathcal{N})$ if and only if $\ell_{s,i} = \ell$, or $\nu_s \models \varphi$, respectively. A *reachability query* over $\mathcal{N}$ is $\exists \Diamond CF$ where CF is a *configuration formula* over $\mathcal{N}$, i.e. any logical connector of basic formulae. We use $\beta(CF)$ to denote the set of basic formulae in CF. $\mathcal{N}$ satisfies $\exists \Diamond CF$, denoted by $\mathcal{N} \models \exists \Diamond CF$, if and only if there is a configuration s reachable in $\mathcal{T}(\mathcal{N})$ s.t. $s \models CF$.

We recall from [2] the following definitions. Given a network $\mathcal{N}$ with clocks $\mathcal{X}$, two clocks $x, y \in \mathcal{X}$ are called *quasi-equal*, denoted by $x \simeq y$, if and only if for all computation paths of $\mathcal{N}$, the valuations of x and y are equal, or the valuation of one of them is equal to 0, i.e. if $\forall s_0 \xrightarrow{\lambda_1} s_1 \xrightarrow{\lambda_2} s_2 \cdots \in \Pi(\mathcal{N}) \; \forall i \in \mathbb{N}_0 \bullet \nu_{s_i} \models (x = 0 \vee y = 0 \vee x = y)$. In the following, we use $\mathcal{EC}_\mathcal{N}$ to denote the set $\{Y \in \mathcal{X}/\simeq \; | \; 1 < |Y|\}$ of equivalence classes of *quasi-equal* clocks of $\mathcal{N}$ with at least two elements. For each $Y \in \mathcal{X}/\simeq$, we assume a designated representative denoted by $rep(Y)$. For $x \in Y$, we use $rep(x)$ to denote $rep(Y)$. An edge e of a timed automaton $\mathcal{A}$ in network $\mathcal{N}$ is called *resetting edge* if and only if e resets a clock, i.e. if $\exists e = (\ell, \alpha, \varphi, \vec{r}, \ell') \in E(\mathcal{A}) \bullet clocks(\vec{r}) \neq \emptyset$. A location ℓ (ℓ') is called *reset (successor) location* wrt. $Y \in \mathcal{EC}_\mathcal{N}$ in $\mathcal{N}$ if and only if there is a resetting edge in $E(\mathcal{N})$ from (to) ℓ (ℓ'). A configuration $s \in Conf(\mathcal{N})$ is called *stable* wrt. $Y \in \mathcal{EC}_\mathcal{N}$ if and only if all clocks in Y have the same value in s, i.e. if $\forall x \in Y \bullet \nu_s(x) = \nu_s(rep(x))$. We use $\mathcal{SC}_\mathcal{N}^Y$ to denote the set of all configurations that are stable wrt. Y. A configuration not in $\mathcal{SC}_\mathcal{N}^Y$ is called *unstable* wrt. Y.

3   Reducing Clocks in Networks of Timed Automata

Consider the following motivating example of the network $\mathcal{N}_1$ depicted in Fig. 1. Network $\mathcal{N}_1$ consists of automata $\mathcal{A}_1$ and $\mathcal{A}_2$ with respective clocks x and y, rendez-vous channel c, and global variable a. Note that after delaying ten time units at their respective initial locations, automata $\mathcal{A}_1$ and $\mathcal{A}_2$ interleave by taking their simple edges which exclusively reset their respective clocks. This interleaving induces intermediate configurations where clocks x and y differ on their valuations. Automata $\mathcal{A}_1$ and $\mathcal{A}_2$ after a delay of five time units at locations ℓ_1 and ℓ_5 interleave once again by taking their complex edges which reset their respective clocks together with updates of the variable a. Note that automata $\mathcal{A}_1$ and $\mathcal{A}_2$ can reset once again their respective clocks and transit simultaneously to their respective locations ℓ_3 and ℓ_7 at any time, even without delaying at locations ℓ_2 and ℓ_6. Since the valuations of clocks x and y only differ at the point in time when they are reset, therefore they are quasi-equal clocks.

Note that network $\mathcal{N}_1$ cannot be transformed by the approach from [5], since by that approach: (a) the outgoing edges of locations ℓ_2 and ℓ_6 do not fulfill the syntactical pattern of an edge resetting quasi-equal clocks, i.e. there are no clock constraints that guard those edges, and the origin locations of those edges have no invariants; and (b) there must be a delay greater than zero time units at the origin location of any edge resetting a quasi-equal clock.

In this paper we present an approach which: (1) does not require that a network with quasi-equal clocks fulfill certain syntactical assumptions; (2) does not require any delay before resetting quasi-equal clocks; (3) does not restrict the point in time at which quasi-equal clocks are reset; (4) eliminates configurations reachable by taking simple edges, e.g. configurations reachable by taking the simple edges of locations ℓ_0 and ℓ_4 and, (5) preserves configurations reachable by taking complex edges, e.g. configurations reachable by taking the complex edges of locations ℓ_1 and ℓ_5.

In the following we introduce two definitions that allow us to classify edges that reset quasi-equal clocks into *simple* and *complex* edges. Intuitively, an edge

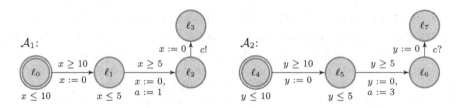

Fig. 1. Network $\mathcal{N}_1$ with quasi-equal clocks x and y.

resetting quasi-equal clocks is called simple if that edge resets exclusively one clock, does not synchronise with other edges and time must pass before taking that edge, otherwise is called complex.

Definition 1 (Pre-delayed Edge). *An edge* $e = (\ell, \alpha, \varphi, \vec{r}, \ell') \in E(\mathcal{N})$ *is called* pre-delayed *if and only if time must pass in* ℓ *before* e *is taken, i.e. if* $\Pi(\mathcal{N}) = \Pi(Z(\mathcal{N}))$, *where* Z *is a transformation that adds a fresh clock* x *in* $\mathcal{N}$, *and for each edge incoming to* ℓ, *a reset* $x := 0$, *and to the guard* φ *the condition* $x > 0$. *We use* $\mathcal{DE}_{\mathcal{N}}$ *to denote the set of pre-delayed edges of* $\mathcal{N}$.

There are *sufficient* syntactic criteria for an edge $e = (\ell_1, \alpha_1, \varphi_1, \vec{r}_1, \ell_2)$ being pre-delayed. For instance, if $(\ell_0, \alpha_0, \varphi_0, \vec{r}_0, \ell_1)$ is the only incoming edge to ℓ_1 and if $\varphi_0 = (x \geq C)$ and $\varphi_1 = (x \geq D)$ and $C < D$, then e is pre-delayed. It is also delayed if $(\ell_0, \alpha_0, \varphi_0, \vec{r}_0, \ell_1)$ is the only incoming edge to ℓ_1, $\vec{r}_0$ is resetting x, and $\varphi_1 = (x > 0)$.

Both patterns occur, e.g., in the FS case-study (cf. Sect. 5). There, the reset location is entered via an edge following the former pattern, and the edges originating at the reset successor location follow the latter pattern. Thus resetting edges are pre-delayed in FS.

Definition 2 (Simple and Complex (Resetting) Edges). *Let edge* $e = (\ell, \alpha, \varphi, \vec{r}, \ell')$ *be an edge which resets at least one quasi-equal clock, i.e. clocks*$(\vec{r}) \cap Y \neq \emptyset$ *for some* $Y \in \mathcal{EC}_{\mathcal{N}}$. *Edge* e *is called* simple edge *if and only if*

- *it is of the form* $(\ell, \tau, x \geq c, \langle x := 0 \rangle, \ell')$ *for some local clock* $x \in \mathcal{X}(\mathcal{A})$,
- *the invariant of* ℓ *is* $x \leq c$,
- *it is pre-delayed, i.e.* $e \in \mathcal{DE}_{\mathcal{N}}$,
- *it is the only outgoing edge of* ℓ, *i.e.* $\forall e_1 = (\ell_1, \alpha_1, \varphi_1, \vec{r}_1, \ell'_1) \in E(\mathcal{A}) \bullet \ell_1 = \ell \implies e = e_1$, *and it is the only incoming edge into* ℓ', *i.e.* $\forall e_1 = (\ell_1, \alpha_1, \varphi_1, \vec{r}_1, \ell'_1) \in E(\mathcal{A}) \bullet \ell'_1 = \ell' \implies e = e_1$.

Otherwise, e *is called* complex edge. *We use* $\mathcal{SE}_Y(\mathcal{A})$ *to denote the set of simple edges of* $\mathcal{A}$ *using a clock from* $Y \in \mathcal{EC}_{\mathcal{N}}$. *We use* $\mathcal{CE}_Y(\mathcal{A})$ *to denote the set of those complex edges which reset at least one clock from* $Y \in \mathcal{EC}_{\mathcal{N}}$.

To avoid really special corner cases in the following we assume that time is not stopped at origin and destination locations of simple edges. We use $\mathcal{RES}_Y(\mathcal{N})$ to denote the set of automata in $\mathcal{N}$ which have simple or complex resetting edges wrt. $Y \in \mathcal{EC}_{\mathcal{N}}$, i.e. $\mathcal{RES}_Y(\mathcal{N}) = \{\mathcal{A} \in \mathcal{N} \mid \mathcal{SE}_Y(\mathcal{A}) \cup \mathcal{CE}_Y(\mathcal{A}) \neq \emptyset\}$. For simplicity we could classify each edge resetting a clock $x \in Y$, with $Y \in \mathcal{EC}_{\mathcal{N}}$, as complex. However, with the above definition we distinguish complex edges from simple ones, and we provide a transformation for networks where interleavings of complex edges are preserved, while interleavings of simple edges are eliminated.

3.1   Algorithm for Transformation of Networks

In the following we present our transformation algorithm. It takes two inputs, a network $\mathcal{N}$ and a set of equivalence classes of quasi-equal clocks $\mathcal{EC}_{\mathcal{N}}$ (which can be obtained by [16]), and outputs a transformed network $\mathcal{N}'$ which from each $Y \in \mathcal{EC}_{\mathcal{N}}$ uses only the representative clock $rep(Y)$ and reflects the truth-value of all queries on $\mathcal{N}$.

Recall that we distinguish stable and unstable configurations per equivalence class Y. In stable configurations, all clocks from Y have the same value, thus in particular the same value as the representative $rep(Y)$. In unstable configurations, some clocks from Y have been reset and some not yet, so each clock from Y either has the value 0 or the same value as $rep(Y)$. We use a fresh boolean token t_x for each quasi-equal clock x to encode clock values in unstable configurations. Configurations in $\mathcal{N}'$ where token t_x is *true* encode configurations of $\mathcal{N}$ where $x = rep(x)$ holds, while the token being *false* encodes that x has already been reset at the current point in time and thus has value 0. Function Γ (cf. Definition 3) transforms guards and conditions based on this encoding.

Definition 3 (Function Γ). *Let $\mathcal{N}$ be a network. Let $Y, W \in \mathcal{EC}_{\mathcal{N}}$ be sets of quasi-equal clocks of $\mathcal{N}$, $x \in Y$ and $y \in W$ clocks, and z a non-quasi-equal clock. Let $t_x, t_y \notin \mathcal{V}(\mathcal{N})$ be boolean variables. Given a clock constraint φ_{clk}, we define:*

$$\Gamma_0(\varphi_{clk}) := \begin{cases} ((rep(x) \sim c \ \wedge \ t_x) \vee (0 \sim c \ \wedge \ \neg t_x)) & \text{, if } \varphi_{clk} = x \sim c, \\ ((rep(x) - rep(y) \sim c \ \wedge \ t_x \ \wedge \ t_y) & \text{, if } \varphi_{clk} = x - y \sim c, \\ \quad \vee \ (0 - rep(y) \sim c \ \wedge \ \neg t_x \ \wedge \ t_y) \\ \quad \vee \ (rep(x) - 0 \sim c \ \wedge \ t_x \ \wedge \ \neg t_y) \\ \quad \vee \ (0 \sim c \ \wedge \ \neg t_x \ \wedge \ \neg t_y)) \\ ((rep(x) - z \sim c \ \wedge \ t_x) & \text{, if } \varphi_{clk} = x - z \sim c, \\ \quad \vee \ (0 - z \sim c \ \wedge \ \neg t_x)) \\ \Gamma_0(\varphi_1) \wedge \Gamma_0(\varphi_2) & \text{, if } \varphi_{clk} = \varphi_1 \wedge \varphi_2. \end{cases}$$

We obtain the transformation Γ by setting $\Gamma(\varphi_{clk} \wedge \psi_{int}) := \Gamma_0(\varphi_{clk}) \wedge \psi_{int}$.

Following [5], we add to transformed networks a resetter automaton $\mathcal{R}_Y$ to whom we delegate the reset of clock $rep(Y)$. Resetter $\mathcal{R}_Y$ has the location $\ell_{nst\mathcal{R}_Y}$ which, as in [5], encodes unstable configurations wrt. Y. In contrast to [5], where the time points for resets were encoded in the resetters, our new approach lets the transformed automata indicate $\mathcal{R}_Y$ when to reset the clock $rep(Y)$ using the following two mechanisms (cf. Fig. 2):

1. *Rendez-vous channel reset$_Y$*. This mechanism is used if at least one transformed automaton assumes the origin location of a simple edge. The origin locations of simple edges obtain self-loops which can synchronise with $\mathcal{R}_Y$ on *reset$_Y$* exactly at those points in time in which the simple edge would be taken in the original network. Since multiple automata may have an edge synchronising on *reset$_Y$* enabled, there is a slight verification time overhead, but all edges induce the exact same follow-up configuration where only $\mathcal{R}_Y$ changes its location. The location which $\mathcal{R}_Y$ reaches by the synchronisation on *reset$_Y$* is the first of a chain of locations. The edges along the chain basically simulate a broadcast to all transformed automata which assume the origin location of a simple edge (as indicated by the flag s_Y^A) using the rendez-vous channels r_Y. The synchronisation on r_Y involves the transformed simple edge if and only if would be enabled in $\mathcal{N}$. Thereby, $\mathcal{N}'$ realises exactly one fixed sequence of simple edges as opposed to the full interleaving of simple edges possible in $\mathcal{N}$. To avoid costly and unnecessary interleavings between these "pseudo-broadcasts", all intermediate locations are committed.

   Note that a better option could be the use of a single broadcast channel on which automata assuming an origin location of a simple edge would be able to send *and* listen, and on which the corresponding $\mathcal{R}_Y$ would listen. Then, all interleavings of simple edges wrt. Y possible in $\mathcal{N}$ would be simulated by only one transition in $\mathcal{N}'$. Unfortunately, the version of Uppaal used in our experiments does not allow clock constraints on edges with inputs on broadcast channels, which is necessary since being at the origin location of a simple edge does not imply that edge is enabled.

2. *Urgent broadcast channel u_Y*. For the case that no transformed simple edge is ready to indicate the reset time, the $\mathcal{R}_Y$ also (indirectly) observes whether complex edges are taken. If the first transformed complex edge is taken at reset time, then the sum of tokens will decrease. The resetter $\mathcal{R}_Y$ uses the urgent broadcast channel u_Y in order to transit to $\ell_{nst\mathcal{R}_Y}$ as soon as the sum of tokens is below $|Y|$. By transiting to the *urgent* location $\ell_{nst\mathcal{R}_Y}$, we ensure that no time elapses unless a configuration corresponding to stability wrt. Y is reached, i.e. until all tokens wrt. Y are 0.

In order to avoid interleavings between resetters and, e.g., complex edges wrt. other equivalence classes which may be unstable at the same point in time, a resetter $\mathcal{R}_Y$ only transits back to $\ell_{ini\mathcal{R}_Y}$ (and resets the representative $rep(Y)$ and the tokens), if all other equivalence classes are stable as expressed by condition $blk(\mathcal{EC}_\mathcal{N})$ in the guard.

Note that simple edges are taken independently from all other edges, this allows us to take all transformed simple edges in $\mathcal{N}'$ before the first transformed complex one, which in turn allows us to support all queries which ask for configurations where some complex edges and none, only some, or all simple edges have been taken. Our choice for this order restricts broadcast synchronisation on edges where the receiver resets clocks from a given equivalence class, and the sender does not reset clocks from that class. To avoid unnecessarily interleavings, we enforce this order using $go(\vec{r})$ in guards of transformed complex edges

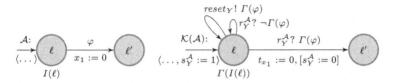

(a) Pattern of a simple edge wrt. Y in automaton $\mathcal{A}$.

(b) Pattern of the simple edge of $\mathcal{A}$ transformed in $\mathcal{K}(\mathcal{A})$.

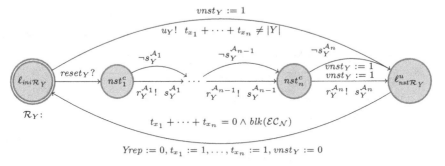

(c) Pattern of resetter $\mathcal{R}_Y$.

Fig. 2. Patterns used to transform a given network $\mathcal{N}$ with $\mathcal{EC}_\mathcal{N}$. In figures (a), (b) and (c) we consider the following quasi-equal clocks $Y = \{x_1, \ldots, x_n\}, Y \in \mathcal{EC}_\mathcal{N}$. Urgent and committed locations are denoted with the superscript u and c in the name of those locations, respectively. We use $Yrep$ as representative clock of Y, and $blk(\mathcal{EC}_\mathcal{N}) := \bigwedge_{W \in \mathcal{EC}_\mathcal{N} \setminus \{Y\}} (\sum_{w \in W} t_w = 0 \vee \sum_{w \in W} t_w = |W|)$.

wrt. Y. The condition $go(\vec{r})$ refers to the sum of all variables $s_Y^\mathcal{A}$ as indicator of whether there are transformed simple edges wrt. Y which must be taken before transformed complex edges wrt. Y or, each of those transformed simple ones has been already taken, thus variable $vnst_Y$ holds value true.

Formally, the transformation algorithm $\mathcal{K}$ works with two given inputs, a network $\mathcal{N}$ and the set $\mathcal{EC}_\mathcal{N}$ of equivalence classes of quasi-equal clocks. The output of $\mathcal{K}$ is the transformed network $\mathcal{N}' = \{\mathcal{K}(\mathcal{A}_1, \mathcal{EC}_\mathcal{N}), \ldots, \mathcal{K}(\mathcal{A}_n, \mathcal{EC}_\mathcal{N})\} \cup \{\mathcal{R}_Y \mid Y \in \mathcal{EC}_\mathcal{N}\}$ where $\mathcal{K}(\mathcal{A}, \mathcal{EC}_\mathcal{N}) = (L(\mathcal{A}), B', \mathcal{X}', \mathcal{V}', I', E_c \cup E_s \cup E_n, \ell'_{ini})$.

- $B' = B(\mathcal{A}) \cup \{reset_Y, r_Y^\mathcal{A} \mid \mathcal{A} \in \mathcal{RES}_Y(\mathcal{N})\}$, i.e. the rendez-vous channels $reset_Y$ and $r_Y^\mathcal{A}$ are added for each equivalence class affected by $\mathcal{A}$,
- $\mathcal{X}' = (\mathcal{X}(\mathcal{A}) \setminus Y) \cup \{rep(Y)\}$, i.e. all quasi-equal clocks but the representative are removed,
- $\mathcal{V}' = \mathcal{V}(\mathcal{A}) \cup \{t_x \mid x \in Y, Y \in \mathcal{EC}_\mathcal{N}\} \cup \{s_Y^\mathcal{A} \mid \mathcal{A} \in \mathcal{RES}_Y(\mathcal{N})\}$, i.e. one boolean (reset-)token for each quasi-equal clock is added (initial value is one), and a boolean simple-edge indicator $s_Y^\mathcal{A}$ (initial value is one iff the initial location of $\mathcal{A}$ is a reset location of a simple edge wrt. Y).
- $I' = \{\ell \mapsto \Gamma(I(\ell)) \mid \ell \in L(\mathcal{A})\}$, i.e. invariants are transformed with Γ to consider the representative and the reset-token of quasi-equal clocks,

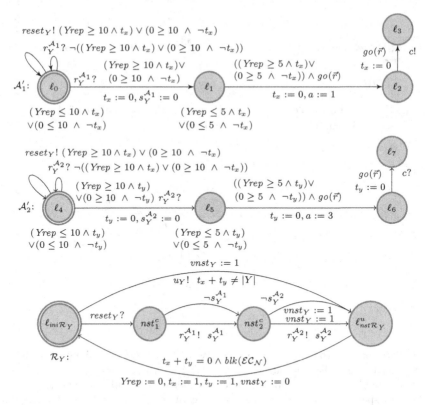

Fig. 3. Transformed network $\mathcal{N}_1' = \mathcal{K}(\mathcal{N}_1, \mathcal{EC}_\mathcal{N})$.

– Complex and non-resetting edges are transformed as follows, and the resulting edges contained in E_c and E_n, respectively. Guards are also transformed using Γ and, for complex edges, extended by the blocking condition $go(\vec{r}) := \bigwedge_{Y \in \mathcal{EC}_\mathcal{N}, clocks(\vec{r}) \cap Y \neq \emptyset} \sum_{\mathcal{A} \in \mathcal{N}} s_Y^\mathcal{A} = 0 \vee vnst_Y$. which ensures that simple edges are pushed first. Reset vectors are transformed to consider reset-tokens instead of the original clock, and extended by r_1 as book-keeping for the simple-edge indicator, where $r_1(\ell')$ is the update $s_Y^\mathcal{A} := 1$ if ℓ' is the origin location of a simple resetting edge, and ϵ otherwise.

$$E_c = \{(\ell, \alpha, \Gamma(\varphi) \wedge go(\vec{r}), \vec{r}[y := 0/t_y := 0] \mid y \in Y, Y \in \mathcal{EC}_\mathcal{N}]; r_1(\ell'), \ell') \mid$$
$$(\ell, \alpha, \varphi, \vec{r}, \ell') \in E(\mathcal{A}) \setminus \mathcal{SE}_Y(\mathcal{A})\},$$

The transformation of simple edges and the construction of the *resetter* $\mathcal{R}_Y$ for equivalence class Y is depicted in Fig. 2. Transformed simple edges contained in E_s.

Example 1. Applying $\mathcal{K}$ to network $\mathcal{N}_1$ from Fig. 1 yields network $\mathcal{N}_1'$ (cf. Fig. 3). Similar to the algorithm in [5], only the representative clock of each equivalence class remains, in our example we use the fresh clock *Yrep* as representative of Y which is reset by resetter $\mathcal{R}_Y$. Note that each guard and invariant in automata $\mathcal{A}'_1$ and $\mathcal{A}'_2$ is transformed by Γ into a disjunction of clauses. For instance, the guard $x \geq 10$ of automaton $\mathcal{A}_1$ in $\mathcal{N}_1$, is transformed in $\mathcal{N}'_1$ into the encoding (*Yrep* $\geq 10 \wedge t_x) \vee (0 \geq 10 \wedge \neg t_x)$. Then the clause (*Yrep* $\geq 10 \wedge t_x$) is effective in configurations in $\mathcal{N}'$ where t_x is true (encoding that clock x has the same value as *Yrep*), while the clause $(0 \geq 10 \wedge \neg t_x)$ is effective in configurations where t_x is false (encoding that x has already been reset and thus has value 0).

Note that in $\mathcal{N}'_1$ the pair of transformed complex edges from locations ℓ_1 and ℓ_5 preserve their original interleavings. Furthermore, the other pair of transformed complex edges, from locations ℓ_2 and ℓ_6, are taken simultaneously even without delaying at their origin locations.

3.2   Transformation of Properties

Definition 4 (Function Ω). *Let $\mathcal{N}$ be a network with a set $\mathcal{EC}_\mathcal{N}$. Let $\mathcal{A}_i$, with $1 \leq i \leq n$, be the i-th automaton of $\mathcal{N}$. Let $x \in Y$ be a clock. Let $\mathcal{N}' = \mathcal{K}(\mathcal{N}, \mathcal{EC}_\mathcal{N})$. Let β be a basic formula over $\mathcal{N}$. Let $\ell_{nst\mathcal{R}_Y}$ be the unique urgent location of resetter $\mathcal{R}_Y$. We define the function Ω as follows where $E^\star = E(\mathcal{A}) \setminus \mathcal{SE}_Y(\mathcal{A}) : \Omega_0(\beta) =$*

$$
\begin{cases}
(\ell' \wedge \tilde{\ell}_i) \vee \ell & , \text{ if } \beta = \ell, (\ell, \alpha, \varphi, \langle x := 0 \rangle, \ell') \in \mathcal{SE}_Y(\mathcal{A}_i). \\
(\ell' \wedge \neg \tilde{\ell}_i) & , \text{ if } \beta = \ell', (\ell, \alpha, \varphi, \langle x := 0 \rangle, \ell') \in \mathcal{SE}_Y(\mathcal{A}_i). \\
\ell_0 & , \text{ if } \beta = \ell_0(\ell'_0), (\ell_0, \alpha_0, \varphi_0, \vec{r}_0, \ell'_0) \in E^\star. \\
\Gamma_0(\varphi_{clk})[t_x/(t_x \vee \tilde{x})] \wedge \varphi_{int} & , \text{ if } \beta = \varphi_{clk} \wedge \varphi_{int}.
\end{cases}
$$

$$
\Omega(CF) = \exists \tilde{\ell}_1, .., \tilde{\ell}_m \; \exists \tilde{x}_1, .., \tilde{x}_k \bullet \Omega_0(CF) \wedge
$$

$$
(\tilde{\ell}_i \implies \bigvee_{(\ell, \alpha, \varphi, \vec{r}, \ell') \in \mathcal{SE}_Y(\mathcal{A}_i)} \ell' \wedge \ell_{nst\mathcal{R}_Y}) \wedge (\tilde{x}_j \implies \bigvee_{(\ell, \alpha, \varphi, \langle x_j := 0 \rangle, \ell') \in \mathcal{SE}_Y(\mathcal{A}_j)} \ell' \wedge \tilde{\ell}_j)
$$

By structural induction Ω_0 transforms configuration formulas CF.

Function Ω syntactically transforms properties over a network $\mathcal{N}$ with a set of equivalence classes of quasi-equal clocks $\mathcal{EC}_\mathcal{N}$ into properties over $\mathcal{N}' = \mathcal{K}(\mathcal{N}, \mathcal{EC}_\mathcal{N})$. Function Ω treats queries for origin and destination locations of simple edges special, and outputs an equivalent property which can be verified in $\mathcal{N}'$. For instance, consider the simple edge $e = (\ell_0, \tau, (x \geq 10), \langle x := 0 \rangle, \ell_1)$ of automaton $\mathcal{A}_1$ of network $\mathcal{N}_1$. The query $\exists \Diamond \phi$, where $\phi : \ell_0$, is transformed after some simplifications into $\Omega(\phi) : \exists \tilde{\ell} \in \{0, 1\} \bullet ((\ell_1 \wedge \tilde{\ell}) \vee \ell_0) \wedge (\tilde{\ell} \implies (\ell_1 \wedge \ell_{nst\mathcal{R}_Y}))$. The logical variable $\tilde{\ell}$ in the transformed query enforces consistent unstable configurations where the location ℓ_0 can be assumed.

The origin location ℓ_0 of e can be assumed in $\mathcal{N}$ in different configurations: either the reset time is not yet reached, or the reset time is reached but $\mathcal{A}_1$ has not reset its clock x yet, while other automata in $\mathcal{RES}_Y(\mathcal{N})$ may have reset their clocks already. In $\mathcal{N}'$, all edges resulting from simple edges are taken in a fixed sequence by rendez-vous synchronisations, so each origin location is left

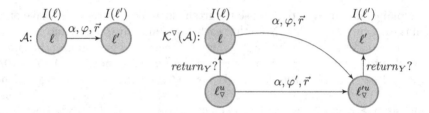

Fig. 4. Transformation pattern of algorithm $\mathcal{K}^\triangledown$ over network $\mathcal{N}' = \mathcal{K}(\mathcal{N}, \mathcal{EC}_\mathcal{N})$, where $\varphi' = \varphi \wedge \bigwedge_{Y \in \mathcal{EC}_\mathcal{N}} \sum_{x \in Y \cap \mathcal{X}(\mathcal{A})} t_x > 0$. Algorithm $\mathcal{K}^\triangledown$ takes each edge of network $\mathcal{N}'$ (excluding edges of resetters), cf. left-hand side and transforms it according to the right-hand side. The edge originally linking locations ℓ and ℓ' is redirected to $\ell_\triangledown^{\prime u}$ if and only if $\exists Y \in \mathcal{EC}_\mathcal{N} \,\exists x \in Y \bullet t_x \in \mathit{vars}(\vec{r})$. In addition, in each resetter $\mathcal{R}_Y$, an output action on broadcast channel return_Y is added to the edge from $\ell_{nst\mathcal{R}_Y}$ to $\ell_{ini\mathcal{R}_Y}$.

one by one. Because the resetter finally moves to $\ell_{nst\mathcal{R}_Y}$ after synchronising with automata $\mathcal{A}_1'$ and $\mathcal{A}_2'$, a configuration of $\mathcal{N}'$ which assumes location $\ell_{nst\mathcal{R}_Y}$ represents all similar unstable configurations of $\mathcal{N}$ where all simple edges are in their origin or destination location. Therefore, from $\Omega(\phi)$, the clause ℓ_0 is effective in configurations of $\mathcal{N}'$ which represent those in $\mathcal{N}$ where the reset time is not yet reached; while the clause $(\ell_1 \wedge \tilde{\ell})$ is effective in configurations of $\mathcal{N}'$ which represent those in $\mathcal{N}$ where the reset time is reached but $\mathcal{A}_1$ has not reset its clock x yet, while other automata in $\mathcal{RES}_Y(\mathcal{N})$ may have reset their clocks already. The latter configurations in $\mathcal{N}$, enforced by the logical variable $\tilde{\ell}$, are assumed in $\mathcal{N}'$, in particular, when resetter $\mathcal{R}_Y$ is located at location $\ell_{nst\mathcal{R}_Y}$ and automaton $\mathcal{A}_1'$ at location ℓ_1.

4   Weak Bisimulation

In order to prove our approach correct we establish a weak bisimulation relation between a network $\mathcal{N}$ with a set of equivalence classes of quasi-equal clocks $\mathcal{EC}_\mathcal{N}$, and its respective transformed network $\mathcal{N}' = \mathcal{K}(\mathcal{N}, \mathcal{EC}_\mathcal{N})$.

Recall that configurations induced when each clock x from $Y \in \mathcal{EC}_\mathcal{N}$ is reset in network $\mathcal{N}$, are summarised in $\mathcal{N}'$ in configurations where the $\ell_{nst\mathcal{R}_Y}$-location is assumed, in particular, when the values of variables $s_Y^\mathcal{A}$ and t_x reflect these resets. Hence with the valuations from those variables we unfold information summarised in these configurations from $\mathcal{N}'$.

Lemma 1. *Any network $\mathcal{N}$ with equivalence classes of quasi-equal clocks $\mathcal{EC}_\mathcal{N}$, is weakly bisimilar to $\mathcal{N}' = \mathcal{K}(\mathcal{N}, \mathcal{EC}_\mathcal{N})$, i.e. there is a weak bisimulation relation $\mathcal{S} \subseteq \mathit{Conf}(\mathcal{N}) \times \mathit{Conf}(\mathcal{N}')$ such that*

1. *$\forall s \in \mathcal{C}_{ini}(\mathcal{N}) \,\exists r \in \mathcal{C}_{ini}(\mathcal{N}) \bullet (s, r) \in \mathcal{S}$ and $\forall r \in \mathcal{C}_{ini}(\mathcal{N}') \,\exists s \in \mathcal{C}_{ini}(\mathcal{N}) \bullet (s, r) \in \mathcal{S}$.*
2. *For all config. formulae CF over $\mathcal{N}$, $\forall(s, r) \in \mathcal{S} \bullet s \models CF \implies r \models \Omega(CF)$ and $\forall r \in \downarrow_2 \mathcal{S} \bullet r \models \Omega(CF) \implies \exists s \in \mathit{Conf}(\mathcal{N}) \bullet (s, r) \in \mathcal{S} \wedge s \models CF$.*

3. For all $(s, r) \in \mathcal{S}$,

  (a) if $s \xrightarrow{\lambda} s'$ and

    i. $\lambda = d > 0$, then there exists a sequence of transitions $r \xrightarrow{\tau}^{*} r' \xrightarrow{\lambda} r''$, with $(s', r'') \in \mathcal{S}$,

    ii. transition is justified by some edges (non-resetting, simple or complex edge wrt. $Y \in \mathcal{EC}_{\mathcal{N}}$). Then there exist $r \xrightarrow{\tau}^{*} r' \xrightarrow{\lambda} r'' \xrightarrow{\tau}^{*} r'''$, with $(s', r''') \in \mathcal{S}$.

  (b) if $r \xrightarrow{\lambda} r'$ then there exists s', such that $s \xrightarrow{\lambda_1} s'$, with $(s', r') \in \mathcal{S}$.

Where $r \xrightarrow{\tau}^{*} r'$ denotes zero or more successive τ-transitions from configuration r to configuration r'.

Proof. (Sketch) For each $Y \in \mathcal{EC}_{\mathcal{N}}$ the weak bisimulation relation $\mathcal{S}$ which relates pairs of configurations $(s, r) \in Conf(\mathcal{N}) \times Conf(\mathcal{N}')$, is based in the following four aspects: (A1) the values of variables and non-quasi-equal clocks. (A2) configurations where both networks assume the same locations, and the value of each clock $x \in Y$ in $\mathcal{N}$ coincides with the value of that clock assumed by $rep(x)$ and token t_x in $\mathcal{N}'$. (A2) also considers configurations where simple edges in $\mathcal{N}$ are enabled, and their corresponding transformed simple edges in $\mathcal{N}'$ have been taken. (A3) stable configurations wrt. Y in $\mathcal{N}$ and configurations in $\mathcal{N}'$ where either no transformed resetting edge wrt. Y has been taken, or all transformed resetting edges wrt. Y have been taken. (A4) consistent values for variables $s_Y^{\mathcal{A}}$ and $vnst_Y$.

During stability phases there is a strong bisimulation (one-to-one) between the networks $\mathcal{N}$ and $\mathcal{N}'$. Only during unstability phases there is a weak bisimulation (one-to-many) from $\mathcal{N}$ to $\mathcal{N}'$. For instance, the reset of a simple edge in $\mathcal{N}$ is simulated in $\mathcal{N}'$ with multiple steps. Artificial steps in $\mathcal{N}'$ such as $reset_Y$-synchronization, u_Y-output and return to ℓ_{iniR_Y} in $\mathcal{R}_Y$ are simulated in $\mathcal{N}$ by a zero delay transition. Steps where $\mathcal{N}'$ takes transformed complex o simple edges are simulated in $\mathcal{N}$ by one step taking the corresponding resetting edge.

Theorem 1. *Let $\mathcal{N}$ be a network with a set $\mathcal{EC}_{\mathcal{N}}$. Let CF be a configuration formula over $\mathcal{N}$. Then $\mathcal{K}(\mathcal{N}, \mathcal{EC}_{\mathcal{N}}) \models \exists \Diamond \Omega(CF) \iff \mathcal{N} \models \exists \Diamond CF.$*

Proof. Use Lemma 1 and induction over the length of paths to show that CF holds in $\mathcal{N}$ if and only if $\Omega(CF)$ holds in $\mathcal{K}(\mathcal{N}, \mathcal{EC}_{\mathcal{N}})$. □

For performance purposes we have transformed our benchmarks with algorithm $\mathcal{K}^{\triangledown}$ which takes the output of algorithm $\mathcal{K}$ and applies the changes depicted in Fig. 4. Algorithm $\mathcal{K}^{\triangledown}$ together with functions $devirQE$ and $\Omega^{\triangledown}$ allow us to state in Lemma 2 a strong bisimulation relation between the networks $\mathcal{N}'$ and $\mathcal{N}^{\triangledown}$ which are output by algorithms $\mathcal{K}$ and $\mathcal{K}^{\triangledown}$, respectively.

Lemma 2. *Given networks: $\mathcal{N}$ with a set $\mathcal{EC}_{\mathcal{N}}$, $\mathcal{N}' = \mathcal{K}(\mathcal{N}, \mathcal{EC}_{\mathcal{N}})$ and $\mathcal{N}^{\triangledown} = \mathcal{K}^{\triangledown}(\mathcal{N}')$. Then $\mathcal{N}'$ is strongly bisimilar to $\mathcal{N}^{\triangledown}$ with $devirQE(r) = r[\ell_{\triangledown}/\ell \mid \ell_{\triangledown} \in L(\mathcal{N}^{\triangledown})]$, and $\mathcal{N}' \models \exists \Diamond \Omega(CF) \iff \mathcal{N}^{\triangledown} \models \exists \Diamond \Omega^{\triangledown}(CF)$, where $\Omega^{\triangledown}$ is defined by replacing in Ω every occurrence of a location ℓ', $(\ell, \alpha, \varphi, \vec{r}, \ell') \in \mathcal{SE}_Y, Y \in \mathcal{EC}_{\mathcal{N}}$, by $\ell'_{\triangledown}$.*

5 Experimental Results

We applied our approach to nine industrial case studies using *sAsEt* [16], our implementation of algorithms $\mathcal{K}$ and $\mathcal{K}^{\triangledown}$ with integrated detection of equivalence classes of quasi-equal clocks and, simple and complex edges. Six case studies *FS* [18], *CR* [19], *CD* [20], *EP* [14], *TT* [21] and *LS* [22] appear in [5]. The interested reader can obtain from [5] more details of those case studies. The elimination of assumptions on networks allowed us to include three new case studies that [5] cannot transform: *FB* [7], *TA* [8] and *PG* [9]. We verified queries as proposed by the respective authors of each case study. Our motivating case study is inspired by the network from [7] which models the Foundation Fieldbus Data Link Layer protocol (FDLL). The network consists of N sensors and one master. Each of them with complex edges which are taken simultaneously by synchronising on a given broadcast channel at the command of the master. Both sender and receiver reset quasi-equal clocks of the same equivalence class. The point in time in which quasi-equal clocks are reset by those complex edges, is neither unique nor explicit in the syntax of those edges. Moreover, those complex edges can be taken even without delaying at their origin locations. Case study [8] is an implementation of a TDMA protocol. Case study [9] is an implementation of the Pragmatic General Multicast (PGM), which is a reliable multicast transport protocol for applications that require multicast data delivery from a single source to multiple receivers.

Table 1 gives figures for the verification of queries in instances of the original and the transformed model (denoted by the suffix K in the name). The rows without results indicate the smallest instances for which we did not obtain results within 24 h. For all examples we achieved significant savings in verification time, sometimes of factor n. However, the verification time in transformed models is less meaningful in benchmarks *TA* and *TT*. The quasi-equal clocks in the *TA* and *TT* models are reset by complex edges, so all interleaving of resets in the original model are preserved in the transformed network, together with the artificial transitions that our transformation introduces. This can explain that our savings in these models are related to a more efficient DBM-management. Still, the verification of the transformed models of *TA* and *TT* *including* transformation time is faster than verification of the original ones.

The biggest savings in terms of verification time are obtained in the transformed models *FS*, *CD*, and *CR*. In these models we have simple edges whose interleaving is reduced to a fixed sequence. Regarding memory consumption, we observe the biggest savings again in the mentioned models for the reasons already explained. Note that the verification of the transformed models *EP*, *LS*, *PG* takes slightly more memory than the verification of the original counterparts. We argue that this is due to all resetting edges being *complex* in these three networks. Thus, our transformation preserves the full interleaving of clock resets and the whole set of unstable locations whose size is exponential in the number of participating automata, and it adds the transitions to and from location $\ell_{nst\mathcal{R}_Y}$. Furthermore, we add extra variables in those networks, namely, boolean tokens for each quasi-equal clock whose management contributes in the

Table 1. Row X-$N(\mathcal{K})$ gives the figures for case study X with N components (and $\mathcal{K}$ applied). 'C' gives the number of clocks in the model, 'kStates' the number of 10^3 visited states, 'M' memory usage in MB, and '$t(s)$' verification time in seconds. sAsEt transformed each of our benchmarks in at most 5 s.

Network	C	kStates	M	$t(s)$	Network	C	kStates	M	$t(s)$
EP-21	21	3,145.7	507.6	444.8	FS-8	14	5,084.3	160.8	1,007.1
EP-21K	1	3,145.7	525.7	89.8	FS-8K	5	1,892.7	78.0	80.3
EP-22	22	6,291.5	1,027.2	1,032.0	FS-10	16	17,474,6	518.6	4,734.0
EP-22K	1	6,291.5	1,060.5	193.8	FS-10K	5	2,152.1	83.7	97.7
EP-23	23	–	–	–	FS-11	17	–	–	–
EP-23K	1	12,582.9	2,146.9	427.3	FS-126K	5	28,510.8	905.6	3,963.3
TT-5	6	436.9	57.9	5.9	CD-14	29	7,078.1	591.7	1,388.0
TT-5K	1	327.1	79.5	4.5	CD-14K	15	1,327.3	142.0	179.1
TT-6	7	2,986.0	116.5	36.9	CD-15	31	8,945.7	1,186.9	1,785.7
TT-6K	1	1,916.6	467.1	30.2	CD-15K	16	6,062.6	529.6	978.9
TT-7	8	16,839.9	612.9	235.3	CD-16	33	–	–	–
TT-7K	1	11,054.9	2,527.7	198.2	CD-16K	17	17,892.1	1,954.9	3,703.0
LS-6	17	145.1	21.6	4.3	CR-6	6	264.5	20.3	2.8
LS-6K	3	151.2	23.0	2.2	CR-6K	1	67.7	12.3	0.8
LS-7	19	553.3	74.6	22.2	CR-7	7	7,223.7	497.5	132.8
LS-7K	3	554.7	81.0	10.1	CR-7K	1	1,300.6	165.2	20.9
LS-9	23	8,897.6	1,285.2	524.9	CR-8	8	–	–	–
LS-9K	3	9,008.2	1,450.8	224.1	CR-8K	1	2,569.7	359.0	52.4
FB-12	14	24.6	6.6	30.9	TA-2	7	42.1	6.3	0.3
FB-12K	3	24.6	6.1	0.4	TA-2K	2	40.1	6.1	0.3
FB-15	17	2,920.3	36.5	3,894.4	TA-3	8	921.5	97.5	10.6
FB-15K	3	196.6	31.7	4.8	TA-3K	2	917.4	59.5	9.7
FB-16	18	–	–	–	TA-4	9	33,547.6	1,827.8	630.0
FB-21K	3	12,582.9	2,138.4	647.5	TA-4K	2	31,397.2	1,405.7	412.7
PG-10	13	85.0	4.6	367.9	Experimental environment: Intel i3, 2.3 GHz, 3 GB, Ubuntu 11.04, verifyta 4.1.3.4577/default options.				
PG-10K	3	160.8	7.1	1.5					
PG-12	15	389.1	9.6	9,560.9					
PG-12K	3	737.3	21.1	8.5					
PG-13	16	–	–	–					
PG-18K	3	65,273.9	1,732.4	1,165.3					

overall memory consumption. The shown reduction of the verification time is due to a smaller size of the DBMs that Uppaal uses to represent zones [6] and whose size grows quadratically in the number of clocks.

Our new technique transforms any network with quasi-equal clocks. It reduces the verification time of properties in transformed networks, and represents all clocks from an equivalence class by one representative. This technique can reduce those configurations induced by automata that reset quasi-equal clocks one by one. Furthermore, our technique supports all properties reflected by original networks. We plan to implement our new approach in hybrid automata.

References

1. Alur, R., Dill, D.: A theory of timed automata. TCS **126**(2), 183–235 (1994)
2. Herrera, C., Westphal, B., Feo-Arenis, S., Muñiz, M., Podelski, A.: Reducing quasi-equal clocks in networks of timed automata. In: Jurdziński, M., Ničković, D. (eds.) FORMATS 2012. LNCS, vol. 7595, pp. 155–170. Springer, Heidelberg (2012)
3. Rappaport, T.S.: Wireless communications, vol. 2. Prentice Hall (2002)
4. Behrmann, G., David, A., Larsen, K.G.: A tutorial on UPPAAL. In: Bernardo, M., Corradini, F. (eds.) SFM-RT 2004. LNCS, vol. 3185, pp. 200–236. Springer, Heidelberg (2004)
5. Herrera, C., Westphal, B., Podelski, A.: Quasi-equal clock reduction: more networks, more queries. In: Ábrahám, E., Havelund, K. (eds.) TACAS 2014 (ETAPS). LNCS, vol. 8413, pp. 295–309. Springer, Heidelberg (2014)
6. Bengtsson, J.E., Yi, W.: Timed automata: semantics, algorithms and tools. In: Desel, J., Reisig, W., Rozenberg, G. (eds.) Lectures on Concurrency and Petri Nets. LNCS, vol. 3098, pp. 87–124. Springer, Heidelberg (2004)
7. Petalidis, N.: Verification of a fieldbus scheduling protocol using timed automata. CI **28**(5), 655–672 (2009)
8. Godary, K.: Validation temporelle de réseaux embarqués critiques et fiables pour l'automobile. PhD thesis, Institut National des Sciences Appliquées de Lyon, France (2004)
9. Bérard, B., Bouyer, P., Petit, A.: Analysing the PGM Protocol with UPPAAL. IJPR **42**(14), 2773–2791 (2004)
10. Daws, C., Yovine, S.: Reducing the number of clock variables of timed automata. In: RTSS, pp. 73–81. IEEE (1996)
11. Daws, C., Tripakis, S.: Model checking of real-time reachability properties using abstractions. In: Steffen, B. (ed.) TACAS 1998. LNCS, vol. 1384, pp. 313–329. Springer, Heidelberg (1998)
12. Braberman, V., Garbervestky, D., Kicillof, N., Monteverde, D., Olivero, A.: Speeding up model checking of timed-models by combining scenario specialization and live component analysis. In: Ouaknine, J., Vaandrager, F.W. (eds.) FORMATS 2009. LNCS, vol. 5813, pp. 58–72. Springer, Heidelberg (2009)
13. Braberman, V.A., Garbervetsky, D., Olivero, A.: Improving the verification of timed systems using influence information. In: Katoen, J.-P., Stevens, P. (eds.) TACAS 2002. LNCS, vol. 2280, p. 21. Springer, Heidelberg (2002)
14. Limal, S., Potier, S., Denis, B., Lesage, J.: Formal verification of redundant media extension of ethernet powerlink. In: ETFA, pp. 1045–1052. IEEE (2007)
15. Muñiz, M., Westphal, B., Podelski, A.: Timed automata with disjoint activity. In: Jurdziński, M., Ničković, D. (eds.) FORMATS 2012. LNCS, vol. 7595, pp. 188–203. Springer, Heidelberg (2012)
16. Muñiz, M., Westphal, B., Podelski, A.: Detecting quasi-equal clocks in timed automata. In: Braberman, V., Fribourg, L. (eds.) FORMATS 2013. LNCS, vol. 8053, pp. 198–212. Springer, Heidelberg (2013)

17. Olderog, E.-R., Dierks, H.: Real-time systems - formal specification and automatic verification. Cambridge University Press (2008)
18. Dietsch, D., Feo-Arenis, S., et al.: Disambiguation of industrial standards through formalization and graphical languages. In: RE, pp. 265–270. IEEE (2011)
19. Gobriel, S., Khattab, S., Mossé, D., et al.: RideSharing: fault tolerant aggregation in sensor networks using corrective actions. In: SECON, pp. 595–604. IEEE (2006)
20. Jensen, H., Larsen, K., Skou, A.: Modelling and analysis of a collision avoidance protocol using SPIN and Uppaal. In: 2nd SPIN Workshop (1996)
21. Steiner, W., Elmenreich, W.: Automatic recovery of the TTP/A sensor/actuator network. In: WISES, pp. 25–37. Vienna University of Technology (2003)
22. Kordy, P., Langerak, R., et al.: Re-verification of a lip synchronization protocol using robust reachability. In: FMA. EPTCS, vol. 20, pp. 49–62 (2009)

Resource-Parameterized Timing Analysis of Real-Time Systems

Jin Hyun Kim[1]([✉]), Axel Legay[1], Kim G. Larsen[2], Marius Mikučionis[2], and Brian Nielsen[2]

[1] INRIA/IRISA, Rennes, France
[2] Alborg University, Aalborg, Denmark
`jin-hyun.kim@inria.fr`

Abstract. Cyber-Physical Systems (CPS) are subject to platform-given resource constraints upon such resources as CPU, memory, and bus, in executing their functionalities. This causes the behavior of a verified application to deviate from its intended timing behavior when the application is integrated on a specific platform. For the same reason, a configuration of platforms cannot be independent from applications in most cases. This paper proposes a new analysis framework of real-time systems where an application and a platform can be analyzed in a fully independent way such that not only the application but also the platform once verified can be exploited by various applications. The dependent behaviors of application and platform are also analyzed by exploiting their individual models transformed from their independent models. To the end, we provide a highly configurable platform model that can be parameterized by various resource configurations. For analysis of application and platform models, we use two model checking techniques: symbolic and statistical model checking techniques of UPPAAL. Our framework is demonstrated by a case study where a turn indicator system is analyzed with respect to various platform resource constraints.

1 Introduction

The more control systems close to human lives adopt Cyber-Physical Systems (CPS), the more important it is to guarantee the safety and integrity of the system. For instance, many automotive system components are required to achieve a designated integrity level through recommended design and analysis methods. In order to achieve a high level of integrity, it is recommended to formally design and analyze all possible properties of the system.

In particular, it is important to take into account the composability of application and platform in an early design phrase prior to implementation. So that the application once verified without the concern about its platform should satisfy its functional and performance requirements when being integrated with a platform. Model-Driven Architecture (MDA) is a model-based approach based

The research presented in this paper has been partially supported by EU Artemis Projects CRAFTERS and MBAT.

N. Piterman (Ed.): HVC 2015, LNCS 9434, pp. 190–205, 2015.
DOI: 10.1007/978-3-319-26287-1_12

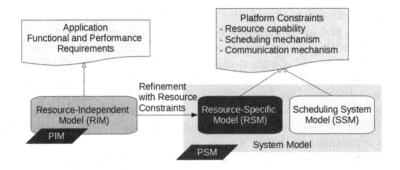

Fig. 1. Analysis methodology using UPPAAL environment.

on the separation of concerns principle. In the approach, an application is captured by two models, a Platform-Independent Model (PIM) and a Platform-Specific Model (PSM). Kim et al. in [5,6] present a formal analysis method utilizing the MDA principle, where the PIM (Platform-Independent Model) and PSM (Platform-Specific Model) of a medical software system are analyzed using a symbolic model checking technique. The platform-concerned aspect of the PSM is abstracted as a delay which postpones the execution time of applications. The PSM of this work is simple but too specific to be used for various platform settings. Also, the PSM of the MDA does not specify a platform even if a platform is more often re-used than applications. So far, platform aspects in the MDA have not been much studied as an independent model so that they are captured for the composability analysis of applications, analysis of a platform cannot be thus independent from applications.

In short, not only application requirements should be platform-independent and define both functional and performance timing requirements, but also a platform should be application-independent. Hence, the development of CPS applications should be leveraged so that if resource constraints are guaranteed by a platform running the application, then the integration of applications and platforms will satisfy both functional and performance requirements of applications.

This paper presents a new analysis framework of real-time CPS using formal analysis techniques, where the platform is verified independently from applications to guarantee given resource constraints, and the application is evaluated under the verified resource constraints to satisfy its functional and timing requirements. In our framework, an application model captures a functional behavior over time, and a platform model captures resource constraints regarding a shared resource, e.g. CPU, and is represented by a scheduling system that manages limited resources for current tasks. The application model is integrated on a platform model and checks its functional and timing properties under resource constraints given by the platform model.

We propose three behavioral models for applications and platforms, as shown in Fig. 1: Resource-Independent behavioral Model (RIM) models a functionality of the system including application-concerned timing requirements, ignoring any platform constraints. Scheduling System Model (SSM) specifies a scheduling mechanism of a given platform. Resource-Specific behavioral Model (RSM) refines a RIM with platform-given constraints in terms of the best- and worst-case execution time and communication mechanisms. In terms of MDA, a platform independent model of applications can be presented by a RIM. A platform specific model is given by both RSM and SSM. For the analysis of platform independent and platform specific models, a behavior model of each application component is first captured by RIM. Second, a (shared) resource constraint of platforms is captured by a SSM. One or more tasks and scheduling mechanisms constitute a SSM, which is checked in terms of the schedulability. Third, a RSM is constructed by refining individual operations of a RIM with timing properties. Finally, a RSM and a SSM are combined into a system model by associating individual components of the RSM to tasks of the SSM, and the system model is checked against application's properties relying on a platform. For the formal analysis, we apply the statistical and symbolic model checking techniques of UPPAAL.

This paper extends our previous work of [7] where a turn indicator system is analyzed using UPPAAL tools so that application model of the system is investigated under platform-given resource constraints. In addition, we propose a scheduling system model as a way of providing resource constraints of platforms for composability analysis of applications.

The rest of the paper is organized as follows: Sect. 2 discuss the background of this work and related work. Section 3 discusses our methodology and proposes a new analysis framework using formal analysis techniques that supports the MDA principle. Section provides a brief description of the case study, Turn Indicator (TI) system, and the properties to be checked. Finally, the paper is concluded in Sect. 5.

2   Backgrounds

This section discusses the formalism of our specification and analysis. We used Timed Automata (TA) and Stopwatch Automata (SWA) for specification and the relevant model checking tools, UPPAAL MC and UPPAAL SMC. *Timed Automaton* (TA) that [1] is a classical formal model for designing real-time systems. It consists of:

- A set of real-time *clocks*. The model uses a continuous time semantics meaning that the clocks are evaluated to real number.
- A set of locations, possibly labeled with an *invariant* constraint over clocks, which restricts the time spent in the location.
- A set of *transitions* between pairs of *locations*, possibly labeled with a *guard* over clocks. This guard specifies from which values of the clocks the transition may be taken. The transition may also be labeled with a synchronization channel and an update of clocks.

In case of preemptive real-time systems, it is necessary to keep track of the execution time of a running process, and SWA comes along with a stopwatch

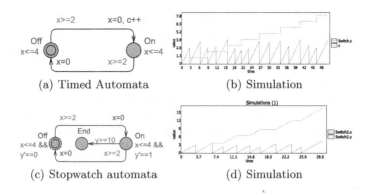

(a) Timed Automata

(b) Simulation

(c) Stopwatch automata

(d) Simulation

Fig. 2. Stopwatch Automata for switch

mechanism where a stopwatch clock keeps the time it stops by a condition so that it resumes from the moment it freezes.

The TA and SWA of Fig. 2 models various quantitative aspect of a simple Switch with two modes On and Off. Figure 2(a) is a timed automaton model of the Switch using a clock x to enforce that the time-separation between mode-switches is between 2 and 4 time-units. In addition an integer variable c counts the number of time the Switch has been in location On. Figure 2(c) introduces a stopwatch y which is running only in location On, thus effectively measuring the accumulated residence-time in On.

Correctness of the system is specified using formal logics that defines which are the admissible executions of the system. We will use a subset of the Computational Tree Logic (CTL) as defined by the model-checker UPPAAL. The grammar of this subset is $\varphi ::= A[]P \mid A<>P \mid E[]P \mid E<>P$. A and E are paths operators, meaning respectively "for all the path" and "there exists a path". [] and <> are state operators, meaning respectively "all the states of the path" and "there exists a state in the path". P is an atomic proposition that is valid in some state. For example the formula "A[] not deadlock" specifies that in all the paths and all the states on these paths we will never reach a deadlock state in which the system is permanently blocked.

Model-checking (MC) is an automated verification technique that explored all the possible executions of a TA to verify if it satisfies a property expressed in a logic like CTL. Probabilistic model-checking can also be used to compute the probability to satisfy a CTL property. However these technique are limited by state-space explosion problems when the model is too large, which can prevent the analysis due to a lack of memory.

Another verification method that we adopt here is Statistical Model-Checking (SMC) [3]. We have two reasons for using SMC analyzing a probabilistic model: First, it somehow mitigates the limitation of MC, the state-explosion problem. Basically, SMC, based on numerous traces from simulations, computes a possibility of system's satisfaction for a property using statistical methods. The model that can be checked by SMC must be probabilistic. However, UPPAAL SMC accepts a non-probabilistic model and transforms the model into a probabilistic model by applying the uniform probability distribution so that SMC techniques is applicable for the model. Using SMC techniques, we can gain a probability of system's satisfaction for a property limited by a specific certainty. Although the 100 % certainty cannot be not obtained, SMC can give a quantified evidence of system's satisfaction for a property Moreover, SMC can return a counterexample that disproves a property of a system so that we can find a way how to fix the identified problem. Second, a non-determinism of timed systems that can not be modeled in an easy way can be modeled with a probability.

2.1 Related Work

This work is a realization of Y-Chart methodology [2,4] targeting at the early phase timing analysis of CPS. Y-Charts methodology recommends the performance check of the combination of platforms and applications. Metropolice [2] is an analysis environment where a system is designed and analyzed in accordance with the Y-Chart principle prior to implementation of applications. However, we are aiming at providing a platform model fully independent from applications such that it can be utilized for any given applications.

In principle, our model of real-time CPS is similar to conservative scheduling systems, such as deferrable server and sporadic server scheduling [8,11]. One of the drawbacks of conservative scheduling systems is to waste some supplied resource when a client task is idling. However, the separation of our framework between application and platform executions brings the advantage that analysis of platforms is independent from that of applications. In addition, the separation makes it possible to provide a verified specification of applications that can be refined with resource constraints of platforms. The behavior of our application models depending on a platform model of scheduling systems is compared to a hierarchical scheduling system, where a scheduling system depends on its nesting scheduling system [9]. Our focus of this work is on the realization and analysis of various combinations of applications and platforms for composability analysis. To the end, we present highly configurable formal models of applications and platforms.

The most recent relevant work is the work of Kim et al. in [5,6]. In this work, a CPS is modeled based on Model-Driven Architecture principle. A PSM is captured by two layers, an application layer and a platform layer, which are distinguished by Input/Output and Monitor/Control variables individually. In this work, the computation and communication time of applications depending on platforms are abstracted by a delay measured physically. Distinguished from [5,6], we propose a combination of a platform behavior model and an application model, where the platform model is represented by an scheduling unit. Thus, the platform layer is so flexible, specified and general as to be adopted by any platforms.

In terms of application model, TIMMO Project [12] also deals with an extension of software architecture models with timing but are not supported by any formal analysis technique. In terms of formal analysis for software architecture, Sokolsky et al. [10] presented a formal method using a process algebraic method,

ACSR-VP and the relevant tool for AADL. However, it focuses on schedulability analysis from application perspective.

To our best knowledges, our work is unique in that we present behavior models of applications that are completely dependent from platforms but transformed for a particular platform in ease. Also, we propose a systematic way of combining an application and a platform that has not been dealt by MDA approaches. Moreover, we present a highly configurable platform is parameterized with various resource configurations for analysis of platform-dependent properties of applications.

3   Resource-Parameterized Timing Analysis

To analyze individual applications, platforms, and their combinations, we capture their individual behaviors and then compose them into a system model. An application is modeled in accordance with functional and performance requirements. A platform is modeled to capture resource constraints in the form of scheduling systems, which is parameterized with configurations of tasks characterized by real-time attributes e.g. an execution time, a period, and a deadline.

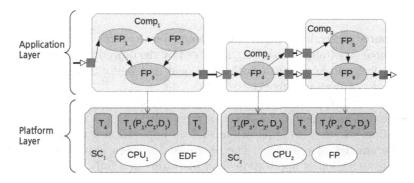

Fig. 3. Our CPS model

Figure 3 shows a Resource-Parameterized Model (RPM) of real-time applications where a platform is configured according to resource constraints. This model is composed of two layers, an application layer and a platform layer. The application layer is composed of a set of components ($Comp_i$) and the platform layer is composed of one or more scheduling units (SC_i). The behavior of an application component is modeled by one or more functional processes (FP_i), which can be any computation models capable of representing a behavior of computations and communications over time. Each component $Comp_i$ is connected to a specific task T_i, which is characterized by real-time attributes, such as a period(P_i), the worst-case execute time (C_i), and a deadline (D_i). As our framework is aiming at an early phase timing analysis, the worst-case execution time of a task is a timing requirement.

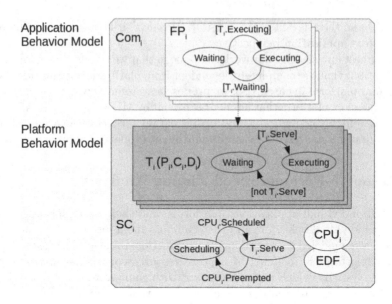

Fig. 4. Resource-Parameterized Model (RPM)

A resource constraint of a platform is denoted by real-time attributes of tasks. The resource constraint should be guaranteed by the objective platform and the application should accomplish both functional and performance requirements under platform-given resource constraints.

In fact, an application is the same object as task but they are separated in our framework as a client and a server, respectively: A task is a server supplying computation resources to applications and an application is a client requiring a specific amount of resources. The separation between application and task enables investigation of applications and platforms in a fully independent way. Also, the platform model can be used as a resource constraint specification for composability analysis of applications prior to their integration. Furthermore, it enables a platform once verified to be used for different applications.

The RPM in Fig. 4 refines the RPM in Fig. 3 in terms of behavior. The task $T_i(P_i, C_i, D_i)$ has a behavior depending on a resource model of CPU. The CPU resource model schedules jobs of tasks using the EDF scheduling policy. If the CPU resource model begins to serve at state T_i.Server, then the task T_i switches to state Executing by the condition $[T_i.\text{Serve}]$ and the functional process FP_i also switches to state Executing by the condition $[T_i.\text{Executing}]$.

3.1 Response Time of Applications

The separation between applications and tasks is similar to a hierarchical scheduling system and a deferrable scheduling system, where a client task demanding a resource assignment cooperates with a server task supplying resources to a client

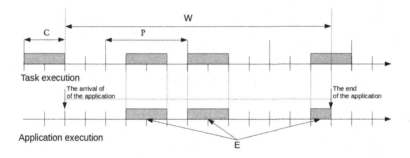

Fig. 5. The WCRT of an application

task. For this reason, the preexisting analysis techniques for such systems can also be used for the application properties of our framework.

The application behavior in this framework does not necessarily synchronize with its relevant task of a platform model, the response time of applications relying on its associated task is hence varying according to the real-time attributes of the task. Figure 5 depicts that the application with execution time E is served by a task in the worst-case. The task runs for C time units every P time units. The application needs E time units to finish its computations. The worst-case is that the application begins as soon as the task (the first execution of the task) finishes one of its executions, and ends with an execution of the task (the last execution of the task) postponed as long as possible. For a given application whose the execution time is E and which relies on a periodic task $T(P,C)$, the worst-case response time (W) of the application can be computed using the *service time bound function* (sbf) [9]:

$$\mathsf{sbf}(E) = (P - C) + P \cdot \left\lfloor \frac{E}{C} \right\rfloor + \epsilon_s \tag{1}$$

$$\epsilon_s = \begin{cases} P - C + E - C \cdot \left\lfloor \frac{E}{C} \right\rfloor & \text{if } t - C \cdot \left\lfloor \frac{E}{C} \right\rfloor > 0 \\ 0 & otherwise \end{cases} \tag{2}$$

However, the response time of applications according to the above equation is the worst-case and not always returned by the actual setting of the system, thus we present a way of estimating a response time close to the actual response time using model checking techniques, which we will explain in Sect. 4.2.

3.2   Behavior Models of PIM and PSM

Modeling Aspects of PIM and PSM. The requirements of CPS that we are concerned about are application requirements and platform constraints. An application requirement includes both functional and performance requirements. A platform constraint is a constraint to be imposed upon applications that characterizes a platform. We distinguish platform constraints by three categories: a resource capability, a scheduling mechanism, and a communication mechanism. A resource capability is a processing capability of resources. In the case of CPU, the resource capability is represented by an execution time for a computation of applications. A scheduling mechanism denotes a resource sharing mechanism. A communication mechanism is a communication protocol supported by a platform.

RIM and RSM in Timed Automata. A RIM captures a functionality of applications, i.e. computation and communication behavior of applications. A RSM refines a RIM with the resource capability and the communication mechanism of a platform.

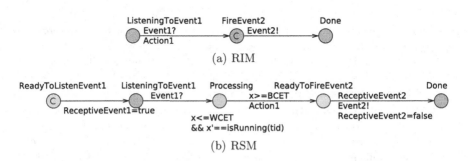

Fig. 6. Refinement of RIM to RSM (Color figure online)

Figure 6 shows a RIM and its corresponding RSM modeled using TA. They have the same functionality, but the RSM includes more information on resource constraints and communication mechanisms. The RIM of Fig. 6(a) has a simple behavior: If it receives the event Event1, then it performs the action Action1. Afterwards, it triggers the event Event2. The action performed during a transition can be any types of actions, such as computations and communications. The action might need a computation resource and time when it is actually implemented. However, a RIM executes such a resource-consuming action instantaneously and it does not need any resources.

A RSM corresponding to RIM takes into account resource capability and communication mechanisms in addition to the functionality and communication of RIM. Thus, the action of a RSM consuming time and resources is guarded by an execution time, such as WCET and BCET, and the availability of a resource. In a RSM, a specific communication mechanism replaces a simple communication of a RIM.

The execution time and the availability of a resource necessary to perform the action of a RSM is represented by a location, an invariant and a guard outgoing from the location. In Fig. 6(b), the location Processing (in blue) proceeds to execute the action Action1, where the WCET of the action is specified as an invariant in the form of $x <=$ WCET and the availability of the relevant resource is represented by the function isRunning(). Also, the BCET of the action Action1 is labeled on the transition outgoing from location Processing in the form of x >= BCET. In a RSM, a specific communication mechanism is considered. In Fig. 6(b), the condition ReceptiveEvent1 is set to true in order to notify that the event Event2 is allowed to synchronize. Compared to the RIM, the RSM adds the condition ReceptiveEvent2 to the outgoing transition from the location ReadyToFireEvent2 in order to specify a specific condition to fire the event Event2.

SSM in Timed Automata. A scheduling system model (SSM) consisting of a task model and scheduler model is modeled using SWA.

The scheduling policy models of EDF (Earliest Deadline First) is shown in Fig. 7. The scheduling policy model is triggered by the event (req_sched[i]) from a task process and selects the highest priority task from the ready queue where tasks are sorted according to their priorities.

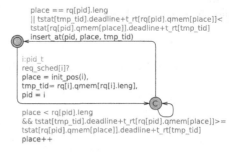

The task model in Fig. 8 simulates a task behavior that depends on the availability of a CPU. The task model releases a job at the location Job-Done by the condition t_rt[tid] >=

Fig. 7. TA Scheduler model

tstat[tid].prd that denotes a new period has begun. Then, the released job accesses to a CPU at the location Executing, where the availability of the resource is checked by the function isSchedSuped(). The stopwatch clock t_et refers to the executing time. If a CPU is available to this task, the clock t_et begin its progress.

Fig. 8. SWA Task model

The clock is running as long as the CPU is available. If t_et reaches the BCET denoted by tstat[tid].bcet, the task model can leave the location Executing and return to the location JobDone.

4 Case Study: Turn Indication Systems

In this section, a case study is conducted to illustrate our framework, extending our previous work in [7]. A turn indicator (TI) subsystem is one of automotive components that indicates the direction of the car when the driver is about to change the direction of his car. In addition, it indicates the emergency situation and the status of the door lock/unlock operated by the driver.

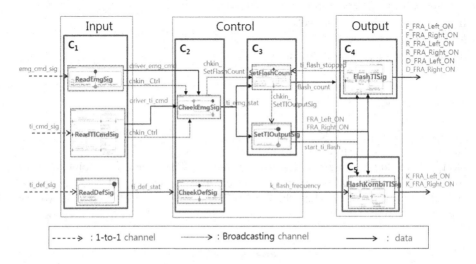

Fig. 9. The architecture of the TI system

Figure 9 shows the software architecture of the TI system model and its data and control flow between functional processes in individual components. The architecture model groups TA functional processes into three groups consisting of five components: **Input, Control**, and **Output**. Each component is composed of one or more functional processes, and a functional process (FP) is a concurrent process capturing functional and communication behavior of components.

For the simplicity, most of data are manipulated by user-defined functions that use the UPPAAL type system supporting data variables using a behavioral description language like C. The interfaces of the components are represented by channel names, and the connectors are modeled using the communication primitives of UPPAAL, a broadcasting channel (long dashed arrow) and a 1-to-1 synchronization (short dashed arrow) channel. The data is communicated by shared data variables (normal arrow).

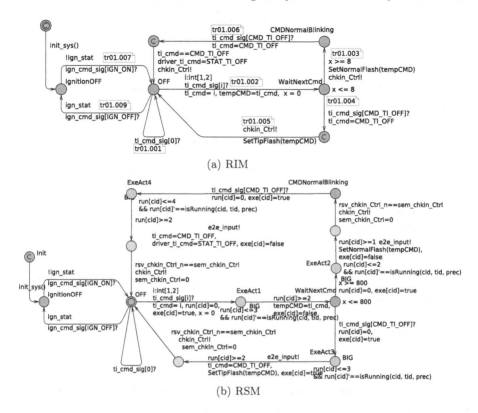

(a) RIM

(b) RSM

Fig. 10. ReadTICmdSig: TI command handler in RIM and RSM (Color figure online)

4.1 PIM Analysis

Firstly, the applications of the TI system are modeled in terms of RIM, and the platform is also analyzed separately from the application analysis. Figure 10(a) shows the RIM of ReadTICmdSig. It (1) responds to a TI command from Single Column Switching, (2) determines the TI operation mode to be activated, and (3) calls on the functional process that determines the occurrence of the emergency.

RIM Analysis. For the verification of safety and liveness properties of the TI system, we construct some additional templates that monitor the violation of system's behavior against required properties. The detailed description of our PIM models can be found from [7].

Table 1 shows the verification results of the safety, liveness, and deadlock-freedom properties checked by UPPAAL MC. The first property UP.001 is proven to show that the system is safe from deadlock. The safety property SP.001.01 is proven to show that only one turn indicator group exclusively flashes when a normal mode or the Tip blinking mode is engaged. The last liveness property LP.001 is also proven to show that one of the turn indicator lamp groups is operated eventually by any command from the driver.

Table 1. CTL properties and model checking results

Property ID	CTL	Results	Analysis time (second)
UP.001	A[] **not deadlock**	Satisfied	1.05
SP.001	A[] **not** FailSafetyReq001.SReq001_1	Satisfied	0.29
LP.001	E<> LivenessReq001.LReq001_1	Satisfied	0.02

Table 2. Assignments of shared resources

Applications			Resource Configuration 1		Resource Configuration 1	
$Comp_i$	FP_i	Precedence	T_i(ExeTime, Period)	CPU_i	T_i(ExeTime, Period)	CPU_i
C_1	ReadEmgSig	1	$T_1(3, 20)$	CPU_1	$T_1(2, 10)$	CPU_1
	ReadTICmdSig	2				
	ReadDefSig	3				
C_2	CheckEmgSig	1	$T_2(3, 20)$		$T_2(2, 10)$	CPU_2
	CheckDefSig	2				
C_3	SetFlashCount	1	$T_3(2, 20)$	CPU_2	$T_3(1, 10)$	
	SetTIOutputSig	2				
C_4	FlashTISig	1	$T_4(3, 20)$		$T_4(2, 10)$	CPU_3
C_5	FlashKombiTISig	1	$T_5(3, 20)$		$T_5(2, 10)$	

SSM Analysis. A platform is parameterized by resource configurations. Table 2 shows two resource configurations to be given the TI applications. The first configuration (Resource Configuration 1) deploys five tasks exploiting 2 CPUs while the second one (Resource Configuration 2) exploits three CPUs. We check the schedulability of each resource configuration using the statistical and the symbolic model checkers of UPPAAL.

Table 3. Results of schedulability analysis for platform configurations

Property ID	Property specifications	Results
Probabilistic schedulability	Pr[<= SimLimit] (<> *error*)	(228 runs) Pr(<> ...) in [0,0.0199955] with confidence 0.99. (Verification time used: 14.7 s)
Schedulability	A[ ] *not error*	Satisfied (Verification time used: 77.93 s)

Table 3 exhibits the results of schedulability analysis for the resource configurations. Firstly, we conduct a quick analysis consuming a relative short time (14.7 s) by means of a small hammer, the statistical model checker of UPPAAL (SMC). As a result, we obtained the probabilistic results regarding the schedulability with 99 % certainty. SMC simulates a given model numerous times and returns a probabilistic answer on how many traces satisfy a given property. Afterwards, we applied a big hammer, the symbolic model checker of UPPAAL, that consumes 77.93 s to return 100 % certainty for the schedulability of the resource configurations.

4.2   PSM Analysis

RSM Construction. Figure 10(b) shows a RSM of the TI system that is refined from its corresponding RIM. Note that some actions in Fig. 10(b) are refined to denote the consumption of time and resources using a resource-consuming location (in blue) given a WCET and associated with a stopwatch clock (run[cid]) that stops and resumes by the function isRunning(). Similar to the task model of Fig. 8, the resource-consuming action of the RSM depends on the associating task, i.e. the action is performed only while the task is running.

Some event channels are also protected by the associated condition variables. For instance, the location ExeAct1 has the invariant run[cid] $<= 3$ and the transition from the location has the guard run[cid] $>= 2$. In the expressions, 3 and 2 are the WCRT and the BCET, respectively, to perform the actions tempCMD=ti_cmd, exe[cid]=false on the transition leaving ExeAct1. In this way, the action to consume time and resource is refined with a logical time.

Composability Analysis: End-to-End Delay Analysis. The RSM of the TI system is composed with a SSM varying resource configurations and checked to see if the TI model satisfy its end-to-end delay requirement. Table 2 maps individual components and their associated tasks. For this case study, we provide two resource configurations for the TI applications. We checked the end-to-end delay requirement that any driver commands for TI operations should be responded within 20 ms.

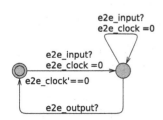

The end-to-end delay is estimated by a new TA template in Fig. 11: The clock e2e_clock begins to progress when the event end2end_input occurs, stops when the event e2e_output occurs, and is reset when a new TI command arrives. The events end2end_input and e2e_output can be annotated upon any transitions of the TI model that denote the start and the end of an operation. The following SMC query is given SMC to check the end-to-end delay:

Fig. 11. TA environment model for end-to-end delay analysis

$$E[<=100000;1000](max:e2e\_clock)$$

It requires UPPAAL SMC to return a probability distribution on the average of the maximum value of the clock e2e_clock from 1,000 individual simulation traces, of which each runs for 100,000 time units.

As results, we obtained two probability distributions, as shown in Fig. 12, from SMC. Figure 12(a) is the probability distribution concerning the first resource configuration and shows that the maximum end-to-end delay is 99.86 ms (Span of display sample [0, 99.86]) and the average of the maximum end-to-end delay over

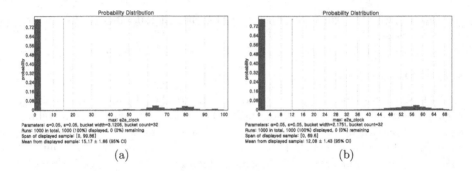

Fig. 12. Probability distributions of the end-to-end delay of the TI system

all produced traced is 15.17 ms. Meanwhile, the end-to-end delay for the second resource configuration is 69.6 ms, as shown in Fig. 12(a), and its average of the maximum end-to-end delay is 12.08. It is because the second configuration operates the TI system using more CPUs than the first one. By checking these configurations, we concluded that, in terms of the end-to-end delay, the performance of the second configuration is 30 % better than the first configuration.

5 Conclusions

In developing safe and reliable real-time CPS, one of significant issues is how to correctly integrate applications with a given platform such that application behavior does not deviate from any requirements. To the end, the application should be developed such that its behavior is correct with respect to resource constraints of a given platform that are guaranteed by the platform.

This paper presented a design and analysis framework for real-time systems. In this framework, the application model and the platform model are analyzed independently from each other, and the application model is then transformed into a platform-concerned application model so that its composability against a given platform is formally analyzed.

To the end, we presented formal behavior models of applications and platforms and a transformation method to refine a platform-independent application model into the corresponding platform-specific application model for composability check. For a platform resource constraint given applications, we proposed a platform model that is a scheduling system model capable of being parameterized with configurations of tasks and showed how the platform model can be associated to an application model for composability check.

This paper contributes to the design and analysis of safe and reliable real-time CPS with:

– A model of real-time systems that distinguishes between task and application such that platform properties are analyzed independently from applications,
– A platform-independent behavior model of applications extensible for its analysis against platform-concerned properties,

– A platform model that can be used as a resource constraint specification and be composed with an application model to check platform-concerned properties of applications.

This framework leverages the analysis of an integration of applications and platforms in advance of their implementation to obtain more functionally correct applications in terms of platforms. In this paper, we realized these models using TA and SWA and checked using the statistical and the symbolic model checker of UPPAAL and conducted a case study to illustrate our framework.

References

1. Alur, R., Dill, D.L.: A theory of timed automata. Theor. Comput. Sci. **126**(2), 183–235 (1994)
2. Balarin, F., Watanabe, Y., Hsieh, H., Lavagno, L., Passerone, C., Sangiovanni-Vincentelli, A.: Metropolis: an integrated electronic system design environment. Computer **36**(4), 45–52 (2003)
3. David, A., Larsen, K., Legay, A., Mikučionis, M., Poulsen, D.: Uppaal SMC tutorial. Int. J. Softw. Tools Technol. Transf. **17**, 1–19 (2015)
4. Kienhuis, B., Deprettere, E.F., van der Wolf, P., Vissers, K.: A methodology to design programmable embedded systems. In: Deprettere, F., Teich, J., Vassiliadis, S. (eds.) SAMOS 2001. LNCS, vol. 2268, pp. 18–37. Springer, Heidelberg (2002)
5. Kim, B., Feng, L., Phan, L.T.X., Sokolsky, O., Lee, I.: Platform-specific timing verification framework in model-based implementation. In: Proceedings of the 2015 Design, Automation and Test in Europe Conference and Exhibition, DATE 2015, pp. 235–240. EDA Consortium, San Jose (2015)
6. Kim, B., Hwang, H., Park, T., Son, S., Lee, I.: A layered approach for testing timing in the model-based implementation. In: 2014 Design, Automation and Test in Europe Conference and Exhibition (DATE), pp. 1–4, March 2014
7. Kim, J.H., Larsen, K.G., Nielsen, B., Mikučionis, M., Olsen, P.: Formal analysis and testing of real-time automotive systems using UPPAAL tools. In: Núñez, M., Güdemann, M. (eds.) FMICS 2015. LNCS, vol. 9128, pp. 47–61. Springer, Heidelberg (2015)
8. Lehoczky, J.P., Sha, L., Strosnider, J.K.: Enhanced aperiodic responsiveness in hard real-time environments. In: RTSS, pp. 261–270. IEEE Computer Society (1987)
9. Shin, I., Lee, I.: Periodic resource model for compositional real-time guarantees. In: RTSS, pp. 2–13. IEEE Computer Society (2003)
10. Sokolsky, O., Lee, I., Clarke, D.: Schedulability analysis of AADL models. In: Proceedings of International Conference on Parallel and Distributed Processing, p. 179. IEEE Computer Society, Washington (2006)
11. Strosnider, J.K., Lehoczky, J.P., Sha, L.: The deferrable server algorithm for enhanced aperiodic responsiveness in hard real-time environments. IEEE Trans. Comput. **44**(1), 73–91 (1995)
12. TIMMO(TIMing MOdel) Project. http://www.timmo-2-use.org

SAT Solving

SAT-Based Explicit LTL Reasoning

Jianwen Li[1,2]([⊠]), Shufang Zhu[2], Geguang Pu[2], and Moshe Y. Vardi[1]

[1] Department of Computer Science, Rice University, Houston, USA
lijwen2748@gmail.com
[2] Shanghai Key Laboratory of Trustworthy Computing, East China Normal
University, Shanghai, People's Republic of China

Abstract. We present here a new explicit reasoning framework for linear temporal logic (LTL), which is built on top of propositional satisfiability (SAT) solving. As a proof-of-concept of this framework, we describe a new LTL satisfiability algorithm. We implemented the algorithm in a tool, Aalta_v2.0, which is built on top of the Minisat SAT solver. We tested the effectiveness of this approach by demonstrating that Aalta_v2.0 significantly outperforms all existing LTL satisfiability solvers.

1 Introduction

Linear Temporal Logic (LTL) was introduced into program verification in [24]. Since then it has been widely accepted as a language for the specification of ongoing computations [20] and it is a key component in the verification of reactive systems [4,14]. Explicit temporal reasoning, which involves an explicit construction of temporal transition systems, is a key algorithmic component in this context. For example, explicitly translating LTL formulas to Büchi automata is a key step both in explicit-state model checking [11] and in runtime verification [30]. LTL satisfiability checking, a step that should take place *before* verification, to assure consistency of temporal requirements, also uses explicit reasoning [25]. These tasks are known to be quite demanding computationally for complex temporal properties [11,25,30]. A way to get around this difficulty is to replace explicit reasoning by symbolic reasoning, e.g., as in BDD-based or SAT-based model checking [22,23], but in many cases the symbolic approach is inefficient [25] or inapplicable [30]. Thus, explicit temporal reasoning remains an indispensable algorithmic tool.

The main approach to explicit temporal reasoning is based on the *tableau* technique, in which a recursive *syntactic* decomposition of temporal formulas drives the construction of temporal transition systems. This approach is based on the technique of *propositional tableau*, whose essence is search via *syntactic splitting* [6]. This is in contrast to modern propositional satisfiability (SAT) solvers, whose essence is search via *semantic splitting* [19]. The tableau approach to temporal reasoning underlies both the best LTL-to-automata translator [8] and the best LTL-satisfiability checker [18]. Thus, we have a situation where in the symbolic setting much progress is being attained both by the impressive improvement in the capabilities of modern SAT solvers [19] as well as new

© Springer International Publishing Switzerland 2015
N. Piterman (Ed.): HVC 2015, LNCS 9434, pp. 209–224, 2015.
DOI: 10.1007/978-3-319-26287-1_13

SAT-based model-checking algorithms [1,3], while progress in explicit temporal reasoning is slower and does not fully leverage modern SAT solving. (It should be noted that several LTL satisfiability solvers,including Aalta_v1.2 [17], TRP++ [15], and ls4 [29] do employ SAT solvers, but they do so as an *aid* to the main reasoning engine, rather than serve as the *main* reasoning engine.)

Our main aim in this paper is to study how SAT solving can be *fully leveraged* in explicit temporal reasoning. The key intuition is that explicit temporal reasoning consists of construction of states and transitions, subject to temporal constraints. Such temporal constraints can be reduced to a sequence of Boolean constraints, which enables the application of SAT solving. This idea underlies the complexity-theoretic analysis in [32], and has been explored in the context of modal logic [12], but not yet in the context of explicit temporal reasoning. Our belief is that SAT solving would prove to be superior to tableau in that context.

We describe in this paper a general framework for SAT-based explicit temporal reasoning. The crux of our approach is a construction of temporal transition system that is based on SAT-solving rather than tableau to construct states and transitions. The obtained transition system can be used for LTL-satisfiability solving, LTL-to-automata translation, and runtime-monitor construction.

As proof of concept for the new framework, we use it to develop a SAT-based algorithm for LTL-satisfiability checking. We also propose several heuristics to speed up the checking by leveraging SAT solvers. We implemented the algorithm and heuristics in an LTL-satisfiability solver Aalta_v2.0.

To evaluate its performance, we compared it against Aalta_v1.2, the existing best-of-breed LTL-satisfiability solver [17,18], which is tableau-based. We also compare it against NuXmv, a symbolic LTL-satisfiability solver that is based on cutting-edge SAT-based model-checking algorithms [1,3], which outperforms Aalta_v1.2. We show that our explicit SAT-based LTL-satisfiability solver outperforms both.

In summary, the contributions in this paper are as follows:

- We propose a SAT-based explicit LTL-reasoning framework.
- We show a successful application of the framework to LTL-satisfiability checking, by designing a novel algorithm and efficient heuristics.
- We compare our new framework for LTL-satisfiability checking with existing approaches. The experimental results demonstrate that our tool significantly outperforms other existing LTL satisfiability solvers.

The paper is organized as follows. Section 2 provides technical background. Section 3 introduces the new SAT-based explicit-reasoning framework. Section 4 describes in detail the application to LTL-satisfiability checking. Section 5 shows the experimental results for LTL-satisfiability checking. Finally Sect. 6 provides concluding remarks. Missing proofs and algorithms are available at our on-line technical report http://arxiv.org/abs/1507.02519.

2   Preliminaries

Linear Temporal Logic (LTL) is considered as an extension of propositional logic, in which temporal connectives X (next) and U (until) are introduced. Let AP be a set of atomic properties. The syntax of LTL formulas is defined by:

$$\phi ::= tt \mid ff \mid a \mid \neg\phi \mid \phi \wedge \phi \mid \phi \vee \phi \mid \phi U \phi \mid X\phi$$

where $a \in AP$, tt is $true$ and ff is $false$. We introduce the R (release) connectives as the dual of U, which means $\phi R\psi \equiv \neg(\neg\phi U \neg\psi)$. We also use the usual abbreviations: $Fa = ttUa$, and $Ga = ffRa$.

We say that a is a *literal* if it is an atomic proposition or its negation. Throughout the paper, we use L to denote the set of literals, lower case letters a, b, c, l to denote literals, α to denote propositional formulas, and ϕ, ψ for LTL formulas. We consider LTL formulas in negation normal form (NNF), which can be achieved by pushing all negations in front of only atoms. Since we consider LTL in NNF, formulas are interpreted here on infinite literal sequences, whose alphabet is $\Sigma := 2^L$.

A *trace* $\xi = \omega_0\omega_1\omega_2\ldots$ is an infinite sequence in Σ^ω. For ξ and $k \geq 1$ we use $\xi^k = \omega_0\omega_1\ldots\omega_{k-1}$ to denote a prefix of ξ, and $\xi_k = \omega_k\omega_{k+1}\ldots$ to denote a suffix of ξ. Thus, $\xi = \xi^k\xi_k$. The semantics of LTL with respect to an infinite trace ξ is given by:

- $\xi \models \alpha$ iff $\xi^1 \models \alpha$, where α is a propositional formula;
- $\xi \models X\ \phi$ iff $\xi_1 \models \phi$;
- $\xi \models \phi_1\ U\ \phi_2$ iff there exists $i \geq 0$ such that $\xi_i \models \phi_2$ and for all $0 \leq j < i$, $\xi_j \models \phi_1$;
- $\xi \models \phi_1\ R\ \phi_2$ iff for all $i \geq 0$, it holds $\xi_i \models \phi_2$ or there exists $0 \leq j \leq i$ such that $\xi_j \models \phi_1$.

The *closure* of an LTL formula ϕ, denoted as $cl(\phi)$, is a formula set such that: (1). ϕ is in $cl(\phi)$; (2). ψ is in $cl(\phi)$ if $\phi = X\psi$ or $\phi = \neg\psi$; (3). ϕ_1, ϕ_2 are in $cl(\phi)$ if $\phi = \phi_1\ op\ \phi_2$, where op can be $\wedge, \vee, U$ and R; (4). $(X\psi) \in cl(\phi)$ if $\psi \in cl(\phi)$ and ψ is an Until or Release formula. We say each ψ in $cl(\phi)$, which is added via rules (1)–(3), is a *subformula* of ϕ. Note that the standard definition of LTL closure consists only of rules (1)–(3). Rule (4) is added in this paper due to its usage in later sections. Note that the size of $cl(\phi)$ is linear in the length of ϕ, even with the addition of rule (4).

3   Explicit LTL Reasoning

In this section we introduce the framework of explicit LTL reasoning. To demonstrate clearly both the similarity and difference between our approach and previous ones, we organize this section as follows. We first provide a general definition of temporal transition systems, which underlies both our new approach and previous approach. We then discuss how traditional methods and our new one relate to this framework.

3.1 Temporal Transition System

As argued in [12,31], the key to efficient *modal* reasoning is to reason about states and transitions *propositionally*. We show here how the same approach can be applied to LTL. Unlike *modal logic*, where there is a clear separation between formulas that talk about the current state and formulas that talk about successor states (the latter are formulas in the scope of $\Box$ or $\Diamond$, i.e. G or F in LTL), LTL formulas do not allow for such a clean separation. Achieving such a separation requires some additional work.

We first define propositional satisfiability of LTL formulas.

Definition 1 (Propositional Satisfiability). *For an LTL formula ϕ, a propositional assignment for ϕ is a set $A \subseteq cl(\phi)$ such that*

- *every literal $\ell \in L$ is either in A or its negation is, but not both.*
- *$(\theta_1 \wedge \theta_2) \in A$ implies $\theta_1 \in A$ and $\theta_2 \in A$,*
- *$(\theta_1 \vee \theta_2) \in A$ implies $\theta_1 \in A$ or $\theta_2 \in A$,*
- *$(\theta_1 U \theta_2) \in A$ implies $\theta_2 \in A$ or both $\theta_1 \in A$ and $(X(\theta_1 U \theta_2)) \in A$. In the former case, that is, $\theta_2 \in A$, we say that A satisfies $(\theta_1 U \theta_2)$ immediately. In the latter case, we say that A postpones $(\theta_1 U \theta_2)$.*
- *$(\theta_1 R \theta_2) \in A$ implies $\theta_2 \in A$ and either $\theta_1 \in A$ or $(X(\theta_1 R \theta_2)) \in A$. In the former case, that is, $\theta_1 \in A$, we say that A satisfies $(\theta_1 R \theta_2)$ immediately. In the latter case, we say that A postpones $(\theta_1 R \theta_2)$.*

We say that a propositional assignment A propositional satisfies ϕ, denoted as $A \models_p \phi$, if $\phi \in A$. We say an LTL formula ϕ is propositionally satisfiable if there is a propositional assignment A for ϕ such that $A \models_p \phi$.

For example, consider the formula $\phi = (aUb) \wedge (\neg b)$. The set $A_1 = \{a, (aUb), (\neg b), (X(aUb))\} \subseteq cl(\phi)$ is a propositional assignment that propositionally satisfies ϕ. In contrast, the set $A_2 = \{(aUb), \neg b\} \subseteq cl(\phi)$ is not a propositional assignment.

The following theorem shows the relationship between LTL formula ϕ and its propositional assignment.

Theorem 1. *For an LTL formula ϕ and an infinite trace $\xi \in \Sigma^\omega$, we have that $\xi \models \phi$ iff there exists a propositional assignment $A \subseteq cl(\phi)$ such that A propositionally satisfies ϕ and $\xi \models \bigwedge A$.*

Since a propositional assignment of LTL formula ϕ contains the information for both current and next states, we are ready to define the *transition systems* of LTL formula.

Definition 2. *Given an LTL formula ϕ, the transition system T_ϕ is a tuple (S, S_0, T) where*

- *S is the set of states $s \subseteq cl(\phi)$ that are propositional assignments for ϕ. The trace of a state s is $s \cap L$, that is, the set of literals in s.*
- *$S_0 \subseteq S$ is a set of initial states, where $\phi \in s_0$ for all $s_0 \in S_0$.*

- $T : S \times S$ is the transition relation, where $T(s_1, s_2)$ holds if $(X\theta) \in s_1$ implies $\theta \in s_2$, for all $X\theta \in cl(\phi)$.

A run of T_ϕ is an infinite sequence $s_0, s_1, \ldots$ such that $s_0 \in S_0$ and $T(s_i, s_{i+1})$ holds for all $i \geq 0$.

Every run $r = s_0, s_1, \ldots$ of T_ϕ induces a trace $trace(r) = trace(s_0), trace(s_1)$, $\ldots$ in Σ^ω. In general, it needs not hold that $trace(r) \models \phi$. This requires an additional condition. Consider an Until formula $(\theta_1 U \theta_2) \in s_i$. Since s_i is a propositional assignment for ϕ we either have that s_i satisfies $(\theta_1 U \theta_2)$ immediately or that it postpones it, and then $(\theta_1 U \theta_2) \in s_{i+1}$. If s_j postpones $(\theta_1 U \theta_2)$ for all $j \geq i$, then we say that $(\theta_1 U \theta_2)$ is *stuck* in r.

Theorem 2. *Let r be a run of T_ϕ. If no Until subformula is stuck at r, then $trace(r) \models \phi$. Also, ϕ is satisfiable if there is a run r of T_ϕ so that no Until subformula is stuck at r.*

We have now shown that the temporal transition system T_ϕ is intimately related to the satisfiability of ϕ. The definition of T_ϕ is, however, rather nonconstructive. In the next subsection we discuss how to construct T_ϕ.

3.2   System Construction

First, we show how one can consider LTL formulas as propositional ones. This requires considering temporal subformulas as *propositional atoms*. We now define the *propositional atoms* of LTL formulas.

Definition 3 (Propositional Atoms). *For an LTL formula ϕ, we define the set of propositional atoms of ϕ, i.e. $PA(\phi)$, as follows:*

1. $PA(\phi) = \{\phi\}$ *if ϕ is an atom, Next, Until or Release formula;*
2. $PA(\phi) = PA(\psi)$ *if $\phi = (\neg\psi)$;*
3. $PA(\phi) = PA(\phi_1) \cup PA(\phi_2)$ *if $\phi = (\phi_1 \wedge \phi_2)$ or $\phi = (\phi_1 \vee \phi_2)$.*

Consider, for example, the formula $\phi = (a \wedge (aUb) \wedge \neg(X(a \vee b)))$. Here we have $PA(\phi)$ is $\{a, (aUb), (X(a \vee b))\}$. Intuitively, the propositional atoms are obtained by treating all temporal subformulas of ϕ as atomic propositions. Thus, an LTL formula ϕ can be viewed as a propositional formula over $PA(\phi)$.

Definition 4. *For an LTL formula ϕ, let ϕ^p be ϕ considered as a propositional formula over $PA(\phi)$.*

We now introduce the *neXt Normal Form* (XNF) of LTL formulas, which separates the "current" and "next-state" parts of the formula, but costs only linear in the original formula size.

Definition 5 (neXt Normal Form). *An LTL formula ϕ is in neXt Normal Form (XNF) if there are no Unitl or Release subformulas of ϕ in $PA(\phi)$.*

For example, $\phi = (aUb)$ is not in XNF, while $(b \vee (a \wedge (X(aUb))))$ is in XNF. Every LTL formula ϕ can be converted, with linear in the formula size, to an equivalent formula in XNF.

Theorem 3. *For an LTL formula ϕ, there is an equivalent formula $xnf(\phi)$ that is in XNF. Furthermore, the cost of the conversion is linear.*

Proof. To construct $xnf(\phi)$, We can apply the expansion rules $(\phi_1 U \phi_2) \equiv (\phi_2 \vee (\phi_1 \wedge X(\phi_1 U \phi_2)))$ and $(\phi_1 R \phi_2) \equiv (\phi_2 \wedge (\phi_1 \vee X(\phi_1 R \phi_2)))$. In detail, we can construct $xnf(\phi)$ inductively:

1. $xnf(\phi) = \phi$ if ϕ is tt, ff, a literal l or a Next formula $X\psi$;
2. $xnf(\phi) = xnf(\phi_1) \wedge xnf(\phi_2)$ if $\phi = (\phi_1 \wedge \phi_2)$;
3. $xnf(\phi) = xnf(\phi_1) \vee xnf(\phi_2)$ if $\phi = (\phi_1 \vee \phi_2)$;
4. $xnf(\phi) = (xnf(\phi_2)) \vee (xnf(\phi_1) \wedge X\phi)$ if $\phi = (\phi_1 U \phi_2)$;
5. $xnf(\phi) = xnf(\phi_2) \wedge (xnf(\phi_1) \vee X\phi)$ if $\phi = (\phi_1 R \phi_2)$.

Since the construction is built on the two expansion rules that preserve the equivalence of formulas, it follows that ϕ is logically equivalent to $xnf(\phi)$. Note that the conversion map $xnf(\phi)$ doubles the size of the converted formula ϕ, but since the conversion puts Until and Release subformulas in the scope of Next, and the conversion stops when it comes to Next subformulas, the cost is at most linear.   □

We can now state propositional satisfiability of LTL formulas in terms of satisfiability of propositional formulas. That is, by restricting LTL formulas to XNF, a satisfying assignment of ϕ^p, which can be obtained by using a SAT solver, corresponds precisely to a propositional assignment of formula ϕ.

Theorem 4. *For an LTL formula ϕ in XNF, if there is a satisfying assignment A of ϕ^p, then there is a propositional assignment A' of ϕ that satisfies ϕ such that $A' \cap PA(\phi) \subseteq A$. Conversely, if there is a propositional assignment A' of ϕ that satisfies ϕ, then there is a satisfying assignment A of ϕ^p such that $A' \cap PA(\phi) \subseteq A$.*

Proof. ($\Rightarrow$) Let A be a satisfying assignment of ϕ^p. Then let A' be the set of all formulas $\psi \in cl(\phi)$ such that A satisfies $(xnf(\psi))^p$. We clearly have that $A' \cap PA(\phi) \subseteq A$. According to Definition 1 and because ϕ is in XNF, we have that A' is a propositional assignment of ϕ that satisfies ϕ.

($\Leftarrow$) Let A' be a propositional assignment of ϕ that satisfies ϕ. Then let A to be the assignment that assign true to $\psi \in cl(\phi)$ precisely when $\psi \in A'$. Again, we clearly have that, $A' \cap PA(\phi) \subseteq A$. According to Definition 1 and because ϕ is in XNF, we have that A is a satisfying assignment of ϕ^p.   □

Theorem 4 shows that by requiring the formula ϕ to be in XNF, we can construct the states of the transition system T_ϕ via computing satisfying assignments of ϕ^p over $PA(\phi)$. Let t be a satisfying assignment of ϕ^p and A_t be the related propositional assignment of ϕ generated from t by Theorem 4, the construction is operated as follows:

1. Let $S_0 = \{A_t \mid t \models \phi^p\}$; and let $S := S_0$,
2. Compute $S_i = \{A_t \mid t \models (xnf(\bigwedge X(s_i)))^p\}$ for each $s_i \in S$, where $X(s_i) = \{\theta \mid (X\theta) \in s_i\}$; and update $S := S \cup S_i$;
3. Stop if S does not change; else go back to step 2.

The construction first generates initial states (step 1), and then all reachable states from initial ones (step 2); it terminates once no new reachable state can be generated (step 3). So S is the set of system states and its size is bounded by $2^{|cl(\phi)|}$.

Our goal here is to show that we can construct the transition system T_ϕ by means of SAT solving. This requires us to refine Theorem 2. A key issue in how a propositional assignment handles an Until formula is whether it satisfies it immediately or postpones it. We introduce new propositions that indicate which is the case, and we refine the implementation of $xnf()$. Given $\psi = (\psi_1 U \psi_2)$, we introduce a new proposition $v(\psi)$, and use the following conversion rule: $xnf(\psi) \equiv (v(\psi) \wedge \psi_2) \vee ((\neg v(\psi)) \wedge \psi_1 \wedge (X(\psi)))$. Thus, $v(\psi)$ is required to be true when the Until is satisfied immediately, and false when the Until is postponed. Now we can state the refinement of Theorem 2.

Theorem 5. *For an LTL formula ϕ, ϕ is satisfiable iff there is a finite run $r = s_0, s_1, \ldots, s_n$ in T_ϕ such that*

1. *There are $0 \leq m \leq n$ such that $s_m = s_n$;*
2. *Let $Q = \bigcup_{i=m}^n s_i$. If $\psi = (\psi_1 U \psi_2) \in Q$, then $v(\psi) \in Q$.*

Proof. Suppose first that items 1 and 2 hold. Then the infinite sequence $r' = s_0, \ldots, s_m, (s_{m+1}, \ldots, s_n)^\omega$ is an infinite run of T_ϕ. It follows from Item 2 that no Until subformula is stuck at r'. By Theorem 2, we have that $r' \models \phi$.

Suppose now that ϕ is satisfiable. By Theorem 2, there is an infinite run r' of T_ϕ in which no Until subformula is stuck. Let $r' = s_0, s_1, \ldots$ be such a run. Each $s_i (i \geq 0)$ is a state of T_ϕ, and the number of states is bounded by $2^{|cl(\phi)|}$. Thus, there must be $0 \leq m < n$ such that $s_m = s_n$. Let $Q = \bigcup_{i=m}^n s_i$. Since no Until subformula can be stuck at r, if $\psi = \psi_1 U \psi_2 \in Q$, then it is must be that $v(\psi) \in Q$. □

The significance of Theorem 5 is that it reduces LTL satisfiability checking to searching for a "lasso" in T_ϕ [5]. Item 1 says that we need to search for a prefix followed by a cycle, while Item 2 provides a way to test that no Until subformla gets stuck in the infinite run in which the cycle $s_{m+1}, \ldots, s_n$ is repeated infinitely often.

3.3 Related Work

We introduced our SAT-based reasoning approach above, and in this section we discuss the difference between our SAT-based approach and earlier works.

Earlier approaches to transition-system construction for LTL formulas, based on tableau [11] and normal form [18], generate the system states explicitly or implicitly via a translation to *disjunctive normal form* (DNF). In [18], the conversion to

DNF is explicit (though various heuristics are used to temper the exponential blow-up) and the states generated correspond to the disjuncts. In tableau-based tools, cf., [7,11], the construction is based on iterative *syntactic splitting* in which a state of the form $A \cup \{\theta_1 \vee \theta_2\}$ is split to states: $A \cup \{\theta_1\}$ and $A \cup \{\theta_2\}$.

The approach proposed here is based on SAT solving, where the states correspond to satisfying assignments. Satisfying assignments are generated via a search process that is guided by *semantic splitting*. The advantage of using SAT solving rather than syntactic approaches is the impressive progress in the development of heuristics that have evolved to yield highly efficient SAT solving: unit propagation, two-literal watching, back jumping, clause learning, and more, see [19]. Furthermore, SAT solving continues to evolve in an impressive pace, driven by an annual competition[1]. It should be remarked that an analogous debate, between syntactic and semantic approaches, took place in the context of automated test-pattern generation for circuit designs, where, ultimately, the semantic approach has been shown to be superior [16].

Furthermore, relying on SAT solving as the underlying reasoning technology enables us to decouple temporal reasoning from propositional reasoning. Temporal reasoning is accomplished via a search in the transition system, while the construction of the transition system, which requires proposition reasoning using SAT solving.

4   LTL Satisfiability Checking

Given an LTL formula ϕ, the satisfiability problem is to ask whether there is an infinite trace ξ such that $\xi \models \phi$. In the previous section we introduced a SAT-based LTL-reasoning framework and showed how it can be applied to solve LTL reasoning problems. In this section we use this framework to develop an efficient SAT-based algorithm for LTL satisfiability checking. We design a depth-first-search (DFS) algorithm that constructs the temporal transition system on the fly and searches for a trace per Theorem 5. Furthermore, we propose several heuristics to reduce the search space. Due to the limited space, we offer here a high-level description of the algorithms. Details are provided in our online technical report.

4.1   The Main Algorithm

The main algorithm, LTL-CHECK, creates the temporal transition system of the input formula on-the-fly, and searches for a lasso in a DFS manner. Several prior works describe algorithms for DFS lasso search, cf. [5,18,27]. Here we focus on the steps that are specialized to our algorithm.

The key idea of LTL-CHECK is to create states and their successors using SAT techniques rather than traditional tableau or expansion techniques. Given the current formula ϕ, we first compute its XNF version $xnf(\phi)$, and then use

---

[1] See http://www.satcompetition.org/.

a SAT solver to compute the satisfying assignments of $(xnf(\phi))^p$. Let P be a satisfying assignment for $(xnf(\phi))^p$; from the previous section we know that $X(P) = \{\theta \mid X\theta \in P\}$ yields a successor state in T_ϕ. We implement this approach in the *getState* function, which we improve later by introducing some heuristics. By enumerating all assignments of $(xnf(\phi))^p$ we can obtain all successor states of P. Note, however that LTL-CHECK runs in the DFS manner, under which only a single state is needed at a time, so additional effort must be taken to maintain history information of the next-state generation for each state P.

As soon as LTL-CHECK detects a lasso, it checks whether the lasso is accepting. Previous lasso-search algorithms operate on the Büchi automaton generated from the input formula. In contrast, here we focus directly on the satisfaction of Until subformulas per Theorem 5. We use the example below to show the general idea.

Consider the formula $\phi = G((Fb) \wedge (Fc))$. By Theorem 3, $xnf(\phi) = xnf(Fb) \wedge xnf(Fc) \wedge X\phi$, where $xnf(Fb) = ((b \wedge v(Fb)) \vee (\neg v(Fb) \wedge X(Fb)))$ and $xnf(Fc) = ((c \wedge v(Fc)) \vee (\neg v(Fc) \wedge X(Fc)))$. Suppose we get from the SAT solver an assignment of $(xnf(\phi))^p$ $P = \{v(Fb), \neg v(Fc), b, \neg c, \neg X(Fb), X(Fc), X\phi\}$. By Theorem 4, we create a satisfying assignment A' that includes all formulas in $cl(\phi)$ that are satisfied by P, and we get the state $s_0 = P \cup \{\phi, Fb, Fc, (Fb) \wedge (Fc)\}$. To obtain the next state, we start with $X(s_0) = \{Fc, \phi\}$, compute $xnf(Fc \wedge \phi)$ and repeat the process. After several steps LTL-CHECK may find a path $s_0 \rightarrow s_1 \rightarrow s_0$, where $s_1 = \{\phi, Fb, Fc, (Fb) \wedge (Fc), \neg v(Fb), v(Fc), \neg b, c, X(Fb), \neg X(Fc), X\phi\}$. Now s_0 and s_1 form a lasso. Let $Q = s_0 \cup s_1$. Both Fb and Fc are in Q, and also $v(Fb)$ and $v(Fc)$ are in Q. By Theorem 5, ϕ is satisfiable.

4.2   Heuristics for State Elimination

While LTL-CHECK uses an efficient SAT solver to compute states of the system in the *getState* function, this approach is effective in creating states and their successors, but cannot be used to guide the overall search. To find a satisfying lasso faster, we add heuristics that drive the search towards satisfaction. The key to these heuristics is smartly choosing the next state given by SAT solvers. This can be achieved by adding more constraints to the SAT solver. Experiments show these heuristics are critical to the performance of our LTL-satisfiability tool.

The construction of state in the transition system always starts with formulas. At the beginning, we have the input formula ϕ_0 and we take the following steps: (1) Compute $xnf(\phi_0)$; (2) Call a SAT solver to get an assignment P_0 of $(xnf(\phi_0))^p$; and (3) Derive a state P_0' from P_0. Then, to get a successor state, we start with the formula $\phi_1 = \bigwedge X(P_0')$, and repeat steps (1–3). Thus, every state s is obtained from some formula ϕ_s, which we call the *representative formula*. Note that with the possible exception of ϕ_0, all representative formulas are conjunctions. Let $\phi_s = \bigwedge_{1 \leq i \leq n} \theta_i$ be the representative formula of a state s; we say that $\theta_i (1 \leq i \leq n)$ is an *obligation* of ϕ if θ_i is an Until formula. Thus, we associate with the state s a set of obligations, which are the Until conjunctive elements of ϕ_s. (The initial state may have obligations if it is a conjunction.) The approach we now describe is to satisfy obligations as early as possible during the search, so that a satisfying lasso is obtained earlier. We now refine the *getState* function, and introduce three heuristics via examples.

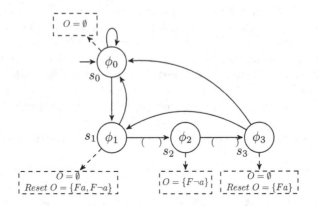

Fig. 1. A satisfiable formula. In the figure $\phi_0 = G((Fa) \land (F\neg a))$, $\phi_1 = ((Fa) \land (F\neg a) \land \phi_0)$, $\phi_2 = ((F\neg a) \land \phi_0)$ and $\phi_3 = ((Fa) \land \phi_0)$. These representative formulas correspond to states s_0, s_1, s_2, s_3, respectively.

The *getState* function keeps a global *obligation set*, collecting all obligations so far not satisfied in the search. The obligation set is initialized with the obligations of the initial formula ϕ_0. When an obligation o is satisfied (i.e., when $v(o)$ is true), o is removed from the obligation set. Once the obligation set becomes empty in the search, it is reset to contain obligations of current representative formula ϕ_i. In Fig. 1, we denote the obligation set by O. O is initialized to $\emptyset$, as there is no obligation in ϕ_0. O is then reset in the states s_1 and s_3, when it becomes empty.

The *getState* function runs in the **ELIMINATION** mode by default, in which it obtains the next state guided by the obligations of current state. For satisfiable formulas, this leads to faster lasso detection. Consider formula $\phi = G((Fa) \land (F\neg a))$. Parts of the temporal transition system T_ϕ are shown in Fig. 1. In the figure, O is reset to $\{(Fa), (F\neg a)\}$ in state s_1, as these are the obligations of ϕ_1. To drive the search towards early satisfaction of obligations, we obtain a successor of s_1, by applying the SAT solver to the formula $(xnf(\phi_1) \land (v(Fa) \lor v(F\neg a)))^p$, to check whether Fa or $F\neg a$ can be satisfied immediately. If the returned assignment satisfies $v(Fa)$, then we get the success state s_2 with the representative formulas ϕ_2, and (Fa) is removed from O. Then the next state is s_3 with the representative formula ϕ_3, which removes the obligation $(F\neg a)$. since O becomes empty, it is reset to the obligations $\{Fa\}$ of ϕ_3. Note that in Fig. 1, there should be transitions from s_2 to s_1 and from s_3 to s_2, but they are never traversed under the ELIMINATION mode.

The *getState* function runs in the **SAT_PURSUING** mode when the obligation set becomes empty. In this mode, we want to check whether the next state can be a state that have been visited before and after that visit the obligation set has become empty. In this case, the generated lasso is accepting, by Theorem 5. In Fig. 1, the obligation set O becomes empty in state s_3. Previously, it has become empty in s_1. Normally, we find a success state for s_3 by applying the SAT solver to $(xnf(\phi_3))^p$. To find out if either s_0 or s_1 can be a successor of s_3, we apply the SAT solver to the formula $(xnf(\phi_3) \wedge (X(\phi_0) \vee X(\phi_1)))^p$. Since this formula is satisfiable and indicates a transition from s_3 to s_1 ($X\phi_1$ can be assigned true in the assignment), we have found that $trace(s_0), (trace(s_1), trace(s_2), trace(s_3))^\omega$ satisfies ϕ. In the figure, the transitions labeled **x** represent failed attempts to generate the lasso when O becomes empty. Although failed attempts have a computational cost, trying to close cycles aggressively does pay off.

The $getState$ function runs in the **CONFLICT_ANALYZE** mode if all formulas in the obligation set are postponed in the ELIMINATION mode. The goal of this mode is to eliminate "conflicts" that block immediate satisfaction of obligations. To achieve this, we use a *conflict-guided* strategy. Consider, for example, the formula $\phi_0 = a \wedge (Xb) \wedge F((\neg a) \wedge (\neg b))$. Here the formula $\psi = F((\neg a) \wedge (\neg b))$ is an obligation. We check whether ψ can be satisfied immediately, but it fails. The reason for this failure is the conjunct a in ϕ, which conflicts with the obligation ψ. We identify this conflict using a *minimal unsat core* algorithm [21]. To eliminate this conflict, we add the conjunct $\neg Xa$ to ϕ, hoping to be able to satisfy the obligation immediately in the next state. When we apply the SAT solver to $(xnf(\phi) \wedge (\neg Xa))^p$, we obtain a successor state with the representative formula $\phi_1 = (b \wedge \psi)$, again with ψ as an obligation. When we try to satisfy ψ immediately, we fail again, since ψ conflicts with b. To block both conflicts, we add $\neg Xb$ as an additional constraint, and apply the SAT solver to $(xnf(\phi) \wedge (\neg Xa) \wedge (\neg Xb))^p$. This yields a successor state with the representative formula $\phi_2 = \psi$. Now we are able to satisfy ψ immediately, and we are able to satisfy ϕ with the finite path $\phi \to \phi_1 \to \phi_2$.

As another example, consider the formula $\phi = (G(Fa) \wedge Gb \wedge F(\neg b))$. Since $F(\neg b)$ is an obligation, we try to satisfy it immediately, but fail. The reason for the failure is that immediate satisfaction of $F(\neg b)$ conflicts with the conjunct Gb. In order to try to block this conflict, we add to ϕ the conjunct $\neg XGb$, and apply the SAT solver to $(xnf(\phi) \wedge \neg XGb)^p$. This also fails. Furthermore, by constructing a minimal unsat core, we discover that $(xnf(Gb) \wedge \neg X(Gb))^p$ is unsatisfiable. This indicates that Gb is an "invariant"; that is, if Gb is true in a state then it is also true in its successor. This means that the obligation $F(\neg b)$ can never be satisfied, since the conflict can never be removed. Thus, we can conclude that ϕ is unsatisfiable without constructing more than one state.

In general, identifying conflicts using minimal unsat cores enables both to find satisfying traces faster, or conclude faster that such traces cannot be found.

5 Experiments on LTL Satisfiability Checking

In this section we discuss the experimental evaluation for LTL satisfiability checking. We first describe the methodology used in experiments and then show the results.

5.1 Experimental Methodologies

The platform used in the experiments is an IBM iDataPlex consisting of 2304 processor cores in 192 Westmere nodes (12 processor cores per node) at 2.83 GHz with 48 GB of RAM per node (4 GB per core), running the 64-bit Redhat 7 operating system. In our experiments, each tool runs on a single core in a single node. We use the Linux command "time" to evaluate the time cost (in seconds) of each experiment. Timeout was set to 60 seconds, and the out-of-time cases are set to cost 60s.

We implemented the satisfiability-checking algorithms introduced in this paper, and named the tool Aalta_v2.0 [2]. We compare Aalta_v2.0 with Aalta_v1.2, which is the latest explicit LTL-satisfiability solver (though it does use some SAT solving for acceleration) [17]. (The SAT engine used in both Aalta_v1.2 and Aalta_v2.0 is Minisat [9].) In the literature, Aalta_v1.2 is shown to outperform other existing explicit LTL solvers, so we omit the comparison with these solvers in this paper. Two resolution-based LTL satisfiability solvers, TRP++ [15] and ls4 [29], also utilize SAT solving, and we include them in our comparison.

As shown in [25], LTL satisfiability checking can be reduced to model checking. While BDD-based model checker were shown to be competitive for LTL satisfiability solving in [25], they were shown later not to be competitive with specialized tools, such as Aalta_v1.2 [18]. We do, however, include in our comparison the model checker NuXmv [2], which integrates the latest SAT-based model checking techniques. It uses Minisat as the SAT engine as well. Although standard bounded model checking (BMC) is not complete for the LTL satisfiability checking, there are techniques to make it complete, for example, *incremental bounded model checking* (BMC-INC) [13], which is implemented in NuXmv. In addition, NuXmv implements also new SAT-based techniques, IC3 [1], which can handle liveness properties with the K-liveness technique [3]. We included IC3 with K-liveness in our comparison.

To compare with the K-liveness checking algorithm, we ran NuXmv using the command "check_ltlspec_klive -d". For the BMC-INC comparison, we run NuXmv with the command "check_ltlspec_sbmc_inc -c". Aalta_v2.0 and Aalta_v1.2 tools were run using their default parameters. For the other tools, ls4 runs with "-r2l" and TRP++ runs with "-sBFS -FSR". Since the input of TRP++ and ls4 must be in SNF (Separated Normal Form [10]), an SNF generator is required for running these tools. A generator *translate* is available from the TRP++ website[3]. The parameters of *translate* are "-s -r".

In the experiments we consider the benchmark suite from [26], referred to as *schuppan-collected*. This suite collects formulas from several prior works, including [25], and has a total of 7446 formulas (3723 representative formulas and their negations). (Testing also the negation of each formula is in essence a check for validity.) In our experiments, we did not find any inconsistency among the solvers that did not time out.

---

[2] It can be downloaded at www.lab205.org/aalta.

[3] http://cgi.csc.liv.ac.uk/~konev/software/trp++/.

5.2   Results

The experimental results are shown in Table 1. In the table, the first column lists the different benchmarks in the suite, and the second to eighth columns display the results from different solvers. Each result in a cell of the table is a tuple $\langle t, n \rangle$, where t is the total checking time for the corresponding benchmark, and n is the number of unsolved formulas due to timeout in the benchmark. Specially the number "0" in the table means all formulas in the given benchmark are solved. Finally, the last row of the table lists the total checking time and number of unsolved formulas for each solver.

The results show that while the tableau-based tool Aalta_v1.2, outperforms ls4 and TRP++, it is outperformed by NuXmv-BMCINC and NuXmv-IC3-Klive, both of which are outperformed by Aalta_v2.0, which is faster by about 6,000 seconds and solves 47 more instances than NuXmv-IC3-Klive.

Our framework is explicit and closest to that is underlaid behind Aalta_v1.2. From the results, Aalta_v2.0 with heuristic outperforms Aalta_v1.2 dramatically, faster by more than 23,000 seconds and solving 371 more instances. One reason is, when Aalta_v1.2 fails it is often due to timeout during the heavy-duty normal-form generation, which Aalta_v2.0 simply avoids (generating XNF is rather lightweight).

Generating the states in a lightweight way, however, is not efficient enough. By running Aalta_v2.0 without heuristics, it cannot perform better than Aalta_v1.2, see the data in column 5 and 7 of Table 1. It can even be worse in some benchmarks such as "/anzu/amba" and "anzu/genbuf". We can explain the reason via an example. Assume the formula is $\phi_1 \vee \phi_2$, the traditional tableau method splits the formula and at most creates two nodes. Under our pure SAT-reasoning framework, however, it may create three nodes which contain $\phi_1 \wedge \neg\phi_1$ or $\neg\phi_1 \wedge \phi_2$, or

Table 1. Experimental results on the Schuppan-collected benchmark. Each cell lists a tuple $\langle t, n \rangle$ where t is the total checking time (in seconds), and n is the total number of unsolved formulas.

Formula type	ls4		TRP++		NuXmv-BMCINC		Aalta_v1.2		NuXmv-IC3-Klive		Aalta_v2.0 without heuristics		Aalta_v2.0 with heuristics	
/acacia/example	155	0	192	0	1	0	1	0	8	0	1	0	1	0
/acacia/demo-v3	68	0	2834	38	3	0	660	0	30	0	630	0	3	0
/acacia/demo-v22	60	0	67	0	1	0	2	0	4	0	2	0	1	0
/alaska/lift	2381	27	15602	254	1919	26	4084	63	867	5	4610	70	1431	18
/alaska/szymanski	27	0	283	4	1	0	1	0	2	0	1	0	1	0
/anzu/amba	5820	92	6120	102	536	7	2686	40	1062	8	3876	60	928	4
/anzu/genbuf	2200	30	7200	120	782	11	3343	54	1350	13	5243	94	827	4
/rozier/counter	3934	62	4491	44	3865	64	3928	60	3988	65	3328	55	2649	40
/rozier/formulas	167	0	37533	523	1258	19	1372	20	664	0	1672	25	363	0
/rozier/pattern	2216	38	15450	237	1505	8	8	0	3252	17	8	0	9	0
/schuppan/O1formula	2193	34	2178	35	14	0	2	0	95	0	2	0	2	0
/schuppan/O2formula	2284	35	2566	41	1781	28	2	0	742	7	2	0	2	0
/schuppan/phltl	1771	27	1793	29	1058	15	1233	21	753	11	1333	21	767	13
/trp/N5x	144	0	46	0	567	9	309	0	187	0	219	0	15	0
/trp/N5y	448	10	95	1	2768	46	116	0	102	0	316	0	16	0
/trp/N12x	3345	52	45739	735	3570	58	768	48	705	0	768	0	175	0
/trp/N12y	3811	56	19142	265	4049	67	7413	110	979	0	7413	100	154	0
/forobots	990	0	1303	0	1085	18	2280	32	37	0	2130	30	524	0
Total	32014	463	163142	2428	24769	376	31208	450	14261	126	31554	455	7868	79

$\phi_1 \wedge \phi_2$. This indicates that the state space generated by SAT solvers may in general be larger than that generated by tableau expansion.

To overcome this challenge, we propose some heuristics by adding specific constraints to SAT solvers, which at the mean time succeeds to reduce the searching space of the overall system. The results shown in column 8 of Table 1 demonstrate the effectiveness of heuristics presented in the paper. For example, the "/trp/N12/" and "/forobots/" benchmarks are mostly unsatisfiable formulas, which Aalta_v1.2 and Aalta_v2.0 with heuristic do not handle well. Yet the *unsat-core extraction* heuristic, which is described in the CONFLICT_ANALYZE mode of *getState* function, enables Aalta_v2.0 with heuristic to solve all these formulas. For satisfiable formulas, the results from "/anzu/amba/" and "/anzu/ genbuf" formulas, which are satisfiable, show the efficiency of the ELIMINA-TION and SAT_PURSUING heuristics in the *getState* function, which are necessary to solve the formulas.

Note that NuXmv-IC3-Klive is able to solve more cases than Aalta_v2.0 with heuristic in some benchmarks, such as "/lift" and "/schuppan/phltl" in which unsatisfiable formulas are not handled well enough by Aalta_v2.0. Currently, Aalta_v2.0 requires large number of SAT calls to identify an unsatisfiable core. In future work we plan to use a specialized MUS (minimal unsatisfable core) solver to address this challenge.

6   Concluding Remarks

We described in this paper a SAT-based framework for explicit LTL reasoning. We showed one of its applicaitons to LTL-satisfiability checking, by proposing basic algorithms and efficient heuristics. As proof of concept, we implemented an LTL satisfiability solver, whose performance dominates all similar tools. Moreover we demonstrate that our approach can be extended from propositional LTL to assertional LTL, yielding exponential improvement in performance. (see technical reprot)

Extending the explicit SAT-based approach to other applications of LTL reasoning, is a promising research direction. For example, the standard approach in LTL model checking [33] relies on the translation of LTL formulas to Büchi automata. The transition systems T_ϕ that is used for LTL satisfiability checking can also be used in the translation from LTL to Büchi automata. Current best-of-breed translators, e.g., [7,8,11,28] are tableau-based, and the SAT approach may yield significant performance improvement.

Of course, the ultimate temporal-reasoning task is model checking. Explicit model checkers such as SPIN [14] start with a translation of LTL to Büchi automata, which are then used by the model-checking algorithm. An alternative approach is to construct the automaton on-the-fly using SAT techniques, using the framework developed here. Current symbolic model-checking tools, such as NuXmv, do rely heavily on SAT solvers to implement algorithms such as BMC [13] or IC3 [1]. The success of the SAT-based explicit LTL-reasoning approach for LTL satisfiability checking suggests that this approach may also be successful in SAT-based model checking. This remains a highly intriguing research possibility.

Acknowledgment. The authors thank anonymous reviewers for useful comments. The work is supported in part by NSF grants CCF-1319459, by NSF Expeditions in Computing project "ExCAPE: Expeditions in Computer Augmented Program Engineering", and by BSF grant 9800096. Geguang Pu is partially supported by the NSFC grants No. 61202069 and No. 61361136002. Jianwen Li is partially supported by Shanghai Collaborative Innovation Center of Trustworthy Software for Internet of Things (ZF1213).

References

1. Bradley, A.R.: SAT-based model checking without unrolling. In: Jhala, R., Schmidt, D. (eds.) VMCAI 2011. LNCS, vol. 6538, pp. 70–87. Springer, Heidelberg (2011)
2. Cavada, R., Cimatti, A., Dorigatti, M., Griggio, A., Mariotti, A., Micheli, A., Mover, S., Roveri, M., Tonetta, S.: The NUXMV symbolic model checker. In: Biere, A., Bloem, R. (eds.) CAV 2014. LNCS, vol. 8559, pp. 334–342. Springer, Heidelberg (2014)
3. Claessen, K., Sörensson, N.: A liveness checking algorithm that counts. In: Cabodi, G., Singh, S. (ed.) FMCAD, pp. 52–59. IEEE (2012)
4. Clarke, E.M., Grumberg, O., Peled, D.: Model Checking. MIT Press, Cambridge (1999)
5. Courcoubetis, C., Vardi, M.Y., Wolper, P., Yannakakis, M.: Memory efficient algorithms for the verification of temporal properties. Formal Methods Syst. Des. **1**, 275–288 (1992)
6. D'Agostino, M.: Tableau methods for classical propositional logic. In: D'Agostino, M., Gabbay, D.M., Hähnle, R., Posegga, J. (eds.) Handbook of Tableau Methods, pp. 45–123. Springer, Netherlands (1999)
7. Daniele, M., Giunchiglia, F., Vardi, M.Y.: Improved automata generation for linear temporal logic. In: Halbwachs, N., Peled, D.A. (eds.) CAV 1999. LNCS, vol. 1633, pp. 249–260. Springer, Heidelberg (1999)
8. Duret-Lutz, A., Poitrenaud, D: SPOT: an extensible model checking library using transition-based generalized büchi automata. In: Proceedings of the 12th International Workshop on Modeling, Analysis, and Simulation of Computer and Telecommunication Systems, pp. 76–83. IEEE Computer Society (2004)
9. Eén, N., Sörensson, N.: An extensible SAT-solver. In: Giunchiglia, E., Tacchella, A. (eds.) SAT 2003. LNCS, vol. 2919, pp. 502–518. Springer, Heidelberg (2004)
10. Fisher, M.: A normal form for temporal logics and its applications in theorem-proving and execution. J. Logic Comput. **7**(4), 429–456 (1997)
11. Gerth, R., Peled, D., Vardi, M.Y., Wolper, P.: Simple on-the-fly automatic verification of linear temporal logic. In: Dembiski, P., Sredniawa, M. (eds.) Protocol Specification, Testing, and Verification, pp. 3–18. Chapman & Hall, Warsaw (1995)
12. Giunchiglia, F., Sebastiani, R.: Building decision procedures for modal logics from propositional decision procedures - the case study of modal K. In: McRobbie, M.A., Slaney, J.K. (eds.) CADE 1996. LNCS, vol. 1104, pp. 583–597. Springer, Heidelberg (1996)
13. Heljanko, K., Junttila, T.A., Latvala, T.: Incremental and complete bounded model checking for full PLTL. In: Etessami, K., Rajamani, S.K. (eds.) CAV 2005. LNCS, vol. 3576, pp. 98–111. Springer, Heidelberg (2005)
14. Holzmann, G.J.: The SPIN Model Checker: Primer and Reference Manual. Addison-Wesley, Reading (2003)

15. Hustadt, U., Konev, B.: TRP++ 2.0: a temporal resolution prover. In: Baader, F. (ed.) CADE 2003. LNCS (LNAI), vol. 2741, pp. 274–278. Springer, Heidelberg (2003)

16. Larrabee, T.: Test pattern generation using Boolean satisfiability. IEEE Trans. Comput. Aided Des. Integr. Circuits Syst **11**(1), 4–15 (1992)

17. Li, J., Pu, G., Zhang, L., Vardi, M.Y., He, J.: Fast LTL satisfiability checking by SAT solvers. CoRR, abs/1401.5677 (2014)

18. Li, J., Zhang, L., Pu, G., Vardi, M., He, J.: LTL satisfibility checking revisited. In: 20th International Symposium on Temporal Representation and Reasoning, pp. 91–98 (2013)

19. Malik, S., Zhang, L.: Boolean satisfiability from theoretical hardness to practical success. Commun. ACM **52**(8), 76–82 (2009)

20. Manna, Z., Pnueli, A.: The Temporal Logic of Reactive and Concurrent Systems: Specification. Springer, New York (1992)

21. Marques-Silva, J., Lynce, I.: On improving MUS extraction algorithms. In: Sakallah, K.A., Simon, L. (eds.) SAT 2011. LNCS, vol. 6695, pp. 159–173. Springer, Heidelberg (2011)

22. McMillan, K.L.: Interpolation and SAT-based model checking. In: Hunt Jr., W.A., Somenzi, F. (eds.) CAV 2003. LNCS, vol. 2725, pp. 1–13. Springer, Heidelberg (2003)

23. McMillan, K.L.: Symbolic Model Checking. Kluwer Academic Publishers, Boston (1993)

24. Pnueli, A.: The temporal logic of programs. In: Proceedings of the 18th IEEE Symposium on Foundations of Computer Science, pp. 46–57 (1977)

25. Rozier, K.Y., Vardi, M.Y.: LTL satisfiability checking. Int. J. Softw. Tools Technol. Transf. **12**(2), 123–137 (2010)

26. Schuppan, V., Darmawan, L.: Evaluating LTL satisfiability solvers. In: Bultan, T., Hsiung, P.-A. (eds.) ATVA 2011. LNCS, vol. 6996, pp. 397–413. Springer, Heidelberg (2011)

27. Schwoon, S., Esparza, J.: A note on on-the-fly verification algorithms. In: Halbwachs, N., Zuck, L.D. (eds.) TACAS 2005. LNCS, vol. 3440, pp. 174–190. Springer, Heidelberg (2005)

28. Somenzi, F., Bloem, R.: Efficient Büchi automata from LTL formulae. In: Emerson, E.A., Sistla, A.P. (eds.) CAV 2000. LNCS, vol. 1855. Springer, Heidelberg (2000)

29. Suda, M., Weidenbach, C.: A PLTL-prover based on labelled superposition with partial model guidance. In: Gramlich, B., Miller, D., Sattler, U. (eds.) IJCAR 2012. LNCS, vol. 7364, pp. 537–543. Springer, Heidelberg (2012)

30. Tabakov, D., Rozier, K.Y., Vardi, M.Y.: Optimized temporal monitors for SystemC. Formal Methods Syst. Des. **41**(3), 236–268 (2012)

31. Vardi, M.: On the complexity of epistemic reasoning. In: Proceedings of the Fourth Annual Symposium on Logic in Computer Science, pp. 243–252. IEEE Press, Piscataway (1989)

32. Vardi, M.Y.: Unified verification theory. In: Banieqbal, B., Barringer, H., Pnueli, A. (eds.) Temporal Logic in Specification. LNCS, vol. 398, pp. 202–212. Springer, Heidelberg (1989)

33. Vardi, M.Y., Wolper, P.: An automata-theoretic approach to automatic program verification. In: Proceedings of the 1st IEEE Symposium on Logic in Computer Science, pp. 332–344 (1986)

Understanding VSIDS Branching Heuristics in Conflict-Driven Clause-Learning SAT Solvers

Jia Hui Liang[✉], Vijay Ganesh, Ed Zulkoski, Atulan Zaman,
and Krzysztof Czarnecki

University of Waterloo, Waterloo, Canada
jliang@gsd.uwaterloo.ca

Abstract. Conflict-Driven Clause-Learning (CDCL) SAT solvers crucially depend on the Variable State Independent Decaying Sum (VSIDS) branching heuristic for their performance. Although VSIDS was proposed nearly fifteen years ago, and many other branching heuristics for SAT solving have since been proposed, VSIDS remains one of the most effective branching heuristics. Despite its widespread use and repeated attempts to understand it, this *additive bumping* and *multiplicative decay* branching heuristic has remained an enigma.

In this paper, we advance our understanding of VSIDS by answering the following key questions. The first question we pose is "what is special about the class of variables that VSIDS chooses to additively bump?" In answering this question we showed that VSIDS overwhelmingly picks, bumps, and learns bridge variables, defined as the variables that connect distinct communities in the community structure of SAT instances. This is surprising since VSIDS was invented more than a decade before the link between community structure and SAT solver performance was discovered. Additionally, we show that VSIDS viewed as a ranking function correlates strongly with temporal graph centrality measures. Putting these two findings together, we conclude that VSIDS picks high-centrality bridge variables. The second question we pose is "what role does multiplicative decay play in making VSIDS so effective?" We show that the multiplicative decay behaves like an exponential moving average (EMA) that favors variables that persistently occur in conflicts (the signal) over variables that occur intermittently (the noise). The third question we pose is "whether VSIDS is temporally and spatially focused." We show that VSIDS disproportionately picks variables from a few communities unlike, say, the random branching heuristic. We put these findings together to invent a new adaptive VSIDS branching heuristic that solves more instances than one of the best-known VSIDS variants over the SAT Competition 2013 benchmarks.

1 Introduction

The Boolean satisfiability (SAT) problem [14] is the quintessential NP-complete problem, a class of decision problems conjectured to be computationally hard. Yet, impressively, modern sequential Conflict-Driven Clause-Learning SAT

© Springer International Publishing Switzerland 2015
N. Piterman (Ed.): HVC 2015, LNCS 9434, pp. 225–241, 2015.
DOI: 10.1007/978-3-319-26287-1_14

solvers [6,9,15,32,34] are able to solve large instances obtained from real-world applications [3,29]. Although hundreds of techniques and heuristics have been proposed over the last five decades to solve the Boolean SAT problem [2,3], modern SAT solvers rely crucially only on a handful of them. Of these, the two most important are Conflict-Driven Clause-Learning with backjumping (CDCL) [34] and Variable State Independent Decaying Sum (VSIDS) branching heuristic [36]. Many systematic experiments have been performed to ascertain the veracity of this observation [29]. Additionally, not only is VSIDS one of the most effective branching heuristics, but many other well-known high-performing branching heuristics are simply variants of VSIDS. Researchers have proposed some theoretical explanations for the impact of clause-learning on the performance of the modern SAT solvers: clause-learning allows SAT solvers to polynomially simulate general resolution propositional proof system [5,7,39]. However, our understanding of the role played by VSIDS heuristic has previously been limited. The motivation for the research presented in this paper is to achieve a better scientific understanding of VSIDS. We focus on two well-known variations of VSIDS, namely cVSIDS and mVSIDS, described in Sect. 2.

Our Scientific Findings and Contributions. In this paper we ask the following questions regarding the behavior of VSIDS.[1] First, what is special about the class of variables that VSIDS chooses to additively bump? (Answered by Contributions I and III.) Second, what role does multiplicative decay play in making VSIDS so effective? (Answered by Contribution IV.) Third, is VSIDS temporally and spatially focused? (Answered by Contribution II.)

Contribution I: Bridge Variables and VSIDS. Community structure is a property exhibited in many real-world graphs, particularly in social networks, where the graph can be partitioned into groups of vertices, called communities, such that each group is densely connected within itself but sparsely connected with other groups. Recent research has shown that the community structure quality of the SAT input correlates with faster solving time [38]. We show that bridge variables connecting distinct communities in the community structure of a SAT instance [21] are high priority targets for both the branching heuristic and clause-learning, which suggests one possible explanation for this correlation.

Contribution II: Community-focused Search and VSIDS. We define two terms, *spatial focus* and *temporal focus*, to describe how a branching heuristic focuses on certain regions of the search space during solving, with respect to the underlying community structure. We refer to this form of locality as focused search, to distinguish it from local search performed by stochastic local search solvers [25]. We show that mVSIDS is more focused than cVSIDS and random branching according to these metrics.

---

[1] All code and experimental data sets are available from our website: https://github.com/JLiangWaterloo/vsids.

Contribution III: Exponentially-smoothed Temporal Graph Central-ity and VSIDS correlate strongly. Third, we show that VSIDS rankings correlate strongly with the variable rankings induced by *exponentially smoothed temporal graph centrality* (TGC) measures over the *temporal variable incidence graphs* (TVIG) of the original and learnt clauses of an input SAT instance. This correlation remains strong throughout the run of the solver. The TVIG extends the well-known *variable incidence graph* over Boolean formulas by incorporat-ing the dynamically evolving aspect of the learnt clause database inside a SAT solver and uses exponential smoothing to focus on recently learnt clauses. TGC is the temporal version of the widely-used graph centrality measures, such as degree and eigenvector centrality, which are used to identify important vertices in a graph. The definitions are inspired by recent research on temporal aspects of social networks [22,42]. For example, the timed PageRank algorithm [42] is used to discover important publications that are likely to be referenced in the future. We show that VSIDS typically selects variables with high *temporal degree centrality* and *temporal eigenvector centrality*. The above-mentioned find-ings essentially tell us that we have a single family of mathematically-precise graph-theoretic measures, namely TGC, that succinctly characterizes both the additive bump and multiplicative decay components of VSIDS family of heuris-tics. Variables that have high centrality correspond to variables in "recent" learnt clauses that are "highly-constrained" and get additively bumped. Variables that are not "persistently" highly-constrained, i.e., do not occur frequently in recent learnt clauses get decayed away quickly. Putting together Contributions I and III, we conclude that *VSIDS picks high-centrality bridge variables*.

Contribution IV: Exponential Moving Average and Multiplicative Decay in VSIDS. Fourth, we show that the multiplicative decay in VSIDS is a form of exponential moving average, and provide a plausible explanation as to why this is crucial to the effectiveness of VSIDS.

Contribution V: A Novel Adaptive Branching Heuristic. Our findings led to a new VSIDS called adaptVSIDS that adapatively adjusts the exponential moving average (a form of adaptive moving average) depending on the quality of the learnt clauses. We show that adaptVSIDS outperforms mVSIDS, by solving 2.4 % more instances over the SAT Competition 2013 benchmarks.

2   Background

Here we describe VSIDS and the variable incidence graph of a CNF formula.

The VSIDS Branching Heuristic and Variants. The term VSIDS refers to a family of branching heuristics widely used in modern CDCL SAT solvers that *rank* all variables of a Boolean formula during the run of a solver. As things stand today, VSIDS is significantly more effective than other well-known heuristics such as DLIS [33], MOM [18], Jeroslow-Wang [28], and BOHM [12]. VSIDS was a major breakthrough when first introduced as part of the Chaff solver [36]. The key idea is to collect statistics over learnt clauses to guide the direction of the search, where recent learnt clauses are favored. The key characteristics of VSIDS is the additive bumping and multiplicative decay behavior, described in more details below. Another positive characteristic of VSIDS is its low computational overhead. We focus on two of the more well-known variants of VSIDS, namely, the variant from Chaff [36] and the variant from MiniSAT version 2.2.0 [15]. We refer to these variants as cVSIDS and mVSIDS respectively. Both variants have the common characteristics listed below.

Activity Score, Initialization and VSIDS Ranking. VSIDS assigns a floating point number, called *activity*, to each variable in the Boolean formula. At the begining of a run of a solver, the activity scores of all variables are typically initialized to 0. We refer to the ranking of variables according to their activity scores in the decreasing order as the VSIDS ranking. VSIDS picks the variable with the highest activity to branch on.

Additive Bump and Multiplicative Decay. When the solver learns a clause, a set of variables is chosen, and their activities are additively increased, typically by 1. The quantum of this increase is called the (additive) *bump*. At regular intervals during the run of the solver, the activities of all variables are multiplied by a constant $0 < \alpha < 1$ called the (multiplicative) *decay factor*.

cVSIDS. The activities of variables occurring in the newest learnt clause are bumped up by 1, immediately after the clause is learnt. The activities of all variables are multiplied by a constant $0 < \alpha < 1$. The decay occurs after every i conflicts. We follow the policy used in recent solvers like MiniSAT and use $i = 1$.

mVSIDS. The activities of all variables resolved during conflict analysis that lead to the learnt clause (including the variables in the learnt clause) are bumped up by 1. The activities of all variables are decayed as in cVSIDS[2].

Variable Incidence Graph (VIG). The VIG of a CNF formula F is defined as follows: vertices of the graph are the variables in the formula. For every clause $c \in F$ we have an edge between each pair of variables in c. In other words, each clause corresponds to a clique between its variables. The weight of an edge is $\frac{1}{|c|-1}$ where $|c|$ is the length of the clause. VIG does not distinguish between positive and negative occurrences of variables. We combine all edges between each pair of vertices into one weighted edge by summing the weights. More precisely, the VIG of a CNF formula F is a weighted graph defined as follows: set of vertices $V = Var$, set of edges $E = \{xy \mid x, y \in c \in F\}$, and the weight function $w(xy) = \sum_{x,y \in c \in F} \frac{1}{|c|-1}$.

---

[2] MiniSAT's actual implementation is slightly different, but has the same effect. Rather than decaying the activities of every variable, it increases the bump quantum of all future conflicts instead [8].

3 Contribution I and II: Community-Focused Search, Bridge Variables, and VSIDS

In this section, we describe the experimental setup, methodology, and results to show the connection between VSIDS and community structure.

The Hypotheses. Here we state the three hypotheses that we tested in this section: **(1) Bridge Experiment:** VSIDS disproportionately picks, bumps, and learns the bridge variables, **(2) Spatial Focus Experiment:** VSIDS disproportionately picks from a smaller number of communities rather than a large fraction of the communities of a SAT instance, and **(3) Temporal Focus Experiment:** VSIDS typically picks from recently-seen communities.

Community Structure of the Graph of SAT Instances, and Bridge Variables. The concept of decomposing graphs into *natural communities* [13,43] arose in the study of complex networks such as the *graph of biological systems*. Informally, a network or graph is said to have community structure if the graph can be decomposed into sub-graphs where the sub-graphs have more internal edges than outgoing edges [38]. We say that a graph has a "good" community structure if the percentage of intra-community edges is significantly higher than inter-community edges. We refer to these inter-community edges as bridges, and the vertices connected by such edges as *bridge vertices*. In the context of the community structure of the VIG of a Boolean formula, bridge vertices are called *bridge variables*. We refer the reader to these papers [13,43] for a more formal introduction to community structure of graphs.

Recently there has been some interesting discoveries regarding the impact of community on CDCL SAT solver performance [38]. Specifically, the authors of the paper [38] showed that the running time of CDCL solvers is strongly correlated with community structures of SAT instances. In light of these discoveries, it was but natural for us ask the question whether VSIDS somehow exploits the community structure of SAT instances. What we discovered and explain below is that VSIDS disproportionately picks, bumps, and learns the bridge variables in the community structure of SAT instances.

Temporal and Spatial Focused Search. We further define two terms, *spatial focus* and *temporal focus*, to describe how a branching heuristic gravitates towards certain regions of the search space during solving, with respect to the underlying community structure. We say a branching heuristic is spatially focused if it disproportionately picks variables from a small set of communities, when normalized for size, throughout the entire run of the solver. A branching heuristic exhibits temporal focus if it typically picks a new decision variable from a small fixed-size *window* of recently-seen communities.

Experimental Setup and Methodology. Experiments were performed over the 1030 instances from SAT Competition 2013 [3], after simplification using MiniSAT simplifying-solver. We use the Louvain method [10] to compute the communities of the VIG of the input SAT formulas. There are many community-detecting algorithms to choose from and we picked Louvain because it scales well with the size of input graphs. For each instance, the Louvain method is given an hour to compute and save the communities it finds. The community information is then given to a modified MiniSAT 2.2.0 so it can track the bridge variables. Due to the high cost, we only compute the communities once at the start.

For the *Bridge-Experiment*, we ran the instances using a modified MiniSAT with a timeout of 5000 seconds, as per the SAT Competition 2013 rules. Before MiniSAT begins its CDCL loop, it reads in the community information stored by the Louvain method. The solver then scans through its the initial input clauses and checks which variables share at least one clause with another variable residing in a different community and marks them as bridge variables. Whenever our modified version of MiniSAT (1) picks a decision variable, (2) bumps a variable, and (3) learns a clause over a variable during the search, it checks whether the variable is a bridge variable. If so, the solver updates its internal counters to keep track of the number of bridge variables in the each of the 3 scenarios. At the end of the run, the solver outputs the percentage of variables that are bridge in each of these scenarios. This additional code adds little overhead and does not change the behavior of MiniSAT. We are simply instrumenting the solver to collect statistics of interest. For the *Temporal-Experiment* and *Spatial-Experiment*, we additionally modified MiniSAT to record all decision variables to a file, in order to post-process the data. We allowed a 10000 second timeout for these experiments due to this additional overhead.

The Reporting of Results. In the *Bridge-Experiment*, for each instance, we compute the percentage of decision variables, bumped variables, learnt clause variables, and number of variables that are also bridges. Then we averaged these percentages over the three SAT 2013 Competition benchmark categories (application, combinatorial, and random) and reported these numbers.

For the *Spatial-Experiment*, for every community i, we compute a community score $cs_i = picks\_from(i)/order(i)$, where $picks\_from(i)$ is the number of times the solver branched on a variable from community i and $order(i)$ is the size of community i in terms of variables. We then use the *Gini coefficient* [20], a statistical measure of inequality, to compute our spatial score $ss = gini(cs_i$ for i $\in communities)$. A score of 1 indicates total disparity (e.g. all picks are from one community), whereas zero indicates total equality. Higher scores therefore favor our hypothesis. We report the average ss value for each benchmark category. The intuition behind this experiment and the use of the Gini coefficient here (used in measuring the inequality of wealth distribution in countries) is that it is an effective method for computing how unequally a branching heuristic favors some communities over others. Using this metric we show for example that VSIDS disproportionately favors a small set of communities (highly unequal distribution of picks) versus random branching heuristic (largely equal distribution of picks).

For the *Temporal-Experiment*, we define our window size ws to be 10 % of the total number of communities, rounded up to the nearest integer. For all instances, our window contains the set of communities from the ws most recent decisions (note that the set may have less than ws elements). At every decision, we increment a counter *window_hits* if the current variable is from a community in the window. We assign a temporal score $ts = window\_hits/decisions$ for each instance. We report the average ts value for each benchmark category. The key idea behind this experiment is to test the hypothesis that VSIDS branching favors picking from recently picked-from communities, versus random which does not display such temporal locality.

Results and Interpretations of Bridge Variable Experiment. Table 1 shows that bridge variables are highly favored in MiniSAT by its branching heuristic, conflict analysis, and clause-learning. It is a surprising result that bridge variables are favored even though the heuristics and techniques in MiniSAT have no notion of communities. While bridge variables certainly make up a large percent of variables, the percent of picked bridge variables is even higher. Table 1 includes only the instances where the Louvain implementation completed before timing out. In total, 229/300 instances in the application category and 238/300 instances in the hard combinatorial category are included in the Table 1. In the random category, every variable is a bridge, hence the results are omitted. This is expected because it is highly improbable to generate random instances where a variable is not neighboring another variable outside its community.

Recent research suggests that CDCL solvers take advantage of good community structure in SAT instances [38] leading to faster solving time. The reason for this phenomenon is not fully understood. One possibility is that good community structure lends itself to divide-and-conquer because the bridges are easier to cut (i.e., satisfy). More precisely, the solver can focus its attention on the bridges by picking the bridge variables and assigning them appropriate values. When it eventually assigns the correct values to enough bridges, the VIG is divided into multiple components, and each component can be solved with no interference from each other. Even if the VIG cannot be completely separated, it may still be beneficial to the cut bridges between communities so that these communities can be solved relatively independently.

Results and Interpretations of Temporal and Spatial Focused Search Experiments. Table 2a depicts the average Gini coefficient for the *Spatial-Experiment*. Both VSIDS techniques exhibit much more inequality relative to random branching for the application and combinatorial instances, indicating that VSIDS may be attempting to *hone in* on certain communities. The very

Table 1. MiniSAT's CDCL and mVSIDS techniques prefers to pick, bump, and learn over bridge variables.

Category	% of variables that are bridge	% of picked variables that are bridge	% of bumped variables that are bridge	% of learnt clause variables that are bridge
Application	61.0	79.9	71.6	78.4
Combinatorial	78.2	87.6	84.3	88.2

Table 2. (a) VSIDS heuristics are more spatially focused than random branching. (b) VSIDS heuristics tend to pick from recently-picked communities.

Category	mVSIDS	cVSIDS	random	Category	mVSIDS	cVSIDS	random
Application	0.592	0.560	0.216	Application	0.580	0.551	0.268
Combinatorial	0.275	0.261	0.099	Combinatorial	0.505	0.473	0.265
Random	0.029	0.023	0.006	Random	0.269	0.268	0.219

(a) *Spatial-Experiment* average ss score.   (b) *Temporal-Experiment* average ts score.

low values for random instances indicate that none of the branching heuristics typically favor certain communities, likely due to the poor community structures exhibited by such instances. Table 2b demonstrates that VSIDS techniques are much more temporally focused on average than random branching. It is commonly believed that VSIDS improves the *search locality* [32,37] which in turn improves solver performance. However, this term *search locality* has previously been not rigorously defined. We precisely defined spatial focus and temporal focus, and show that VSIDS displays high search locality in terms of these definitions.

4   Contribution III: Experimental Evidence Supporting Strong Correlation Between TGC and VSIDS

In this section, we describe the experiments to support the hypothesis that the VSIDS variants cVSIDS and mVSIDS, viewed as ranking functions, correlate strongly with both temporal degree centrality and temporal eigenvector centrality according to Spearman's rank correlation coefficient and top-k measures. Combining the results of this section with Contribution I (namely, VSIDS picks, bumps and learns over bridge variables), we conclude that VSIDS picks *high-centrality bridge variables*.

Temporal Variable Incidence Graph (TVIG). To incorporate the temporal aspect of learnt clauses we introduce *temporal variable incidence graph* (TVIG) here, that extends the VIG by encoding temporal information into its structure. In the TVIG, every clause is labeled with a timestamp denoted $t(c)$. The $t(c)$ is equal to 0 if c is a clause from the original input formula, otherwise $t(c)$ is equal to the number conflicts up to the learning of c. We refer to the difference between the current time t and the timestamp of a clause $t(c)$ as the age of the clause: $age(c) = t - t(c)$. Fix an *exponential smoothing factor* $0 < \alpha < 1$. The TVIG is a weighted graph constructed in the same manner as the VIG except the weight of an edge is $\frac{\alpha^{age(e)}}{|c|-1}$. Like the VIG, multiple edges between a pair of vertices are combined into one weighted edge. More precisely, the TVIG of a clause database at time t is defined in the same way as VIG except with a modified weight function that takes the ages of clauses into account: $w(xy) = \sum_{x,y \in c \in F} \frac{\alpha^{age(c)}}{|c|-1}$. Observe that the TVIG evolves throughout the solving process: as new learnt clauses are added, new edges are added to the graph, and all the ages increase.

As an edge's age increases, its weight decreases exponentially with time assuming no new learnt clause contains its variables. In many domains, it is often the case that more recent data points are more useful than older data points.

(Temporal) Degree and Eigenvector Centrality. A graph centrality measure is a function that assigns a real number to each vertex in a graph. The number associated with each vertex denotes its relative importance in the graph [16,19,41]. For example, the degree centrality [16] of a vertex in a graph is defined as the degree of the vertex. The eigenvector centrality of a vertex in a graph is defined as its corresponding value in the eigenvector of the greatest eigenvalue of the graph's adjacency matrix. We similarly define the temporal versions of degree and eigenvector centrality. The key idea needed to define temporal graph centrality measures is to incorporate temporal information inside the TVIG. The temporal degree centrality (TDC) and (resp. temporal eigenvector centrality (TEC)) of a vertex at time t is defined as the degree centrality (resp. eigenvector centrality) of the vertex in the TVIG at time t.

Experimental Setup and Methodology. We implemented the VSIDS variants and TGC measures in MiniSAT 2.2.0 [15]. All the experiments were performed using MiniSAT on all 1030 Boolean formulas obtained from all three categories (application, combinatorial, and random) of the SAT Competition 2013 [3]. Before beginning any experimentation, the instances are first simplified using MiniSAT's inbuilt preprocessor with the default settings. All experiments were performed on the SHARCNET cloud [4], where cores range in specs between 2.2 to 2.7 GHz with 4 GB of memory, and 4 hour timeout. We use 100 iterations of the power iteration algorithm [23] to compute TEC, and 1 iteration for TDC. We use MiniSAT's default decay factor of 0.95 for VSIDS. We also use 0.95 as the exponential smoothing factor for the TVIG. We take measurements on the current state of the solver after every 5000 iterations, where an iteration is defined as a decision or a conflict. Observe that we take measurements dynamically as the solver solves an instance, and not just once at the beginning. Such a dynamic comparison gives us a much better picture of the correlation between two different ranking functions or measures than a single point of comparison.

Methodology for Comparing Rankings based on Spearman's Rank Correlation Coefficient. For each set of experiments, for each SAT instance, for every measurement made, we compute the Spearman's rank correlation coefficient [40] between the VSIDS and TGC rankings. Spearman's rank correlation coefficient is a widely-used correlation coefficient in statistics for measuring the degree of relationship between a pair of rankings. The strength of Spearman's correlation is conventionally interpreted as follows: 0.00–0.19 is very weak, 0.20–0.39 is weak, 0.40–0.59 is moderate, 0.60–0.79 is strong, 0.80–1.00 is very strong. We compute the average of the Spearman's correlation over the execution of a SAT solver on each instance. We follow the standard practice of applying the Fisher transformation [17] when aggregating the correlations.

Methodology for Comparing Rankings based on Top-k. Let v be the unassigned variable with the highest ranked according to some VSIDS variant. Let i be the position of variable v according to a specific TGC ranking, excluding assigned variables. Then the *top-k measure* is 1 if $i \leq k$, otherwise 0. The rationale for this metric is that SAT solvers typically only choose the top-ranked unassigned variable, according to the VSIDS ranking, to branch on. If the VSIDS top-ranked unassigned variable occurs very often among the top-k ranked variables according to TGC, then we infer that VSIDS picks variables that are highly ranked according to TGC. In our experiments, we used various values for k. Again, we compute the average of top-k measure over the execution of a SAT solver on each instance.

The Reporting of Results. For every pair of rankings, one from the VSIDS family and the other from the TGC family, we report the top-k measure and Spearman's rank correlation coefficient between the pair of rankings every 5000 iterations. On termination, we compute the average for the instance. We take all the instance averages and average them again, and report the average of the averages. The final numbers are labeled as "mean top-k" or "mean Spearman". For example, a mean top-10 of 0.912 is interpreted as "for the average instance in the experiment, 91.2 % of the measured top-ranked variables according to VSIDS are among the 10 unassigned variables with the highest centrality". Likewise, a high mean Spearman implies the average instance has a strong positive correlation between VSIDS and TGC rankings.

Results and Interpretations. In Table 3 (resp. Table 4), we compare VSIDS and TDC (resp. TEC) rankings. The data shows a strong correlation between VSIDS and TDC, in particular, the 0.818 mean Spearman between cVSIDS and TDC is high. The metrics are lower with TEC, but the correlation remains strong. mVSIDS has a better mean Spearman with TEC than TDC in the application category. We have also conducted this experiment with non-temporal degree/eigenvector centrality and the resulting mean Spearman and mean top-k are significantly lower than their temporal counterparts.

It is commonly believed that VSIDS focuses on the "most constrained part of the formula" [24], and that this is responsible for its effectiveness. However, the term "most constrained part of the formula" has previously not been well-defined in a mathematically precise manner. One intuitive way to define the constrainedness of a variable is to analyze the Boolean formula, and count how many clauses a variable occurs in. The variables can then be ranked based on this measure. In fact, this measure is the basis of the branching heuristic called DLIS [33], and was once the dominant branching heuristic in SAT solvers. We show that graph centrality measures are a good way of mathematically defining this intuitive notion of syntactic "constrainedness of variables" that has been

Table 3. Results of comparing VSIDS and TDC.

	cVSIDS vs TDC			mVSIDS vs TDC		
	Application	Combinatorial	Random	Application	Combinatorial	Random
Mean Spearman	0.818	0.946	0.988	0.629	0.791	0.864
Mean Top-1	0.884	0.865	0.949	0.427	0.391	0.469
Mean Top-10	0.912	0.898	0.981	0.705	0.735	0.867

Table 4. Results of comparing VSIDS and TEC.

	cVSIDS vs TEC			mVSIDS vs TEC		
	Application	Combinatorial	Random	Application	Combinatorial	Random
Mean Spearman	0.790	0.926	0.987	0.675	0.764	0.863
Mean Top-1	0.470	0.526	0.794	0.293	0.304	0.418
Mean Top-10	0.693	0.746	0.957	0.610	0.670	0.856

used by the designers of branching heuristics. Degree centrality of a vertex in the VIG is indeed equal to the number of clauses it belongs to, hence it is a good basis for guessing the constrained variables for the same reason. Eigenvector centrality extends this intuition by further increasing the ranks of variables close in proximity to other constrained variables in the VIG. Additionally, as the dynamic structure of the VIG evolves due to the addition of learnt clauses by the solver, the most highly constrained variables in a given instance also change over time. Hence we incorporated learnt clauses and temporal information into the TVIG to account for changes in variables' constrainedness over time.

Besides the success of branching heuristics like VSIDS and DLIS, there is additional evidence that the syntactic structure is important for making good branching decisions. For example, Iser et al. discovered that initializing the VSIDS activity based on information computed on the abstract syntax tree of their translator has a positive impact on solving time [27]. In a different paper [38], the authors have shown that the graph-theoretic community structure strongly influences the running time of CDCL SAT solvers. This is more evidence of how CDCL SAT solver performance is influenced by syntactic graph properties of input formulas. Finally, by combining the results of this section with Contribution I, we conclude that VSIDS picks *high-centrality bridge variables*.

5   Contribution IV: Exponential Moving Average and Multiplicative Decay

In this section, we argue that the multiplicative decay aspect of the VSIDS branching heuristic is a form of exponential moving average (EMA) [11]. It is the inclusion of multiplicative decay in VSIDS that gives it its distinctive feature of focusing its search based on recent conflicts. The original Chaff paper [36] and patent [35] rather cryptically mentioned that VSIDS acts like a "low-pass filter". They do not specify wh at signals are being fed to this filter, and why the high-frequency components are being filtered out and discarded.

In his paper [8], Armin Biere was perhaps the first to articulate the idea that additive bumping of variable scores can be viewed as a signal (a square wave, to be more precise) over the run of the solver. More precisely, at every time step, the signal of a variable is 1 if it is bumped, or 0 otherwise. Armin Biere formalized *normalized VSIDS* [8] as $s_n = (1 - f) \times \sum_{k=1}^{n} \delta_k \times f^{n-k}$. s_n is the normalized VSIDS activity of a variable v after the nth conflict. $\delta_k = 1$ if variable v was bumped in the kth conflict, otherwise $\delta_k = 0$. f is the decay factor.

While Huang et al. [26] referred to VSIDS as an EMA, we will show this explicitly. We not only characterize VSIDS as an EMA explicitly, but also describe why this is crucial to the effectiveness of VSIDS as a branching heuristic. In the next section we leverage this connection between EMA and VSIDS to propose an adaptive VSIDS branching heuristic inspired by an adaptive version of EMA.

EMA is a form of exponential smoothing, used in getting rid of noise (variables whose VSIDS scores are akin to high-frequency signals) in time series data (the signals due to VSIDS scores). Exponential smoothing is a class of techniques to mitigate the effect of random noise in time series data for the purpose of analysis and forecasting. Armin Biere's normalized VSIDS equation can be rewritten to the following recursive formula: $s_n = (1 - f) \times \delta_n + f \times s_{n-1}$. This formula fits exactly the definition of Brown's simple exponential smoothing, also known as exponential moving average. Therefore normalized VSIDS is exactly an EMA over the δ time series. The EMA causes VSIDS to favor variables that "persistently" occur in "recent" conflicts. A rationale why this is effective could be as follows: A conflict essentially points to faulty judgment by the solver in assigning values to variables. If a set of variables are at the root of a faulty judgment and thus occurs in a conflict, then they would repeatedly occur in related faulty judgments and hence in related conflicts. Variables that occur persistently in "recent" conflicts could be a good guess for the root cause of those conflicts. Hence, perhaps the most effective search strategy is to focus on determining this root cause. The learnt clauses that result from such a strategy improve in quality with time, until such time that the root cause of a set of faulty judgment has been determined and enshrined as a learnt clause.

6   Contribution V: A Faster Branching Heuristic Based on Adaptive Moving Average

In this section, we report on our design of a better VSIDS based on the knowledge that VSIDS decay is a form of EMA. The EMA is integral to VSIDS performance as a branching heuristic, and now that the connection between EMA and VSIDS is established, all the literature on EMA and other time series data analysis are directly applicable to VSIDS.

Adaptive Moving Average. Given that VSIDS decay is a form of EMA, we studied the literature of EMA from the financial domain [31], where it is known that the fixed decay factor can be undesirable. A moving average with a large decay factor would lag behind fast moving markets whereas a small decay factor would fail to smooth out a lot of noise. Kaufman [31] noted that a fixed decay factor performs poorly when the market volatility changes. He devised *adaptive moving average* where the decay factor (also known as smoothing constant) is determined by the market volatility to minimise lag and noise. By fluctuating the decay factor when necessary, adaptive moving average is better than EMA at uncovering trends in the market.

Just like how markets can go up and down, a CDCL SAT solver can go up and down in "productivity" over time. For example, Audemard and Simon [6] discovered that a learnt clause with lower literals blocks distance (LBD) [6] is of higher quality. LBD of a clause is defined to be the number of decision levels that its variables span. If the solver is in a search space that produces many learnt clauses with low LBD, then we want to encourage the solver to stay within that search space. We do so by adjusting the VSIDS decay factor to be closer to 1, i.e., decay slower. On the other hand, if the solver is in a search space that produces many learnt clauses with high LBD, it is best to choose a smaller decay factor, i.e., decay faster. Based on this insight, we devised a new VSIDS heuristic called adaptVSIDS by extending mVSIDS with an adaptive moving average. adaptVSIDS maintains a floating-point number lbdema equal to the exponential moving average of the learnt clause LBDs. lbdema is updated after every learnt clause and this number will be used to adjust the decay factor of the variables' activities. In mVSIDS, the variables' activities are decayed by multiplying with a constant decay factor, typically 0.95, after each conflict. Whereas in adaptVSIDS, the decay factor is adjusted based on the LBD of the learnt clause. If the LBD of the learnt clause is greater than lbdema, then use a decay factor of 0.75, otherwise use a decay factor of 0.99. Our website has all the code.

Experimental Setup and Methodology. The experiments were performed on the application and combinatorial categories of the SAT Competition 2013. For each instance with a timeout of 5000 seconds as per competition rules, we ran an unmodified MiniSAT 2.2.0 and a modified MiniSAT 2.2.0 with adaptVSIDS on StarExec [1].

Results and Interpretations. Our adaptVSIDS solved 351 instances whereas mVSIDS solved 343 instances, an increase of 2.4 % more solved instances.

7 Interpretation of Results

We began our research by posing a series of questions regarding VSIDS, and we now interpret the results obtained in light of these questions.

What is special about the class of variables that VSIDS chooses to additively bump? (Answered by Contributions I and III.) In the bridge variables experiment (Sect. 3), we showed that VSIDS disproportionately favored bridge variables. Even though SAT instances have large number of bridge variables on average, the frequency with which VSIDS picks, bumps, and learns bridge variables is much higher. There is no a priori reason to believe that VSIDS would behave like this. This surprising result, plus a previous result that good community structure correlates with faster solving time [38], suggests CDCL solvers exploit community structure. More precisely, they target variables linking distinct communities, possibly as a way to solve by divide-and-conquer approach.

In the VSIDS vs. TGC experiments (Sect. 4), we used the Spearman's rank correlation coefficient to show that the VSIDS and TGC rankings are *strongly correlated.* From our experiments, we can say that for all the VSIDS variants considered in this paper, additive bumping matches with the increase in centrality of the chosen variables. We also observe from our results that the variables that solvers pick for branching have very high TGC rank. The concept of centrality allows us to define in a mathematically precise the intuition many solver developers have had, i.e., that branching on "highly constrained variables" is an effective strategy. Our bridge variable experiment combined with the TGC experiment suggests that VSIDS focuses on *high-centrality bridge variables*.

What role does multiplicative decay play in making VSIDS so effective? (Answered by Contribution IV, that in turn led to a new adaptive VSIDS presented as Contribution V.) We show that multiplicative decay is essentially a form of exponential smoothing (Sect. 5). We add an explanation as to why this is important, namely, that exponential smoothing favors variables that persistently occur in conflicts and this is a better strategy for root-cause analysis. We designed a new VSIDS technique, we call adaptVSIDS, based on the above results, wherein we rapidly decay the VSIDS activity if the learnt clause LBDs are large (Sect. 6). We showed that this technique is better than mVSIDS on the SAT Competition 2013 benchmark.

Is VSIDS temporally and spatially focused? (Answered by Contribution II.) We show that VSIDS exhibits *spatial focus* and *temporal focus* (Sect. 3), forms of locality in search. While there has been speculation among solver researchers that CDCL with VSIDS solvers perform local search, we precisely define spatial and temporal locality in terms of the community structure.

8   Related Work

Marques-Silva and Sakallah are credited with inventing the CDCL technique [34]. The original VSIDS heuristic was invented by the authors of Chaff [36]. Armin Biere [8] described the low-pass filter behavior of VSIDS, and Huang et al. [26] stated that VSIDS is essentially an EMA. Katsirelos and Simon [30] were the first to publish a connection between eigenvector centrality and branching heuristics. In their paper [30], the authors computed eigenvector centrality (via Google PageRank) only once on the original input clauses and showed that most of the decision variables have higher than average centrality. Also, it bears stressing that their definition of centrality is not temporal. By contrast, our results correlate VSIDS ranking with temporal degree and eigenvector centrality, and show the correlation holds dynamically throughout the run of the solver. Also, we noticed that the correlation is also significantly stronger after extending centrality with temporality. Simon and Katsirelos do hypothesize that VSIDS may be picking bridge variables (they call them fringe variables). However, they do not provide experimental evidence for this. To the best of our knowledge, we are the first to establish the following results regarding VSIDS: first, VSIDS picks, bumps, and learns high-centrality bridge variables; second, VSIDS-influenced search is more spatially and temporally focused than other branching heuristics we considered; third, explain the importance of EMA (multiplicative decay) to the effectiveness of VSIDS; and fourth, invent a new adaptive VSIDS branching heuristic based on our observations.

9   Conclusions and Future Work

In this paper we present various empirically-verified findings on VSIDS. We show that VSIDS tends to favor the high-centrality bridge variables in the community structure of the Boolean formula. In addition, we show that VSIDS focuses on a small subset of communities in the graph of a SAT instance during search. Lastly, we explain the multiplicative decay of VSIDS with EMA and use this finding to devise a new branching heuristic we call adaptVSIDS. These results put together show that community structure, graph centrality, and exponential smoothing are important lenses through which to understand the behavior of the VSIDS family of branching heuristics and CDCL SAT solving. In the future, we plan to strengthen our results by considering a larger number of benchmarks, solvers, branching heuristics, and graph representations.

Acknowledgement. We thank Kaveh Ghasemloo for his help in refining our TGC model and for his insight on the connection between VSIDS decay and exponential moving average.

References

1. Starexec. http://www.starexec.org/
2. Proceedings of Past SAT Conferences (2013). http://www.satisfiability.org
3. SAT Competition Website (2013). http://www.satcompetition.org
4. SHARCNET Website (2013). https://www.sharcnet.ca
5. Atserias, A., Fichte, J.K., Thurley, M.: Clause-learning algorithms with many restarts and bounded-width resolution. In: Kullmann, O. (ed.) SAT 2009. LNCS, vol. 5584, pp. 114–127. Springer, Heidelberg (2009)
6. Audemard, G., Simon, L.: Glucose: a solver that predicts learnt clauses quality. IJCAI **9**, 399–404 (2009)
7. Beame, P., Kautz, H.A., Sabharwal, A.: Towards understanding and harnessing the potential of clause learning. J. Artif. Intell. Res. (JAIR) **22**, 319–351 (2004)
8. Biere, A.: Adaptive restart strategies for conflict driven SAT solvers. In: Kleine Büning, H., Zhao, X. (eds.) SAT 2008. LNCS, vol. 4996, pp. 28–33. Springer, Heidelberg (2008)
9. Biere, A.: Lingeling (2010)
10. Blondel, V.D., Guillaume, J.L., Lambiotte, R., Lefebvre, E.: Fast unfolding of communities in large networks. J. Stat. Mech. Theor. Exp. **2008**(10), P10008 (2008)
11. Brown, R.G.: Exponential Smoothing for Predicting Demand. Little, Cambridge (1956)
12. Buro, M., Büning, H.K.: Report on a SAT competition. Fachbereich Math.-Informatik, Univ. Gesamthochschule (1992)
13. Clauset, A., Newman, M.E., Moore, C.: Finding community structure in very large networks. Phys. Rev. E **70**(6), 066111 (2004)

14. Cook, S.A.: The complexity of theorem-proving procedures. In: Proceedings of the Third Annual ACM Symposium on Theory of Computing, STOC 1971, pp. 151–158. ACM, New York (1971)
15. Een, N., Sörensson, N.: MiniSat: a SAT solver with conflict-clause minimization. In: SAT 2005 (2005)
16. Faust, K.: Centrality in affiliation networks. Soc. Netw. 19(2), 157–191 (1997)
17. Fisher, R.A.: Frequency distribution of the values of the correlation coefficient in samples from an indefinitely large population. Biometrika 10(4), 507–521 (1915)
18. Freeman, J.W.: Improvements to propositional satisfiability search algorithms. Ph.D. thesis, Philadelphia, PA, USA (1995). uMI Order No. GAX95-32175
19. Freeman, L.: Centrality in social networks conceptual clarification. Soc. Netw. 1(3), 215–239 (1979)
20. Gini, C.: Measurement of inequality of incomes. Econ. J. 31(121), 124–126 (1921)
21. Girvan, M., Newman, M.E.: Community structure in social and biological networks. Proc. Natl. Acad. Sci. 99(12), 7821–7826 (2002)
22. Gloor, P., Krauss, J., Nann, S., Fischbach, K., Schoder, D.: Web science 2.0: identifying trends through semantic social network analysis. In: 2009 International Conference on Computational Science and Engineering, CSE 2009, vol. 4, pp. 215–222, August 2009
23. Golub, G.H., Van Loan, C.F.: Matrix Computations. JHU Press, Baltimore (2012)
24. Hamadi, Y., Jabbour, S., Sais, L.: ManySAT: a parallel SAT solver. JSAT 6(4), 245–262 (2009)
25. Hoos, H.H., Stützle, T.: Stochastic Local Search: Foundations & Applications. Morgan Kaufmann Publishers Inc., San Francisco (2004)
26. Huang, R., Chen, Y., Zhang, W.: SAS+ planning as satisfiability. J. Artif. Int. Res. 43(1), 293–328 (2012)
27. Iser, M., Taghdiri, M., Sinz, C.: Optimizing MiniSAT variable orderings for the relational model finder kodkod. In: Cimatti, A., Sebastiani, R. (eds.) SAT 2012. LNCS, vol. 7317, pp. 483–484. Springer, Heidelberg (2012)
28. Jeroslow, R.G., Wang, J.: Solving propositional satisfiability problems. Ann. Math. Artif. Intell. 1(1–4), 167–187 (1990)
29. Katebi, H., Sakallah, K.A., Marques-Silva, J.P.: Empirical study of the anatomy of modern SAT solvers. In: Sakallah, K.A., Simon, L. (eds.) SAT 2011. LNCS, vol. 6695, pp. 343–356. Springer, Heidelberg (2011)
30. Katsirelos, G., Simon, L.: Eigenvector centrality in industrial SAT instances. In: Milano, M. (ed.) CP 2012. LNCS, vol. 7514, pp. 348–356. Springer, Heidelberg (2012)
31. Kaufman, P.J.: Trading Systems and Methods. Wiley, New York (2013)
32. Mahajan, Y.S., Fu, Z., Malik, S.: Zchaff2004: an efficient SAT solver. In: H. Hoos, H., Mitchell, D.G. (eds.) SAT 2004. LNCS, vol. 3542, pp. 360–375. Springer, Heidelberg (2005)
33. Marques-Silva, J.: The impact of branching heuristics in propositional satisfiability algorithms. In: Barahona, P., Alferes, J.J. (eds.) EPIA 1999. LNCS (LNAI), vol. 1695, pp. 62–74. Springer, Heidelberg (1999)
34. Marques-Silva, J.P., Sakallah, K.A.: Grasp: a search algorithm for propositional satisfiability. IEEE Trans. Comput. 48(5), 506–521 (1999)
35. Moskewicz, M.W., Madigan, C.F., Malik, S.: Method and system for efficient implementation of boolean satisfiability (26 August 2008), US Patent 7,418,369
36. Moskewicz, M.W., Madigan, C.F., Zhao, Y., Zhang, L., Malik, S.: Chaff: engineering an efficient SAT solver. In: Proceedings of the 38th Annual Design Automation Conference, DAC 2001, pp. 530–535. ACM, New York (2001)

37. Nadel, A., Ryvchin, V.: Assignment stack shrinking. In: Strichman, O., Szeider, S. (eds.) SAT 2010. LNCS, vol. 6175, pp. 375–381. Springer, Heidelberg (2010)
38. Newsham, Z., Ganesh, V., Fischmeister, S., Audemard, G., Simon, L.: Impact of community structure on SAT solver performance. In: Sinz, C., Egly, U. (eds.) SAT 2014. LNCS, vol. 8561, pp. 252–268. Springer, Heidelberg (2014)
39. Pipatsrisawat, K., Darwiche, A.: On the power of clause-learning SAT solvers with restarts. In: Gent, I.P. (ed.) CP 2009. LNCS, vol. 5732, pp. 654–668. Springer, Heidelberg (2009)
40. Spearman, C.: The proof and measurement of association between two things. Am. J. Psychol. **15**(1), 72–101 (1904)
41. Straffin, P.D.: Linear algebra in geography: eigenvectors of networks. Math. Mag. **53**(5), 269–276 (1980)
42. Yu, P.S., Li, X., Liu, B.: Adding the temporal dimension to search - a case study in publication search. In: Skowron, A., Agrawal, R., Luck, M., Yamaguchi, T., Morizet-Mahoudeaux, P., Liu, J., Zhong, N. (eds.) Web Intelligence, pp. 543–549. IEEE Computer Society (2005)
43. Zhang, W., Pan, G., Wu, Z., Li, S.: Online community detection for large complex networks. In: Proceedings of the Twenty-Third international joint conference on Artificial Intelligence, pp. 1903–1909. AAAI Press (2013)

Multi Domain Verification

Multi-Domain Verification of Power, Clock and Reset Domains

Ping Yeung[1]([⊠]) and Eugene Mandel[2]

[1] Mentor Graphics, Fremont, USA
ping_yeung@mentor.com
[2] Mentor Graphics, Petah Tikva, Israel

Abstract. Multi-Domain Verification (MDV) is a comprehensive approach that specializes in verifying design logic that straddles heterogeneous domains. An integrated circuit design can be conceptually disintegrated into multiple types of partition for domain analysis. For example, a modern design typically has a power domain partition, a clock domain partition, and a reset domain partition. Historically, domain analysis is confined to verification of the same domain (homogeneous domain): for example, power domain verification and clock domain crossing verification are performed separately. As designs become highly sophisticated and domains are inter-dependence of each other, this practice is no longer sufficient. Interactions between different types of domains (heterogeneous domains) is exceptionally complex and critical to the success of the device. Hence, a new methodology is required to verify them effectively. Multi-domain verification uses power domain information from the Unified Power Format (UPF) specifications, clock domain information from the clock tree models and reset domain information from the reset tree models. It employs specialized domain analysis and methodologies to examine the complex interactions of logic that straddles domain boundaries—among both homogeneous domains and heterogeneous domains. Multi-domain verification is an efficient way to ensure that all inter-domain issues are explored and verified with complete confidence.

1 Introduction

To meet the rigorous functionality and power requirements, SoC designs typically operate in a spectrum of clock frequencies and uses a set of sophisticated power management strategies. It can incorporate advanced design technologies, such as asynchronous clocks, ratio-synchronous clocks, clock gating, multiple voltages, power switching, dynamic voltage and frequency scaling (DVFS) and so on. Interaction of logical function spanning out in different power, clock and reset domains can potentially cause spectacular chip failures. Yet, design teams face several challenges to ensure these domains are working correctly with respect to each other. Although design teams usually do a good job partitioning a design into multiple power, clock and reset domains at the chip-level, it is challenging to understand how these domains interact with each other at the block or lower levels. The situation is made worse when design teams are integrating multiple IPs that they know little about together. In order to save power in today's designs, blocks are switched on and off continuously. Power-aware

© Springer International Publishing Switzerland 2015
N. Piterman (Ed.): HVC 2015, LNCS 9434, pp. 245–255, 2015.
DOI: 10.1007/978-3-319-26287-1_15

simulation is a good start, but it is impossible to achieve sufficient coverage with simulation to verify the inter-domain interaction dynamically. Hence, static domain analysis is essential to examine the design space thoroughly. Multi-Domain Verification (MDV) is developed to address the challenges in this area (Fig. 1).

This paper has three sections.

- In the first section, we summarize the current power domain verification, clock domain verification and reset domain verification methods. They provide comprehensive verification of the homogeneous domains, but they fail to consider the presence of the other domains.
- In the second section, we explain the general concept of multi-domain representation, its data model and verification methods. It addresses two limitations in existing tools: (1) what are the effects of other heterogeneous domain, and (2) what will happen to the domain-controlling signals (such as clock gating signals) when they are crossing other domains?
- In the final section, we describe some of the issues found in the designs from our development partners. They are good examples to demonstrate the necessity and benefits of multi-domain verification.

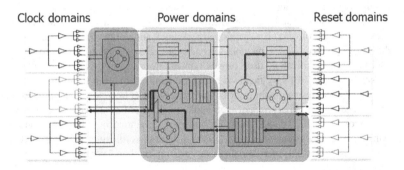

Fig. 1. Multi-domain verification

2   Individual Domain Verification

2.1   Clock Domain Crossing

Today's SoC designs have a large number of clock domains. In addition, it also integrates a lot of internal and external IPs from multiple sources. As a result, a significant number of asynchronous clock domains and clock domain crossing (CDC) signals are introduced into the design. CDC logic must follow strict design principles for reliable operation [5, 6]. And because of transistor-level effects in circuits, verifying CDC logic is not possible with standard simulation or static timing analysis techniques (Fig. 2).

To handle this dilemma, CDC verification can be divided into three parts [7]: 1. identify all CDC signals in the design; statically recognize the synchronizers and validate the intended CDC schemes. 2. Dynamically and/or formally verify the CDC

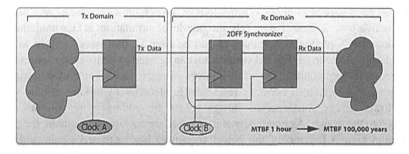

Fig. 2. Clock domain crossing

protocols. This step ensures that the CDC control and data signals are stable when crossing the domain boundaries. 3. Dynamically simulate the design with metastability injection and/or formally verify reconvergent structures. This step ensures that the chip is tolerant of unpredictable delays from the synchronizers embedded in the CDC paths.

CDC verification is commonly deployed by advanced design teams; CDC structures and schemes are well understood. But when a design with hundreds of asynchronous clock domains and thousands clock gating signals operate in various power domains, their interactions are difficult to predict.

2.2 Reset Domain Crossing

System level reset strategy becomes increasingly complex as they combine various sources of reset requirements [8]. For example, reset signals are needed for each power domain and they also must be synchronized to their target clock domains before use.

When a set of data dependent registers in the same clock domain, are driven by different reset signals, Fig. 3, the asynchronous reset signal on the source register will cause an asynchronous event to happen at the receiving register. If *rstn1* is asserted while *rstn2* is not asserted, the asynchronous output data from *dff1* can cause metastability on *dff2*. This is the reset domain crossing we are concerned about.

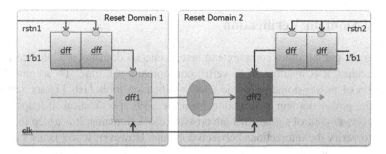

Fig. 3. Reset domain crossing

Reset domain crossing verification can be divided into three parts [9]: 1. Static analysis is used to find and build the tree structure of all the reset signals in the design.

Resets can be classified as either synchronous or asynchronous resets, as well as active high or active low. 2. Rather than rely on gate level simulation, RTL simulation with silicon-accurate X-propagation semantics can be used to find issues related to uninitialized design elements. 3. Formal verification can be used to verify many aspects of the reset tree, including: connectivity of all sources of resets to their intended destinations and detecting corruption of correctly reset storage elements by unknown logic values.

To lower power consumption, design teams are adding more complex power domains into the design. As a reset signal is required for each power domain, the activity of the reset signals (as part of the power sequence) has increased significantly. It is difficult to foresee all the possible interactions of the reset signals with other domains.

2.3   Power Domain Crossing

With the Unified Power Format (UPF) standard [2], project teams are able to capture the power intent of the design. The power intent specification consists of power domains, supply networks, power structures, and power states. The verification goal is to check the functionality of the power management elements to ensure they are working properly. Also, each subsystem can be turned-on, transitioned into its power-modes and shut-down independently.

A power-aware verification tool can check the placement of isolation cells and level shifters on the power domain crossing signals. The isolation cells will be controlled by the power controller with respect to the power-up and power-down sequences. If retention registers are used, the save and restore operations will also need to be verified. To help guide design teams on this new challenge, a power verification checklist is presented in [3]. It focuses on various aspects of power domain toggling, isolation cells, memories, and retention of registers.

As the number of power domain increases in designs, they have created a heavy burden for both the design and the verification teams. By supporting the UPF standard, we enable project teams to verify the power intent early in the design cycle with other domains.

3   Multi-Domain Verification

As designs are getting more complex and heterogeneous domains are interacting more with each other, it is insufficient to verify one domain at a time. To account for the introduction of power domains, some CDC verification tools [10, 11] are starting to leverage the power domain information from the UPF specification. It helps identify and verify power control signals that are crossing clock domains. It is a step in the right direction to verify the interactions between domains. However, it still lacks a complete domain specific view of the design. Hence, we take a step forward to architect a new verification environment. It has all the domain information extracted and represented persistently. This allows the environment to verify all the domain interactions comprehensively. At the same time, extra information from a different domain can be pulled in on-demand to refine and understand the severity of an identified situation.

We named this approach Multi-Domain Verification (MDV). It extracts the power domain information from the Unified Power Format (UPF) specification, the clock domain information from the clock trees and the reset domain information from the reset trees. It is equally important to represent the logic functions controlling the different domains: power control signals, clock gating signals and reset enabling signals. To truly understand the interaction between domains, it has to understand the functionality of the control signals. For instance, if the clock to a register is gated off or the register is in retention mode, the register is going to be very stable. Hence, clock domain crossing or reset domain crossing from the register will not be a problem.

As shown in Fig. 4, the multi-domain verification process is divided vertically into three phases: domain structure verification, domain control verification and domain crossing verification. Instead of verifying one domain at a time, this vertical phase by phase (heterogeneous) approach allows users to focus on the big picture first. For instance, if the power domain specification is wrong, or the clock tree is not well defined yet, it is not going to be productive examining the detail violations generated from the power or clock domain crossing signals. Users should focus on refining the UPF specification, the clock trees and the reset trees first. Once the early phase has been finalized, users can move onto the latter phase. Consequentially, the latter phases can leverage all the information, augmentation, and refinement done in the previous phases.

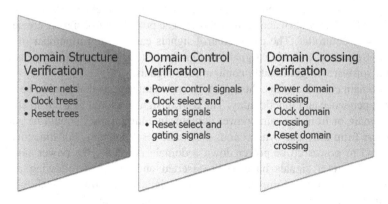

Fig. 4. The 3 phases of multi-domain verification

3.1 Domain Structure Verification

Multi-domain verification extracts, represents and verifies the structures of the power domain, clock domain and reset domain concurrently. It allows users to understand how the domain structures, such as clock trees and reset trees, is affected by the presence of the other domains.

The objective of structure verification is to ensure that the power supply nets, clock signals and reset signals are distributed to different parts of the design correctly. During this process, domains are colored, the domain boundaries are carved, and the number of domains is calculated. Then, for each design element in the design (such as register, memory array, and module), we will know the power, clock and reset domains it is associated with.

Domain structure checks include:

1. Registers without explicitly connected clock or reset signals
2. Reset used both active-high and active-low levels
3. Reset used both asynchronously and synchronously
4. Reset not synchronized to targeted clock domain (wrong clock or polarity)
5. Clock or reset tree with combinational feedback loop
6. Clock or reset tree with unexpected combinational logic
7. Clock or reset tree with re-convergent paths
8. Clock or reset tree crossing power domains
9. Clock tree crossing reset domains
10. Reset tree crossing clock domains
11. Consistence of power supply network (ports, nets, and switches)
12. Power management elements (power controller, retention cells, level shifters or isolation cells) are not in always-on power domain.

3.2 Domain Control Verification

As power switching, frequency switching and clock gating are common practices for low-power designs, it is important to understand the domain control signals, such as power switch signals, isolation and retention control signals; clock select, control and gating signals; reset control and gating signals. The power control signals are generated by the power controller. The clock control signals can be from a number of sources including frequency switching signals, design-for-test signals, mode of operation signals, and software programmable configuration signals.

For domain control signals, there are two important aspects that need to be verified: domain dependence and functionality. The control signals should be from an always-on power domain or from the same power domain. In addition, they should be generated by registers from the same synchronous clock and reset domains. For functionality, to operate and to power up or power down a domain correctly, the power supply, the clock and the reset signals have to be asserted and removed following a precise sequence. To do so, the corresponding control signals, the power switch, clock and reset gating logic have to have the right values at the right time.

With a lot of clock gating and frequency switching, the domain control logic, especially the clock control logic, can be complex. It is impossible to simulate all the possible functional scenarios and corner cases. Hence, static and formal connectivity verification are more effective ways to verify the conditional connectivity of the domain structures.

Domain control checks include:

1. Identifying internally generated multiplexed clock or reset
2. Identifying internally generated gated clock or reset
3. Clock control signals from different power domains
4. Reset control signals from different power domains
5. Power control signal from different clock domains
6. Undefined, undriven or unknown value on all control signals

7. Connectivity check the distribution of power control signals with respect to the power state information
8. Connectivity check the distribution of clock and reset with respect to their control signals (different configurations, power-up and power-down scenarios)
9. Ordering of events in the power control sequence (power-up and power down)

3.3 Domain Crossing Verification

After domain structure verification, the set of domain, (power, clock and reset), associated with each design element in the design has been defined. Domain crossing analysis will examine the connectivity and data dependence in the design. For each data signal, the domain set of the TX register will be compared with the domain set of the RX register.

$$TX(power_{[on/off]}, clock_{[on/off]}, reset_{[on/off]}) \rightarrow RX(power_{[on/off]}, clock_{[on/off]}, reset_{[on/off]})$$

If the RX domains are *significantly* different from the TX domains, corresponding domain crossing analysis will be performed. The objective is to ensure that an appropriate domain crossing scheme is in-place to mediate the risk associated with each type of domain crossing. For instance, for each CDC signal, the domain crossing analysis will ensure that a suitable synchronization scheme has been applied.

At the same time, in order to understand the interactions between TX and RX domains, the domain control signals will also be evaluated to determine whether a domain is active or not. To illustrate why, let us examine Fig. 5; an interface module is connected to a memory controller. In certain mode of operation, if the interface module is powered off completely, only power domain crossing analysis needs to be performed between these modules. On the other hand, if the interface module and the memory controller are both powered on with the same voltage, their clock and reset domains will be examined to determine whether clock or reset domain crossing verification is required.

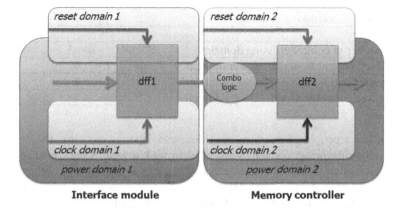

Fig. 5. Power, clock and reset domain crossing

Domain crossing checks include:

1. Clock domain crossing signal without proper synchronizer
2. Clock domain crossing reset signal without proper synchronizer
3. Clock domain crossing control signal without proper synchronizer
4. Reset domain crossing signal without proper guarding or isolation
5. Power domain crossing signal without proper isolation or level shifter
6. Potential signal corruption to and from retention register.

4 Results

We have applied multi-domain verification on a few designs from our development partners with various combinations of power, clock and reset domains. The verification was performed at the RT level with UPF specifications. Results from 3 of the blocks are summarized in Table 1 below. With multi-domain verification, the tool was able to identify all the power, clock and reset domains correctly. Users can amend the power net groupings, clock and reset tree groupings within each domain by assigning explicit values to the control signals, or by grouping the clock and reset signals explicitly with directives.

Table 1. Summary of multi-domain verification

	Number of domains	Block 1	Block 2	Block 3
1	Power domains	2	3	4
2	Asynchronous Clock domains	3	4	16
3	Asynchronous Reset domains	2	11	9

	Number of trees crossing domains	Block 1	Block 2	Block 3
4	Clock trees crossing power domains	2	2	6
5	Clock trees crossing reset domains	2	3	5
6	Reset trees crossing power domains	1	2	7
7	Reset trees crossing clock domains	2	5	16

	Number of control crossing domains	Block 1	Block 2	Block 3
8	Clock control from diff. power domain	0	4	5
9	Reset control from diff. power domain	0	2	13
10	Power control from diff. clock domain	2	4	6

Block 1 is a peripheral interface controller with 2 power domains. The clock and reset trees cross the power domains a few times (row#4, row#6). They are mainly going from the always-on power domain to other switchable power domains. When a clock tree is crossing reset domains (row#5), it means that different reset signals are used to initialize registers within the same clock domain. If some of the registers are depending on each other, this will lead to reset domain crossing problems. Reset trees crossing power and clock domains are normally done by design (row#6, row#7). It means that the same reset tree is being used in different clock or power domains. This will be a problem however if the power domain needs to be reset independently with respect to other domains in the design.

There are two issues with the power control signals (row#10). From the schematic in Fig. 6, an isolation cell is used to isolate the switchable and the always-on power domains. Although the two power domains belong to the same clock domain, the isolation signal is from a different clock domain (such as the power controller clock domain). As a result, the isolation signal introduced a clock domain crossing signal into the design. To design this correctly, the isolation signal should be synchronized to the RX clock before used. Hence, using a single isolation signal for all the output ports can easily lead to this problem.

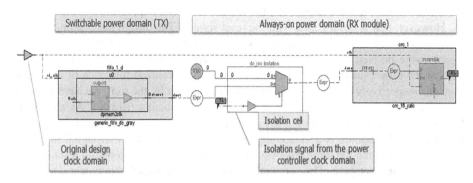

Fig. 6. Clock domain crossing power isolation signal

Block 2 is a functional controller for a design. It has a few clock and power domains, but it generates a lot of reset signals to control structures locally and to other blocks of the design (row#3). For this block, we were focusing on verifying the reset structures. Power domains and reset signals are closely related. Each switchable power domain should have a reset signal to initialize the storage elements every time when it is powered on. However, when data is flowing from one power domain to another, it is not a good idea to use different reset signals to initialize the registers when they are residing within a same clock domain (row#5). In Fig. 7, a reset signal is needed for the RX module in the switchable power domain. Instead of using reset1 from the TX module, the designer synchronized an external reset, reset2, for RX module. As a result, different reset signals are used for the data path from TX module to RX module. An undesirable reset domain crossing path is introduced.

Block 3 is part of an interconnect controller for multiple processor cores. The design has 16 primary clock signals. Some of the clock signals are interface specific and they only go to the specific interface modules. Other system level clock signals are distributed widely. Since the top-level of the design is in an always-on power domain, most of the clock trees going from the top to a switch-able power domain are not a concern. We were particularly worrying about clock trees going from one switch-able

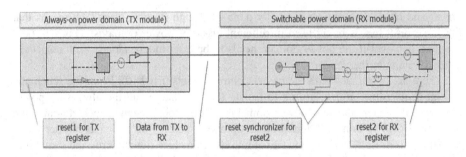

Fig. 7. Reset domain crossing between two power domains

power domain to another switch-able power domain (row#4). After reviewing the results carefully, we were happy that the scenario had not happened.

However, that is not the case with the reset signals. The design has 3 primary reset signals. From them, internal reset signals, warm reset signals, and synchronized reset signals were derived internally. From the top-level, the reset signals are driven into each of the power domains and at the same time, synchronized into each of the clock domains respectively. After reviewing the issues reported by the tool, we have found a few cases that the reset signals are crossing power domains (row#6). As shown in Fig. 8, the two reset signals for the RX module are passing through a switchable power domain. The IP module is a data computational unit. It gets its reset signal from the top-level module and the input reset signal is also used to drive two output reset signals for the receiving datapath. The potential problem is: if the switchable power domain is powered down, it will be impossible to reset the RX module any more. From the schematic, it is quite clear that the RX module does not need to get the reset signals from the IP module, instead, it can get the reset signals directly from the top-level. When we reviewed this situation with the design team, they told us that they do not know the functionality of the IP module. They used the reset signals from the IP module to ensure that the receiving datapath will be in-sync with the computation in the IP module.

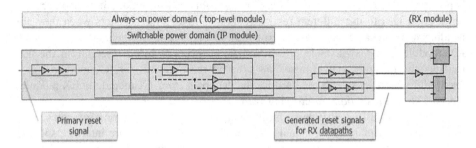

Fig. 8. Reset signals crossing different power domains

5   Conclusion

In this paper, we have presented the Multi-Domain Verification approach that verifies the power, clock and reset domains concurrently at the RT level. It analyzes data signals and structures that straddles heterogeneous domains. By representing and verifying these domains together, it is more intuitive to understand the interaction between them and hence, anticipate any domain issue as early as possible in the design cycle. The process is divided into three steps: domain structure verification, domain control verification and domain crossing verification. This divide-and-conquer approach encourages users to focus on verifying and refining the domain structures first. With well-understood domain structures and controls, domain crossing signals can then be verified efficiently.

References

1. ARM® Cortex®-A17 MPCore Processor Technical Reference Manual Revision: r1p0. http://infocenter.arm.com
2. Unified Power Format: 1801–2013 IEEE Standard for Design and Verification of Low-Power Integrated Circuits. IEEE (2013)
3. Bembaron, F., Kakkar, S., Mukherjee, R., Srivastava, A.: Low power verification methodology using UPF. In: DVCon (2011)
4. Srivastava, A., Bhargava, M.: Stepping into UPF 2.1 world: easy solution to complex power aware verification. In: DVCon (2014)
5. Ginosar, R.: Metastability and synchronizers, a tutorial. IEEE Des. Test Compt. **28**(5), 23–35 (2011)
6. Cummings, C.: Clock domain crossing (CDC) design and verification techniques using SystemVerilog. In: Synopsys User Group Meeting (SNUG) (2008)
7. Kwok, C., Gupta, V., Ly, T.: Using assertion-based verification to verify clock domain crossing signals. In: DVCon (2003)
8. Liu, K., Yang, P., Levitt, J., Berman, M., Eslinger, M.: Using formal techniques to verify system on chip reset schemes. In: DVCon (2013)
9. Kwok, C., Viswanathan, P., Yeung, P.: Addressing the challenges of reset verification in SoC designs. In: DVCon (2015)
10. Chakraborty, A., Jain, N., Goel, S.: Power aware CDC verification at RTL for Faster SoC verification closure. In: DVCon India (2014)
11. Takara, K.: Next-generation power aware CDC verification – what have we learned. In: DVCon (2015)
12. Cummings, C., Mills, D., Golson, S.: Asynchronous and synchronous reset design techniques. In: SNUG 2003, Boston (2003)

Synthesis

FudgeFactor: Syntax-Guided Synthesis for Accurate RTL Error Localization and Correction

Andrew Becker[1]([✉]), Djordje Maksimovic[2], David Novo[1], Mohsen Ewaida[1],
Andreas Veneris[2], Barbara Jobstmann[1], and Paolo Ienne[1]

[1] Ecole Polytechnique Fédérale de Lausanne, Lausanne, Switzerland
andrew.becker@epfl.ch
[2] University of Toronto, Toronto, Canada

Abstract. Functional verification occupies a significant amount of the digital circuit design cycle. In this paper, we present a novel approach to improve circuit debugging which not only localizes errors with high confidence, but can also provide semantically-meaningful source code corrections. Our method, which we call FUDGEFACTOR, starts with a buggy design, at least one failing and several correct test vectors, and a list of suspect bug locations. We obtain the suspect location from a state-of-the-art debugging tool that includes a significant number of false positives. Using this list and a library of rules empirically characterizing typical source-code mistakes, we instrument the buggy design to allow each potential error location to either be left unchanged, or replaced with a set of possible corrections. FUDGEFACTOR then combines the instrumented design with the test vectors and solves a 2QBF-SAT problem to find the minimum number of source-level changes from the original code which correct the bug. Our 13 benchmarks demonstrate that our method is able to correct a sizable portion of realistic bugs within a reasonable computational time. With the aid of available golden reference designs, we show that those corrections are, at least on these benchmarks, always valid and non-trivial fixes. We believe that our technique significantly improves over other debugging tools in two respects: When we succeed, we obtain a much more precise bug localization with no false positives and little or no ambiguity. Additionally, we offer bug corrections that are inherently meaningful to the designers and enable designers to quickly recognize and understand the root cause of the bug with a high level of confidence.

1 Introduction

Functional verification is a traditionally thorny process which occupies up to two thirds of the digital circuit design cycle [9]. There are at least two ways to reduce the time spent on ensuring functional correctness: either ease the process of developing functionally-correct circuits from the beginning, or improve circuit debug and verification tools. This paper takes the latter approach. Although formal verification tools typically return a counterexample when verification fails,

© Springer International Publishing Switzerland 2015
N. Piterman (Ed.): HVC 2015, LNCS 9434, pp. 259–275, 2015.
DOI: 10.1007/978-3-319-26287-1_16

the subsequent debugging process (i.e., error localization and correction) is typically lengthy and heavily reliant on designers' expertise and experience. Tools exist to help in error localization and correction, but most work on the subject has either suggested repairs at the netlist level [6,7], or tried to map netlist repairs back to RTL source code (e.g., [10,17]), which is not always possible and can lead to incomprehensible repair suggestions. We see this as problematic, as designers rarely work directly with netlists: even if tools find errors and suggest appropriate corrections in the netlist, designers must still spend an inordinate amount of time finding the true root cause at the register transfer level to be able to implement a correction they understand and can vouch for. Thus, we think it essential to locate and correct errors directly at the register transfer level, where designers typically work.

In this work, we present FUDGEFACTOR, a syntax-guided synthesis tool for source-level error localization and correction. It takes as input a buggy circuit design, at least one failing test vector, some correct test vectors, and a list of suspect error locations. This list may come from any state-of-the-art error localization tools. These tools are usually remarkably efficient and can handle very large designs but lack precision. This leads to tens—or more—of fairly vague false-positive suspect locations. In our case, we use a commercial verification tool based on the work of Smith et al. [15] to obtain the list of suspect locations. Using this list and a library of rules characterizing typical source code mistakes, we automatically instrument the buggy design to allow each potential bug to either be left unchanged, or replaced with a set of possible corrections. FUDGEFACTOR then combines the instrumented design with the test vector(s) and solves a 2QBF-SAT problem to find the minimum number of source-level changes from the original code which correct the bug. Because all correction rules describe semantically meaningful transformations, changes FUDGEFACTOR presents to the user are highly likely to address the root cause and remove the error. Definitely, not all design errors are typical, "standard" mistakes, and thus our approach can never be complete, regardless of the number of rules in our library. Yet, we provide a quick, high-confidence initial debug pass which virtually eliminates a lengthy root cause analysis for a significant number of frequently recurring design errors. We have tested our tool with 13 different benchmarks from 3 real-world designs available on OpenCores [12] and demonstrate here that FUDGEFACTOR suggests valid corrections for a sizeable portion of the bugs within a reasonable computational time.

FUDGEFACTOR significantly owes to the approach used by Singh et al. to give meaningful automatic feedback to students of a programming course using Python [14]—in fact, the ability to "teach" the designer in which respect the design fails is exactly what drives our efforts and distinguishes our goal. Yet, our approach in the context of digital design results in at least a couple of significant advantages: (1) Our source-level correction-rules are not at all problem-specific but empirically represent an extensible library of typical mistakes that may occur in any design, such as using a wrong compatible signal in an expression, invoking the incorrect Boolean operator, or instantiating a wrong constant.

(2) The broadness of our rules is key to be able to debug arbitrary circuits but, if applied indiscriminately, would naturally catastrophically restrict our scalability. This does not happen because, in this domain, we can leverage many tools, some even commercial, which return approximate error location information using totally different techniques that happen to be scalable to industrial size designs. Thus, we only very selectively apply our generous set of correction rules to the candidate locations and, as our experiments show, incur perfectly acceptable run times.

The rest of the paper is organized as follows: We discuss additional related work in Sect. 2. Sections 3 and 4 describe FUDGEFACTOR in more detail: the former addresses the basic methodology while the latter describes how we solve some fundamental scalability issues. We present our experimental setup in Sect. 5 and discuss results in Sect. 6. Finally, Sect. 7 concludes the paper.

2   Related Work

Debugging of hardware designs has been studied extensively in the previous three decades. This field typically focuses on two related but distinct facets of the problem: finding potential error locations (at whatever level of the design), and proposing corrections which eliminate the errors.

Error Localization. Early works on design error localization were targeted at gate-level representations. Work by Chung et al. [6,7] proposed a localization technique which expresses the problem as a set of Boolean equations, where the existence of a solution determines if the gate or wire is a potential error source or not. Smith et al. [15] improved on the scalability and quality of gate-level error localization using Boolean satisfiability (SAT). Fixing design errors at the gate level produces obscure corrections that are very hard for the circuit designer to understand. Our approach tackles the problem of returning meaningful corrections for the designer. Given the popularity of HDLs among hardware designers, source-level error localization has become increasingly attractive. Works by Bloem et al. [3] and Peischl et al. [13] discussed *Model-Based Diagnosis (MBD)* methods for error localization in VHDL descriptions. Several works [5,15] adapted the concept of gate-level fault modeling to source-level error localization by mapping gates to their HDL description. Our approach adopts the same concept of inserting multiplexers, but instead of having a single free signal, we insert proper error corrections based on an error library model. In this way we restrict the number of possible solutions and improve solver scalability.

Error Correction. Error localization techniques usually generate a design component set: either RTL locations, gates in the netlist or combinational paths that can be modified to correct the error. Chang et al. [4] proposed an approach for correcting gate-level errors using signatures of candidate faulty gates. A signature is a list of bits each corresponding to the gate output for a given set of test vectors. Their approach corrects signatures and re-synthesizes them to replace the gate with one represented by the corrected signature. The idea has been applied to source-level error correction and extended to hierarchal and sequential designs [5]. Jobstmann et al. [10] suggested an approach to correct erroneous Verilog designs. Like our work, this approach assumes access to a list of suspect error locations but uses a different error and reference model. It allows corrections that can be represented by arbitrary functions in terms of the state and input variables. This leads to a very general correction model at the expense of readability and reasonability of correction suggestions. We believe that our correction rules lead to corrections that are more meaningful and much easier to understand. In addition, their approach relies on a formal specification (given in Linear Temporal Logic) that describes the desired behavior of the design. Since formal specifications are often unavailable, we focus on simulation vectors, the de facto standard technique in industry to verify digital designs. Staber et al. [17] have extended the above-mentioned repair approach to error localization by assuming that only a location that can be corrected can be an actual error location. This approach is more precise but also more expensive than other error localization approaches. It is similar to our approach as it also aims to increase the precision of error locations by searching for correction suggestions. However, there are significant differences in the setup and underlying technique. Furthermore, our approach is a SAT-based technique, while their approach used BDD-based methodologies, which are known to be less scalable for large designs.

The related work probably most relevant to this paper are mutation-based approaches. *Mutations* were introduced by Debroy and Wong in the software world [8] and closely resemble our "fudging" rules (Sect. 3.1), but their mutations are extremely simple and success is determined with some test cases, with no formal verification. More recently, Alizadeh et al. [1] have used mutations to create potentially working hardware designs from a failing one; their mutations, essentially targeting signal processing designs, are a restricted and predetermined version of our rules, the latter being much more articulated and constituting an expansible library. And, again, successful mutations are identified by enumeration, whereas our use of 2QBF-SAT is more efficient and also corrects situations where multiple rules or mutations are needed for a single bug.

3   "Fudging" Buggy RTL Circuits

Figure 1 shows the complete FUDGEFACTOR flow from a buggy RTL circuit to a (list of) suggested source-code correction(s) which fix the error(s) in the circuit. The buggy circuit must come with some test vectors and at least one of them must be failing and expose the error(s).

The approach behind FUDGEFACTOR is *syntax-guided synthesis* [2]: we tweak (or "fudge") the original buggy RTL specification in many different ways to try to synthesize a new RTL specification which is syntactically as close as possible to the buggy one yet which does not exhibit the error, and is therefore a candidate correction. In the spirit of syntax-guided synthesis, we follow the intuition that acting at the source-code level, respecting the syntactic template provided by the human designer(s) who inadvertently introduced the error in the first place,

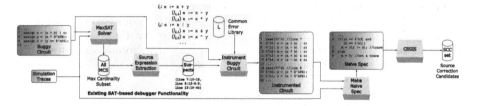

Fig. 1. The overall flow for FUDGEFACTOR. The inputs are a buggy Verilog design and one or more error traces and the output are candidates to correct the RTL source code.

makes it possible to find good corrections much more easily. More specifically, in our application, we note how some erroneous RTL designs may be extremely "close" to the correct one in the syntactic space and yet fundamentally "far" in the netlist space. A case in point is a missing condition of assignment in a *case* construct: a one-character difference in RTL can have such a drastic effect as transforming a combinational circuit into an erroneous sequential circuit. As we will show, our approach is perfectly capable of providing *meaningful* corrections in such cases.

3.1   Common Error Library

The key intuition of our approach is that many of the errors we make as programmers and designers are relatively predictable in nature: we may mistake one signal for another one which is electrically compatible (i.e., the same number of bits and doesn't cause a logic loop), and this may happen both on the right side of an expression (a wrong input being used in the calculation) as well as on the left side (the wrong signal being assigned). Or we may compute a wrong logic or arithmetic function by replacing, for instance, an OR with an AND or specifying a subtraction for an addition. Or, as already mentioned, we may forget some clauses in a conditional statement, leading to a variety of errors at the netlist level including the potential for circuits (or subcircuits) to switch across the combinational to sequential border. In different contexts, researchers have already noted that this is an effective way to capture a large fraction of programming errors [14]. Self-evidently, this approach cannot capture all possible errors. For example, errors of omission (missing conditions in an expression, etc.) are unlikely to be corrected with our general rules. However, we think there is great practical value in efficiently capturing and correcting common errors and thus freeing precious designer time for concentrating on only a relatively few hard cases.

Our common error library has been developed by reflecting on our experience as RTL designers and by manually inspecting a large number of buggy designs, including student assignments and bug fixes in open-source RTL repositories. (We have excluded most of the circuits which we use as benchmarks; more details about this aspect are given in Sect. 5.) At this point, the extensible library contains only a few very general source-code trasformation rules

Table 1. The common error library rules currently implemented in FudgeFactor. Note that this is by no means a list of all rules one may add, or even an attempt at capturing all of the most common RTL errors. Also note that the transformer rules do not necessarily *replace* the subgraph matched on: the transformer rules insert the *possibility* of using such a change, for which it is often necessary to add multiplexers, signals, etc. to the AST.

Rule	Checker (if the subgraph looks like...)	Transformer (insert these options...)
A	Signal indexing operation	Indices and ranges may be shifted to the left or right by one
B	Incomplete case without default	Signals assigned in case get a default assignment of any compatible signal, or a pure free variable
C	If ... If ... Else assigning the same signal	Allow use of a parallel If ... Else If ... Else with the same conditions
D	Signal in any statement explicitly mentioned in candidate set	Allow referring instead to any compatible signal
E	A bitwise comparison operator	Allow comparing with any other bitwise comparison operator instead
F	A constant value on right-hand side; not an index/range	Allow using instead any constant value (a pure free variable)
G	A ternary expression	Allow using instead the same ternary expression, but with the condition inverted

described in Table 1. Although limited, it turns out that this is already very effective.

3.2   Error Modeling

Error rules model common designer errors as modifications to the *abstract syntax tree (AST)* obtained by parsing the input RTL. Because we work directly on the AST, our rules are not limited to identifying line-by-line modifications. Our rules can happily identify and propose corrections for errors spanning multiple lines. Each rule is composed of two different parts: The first part, the *rule checker*, determines whether the particular rule is applicable. The second part, the *rule transformer* expresses the modifications to the AST necessary to include a set of potential corrections. For example, the rule checker of the rule in Fig. 2 checks whether an AST node represents a bitwise OR operator. If the rule checker matches a particular node of the AST, the corresponding rule transformer is executed and the AST is modified. Figure 2 is a simplified example of a rule one might really want to implement; in practice, the rule checker would probably match all bivariate Boolean operator nodes and allow the choice of any shows

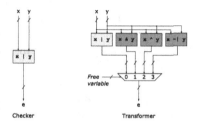

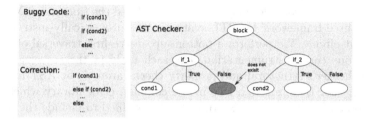

Fig. 2. A visual example of an error rule. The designer has written the expression $e :=$ $x \mid y$ and this rule suggests that what he or she *might have meant* was any other Boolean function (e.g., AND, XOR, NOR) instead of OR. The *rule checker* is represented in the left part of the figure and, in this elementary case, essentially says that this rule applies potentially to any OR operation. The right part of the figure is the *rule transformer*, which describes how the AST can be rewritten to allow the choice of such an alternative Boolean operator. Note that this figure shows, for convenience, the rule in the form of circuits, but rules are actually described and implemented using AST nodes and some rule-specific ad-hoc code.

Fig. 3. A more complex rule checker. This rule checker is shown as an AST subtree to match in the design AST. It approximately corresponds to rule **C** expressing the fact that the designer might have forgotten an *else* clause in an *if* statement. This shows some of the advanced quantifiers we use in our rules, such as the fact that two *if* statement *must* exist in immediate succession within a block but the first one *must not* have already an *else* clause. The example is slightly simplified compared to the actual AST of the parser to improve readability.

the rule checker and rule transformer for a simplified version of such a rule matching only an OR operator.

Rule checkers can perform both structural and property checks. Structural checks are based on tree isomorphism (i.e., detecting if the structure of the AST subtree matches a reference one): they detect subtrees of interest and discard cases where the rule transformer should not be applied. We implement rule checkers programmatically, although we think that it could be possible (but not necessarily truly advantageous) to define a formal language syntax to succinctly express the conditions desired. Property checks are used to gather relevant non-structural information which is also needed to determine if the rule transformer should be applied, such as checking whether two identifiers in the matched subtree refer to the same constant value. Figure 3 shows the rule checker for rule **C** and shows an application of some of the matching features described above.

Rule transformers always instantiate the multiplexer structure illustrated in Fig. 2, though not necessarily in the same AST location on which the rule matched. These multiplexers select an input depending on some free variables. If an assignment to these free variables is necessary to correct the design, the 2QBF solver will find the required assignment (this is described later in Sect. 3.4). Some transformers include a second type of free variable—a *pure free variable*—which can be used to correct constant values (see rule **F**). For example, the condition check $x < y + 3$ can be corrected to $x < y + 5$ with this second type of free variable.

As multiple rules may be triggered on the same AST node, we propose applying the rules following a predetermined ordering roughly going from rules that are more specific to those that are more general. Although this case does not happen with the common error library described here, Table 1 is ordered by priority (the first rule is checked/applied first).

3.3   Instrumentation of the Buggy Circuit

To implement the error rules above, we have modified the frontend of Yosys [18], an open source framework for RTL synthesis, to automatically instrument the buggy input circuit. We perform a bottom-up, depth-first traversal of the AST to trigger our code instrumentation. For each node in the traversal, we run each rule checker's structural and property checks around the AST location to identify whether there exists a rule in the common error library which can be applied. When a rule is triggered, the AST is modified to include the option of replacing or modifying the original AST with multiple potential corrections. All modifications result in additional primary inputs added to the faulty circuits: these free variables control whether the circuit retains the original erroneous behavior or is modified by some combination of changes caused by the rule transformers.

The word "combination" above is important: our technique works perfectly well to handle multiple simultaneously bugs, so long as they are each correctable with the available rules. To ensure the solver not only chooses free variables which give correct behavior, but also employ the minimal necessary number of changes, we also add an extra primary output to the instrumented design that is asserted when the number of non-zero free variables is less than some specified threshold. This threshhold is then swept, beginning with only one change allowed and ending with a user-specified maximum number of allowed changes. We arbitrarily chose a maximum threshold of three changes for our experiments.

The next step is to construct a miter: a circuit where, through the solution of a particular satisfiability problem, one can determine a concrete value for all such free variables which render the circuit correct over all inputs.

3.4   The 2QBF Problem

SAT-based combinational equivalence checking is usually performed by constructing a special circuit, called *miter*, composed of the circuit under test and a

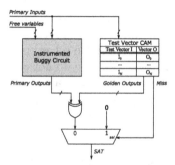

Fig. 4. Constructing a miter with test vectors. Since we have no functional reference, we build some golden outputs from a small subset of passing test vectors and all the failing test vectors we are trying to correct. The existance of a particular golden output for a given set of primary input is used to determine whether the output comparison is relevant or not.

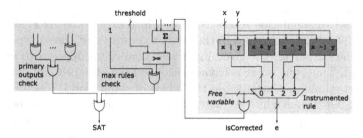

Fig. 5. Minimizing source-code interventions. The implementation of each rule transformer stores the free variables used to select a candidate change. Once all of a module's AST has been checked and transformed, these free variables are collected and their Boolean reduction is summed. The signal "isCorrected" above represents the negated Boolean reduction we actually use. A non-zero Boolean reduction (thus, a non-zero free variable) signifies that a multiplexer is configured to change the behavior of some part of the circuit. The miter then counts the number of corrections applied to the circuit and forces it to be below a fixed threshold.

functional reference circuit. In short, the solver determines if there is any input assignment which violates the expected output value of the miter. A buggy circuit will result in a satisfiable instance and any 'witness' returned is a counterexample, or error trace. Formally stated, SAT solvers determine the truth of the propositional formula:

$$\forall \boldsymbol{x} : \text{test}(\boldsymbol{x}) \Leftrightarrow \text{reference}(\boldsymbol{x}). \tag{1}$$

In contrast, syntax-guided synthesis uses SAT solvers to determine the truth of a slightly different propositional formula (formally, an *exists-forall 2QBF*) in which the circuit test also consumes some vector of free variables $\boldsymbol{h}$:

$$\exists \boldsymbol{h} \ \forall \boldsymbol{x} : \text{test}(\boldsymbol{h}, \boldsymbol{x}) \Leftrightarrow \text{reference}(\boldsymbol{x}). \tag{2}$$

This is equivalent to answering the question "does there exist some value for the special inputs h such that for all inputs x, test and reference behave identically?" The internal mechanics of the solver used in this work (see Sect. 5) are beyond the scope of this paper and we do not claim any innovation on this front. Yet, we need to construct the miter in a slightly particular way given our context.

3.5   Miter Construction

Although the basic idea of the miter we use is pretty conventional for syntax-guided problems, there are two aspects which are peculiar to our situation. First, in our case we assume that a reference design is not available and that the error is exposed by an error vector or trace used for functional simulation. Second, we want to control (and thus minimize) the number of individual corrections to the buggy code.

Figure 4 shows how we build the miter from the instrumented buggy circuit and a set of simulation traces, some of which expose the error. We add an extra multiplexer at the output of the miter to ensure that the solver only tries to match the output for the given input test vectors (as opposed to any input assignment). Thus, our miter is trivially satisfied (i.e., the primary output is 0) for all input stimuli not included in the subset of simulation traces we consider. For those input stimuli which *do* match one of the simulation traces, the primary outputs of the template are XORed with the correct output response. Accordingly, our miter is satisfied by a given vector of free variables (i.e., by a specific set of error rules correcting the error) when the functionality of the instrumented circuit matches the correct output response for all input stimuli in our restricted domain. One key advantage to using this construction as opposed to a golden reference, aside from the typically-limited availability of such a golden reference, is it enhances scalability. Of course, there is a trade off between scalability and the ability of our method to find a real correction as opposed to simply turning the buggy circuit into another buggy circuit which only works correctly for the formerly failing vector and for a handful of other vectors. We will discuss later our very encouraging practical findings, largely dependent on the selective application of the error rules which we will describe soon in Sect. 4. Yet, irrespective of our positive results, one should notice two points: First, we aim to provide *meaningful* solutions to the designer and we assume that false solutions, such as those potentially produced using too few passing test vectors, would be immediately identified and discarded. Secondly, if this were not the case, it would be easy for the designer to tentatively implement the correction and verify with his or her standard verification flow if otherwise passing vectors now fail.

Besides the functional equivalence constraint, we also encode a second type of constraint to force a minimum number of corrections in the buggy RTL code. Figure 5 shows the logic responsible for this second check, mostly in the shaded area annotated as "max rules check". We simply sweep the value of the constant *threshold* in successive runs of the 2QBF solver until we find the minimum number of changes. We are thereby able to find the minimal source code modification(s), which we intuit is/are closest to what a human would do, and try our best to rule out less general but still legal solutions.

One final type of constraint may be desirable. We do not consider multiple solutions, but they can be easily handled. At each tested threshhold value, multiple feasible solutions might exist for a couple reasons: either there is one or more false solutions caused by eschewing an exact golden reference design in favor of the test vector CAM, or there are simply multiple legitimate corrections which each require the same number of RTL changes. In either case, at each solution, the previous choice for non-zero free variables can be 'blocked', thus excluding that same combination of RTL changes, until no more solutions exist. If multiple solutions with the same number of changes are found, the user can be presented with all of them, possibly ordered by some heuristic priority.

4 Selecting Areas for "Fudging"

Applying the error models described in Sect. 3 to the complete AST of a circuit may possibly identify the right correction of the buggy circuit. Yet, both the ability to generate any possible correction and the likelyhood that the correction is the intended one may be jeopardized by this naïve implementation of our idea for a couple of reasons, both of practical and fundamental nature. First, we deliberately selected in our common error library very general rules (Sect. 3.1). This is key in capturing sufficiently broad cases which are typical of erroneous implementations: we definitely meant to be generous with our rules (for instance, as already mentioned, we imagine the library to be extended progressively with new rules as their usefulness becomes apparent). The consequence of this "generosity" is that, were we to apply every rule on every possible AST node where it can be applied, the 2QBF problem would soon become intractable even for extremely simple circuits. A second, more fundamental problem, is that an indiscriminate application of our error rules would arguably lead, in most practical cases, to multiple possible solutions, some potentially quite far (both in terms of RTL and netlist location) from the "natural" correction. We solve this issue by relying on prior work in circuit debugging and using approximate and netlist-based solutions to guide our instrumentation of the buggy specification.

4.1 SAT-Based Debugger

As Fig. 1 shows, we feed the output of a state-of-the-art debugger into FUDGE-FACTOR. This output (also called a solution) of a SAT-based debugger [15] is a set of design components (RTL blocks, RTL code) that cause the propagation of a failure. This debugger takes as input the RTL description of the design, the expected behavior of the design over a set of test vectors, and returns an over-approximate—but not necessarily precise—set of solutions (i.e., the design component where the actual error is located is within this set). We use this tool to determine the locations on which our methodology should focus to try to correct the failure. The details of the particular SAT-based debugger we use are out of the scope of this paper and the interested reader can refer to Smith et al. [15]. All we care for is that the solution it returns is useful to the designer in most cases but contains enough ambiguity to require significant human analysis effort to lead to the actual error correction. Specifically, we parse and load the output of the SAT-based debugger and use this information to mark the corresponding AST nodes of the input circuit description as suspect. We then simply add one additional check when we implement the instrumentation pass described in Sect. 3.3: we only apply a rule checker if the node is marked as suspect.

5   Experimental Methodology

We evaluated the performance and scalability of our approach on a range of Verilog benchmarks taken from OpenCores [12]. Each benchmark has one bug either injected artificially or taken from the version control history. These buggy designs were not used to develop our common error library; they were obtained from a third party, and we do not know which bugs were injected and which are "organic". We believe our results are broadly representative of how our approach works for simple bugs in realistic circuits.

We rely on a commercial verification tool based on the work of Smith et al. [15] to obtain an initial set of error candidate locations in the input Verilog. This initial set is significantly over-approximate or, in other words, contains many false positives: most of the usually dozens of candidates are not actually part of the error. We use this set in the instrumentation process as discussed in Sect. 3.3 and unroll the resulting logic with ABC to handle sequential designs. This unrolled circuit is then passed to the CEGIS 2QBF-SAT solver [16].

Importantly, as mentioned in Sect. 3.5, we do not rely on availability of a golden reference circuit: we build a miter from only three passing test vectors. The choice of three vectors is arbitrary here, and is a trade-off between avoiding trivial, incorrect solutions, and scalability. While the topic of determining which and how many vectors to include is certainly interesting, we leave a thorough investigation to future work. The results described below appear to validate our assumption that a few test vectors are enough to properly correct most circuits with our approach: each correction found is exactly what a reasonable human designer would write, and fixes the bug most generally.

SPI (Serial Peripheral Interface) is a serial, synchronous, full-duplex communication protocol very widely used as a board-level interface between different devices such as microcontrollers, DACs, ADCs, and others. This core is an SPI/Microwire compliant master serial-communication controller with some additional functionality. There are four different buggy versions. The *bug1* design assigns the wrong signal to a control register; *bug3* contains multiple erroneous data assignments in the controller FIFO, and cannot be corrected with our restrictive threshold.

AES (Advanced Encryption Standard) is a widely used block cipher with a block size of 128 bits and a selectable key size of 128 to 256 bits. This is a pipelined 128-bit AES design from OpenCores. This core has two buggy versions. The *bug1* design is missing a subexpression in an assignment—something our methodology is poorly suited to correcting. The *bug2* design contains an XOR which erroneously references the signal used in the immediately preceding operation (a likely copy-paste error).

The *Integer Divider Core* is a parameterizable non-restoring signed-by-unsigned integer division core. In our experiments we used a 16-bit dividend and an 8-bit divisor. This design comes with seven different buggy circuits, some of which we describe here:

- *bug1*. The bug erroneously clips a signal range by one, and concatenates a two-bit constant instead of a one-bit constant. It is difficult to see how this error would be likely to occur, or how it could be corrected with a general rule.
- *bug2*. The bug is an erroneously switched set of function parameters; their order should have been reversed. Because both parameters can be changed to compatible signals, this can be corrected.
- *bug3*. In this version, the arguments of a function are both reversed, but consist of array-indexing expressions. Our rules do not capture the possibility of reversing the operands per se, although this could conceivably be corrected with another fairly-general rule.
- *bug4*. The bug references the wrong array for computing the divisor. Instead of reading the array *s_pipe*, the designer made the mistake of reading from array *d_pipe*—a typo off by one key on a keyboard.

The MIPS CPU is available on GitHub [11]. We used the CPU design to develop rules, prototype our tool flow, and validate our ability to actually solve the problems we formulate. We injected simple errors that designers commonly make and which we believe traditional debugging tools would have difficulty with: leaving out a default statement in a *case* block (in *bug1*), and mistakenly writing an *if* condition instead of an *else if* condition (in *bug2*).

6   Experimental Results

Tables 2 and 3 summarize the experimental results. The *"# Free Var. Bits"* column gives the total number of free variables used in the instrumented design (including both the control signals of all multiplexers and all pure free variables representing constants). The *"Solver Time"* column shows the cumulative solver time spent on each experiment. For example, those experiments which failed include the solver time used sequentially for all three attempted threshold values (1, 2, and 3). The *"# RTL Changes"* column describes the number of error candidate locations in the Verilog which needed fixing (for the benchmarks where a correction was found)—in other words, it is the minimum number of multiplexer free variables ("isCorrected" in Fig. 5) which need to be non-zero in order to correct the bug. The *"Solved?"* column reports if the solver was actually able to find a solution with three or fewer changes. Note that even with our relatively sparse common error library, FUDGEFACTOR was able to correct nearly half the simple bugs in the third-party designs.

Table 2. Those experiments listed above the break were provided by a third-party and not used to develop rules; those below the break are contrived, but show meaningful results. Note that we correct nearly half of the non-contrived experiments. Note also that all solutions are indeed those which an oracle would provide: exactly what any reasonable human designer would provide. "# Matched Nodes" lists how many AST nodes matched one (or more) of our rules. Finally, "SLOC" represented the lines of RTL source code (excluding comments, etc.).

Buggy Design	# RTL Changes	Solved?	Oracle Soln.?	Fixing Rule(s)	Applied Rules	Total AST Size	# Matched AST Nodes	SLOC
spi_bug1	1	✓	✓	D	ABDEF	2968	20	271
spi_bug2	–	✗	–	–	BD	2964	2	266
spi_bug3	–	✗	–	–	DEF	2968	10	266
spi_bug4	1	✓	✓	F	ABDF	2968	13	266
aes_bug1	–	✗	–	–	ADFG	5080	19	467
aes_bug2	1	✓	✓	D	ABDG	5251	33	467
div_bug1	–	✗	–	–	ADF	2486	13	163
div_bug2	2	✓	✓	DD	AD	2478	8	165
div_bug3	–	✗	–	–	ADF	2486	13	165
div_bug4	1	✓	✓	D	ADF	2502	10	165
div_bug5	–	✗	–	–	ADF	2516	15	168
div_bug6	–	✗	–	–	ADF	2528	20	165
div_bug7	2	✓	✓	DD	ADF	2510	12	165
cpu_bug1	1	✓	✓	B	BDG	3842	4	530
cpu_bug2	1	✓	✓	C	CDEF	3846	5	531

The *"Fixing Rule(s)"* column describes which rule(s) were essential to correct the bug. In this column, we see that one rule appears with striking regularity: rule **D** (see Table 1). This should come at no surprise, as this is one of the most general rules in our library. *"Applied Rules"* lists all rules which were employed in the instrumentation phase for each experiment. Finally, *"Oracle Sol."* indicates whether the correction returned matches that which an oracle would give: if the changes were what any reasonable designer would do, we say, "yes" here. Importantly, all of the solutions found were indeed "oracle solutions". Although we do not, and will never, solve every bug, FUDGEFACTOR reports *no* false positives while maintaining a reasonable true positive rate. We should also emphasize that the true positive rate is artificially lowered by our decision to develop the rules with only a limited set of examples and mostly based on our intuition as designers: as mentioned, we have treated all buggy designs above the

Table 3. More information on the experiments. We show the total number of free variable bits inserted, the total solver time, the size (in And-Invert gates as reported by ABC) of the associated golden reference design, the number of frames it was unrolled, and the total blowup (i.e., how much larger the instrumented circuit is than the unrolled golden reference design.

Buggy Design	# Free Var Bits	Total Solver Time (s)	# Golden Gates	Unroll Frames	Blowup
spi_bug1	92	1.90	14468	20	2.94x
spi_bug2	8	1.69	14468	20	1.20x
spi_bug3	35	2.23	14468	20	1.90x
spi_bug4	65	1.66	14468	20	2.14x
aes_bug1	373	18.71	86878	6	1.07x
aes_bug2	62	517.40	86878	6	1.29x
div_bug1	33	32.28	96767	48	2.30x
div_bug2	20	71.47	96767	48	2.12x
div_bug3	30	21.82	96767	48	2.28x
div_bug4	26	78.90	96767	48	2.24x
div_bug5	37	49.05	96767	48	3.20x
div_bug6	32	17.75	96767	48	1.99x
div_bug7	30	101.46	96767	48	3.15x
cpu_bug1	12	87.53	34294	15	2.28x
cpu_bug2	46	60.05	34294	15	2.56x

break as a clean test-set which has not been used to develop rules. On the other hand, in practice, the extensibility of the common error library is a fundamental part of our approach and many (but not all) of the unsolved designs could be fixed by developing additional general rule.

These tables also include some information which can be useful in determining how practical our approach is and validating our use of the SAT-based debugger to compute an over-approximate error set; our general rules would not scale if they matched many more nodes. As rule **D** shows, our strength is in using fairly general rules, but this comes at a cost: Without hints of where to look, we would be forced to use less general rules and fundamentally limit our ability to find bugs.

7   Conclusions

Since humans introduce bugs in the language they use to describe their designs, we formulated the problem of error localization and correction of a buggy RTL circuit as the problem of synthesizing a correct circuit with minimal syntactic distance from the buggy specification. To "fudge" the buggy specification into a rich variety of possible alternate circuits, we have used an empirical library of error models that tries to capture common errors humans make. Although our rules are quite general and produce a very generous set of alternate versions, we use them sparingly by leveraging other over-approximate, better-scalable bug localization tools. We have shown, though a controlled test-set that we have not used to develop the inital set of rules, that we can correct a reasonably large set of errors and, most strikingly, in all cases we can correct, we obtain *exactly* the RTL code a human designer would have produced. As the library of common errors is extensible, we think that the success rate could be improved significantly with acceptable impact on runtimes. Nevertheless, this technique is clearly not a complete solution—it will never find all possible bugs; yet, we believe it could be invaluable in presenting, in most cases, intuitive and immediately understandable solutions to the designers and thus in freeing up precious time for them to focus on the comparatively rare hard cases where we would inherently fail.

References

1. Alizadeh, B., Behnam, P., Sadeghi-Kohan, S.: A scalable formal debugging approach with auto-correction capability based on static slicing and dynamic ranking for RTL datapath designs. IEEE Trans. Comput. **64**(6), 1564–1578 (2015)
2. Alur, R., Bodik, R., Juniwal, G., Martin, M.M.K., Raghothaman, M., Seshia, S.A., Singh, R., Solar-Lezama, A., Torlak, E., Udupa, A.: Syntax-guided synthesis. In: Proceedings of the 13th Conference on Formal Methods in Computer-Aided Design, Portland, OR, pp. 1–8, October 2013
3. Bloem, R., Wotawa, F.: Verification and fault localization in VHDL programs. J. Telematics Eng. Soc. **2**, 30–33 (2002)
4. Chang, K.H., Markov, I., Bertacco, V.: Fixing design errors with counterexamples and resynthesis. In: Proceedings of the Asia and South Pacific Design Automation Conference, Yokohama, Japan, pp. 944–949, January 2007
5. Chang, K.H., Wagner, I., Bertacco, V., Markov, I.: Automatic error diagnosis and correction for RTL designs. In: Proceedings of the High Level Design Validation and Test Workshop, Irvine, CA, pp. 65–72, November 2007
6. Chung, P.Y., Hajj, I.N.: ACCORD: Automatic catching and correction of logic design errors in combinational circuits. In: Proceedings of the International Test Conference, Baltimore, MD, pp. 742–751, September 1992
7. Chung, P.Y., Wang, Y.M., Hajj, I.N.: Logic design error diagnosis and correction. IEEE Trans. Very Large Scale Integr. (VLSI) Syst. **2**(3), 320–332 (1994)
8. Debroy, V., Wong, W.E.: Using mutation to automatically suggest fixes for faulty programs. In: Proceedings of the Third International Conference on Software Testing, Verification and Validation, pp. 65–74, April 2010
9. Foster, H.: Trends in functional verification: a 2014 industry study. In: 2015 52nd ACM/EDAC/IEEE Design Automation Conference (DAC), pp. 1–6, June 2015
10. Jobstmann, B., Griesmayer, A., Bloem, R.: Program repair as a game. In: Etessami, K., Rajamani, S.K. (eds.) CAV 2005. LNCS, vol. 3576, pp. 226–238. Springer, Heidelberg (2005)
11. Mahler, J.: A MIPS CPU written in Verilog. https://github.com/jmahler/mips-cpu. Accessed 24 April 2015
12. OpenCores: Opencores database. http://www.opencores.org

13. Peischl, B., Wotawa, F.: Automated source level error localization in hardware designs. J. IEEE Des. Test Comput. **23**(1), 8–19 (2006)
14. Singh, R., Gulwani, S., Solar-Lezama, A.: Automated feedback generation for introductory programming assignments. In: Proceedings of the 34th ACM SIGPLAN Conference on Programming Language Design and Implementation, Seattle, WA, pp. 15–26, June 2013
15. Smith, A., Veneris, A., Ali, M.F., Viglas, A.: Fault diagnosis and logic debugging using Boolean satisfiability. IEEE Trans. Comput. Aided Des. Integr. Circ. Syst. CAD **24**(10), 1606–1621 (2005)
16. Lezama, A.S.: Program synthesis by sketching. Ph.D. thesis, UC Berkeley, December 2008. http://eecs.berkeley.edu/Pubs/TechRpts/2008/EECS-2008-177.html
17. Staber, S., Jobstmann, B., Bloem, R.: Finding and fixing faults. J. Comput. Syst. Sci. **78**(2), 441–460 (2012)
18. Wolf, C., Glaser, J., Kepler, J.: Yosys - a free Verilog synthesis suite. In: Proceedings of 21st Austrian Workshop on Microelectronics, Linz, Austria, October 2013

On Switching Aware Synthesis
for Combinational Circuits

Jan Lanik[✉] and Oded Maler

VERIMAG CNRS and University of Grenoble, Grenoble, France
{jan.lanik,oded.maler}@imag.fr

Abstract. We propose a synthesis algorithm for combinational circuits which optimizes the expected number of gate switchings induced by typical sequences of input vectors. Our algorithm, which is based on simple observations concerning AND gates, performs quite well on sequences produced by the same probabilistic models used to generate the training sequences.

1 Introduction

Digital circuit synthesis [3,7,8,15] from higher level descriptions to technology dependent standard cells is one of the core activities in Electronic Design Automation (EDA), well-studied in academic research and implemented in powerful commercial tools. This is the hardware analog of optimizing compilation, and indispensable tool in producing efficient chips. Traditionally, the major optimization objectives in synthesis have been area and speed, associated with the depth of the circuit from primary inputs to outputs. In the last decades, power consumption has become a no less important performance measure for reasons that need not be repeated here [1,2,4,14]. In this work we develop a new synthesis algorithm geared toward reducing the expected number of switchings in the circuit, an important ingredient in its power consumption. This work can be viewed as part of the trend to apply formal technology (abstract reasoning on Boolean functions and automata) outside the traditional scope of verification, namely handling *quantitative* properties such as timing and power consumption that were considered non-functional properties, and applying optimization/synthesis rather than evaluation/verification with respect to them.

Figure 1 sketches a possible logic synthesis flow. Starting from a multi-level logic specification, the circuit is brought into a form of an And-Inverter Graph (AIG) consisting solely of AND and NOT gates. This representation is than mapped into a concrete technology of standard cells admitting physical properties such as size and electrical characteristics. Syntactically AIGs are composed from 2AND gates but by collapsing together all NOT-free "cones", we obtain a semantically-equivalent function constructed from AND gates of unbounded fan-in (arity). Part of the technology-dependent mapping can be viewed as decomposing those ANDs into networks of 2ANDs and this is the problem we address in this paper.

© Springer International Publishing Switzerland 2015
N. Piterman (Ed.): HVC 2015, LNCS 9434, pp. 276–291, 2015.
DOI: 10.1007/978-3-319-26287-1_17

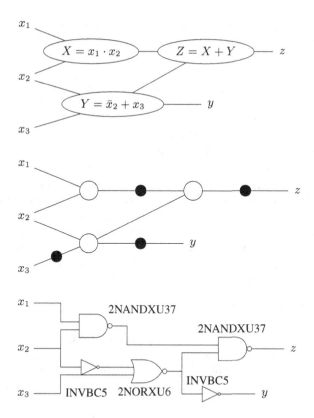

Fig. 1. A logic synthesis design flow: from multilevel logic specification to And-Inverter graphs to standard cells.

Dynamic power consumption of Boolean gates is associated essentially with their switchings between 0 and 1. In this work we consider synchronous combinational circuits that process sequences of input vectors. For each input vector, a circuit propagates values from input to output ports until it stabilizes and then reads the next input. The overall number of switchings associated with a pair of inputs is the number of gates whose stable value for one input is different from their value for the next input. For one such pair it is possible to steer the synthesis process and obtain a circuit with significantly less switchings compared to other arbitrary circuits that realize the same function. But of course, any circuit will process during its lifetime a long sequence consisting of diverse consecutive pairs of input vectors and optimizing synthesis with respect to all those is a challenging problem.

One natural approach is to define some probability function over sequences of input sequences, induced, for example, by a Markov chain which generates them. However, even the evaluation of the expected number of switchings in a *given* circuit is an intractable problem for non-trivial probabilistic generators with many input variables. As an alternative we develop in this paper a switching-aware synthesis procedure which optimizes the circuit relative to a *reference sequence* supposed to represent a typical input. In essence, the algorithm estimates the expected amount of switchings associated with a conjunction of any pair of input variables and then solves an optimal perfect matching problem to decide which variables to pair together as inputs to a 2AND gate. The procedure obtains quite a good switching reduction compared to arbitrary realizations of the same function by circuits of the same topology.

We then study the question of optimization with respect to inputs generated by Markov chains of small description size, that is, networks of sparsely-interacting 2-state probabilistic automata. We use such networks to generate the reference (training) sequences and then measure the performance gains on other sequences generated from the same model. We perform experiments on models of varying degree of variable dependencies and other assumptions on the inputs and we obtain significant reduction in switching activity. Finally, we introduce a reduced model of an instruction decoder and evaluate our procedure under probabilistic assumptions concerning the instruction stream.

2   Problem Statement

Our starting point is a Boolean circuit constructed from unbounded fan-in AND gates and NOT gates and our goal is to replace the AND gates by 2AND gates, yielding a semantically equivalent circuit C. Once we have a good solution for the AND-to-2AND problem we can apply it to any AND in the AIG and solve the synthesis problem for the whole circuit. From now on we consider a function $f : (x_1, \ldots, x_n) \mapsto x_1 \wedge \cdots \wedge x_n$ and a target circuit C which is a properly structured directed acyclic graph whose nodes are 2ANDs of the form $g : (x_1, x_2) \mapsto x_1 \wedge x_2$. We denote the input space $\mathbb{B}^n$ by X and the state-space of C, that is, the set of possible values in the output ports of all its gates, as $Y = \mathbb{B}^m$. The synthesized circuit C can be viewed as a memoryless transducer from X^* to Y^* such that for every t, $y[t]$ is the stable state of the circuit after processing $x[t]$. The amount of switching in C relative to input x and at time t is

$$S(C, x, t) = \Delta(y[t-1], y[t])$$

where Δ is the Hamming distance between Boolean vectors. The total amount of switching while reading a sequence $x \in X^*$ is

$$S(C, x) = \sum_{t=1}^{|x|} S(C, x, t).$$

A circuit C is better than C' relative to x if $S(C, x) < S(C', x)$. We want to build circuits which are optimal or reasonable in this sense. A major issue is what to assume about the set of inputs used to evaluate $S(C, .)$. One can think of two approaches.

1. Assume some probability function P on X^*, or more precisely a family of probabilities $P_k : X^k \to [0,1]$, defined for example via a Markov chain, and then attempt to optimize the expected number of switchings per time step

$$S(C,P) = \lim_{k \to \infty} \sum_{x \in X^k} P_k(x) \cdot S(C,x)/k.$$

2. Use a long reference sequence $\underline{x}$ and evaluate C according to $S(C,\underline{x})$.

We will use a mixture of these two approaches. We optimize $S(C,\underline{x})$ for some training sequence $\underline{x}$ generated by a Markov chain and then evaluate the synthesized circuit according to the number of switchings that occur while processing other sequences generated from the same chain.

3   Input Pairing for AND Gates

The principle underlying switching reduction for AND gates is simple. Among all elements of X only a single vector $\mathbf{1} = (1, \ldots, 1)$ satisfies $f(x) = 1$. Input transitions of the form $x \to x'$ such that $x \neq \mathbf{1}$ and $x' \neq \mathbf{1}$ will not change the primary output. They can change, however, the values of intermediate gates that realize a conjunction of a *subset* of the input variables. We call such transitions *useless* and our goal is to "abort" them as soon as possible.

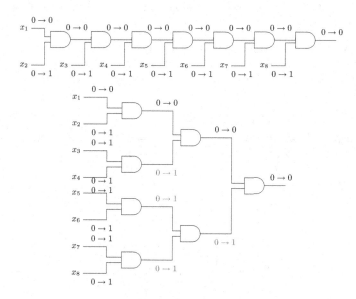

Fig. 2. For an input transition $(0,0,0,0,0,0,0,0) \to (0,1,1,1,1,1,1,1)$ a chain realizations can abort all switchings but a tree cannot.

There are numerous realizations of f by 2ANDs, all using $n-1$ gates. Among those, one can single out two extreme topologies, the sequential chain, whose depth is $n-1$ and the balanced tree with depth $d = \log n$. Since circuit depth determines propagation delay from input the output, speed considerations favor balanced trees and we will focus in this paper on those. Balanced trees bring some regularity to the problem, allowing us to work recursively on the levels of the tree from 0 (primary inputs) to $d-1$. Note, however, that chains tend to be more efficient in switching reduction in AND gates because they can abort useless switchings earlier as shown in Fig. 2. We have implemented also a version of our procedure, not reported here, which does not commit a priori to the circuit topology and which can be applied when power consumption is considered much more important than latency.

For the fixed balanced tree topology, the synthesis problem reduces to mapping input variables to the circuit input ports. The problem can be phrased recursively as follows. At level i of the tree, 2^{d-i} inputs should be partitioned into pairs to be mapped into 2^{d-i-1} 2AND gates. To understand which input signals should be paired together, let us look at Table 1-(A) which shows which transitions are taken by the output as a function of the transitions taken by the inputs. Table 1-(B) shows the number of output switchings in each case while Table 1-(C) shows the net switching reduction effect, namely, the number of input switchings minus the number of output switchings. It is intuitively clear that for one consecutive pair of inputs, we should pair together variables taking respective transitions $1 \to 0$ and $0 \to 1$. Such transitions cancel each other and send as inputs to the next level a variable doing $0 \to 0$ which will not trigger

Table 1. (A) The output transitions of an AND-gate as a function of the input transitions; (B) The number of switchings associated with every pair $(u \to u', v \to v')$ of input transitions; (C) the net switching reduction: number of input switchings minus output switching.

	$0 \to 0$	$0 \to 1$	$1 \to 0$	$1 \to 1$
$0 \to 0$	$0 \to 0$	$0 \to 0$	$0 \to 0$	$0 \to 0$
$0 \to 1$	$0 \to 0$	$0 \to 1$	$0 \to 0$	$0 \to 1$
$1 \to 0$	$0 \to 0$	$0 \to 0$	$1 \to 0$	$1 \to 0$
$1 \to 1$	$0 \to 0$	$0 \to 1$	$1 \to 0$	$1 \to 1$

(A)

	$0 \to 0$	$0 \to 1$	$1 \to 0$	$1 \to 1$
$0 \to 0$	0	0	0	0
$0 \to 1$	0	1	0	1
$1 \to 0$	0	0	1	1
$1 \to 1$	0	1	1	0

(B)

	$0 \to 0$	$0 \to 1$	$1 \to 0$	$1 \to 1$
$0 \to 0$	0	1	1	0
$0 \to 1$	1	1	2	0
$1 \to 0$	1	2	1	0
$1 \to 1$	0	0	0	0

(C)

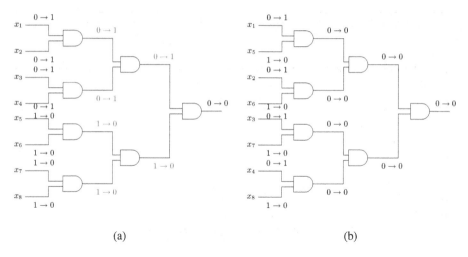

Fig. 3. Two pairings for input transition $(0, 1, 0, 1, 0, 1, 0, 1) \rightarrow (1, 0, 1, 0, 1, 0, 1, 0)$: (a) a bad pairing with 6 switchings; (b) a good pairing with no switchings.

further switching with any other input it will be paired with Fig. 3 shows two circuits and their performance differences with respect to a single consecutive pair of input vectors.

Let $R_{jk}(u, u', v, v')$ be the probability that a pair (x_j, x_k) of input variables takes the joint transition $(u \rightarrow u', v \rightarrow v')$. When the inputs are generated by a Markov chain, these probabilities can be derived from the steady state of the chain which is, however, typically too hard to compute. Given a reference sequence $\underline{x}$, we can approximate $R_{jk}(u, u', v, v')$ by computing the number of occurences of the given transition in the sequence. Denoting the number of switchings associated with a pair of transition $u \rightarrow u'$ and $v \rightarrow v'$ (Table 1-(B)) by $s(u, u', v, v')$ (always 0 or 1), the expected number of switchings in $x_j \wedge x_k$ is

$$\mu_{jk} = \sum_{u, u', v, v'} R_{jk}(u, u', v, v') \cdot s(u, u', v, v').$$

Let $G = (V, E, \mu)$ be a complete graph with n nodes where each edge (j, k) is labeled by μ_{jk}. For the first level of the tree, the problem of finding input pairing which is optimal in terms of expected total number of switching is equivalent to the optimization problem known as *minimal-weight perfect matching* [12] for G. Once such an optimal pairing is found for level i, the outputs of the gates at this level serve as inputs for the pairing problem of the next level as summarized in Algorithm 1. The first polynomial algorithm for the optimal matching problem dates back to [5] using linear programming. The complexity of the algorithm has been improved in [10] from $O(n^4)$ to $O(n^3)$. Thus, together with the computation of μ from the training sequence the complexity of our procedure is $O(n^2 \cdot |\underline{x}| + n^3)$.

The results of the algorithm may deviate from the optimal expected number of switchings for three reasons. First, it is not based on the real value of μ but on its approximation from the training sequence. Secondly, it works by levels in a

---

Algorithm 1. Synthesizing a balanced-tree circuit for a conjunction of n variables.

---

procedure $Synthesize(\underline{x})$
Input: A Boolean sequence $\underline{x}$ of dimension $n = 2^d$
Output: A balanced-tree circuit C realizing $x_1 \wedge \cdots \wedge x_n$

$i := 0$
while $i < d - 1$ **do**
   $\underline{x} := Reduce(\underline{x}, d - i)$
   $i := i + 1$
end

function $Reduce(x, i)$
Input: A Boolean sequence x of dimension $m = 2^i$
Output: An optimal pairing and a Boolean sequence y
         of dimension 2^{i-1}

forall $j \neq k \in [1..i]$ compute μ_{jk}
let $G = (N, E, \mu)$ be the corresponding weighted graph
$M := optimal\_match(G) = \{(x_{r_1}, x_{r_2}), \ldots, (x_{r_{m-1}}, x_{r_m})\}$
$y := (x_{r_1} \wedge x_{r_2}, \ldots, x_{r_{m-1}} \wedge x_{r_m})$
return(y)

---

level-greedy fashion and hence, in principle, it is not guaranteed to produce the optimal among all circuits. Finally it does only statistics for pairs of variables and ignores more complex dependencies between three or more variables that may influence the outcome. However, as the experimental results show, it constitutes a very effective heuristics. We have implemented the algorithm and evaluated it empirically on purely synthetic examples and then on a realization of an instruction decoder. In the current implementation, since we limit the evaluation to $n = 16$, we find the optimal matching by enumeration.

4   Evaluation: Synthetic Boolean Models

We evaluate our algorithm against different classes of probabilistic 16-dimensional input generators. To define probabilities over X^* using arbitrary Markov chains we need to handle transition matrices of size at least $2^n \times 2^n$. For large n even writing down such a matrix is infeasible, not to mention computing its steady state probability. As is common in domains such as probabilistic verification and performance analysis, we use a compositional model consisting of a network of sparsely-interacting probabilistic automata. A probabilistic automaton $\mathcal{A} = (Q, \Sigma, \delta)$ is an input-dependent Markov chain where every input letter $\sigma \in \Sigma$ induces a different transition matrix over state-space Q. The probabilistic transition function is thus of the form $\delta : Q \times \Sigma \times Q \to [0, 1]$ satisfying

$$\sum_{q' \in Q} \delta(q, \sigma, q') = 1$$

for every q and σ. A Markov chain can be viewed as a degenerate probabilistic automaton without an alphabet and a transition function of the form $\delta : Q \times Q \rightarrow [0,1]$.

Let $N = \{1, \ldots, n\}$. A network of n interacting probabilistic automata is given as $\mathcal{A} = (\mathcal{A}_1, \ldots, \mathcal{A}_n, h)$ where $\mathcal{A}_i = (Q_i, \Sigma_i, \delta_i)$ and $h : N \rightarrow 2^N$ is an *influence function* such that $h(i)$ is the set of the other automata (besides itself) whose states are observed by $\mathcal{A}_i$ and influence its transitions. In our network each automaton has a state-space encoded by one bit, $Q_i = \mathbb{B}$, and an input alphabet $\Sigma_i = \mathbb{B}^{|h(i)|}$ which is the state-space of the influencing automata. The composition of the automata yields a global Markov chain (Q, δ) with $Q = Q_1 \times \ldots Q_n = \mathbb{B}^n$. The local input letter read by automaton $\mathcal{A}_i$ in a global state q is the projection of q on the variables in $h(i)$ that we denote by $\pi_i(q)$. The transition function of the global Markov chain is defined as

$$\delta((q_1, \ldots, q_n), (q'_1, \ldots, q'_n))$$
$$=$$
$$\delta_1(q_1, \pi_1(q), q'_1) \cdot \delta_2(q_2, \pi_2(q), q'_2) \cdots \delta_n(q_n, \pi_n(q), q'_n).$$

The structure of $h(i)$ can be used to classify models according to variable interaction. When the maximum of $|h(i)|$ is small, the system admits a small description from which random sequences for training and evaluation can be generated.

For each class of models we draw model instances randomly and measure the reduction obtained by our algorithm with respect to inputs generated by the model. All model classes share a tuning parameter $\alpha \in [0,1]$ intended to quantify the degree of regularity in the input sequences which can be exploited to come up with good input pairing. Whenever we need to fix a probability while defining a model instance, we draw it from I_α defined as

$$I_\alpha = \begin{cases} [0, \alpha] \cup [1 - \alpha, 1] & \text{when } \alpha \leq \frac{1}{2} \\ [\alpha - \frac{1}{2}, 1 - (\alpha - \frac{1}{2})] & \text{when } \alpha \geq \frac{1}{2} \end{cases}$$

The regularity in the inputs (and the potential effectiveness of our procedure) is monotone decreasing with α. When $\alpha = 0$ the probabilities are taken from $\{0, 1\}$ and the resulting model is deterministic. When $\alpha = 1/2$ the probabilities are drawn from the whole interval $[0,1]$ and when $\alpha = 1$ all probabilities in the model instances are equal to $1/2$. In this case there is no regularity in the input, all sequences of states and transitions are uniformly distributed and no switching reduction is expected because any input pairing would be as good as another.

The whole experimental protocol is summarized in Algorithm 2. For each model class and value of α, we draw randomly a set $\{M_1, \ldots, M_{50}\}$ of model instances. For each instance M_i we generate a training sequence $\underline{x}_i$ of length 10000, apply our algorithm and synthesize an optimized circuit C_i. We generate an evaluation sequence x_i of length 10000 and let $\underline{S}_i$ be the number of switchings it induces in C_i. Then we draw a set $\{C_{i1}, \ldots C_{i20}\}$ of arbitrary circuits, let S_i be the average number of switchings induced by x_i in these circuits and let R_i be

Algorithm 2. Average switching reduction evaluation for a class of probabilistic input generators.

Input: A class of probabilistic input generators
Output: An estimation R of the average switching
  reduction obtained by our algorithm
for $i := 1$ to 50
  draw a model M_i
  generate a training sequence $\underline{x}_i$ of length 10000
  $C_i := Synthesize(\underline{x}_i)$
  generate an evaluation sequence x_i of length 10000
  $\underline{S}_i := S(C_i, x)$
  for $j = 1$ to 20
    draw a circuit C_{ij}
    $S_{ij} := S(C_{ij}, x)$
  end
  $S_i := average_j\ S_{ij}$
  $R_i := (S_i - \underline{S}_i)/S_i$
end
$R := average_i\ R_i$

---

the relative improvement in $\underline{S}_i$ relative to S_i. Finally R is the average reduction over all model instances of the same class.

Independent Inputs. We start by evaluating the switching reduction for two simple cases where the input variables are independent of each other. The first is the case where the value of each x_i is drawn according to a stateless Bernoulli process with parameter a_i while in the second model each bit is generated by an independent Markov chain with parameters a_i and b_i. The respective transition matrices are:

$$\begin{pmatrix} a_i & 1 - a_i \\ a_i & 1 - a_i \end{pmatrix} \quad \text{and} \quad \begin{pmatrix} a_i & 1 - a_i \\ 1 - b_i & b_i \end{pmatrix}$$

For these models μ_{jk} is computed analytically (see Table 2) without a training sequence. Figure 4-(a) shows for these two model classes the average reduction obtained by our algorithm as a function of α. In both cases the reduction is around 70 % when the system is close to deterministic and 30 % when probabilities are taken from $[0, 1]$.

Cascades. Next we explore the class of cascade structures where the automata are ordered and each automaton observes the state of some of its predecessors. A network is a cascade of depth k if $h(i) = \{i - k, \dots, i - 1\}$ and the number transition matrices for each automaton is 2^k. The results for cascades of depth 1 and 2 are plotted in Fig. 4-(b). For depth 1 the reduction ranges from 70 % for close to deterministic inputs to 15 % for $\alpha = 1/2$ while for depth 2 the range is from 50 % to 10 %.

Table 2. (a) The probabilities of transition pairs for two sequences generated by: (a) Bernoulli processes with parameters a_j and a_k; (b) independent Markov chains with parameters a_j, b_j and a_k, b_k.

	$0 \to 0$	$0 \to 1$	$1 \to 0$	$1 \to 1$
$0 \to 0$	$(1-a_j)^2(1-a_k)^2$	$(1-a_j)^2 a_k(1-a_k)$	$(1-a_j)^2$	$(1-a_j)^2 a_k^2$
$0 \to 1$	$a_j(1-a_j)(1-a_k)^2$	$a_j(1-a_j)a_k(1-a_k)$	$a_j(1-a_j)a_k(1-a_k)$	$a_j(1-a_j)a_k^2$
$1 \to 0$	$a_j(1-a_j)(1-a_k)^2$	$a_j(1-a_j)a_k(1-a_k)$	$a_j(1-a_j)a_k(1-a_k)$	$a_j(1-a_j)a_k^2$
$1 \to 1$	$a_j^2(1-a_k)^2$	$a_j^2 a_k(1-a_k)$	$a_j^2 a_k(1-a_k)$	$a_j^2 a_k^2$

(a)

	$0 \to 0$	$0 \to 1$
$0 \to 0$	$\dfrac{a_j a_k(1-b_j)(1-b_k)}{(a_j+b_j-2)(a_k+b_k-2)}$	$\dfrac{a_j(1-a_k)(1-b_j)(1-b_k)}{(a_j+b_j-2)(a_k+b_k-2)}$
$0 \to 1$	$\dfrac{(1-a_j)a_k(1-b_j)(1-b_k)}{(a_j+b_j-2)(a_k+b_k-2)}$	$\dfrac{(1-a_j)(1-a_k)(1-b_j)(1-b_k)}{(a_j+b_j-2)(a_k+b_k-2)}$
$1 \to 0$	$-\dfrac{(a_j-1)a_k(1-b_j)(1-b_k)}{(a_j+b_j-2)(a_k+b_k-2)}$	$-\dfrac{(a_j-1)(1-a_k)(1-b_j)(1-b_k)}{(a_j+b_j-2)(a_k+b_k-2)}$
$1 \to 1$	$-\dfrac{(a_j-1)a_k b_j(1-b_k)}{(a_j+b_j-2)(a_k+b_k-2)}$	$-\dfrac{(a_j-1)(1-a_k)b_j(1-b_k)}{(a_j+b_j-2)(a_k+b_k-2)}$

	$1 \to 0$	$1 \to 1$
$0 \to 0$	$-\dfrac{a_j(a_k-1)(1-b_j)(1-b_k)}{(a_j+b_j-2)(a_k+b_k-2)}$	$-\dfrac{a_j(a_k-1)(1-b_j)b_k}{(a_j+b_j-2)(a_k+b_k-2)}$
$0 \to 1$	$\dfrac{(a_j-1)(a_k-1)(1-b_j)(1-b_k)}{(a_j+b_j-2)(a_k+b_k-2)}$	$\dfrac{(a_j-1)(a_k-1)(1-b_j)b_k}{(a_j+b_j-2)(a_k+b_k-2)}$
$1 \to 0$	$\dfrac{(a_j-1)(a_k-1)b_j(1-b_k)}{(a_j+b_j-2)(a_k+b_k-2)}$	$\dfrac{(a_j-1)(a_k-1)b_j b_k}{(a_j+b_j-2)(a_k+b_k-2)}$
$1 \to 1$	$-\dfrac{(1-a_j)(a_k-1)(1-b_j)(1-b_k)}{(a_j+b_j-2)(a_k+b_k-2)}$	$-\dfrac{(1-a_j)(a_k-1)(1-b_j)b_k}{(a_j+b_j-2)(a_k+b_k-2)}$

(b)

Partitioned Variables. Next we applied our procedure to a network where the variables are partitioned into clusters of size 2 and 4 and each automaton observes only the states of the automata in its cluster. The results are plotted in Fig. 4-(c). For 2-clusters the range or reduction is between 65 % for almost deterministic inputs and 15 % for $\alpha = 0.5$, while for 4-clusters the corresponding reductions are less than 50 % and 10 %.

Arbitrary Sparse Network. In the last class of examples we consider arbitrary networks where each automaton observes the states of k randomly chosen other automata. Figure 4-(d) shows the results obtained for $k = 2$ and 4. In the former case we obtain 45 % for $\alpha = 0.05$ and around 5 % for $\alpha = 0.5$, while for the latter we obtain the worst results: less than 10 % for quasi-deterministic inputs and less than 5 % when probabilities are drawn anywhere in $[0, 1]$.

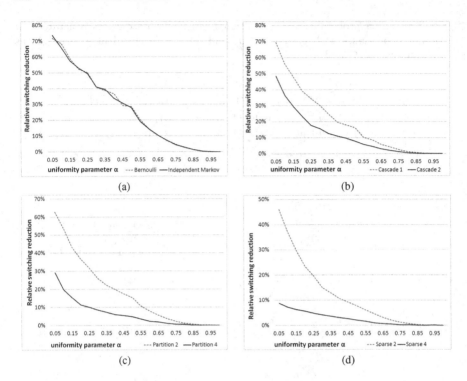

Fig. 4. The average switching reduction as a function of the uniformity parameter α for different input models: (a): Independent inputs – Bernoulli (dashed red) and Markov processes. (b): Variables are arranged in a cascade structure of depth 1 (dashed red) and 2 (c): Variables are partitioned into mutually-dependent clusters of size 2 (dashed red) and 4 (d): Each variable depends on 2 (dashed red) and 4 other arbitrary variables(Color figure online).

Table 3 shows the average number of *absolute* switching elimination per gate in one time step. Upon closer inspection we observe that the results become consistently worse as the number of variables observed by an automaton becomes larger, quite independently of the interaction pattern. This may be an artifact of the way we generate model instances. The reason is that when an automaton has several transition matrices, the values of an entry (u, v) in different matrices may be taken from opposite sides of I_α, cancel each other an render the behavior of the variables more random and less regular.

5   Evaluation: A Mini Instruction Decoder

Finally, we synthesize a mini instruction decoder, where we apply our procedure to a full AIG. We consider a very simple hand-held calculator whose instructions are listed in Table 4. The instruction are encoded using 4 bits although 3 bits would suffice, to reflect the fact that in a real application often not all the possible input combinations are used.

Table 3. The *absolute* reduction in number of switching per gate per time step for all the models.

α	Bern	iMar	casc1	casc2	part2	part4	spar2	spar4
0.05	0.115	0.110	0.117	0.102	0.118	0.060	0.093	0.020
0.10	0.106	0.104	0.105	0.076	0.091	0.041	0.075	0.017
0.15	0.095	0.097	0.089	0.060	0.081	0.037	0.057	0.015
0.20	0.093	0.091	0.079	0.050	0.074	0.029	0.047	0.013
0.25	0.084	0.088	0.066	0.041	0.061	0.023	0.040	0.011
0.30	0.084	0.081	0.063	0.032	0.055	0.019	0.032	0.009
0.35	0.071	0.071	0.048	0.029	0.049	0.016	0.027	0.008
0.40	0.065	0.067	0.040	0.022	0.043	0.013	0.023	0.007
0.45	0.063	0.061	0.037	0.021	0.036	0.012	0.021	0.006
0.50	0.054	0.057	0.036	0.019	0.031	0.011	0.018	0.005
0.55	0.040	0.044	0.026	0.013	0.024	0.008	0.014	0.004
0.60	0.031	0.031	0.018	0.010	0.017	0.006	0.010	0.002
0.65	0.023	0.024	0.013	0.007	0.013	0.004	0.006	0.002
0.70	0.016	0.017	0.009	0.005	0.009	0.002	0.004	0.001
0.75	0.010	0.011	0.006	0.003	0.005	0.001	0.003	0.001
0.80	0.007	0.007	0.003	0.002	0.003	0.000	0.001	0.000
0.85	0.003	0.003	0.001	0.000	0.001	0.000	0.000	0.000
0.90	0.001	0.001	0.000	0.000	0.000	0.000	0.000	0.000
0.95	0.000	0.000	0.000	0.000	0.000	0.000	0.000	0.000

Table 4. The instruction set of the calculator.

Instruction	Code	Meaning
LOAD	1001	Loading from numerical keys
LOADM	1010	Loading from memory
SET_ADD	1100	Pressing '+'
SET_SUB	1101	Pressing '−'
SET_MUL	1110	Pressing '×'
SET_DIV	1111	Pressing '÷'
EVAL	0000	Pressing '='
STORE	0101	Saving result to memory

We assume that the typical use of the calculator will be just to perform an operation (add, subtract, multiply, divide) on two numbers entered from the numeric keypad. More sophisticated users might perform more complex operations, say add three numbers at once, but with a lower probability. The Markov model for instruction sequences is depicted in Fig. 5 and explained below:

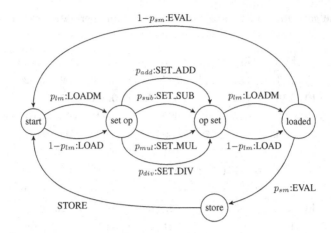

Fig. 5. The probabilistic model of the instruction generator.

1. With probability p_{lm} load an argument previously stored in memory, otherwise just type in some number as the first argument.
2. Press one of $\{+, -, \times, \div\}$ with respective probabilities $\{p_{add}, p_{sub}, p_{mul}, p_{div}\}$.
3. Load the second argument either from memory (probability p_{lm}) or by typing the number.
4. Evaluate by pressing '=' and then with probability P_{sm} store the result in memory.

For the experiment we set the parameters of the model as follows:

$$p_{lm} = 0.1 \quad p_{add} = 0.4 \; p_{sub} = 0.3$$
$$p_{mul} = 0.2 \; p_{div} = 0.1 \; p_{sm} = 0.1$$

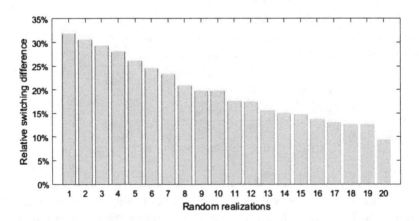

Fig. 6. A comparison of the number of switchings in the optimized instruction compared to 20 other arbitrary realizations. The height of bars shows how much switching can be saved using the optimized circuit compared to that realization.

We generate from the model a training sequence of size 20000 and use it to synthesize an optimized circuit denoted by OC. For evaluation purposes we generate an input sequence of length 100000 and compare the number of switchings it induces in OC with 20 randomly drawn implementations of the decoder. The results are shown in Fig. 6. Note that there is a large variation in the number of switchings among the different realizations. Circuit OC was always better than any of the other circuits and on the average achieved a reduction of 16.49 %. Naturally these results are also sensitive to the uniformity of the probabilities. For example when we set $p_{lm} = 0.25$ and $P_{sm} = 0.2$ we obtained a smaller reduction of 12.53 %.

6   Discussion

The interest in switching reduction and in the evaluation of circuit behavior against probabilistic models in general [6] is not new. Concerning switching reduction we can distinguish between an abstract approach like ours which focuses only on the number of transitions as an approximate indicator of power consumption and more physical approaches that map abstract circuits onto a concrete technology where power consumption can be measured more accurately. The work of [16] which belongs to the second category, mentions the abstract problem that we solve here as a suggestion for future work that could be plugged upstream to their own work on power-aware mapping using a real technology library. The work of [19] is also of this type, mapping abstract AIGs to real gates. The input is specified as a set of input vectors (patterns) and simulation with these patterns is used to estimate power consumption for different mappings alternatives onto real gates from a library.

The work of [17,18] applies a similar reasoning concerning input pairing for 2AND gates and uses a variant of Huffman's algorithm for constructing a binary tree with minimal average weighted path length [9]. However, this work is restricted to the case were variables are assumed to be generated by independent Bernoulli processes while our approach is applicable to any small-description Markov process or any user-provided training sequence. Moreover, they use a greedy pairing algorithm such that at each step of the algorithm one pair of variables, the one which induces the least expected number of switching is selected as an input to an AND gate. Experiments show that our scheme which treats at once a complete level of the tree via optimal matching is significantly more efficient.

The work of [11] also uses Huffman's algorithm but in a different way that seems to yield a random balanced tree. They do not give any explicit probabilistic model but introduce some delay assumptions and claim their algorithm to be optimal in terms of reducing only the switching activity which is due to glitches. This is the place to mention that as we do not model gate delays, we cannot detect glitches but one may argue that their importance in balanced trees structures is less pronounced. The work of [18] is extended significantly in [20] who give an optimal algorithm for unbounded depth 2AND synthesis, restricted to a Bernoulli input model. Their algorithm tends to produce deep circuits with long delays.

To summarize, we devised a novel procedure for an early step in the synthesis flow for digital circuits/functions. The major novelty of the algorithm is its ability to approximate in a tractable manner, polynomial in the number of inputs to an AND gate, the minimal average-case number of switchings, based on a training input sequence. The approach can be applied, in principle to any probabilistic model of the input but, of course, formal guarantees of approximation quality can be given only in restricted cases.

For synthetic empirical evaluation we developed an original framework based on sparsely interacting networks of probabilistic automata and ran extensive experiments under various probabilistic models of the input. The reduction obtained on these synthetic examples were quite impressive, reaching, in some cases, dozens of percents. Two major open questions remain concerning their transfer to real life:

1. Can such reduction be pushed downstream to the more physical steps of synthesis? This question has two versions: can it be done using existing commercial tools that carry a lot of legacy, or can it done in principle by new tools if this type of optimization criterion is considered important.
2. How do real applications look like in terms of circuit structure and input model?

We made a preliminary exploration of the second question using the instruction decoder model and the results seem encouraging. We believe the behavior of real circuits is much more regular than arbitrary Markov chains. In the future we intend to attack larger industrial-scale examples and follow them, as far as possible, down to technology-dependent mapping, being able to detect timing effects and measure real power consumption. It has already been observed that synthesis is an old technology and the outcome of commercial synthesis tools is sensitive to many syntactic features [13] and we hope that this work will bring a fresh look on the topic.

On the theoretical side we intend see under what assumptions our level-greedy algorithm is optimal and to give bounds on its deviation from the optimum when it is not. Another potential direction for exploration is to present trade-offs between speed and switching reduction by being less committed to the circuit topology. Although typically the number of inputs to a single AND cone need not be very large, it would be interesting to explore how far we can go with the number of inputs using the polynomial algorithm for optimal matching. Finally we intend to extend this work to sequential machines and to explore the application of switching-oriented reasoning to the encoding of states and symbolic inputs.

References

1. Bellaouar, A., Elmasry, M.I.: Low-power digital VLSI design: Circuits and Systems. Springer, US (1995)
2. Benini, L., Bogliolo, A., De Micheli, G.: A survey of design techniques for system-level dynamic power management. IEEE Trans. VLSI **8**(3), 299–316 (2000)
3. Brayton, R.K., Hachtel, G.D., McMullen, C., Sangiovanni-Vincentelli, A.: Logic Minimization Algorithms For VLSI Synthesis. The Springer International Series in Engineering and Computer Science, vol. 2. Springer, US (1984)
4. Anantha, P., Chandrakasan, A.P., Brodersen, R.W.: Low Power Digital CMOS Design. Springer, US (1995)
5. Edmonds, J.: Maximum matching and a polyhedron with 0, l-vertices. J. Res. Nat. Bur. Stand. B **69**, 125–130 (1965)
6. Hachtel, G.D., Macii, E., Pardo, A., Somenzi, F.: Markovian analysis of large finite state machines. IEEE Trans. Comput. Aided Des. Integr. Circuits Syst. **15**(12), 1479–1493 (1996)
7. Hachtel, G.D., Somenzi, F.: Logic Synthesis and Verification Algorithms. Springer, US (1996)
8. Kohavi, Z., Jha, N.K.: Switching and Finite Automata Theory. Cambridge University Press, Cambridge (2010)
9. Larmore, L.L., Hirschberg, D.S.: A fast algorithm for optimal length-limited huffman codes. J. ACM **37**(3), 464–473 (1990)
10. Lawler, E.L.: Combinatorial Optimization: Networks and Matroids. Courier Dover Publications, New York (1976)
11. Murgai, R., Brayton, R.K., Sangiovanni-Vincentelli, S.: Decomposition of logic functions for minimum transition activity. In: Proceedings of the 1995 European Conference on Design and Test, pp. 404. IEEE Computer Society (1995)
12. Papadimitriou, C.H., Steiglitz, K.: Combinatorial Optimization: Algorithms and Complexity. Courier Dover Publications, New York (1998)
13. Puggelli, A., Welp, T., Kuehlmann, A., Sangiovanni-Vincentelli, A.: Are logic synthesis tools robust? In: 2011 48th ACM/EDAC/IEEE Design Automation Conference (DAC), pp. 633–638, June 2011
14. Rabaey, J.M., Pedram, M. (eds.): Low Power Design Methodologies. The Springer International Series in Engineering and Computer Science. Springer, US (1996)
15. Sasao, T.: Switching Theory for Logic Synthesis, vol. 1. Springer, US (1999)
16. Tiwari, V., Ashar, P., Malik, S.: Technology mapping for low power. In: 30th Conference on Design Automation, pp. 74–79. IEEE (1993)
17. Tsui, C.-Y., Pedram, M., Despain, A.M.: Technology decomposition and mapping targeting low power dissipation. In: Proceedings of the 30th International Design Automation Conference, pp. 68–73. ACM (1993)
18. Tsui, C.-Y., Pedram, M., Despain, A.M.: Power efficient technology decomposition and mapping under an extended power consumption model. IEEE Trans. Comput. Aided Des. Integr. Circuits Syst. **13**(9), 1110–1122 (1994)
19. Yeh, C., Chang, C.-C., Wang, J.-S.: Technology mapping for low power. In: Proceedings of the ASP-DAC 1999 Design Automation Conference, Asia and South Pacific, pp. 145–148. IEEE(1999)
20. Zhou, H., Wong, DF: An exact gate decomposition algorithm for low-power technology mapping. In: Proceedings of the 1997 IEEE/ACM International Conference on Computer-Aided Design, pp. 575–580. IEEE Computer Society (1997)

Author Index

Printed in the United States
By Bookmasters